Division III of Heidegger's *Being and Time*

Division III of Heidegger's *Being and Time*

The Unanswered Question of Being

edited by Lee Braver

The MIT Press
Cambridge, Massachusetts
London, England

This book was set in Stone Serif and Stone Sans by Toppan Best-set Premedia Limited. Printed and bound in the United States of America.

Library of Congress Cataloging-in-Publication Data

Division III of Heidegger's Being and time : the unanswered question of being / [edited by] Lee Braver.
    pages   cm
Includes bibliographical references and index.
ISBN 978-0-262-02968-1 (hardcover : alk. paper)
1. Heidegger, Martin, 1889–1976. Sein und Zeit. 2. Ontology. I. Braver, Lee, editor. II. Badiou, Alain. Heidegger's Parmenides. III. Title: Division 3 of Heidegger's Being and time. IV. Title: Division three of Heidegger's Being and time.
B3279.H48S44335   2015
111—dc23

2015011500

10   9   8   7   6   5   4   3   2   1

"Being and time" means not a book but the task that is given. The authentic task given here is what we do not know; and insofar as we know this *genuinely*—namely *as* a given task—we always know it only in *questioning*.
—Heidegger, *Introduction to Metaphysics*, 220–221

Contents

Acknowledgments

I thank Alex Levine and Roger Ariew for their generous help with translations, and Phil Laughlin and Judy Feldmann for making the transition from idea to book as smooth as possible. I thank William Parkhurst for creating the index for the book. I thank my children, Julia, Ben, and Sophia, for being, and my wife, Yvonne, for being my wife.

Abbreviations

AM   *Aristotle's* Metaphysics Θ 1–3 (GA33)

BC   *Basic Concepts* (GA51)

BaT   *Being and Truth* (GA36/37)

BCAP   *Basic Concepts of Aristotelian Philosophy* (GA18)

BH   *Becoming Heidegger: On the Trail of His Early Occasional Writings, 1910–1927*

BP   *The Basic Problems of Phenomenology* (GA24)

BQ   *Basic Questions of Philosophy: Selected "Problems" of "Logic"* (GA45)

BT   *Being and Time* (GA2)

BT2   *Being and Time* (Stambaugh translation; GA2)

BW   *Basic Writings*, Revised ed.

CP   *Contributions to Philosophy* (GA65)

CPC   *Country Path Conversations* (GA77)

CT   *The Concept of Time* (GA64)

CV   Curriculum Vitae (in BH)

DT   *Discourse on Thinking*

E   *The Event*

EF   *The Essence of Human Freedom: An Introduction to Philosophy* (GA31)

EG   "On the Essence of Ground" (in PA)

EGT   *Early Greek Thinking* (GA5, 7)

EHP   *Elucidations of Hölderlin's Poetry* (GA4)

ET   *The Essence of Truth* (GA34)

FCM   *The Fundamental Concepts of Metaphysics* (GA29/30)

FS   *Four Seminars* (GA15)

GA   *Gesamtausgabe*

H   *Heraclitus Seminar* (GA15)

HCE   *Hegel's Concept of Experience* (GA5)

HCT   *History of the Concept of Time* (GA20)

HH   *Hölderlin's Hymn "The Ister"* (GA53)

HPS   *Hegel's* Phenomenology of Spirit (GA32)

HR   *The Heidegger Reader*, ed. Günter Figal

ID   *Identity and Difference* (GA11)

IM   *Introduction to Metaphysics* (GA40)

IPR   *Introduction to Phenomenological Research* (GA17)

ITP   *Introduction to Philosophy—Thinking and Poetizing* (GA50)

KPM   *Kant and the Problem of Metaphysics*, 5th ed. (GA3)

LEL   *Logic as the Question Concerning the Essence of Language* (GA38)

LQT   *Logic: The Question of Truth* (GA21)

LR   "Letter to William J. Richardson, April 1962" (in HR)

M   *Mindfulness* (GA66)

MFL   *The Metaphysical Foundations of Logic* (GA26)

MHC   *Martin Heidegger in Conversation*

N   *Nietzsche*, 4 vols., volume denoted by Roman numeral (GA6.1–6.2)

OBT   *Off the Beaten Track* (GA5)

OET   "On the Essence of Truth" (in BW)

OG   "Only a God Can Save Us": The *Der Spiegel* Interview (in HR)

OWL   *On the Way to Language* (GA12)

P   *Parmenides* (GA54)

PIK   *Phenomenological Interpretation of Kant's* Critique of Pure Reason (GA25)

PIRA   "Phenomenological Interpretations with Respect to Aristotle: Indication of the Hermeneutical Situation" (in BH)

PLT   *Poetry, Language, Thought*

PM   *Pathmarks* (GA9)

PR   *The Principle of Reason* (GA10)

PRL   *The Phenomenology of Religious Life* (GA60)

PS   *Plato's Sophist* (GA19)

PT   *The Piety of Thinking*

Q&A   *Martin Heidegger and National Socialism: Questions and Answers*

QT   *The Question Concerning Technology and Other Essays*

R   Richardson, *Heidegger: Through Phenomenology to Thought*

S   Sheehan, "A Paradigm Shift in Heidegger Research"

STF   *Schelling's Treatise on the Essence of Human Freedom* (GA42)

Supp   *Supplements: From the Earliest Essays to* Being and Time *and Beyond*

SZ   *Sein und Zeit* (GA2)

TB   *On Time and Being* (GA14)

TDP   *Toward the Definition of Philosophy* (GA56/57)

WCT *What Is Called Thinking?* (GA8)

WDR "Wilhelm Dilthey's Research and the Struggle for a Historical Worldview" (in Supp)

WIP *What Is Philosophy?*

WM "What Is Metaphysics?" (in BW)

WT *What Is a Thing?* (GA41)

Zo *Zollikon Seminars: Protocols—Conversations—Letters* (GA89)

Bibliography of Heidegger's Works

Aristotle's "Metaphysics" Θ *1–3: On the Essence and Actuality of Force.* Trans. Walter Brogan and Peter Warnek. Bloomington: Indiana University Press, 1995.

Basic Concepts. Trans. Gary E. Aylesworth. Bloomington: Indiana University Press, 1993.

Basic Concepts of Aristotelian Philosophy. Trans. Robert D. Metcalf and Mark B. Tanzer. Bloomington: Indiana University Press, 2009.

The Basic Problems of Phenomenology. Trans. Albert Hofstadter. Bloomington: Indiana University Press, 1982.

Basic Questions of Philosophy: Selected "Problems" of "Logic." Trans. Richard Rojcewicz and André Schuwer. Bloomington: Indiana University Press, 1994.

Basic Writings. Rev. ed. Ed. David Farrell Krell. San Francisco: HarperSanFrancisco, 1993.

Being and Time. Trans. John Macquarrie and Edward Robinson. San Francisco: HarperSanFrancisco, 1962.

Being and Time. Trans. Joan Stambaugh, revised by Dennis Schmidt. Albany: SUNY Press, 2010.

Being and Truth. Trans. Gregory Fried and Richard Polt. Bloomington: Indiana University Press, 2010.

The Concept of Time. Trans. William McNeill. Malden, MA: Blackwell Publishing: 1992.

Contributions to Philosophy (From Enowning). Trans. Parvis Emad and Kenneth Maly. Bloomington: Indiana University Press, 1999.

Country Path Conversations. Trans Bret W. Davis. Indiana University Press, 2010.

Discourse on Thinking. Trans. John M. Anderson and E. Hans Freund. San Francisco: Harper Torchbooks, 1966.

Early Greek Thinking: The Dawn of Western Philosophy. Trans. David Farrell Krell and Frank A. Capuzzi. San Francisco: HarperSanFrancisco, 1975.

Elucidations of Hölderlin's Poetry. Trans. Keith Hoeller. Amherst: Humanity Books, 2000.

The Essence of Human Freedom: An Introduction to Philosophy. Trans. Ted Sadler. New York: Continuum, 2002.

The Essence of Truth: On Plato's Cave Allegory and "Theaetetus." Trans. Ted Sadler. New York: Continuum, 2002.

The Event. Trans. Richard Rojcewicz. Bloomington: Indiana University Press, 2013.

Four Seminars. Trans. Andrew Mitchell and François Raffoul. Bloomington: Indiana University Press, 2003.

The Fundamental Concepts of Metaphysics: World, Finitude, Solitude. Trans. William McNeill and Nicholas Walker. Bloomington: Indiana University Press, 1995.

Gesamtausgabe. Frankfurt am Main: Vittorio Klostermann, 1910–present.

Hegel's Concept of Experience. Trans. K. R. Dove. New York: Harper & Row, 1970.

Hegel's "Phenomenology of Spirit." Trans. Parvis Emad and Kenneth Maly. Bloomington: Indiana University Press, 1994.

The Heidegger Reader. Ed. Günter Figal. Trans. Jerome Veith. Bloomington: Indiana University Press, 2009.

Heraclitus Seminar. Coauthored wth Eugene Fink. Trans. Charles H. Siebert. Evanston, IL: Northwestern University Press, 1993.

History of the Concept of Time. Trans. Theodore Kisiel. Bloomington: Indiana University Press, 1985.

Hölderlin's Hymn "The Ister." Trans. William McNeill and Julia Davis. Bloomington: Indiana University Press, 1996.

Identity and Difference. Trans. Joan Stambaugh. New York: Harper Torchbooks, 1969.

An Introduction to Metaphysics. Trans. Ralph Manheim. New Haven: Yale University Press, 1959.

Introduction to Phenomenological Research. Trans. Daniel O. Dahlstrom. Bloomington: Indiana University Press, 2005.

Introduction to Philosophy—Thinking and Poetizing. Trans. Phillip Jacques Braunstein. Bloomington: Indiana University Press, 2011.

Kant and the Problem of Metaphysics, 5th enl. ed. Trans. Richard Taft. Bloomington: Indiana University Press, 1990.

Logic: The Question of Truth. Trans. Thomas Sheehan. Bloomington: Indiana University Press, 2010.

Logic as the Question Concerning the Essence of Language. Trans. Wanda Torres Gregory. Albany: SUNY Press, 2009.

Martin Heidegger and National Socialism: Questions and Answers. Ed. Günther Neske and Emil Kettering. Trans. Lisa Harries. New York: Paragon House, 1990.

Martin Heidegger in Conversation. Ed. Richard Wisser. Trans. B. Srinivasa Murthy. New Delhi: Arnold-Heinemann, 1977.

The Metaphysical Foundations of Logic. Trans. Michael Heim. Bloomington: Indiana University Press, 1992.

Mindfulness. Trans. Parvis Emad and Thomas Kalary. New York: Continuum, 2002.

Nietzsche. 4 vols. Ed. David Farrell Krell. San Francisco: HarperSanFrancisco, 1979, 1984, 1987, 1982.

Off the Beaten Track. Trans. and ed. Julian Young and Kenneth Haynes. New York: Cambridge University Press, 2002.

On the Way to Language. Trans. Peter D. Hertz. San Francisco: HarperSanFrancisco, 1971

On Time and Being. Trans. Joan Stambaugh. New York: Harper Torchbooks, 1972.

Parmenides. Trans. Richard Rojcewicz and André Schuwer. Bloomington: Indiana University Press, 1992.

Pathmarks. Ed. William McNeill. Cambridge: Cambridge University Press, 1998.

Phenomenological Interpretation of Kant's "Critique of Pure Reason." Trans. Parvis Emad and Thomas Kalary. Bloomington: Indiana University Press, 1997.

The Phenomenology of Religious Life. Trans. Matthis Fritsch and Jennifer Anna Gosetti-Ferencei. Bloomington: Indiana University Press, 2004.

The Piety of Thinking. Trans. James G. Hart and John C. Maraldo. Bloomington: Indiana University Press, 1976.

Plato's Sophist. Trans. Richard Rojcewicz and André Schuwer. Bloomington: Indiana University Press, 1997.

Poetry, Language, Thought. Trans. Albert Hofstadter. New York: Harper & Row, 1971.

The Principle of Reason. Trans. Reginald Lilly. Bloomington: Indiana University Press, 1991.

The Question Concerning Technology and Other Essays. Trans. William Lovitt. New York: Harper Torchbooks, 1977.

Schelling's Treatise on the Essence of Human Freedom. Trans. Joan Stambaugh. Athens: Ohio University Press, 1985.

Sein und Zeit, 12th ed. Tübingen: Max Niemeyer Verlag, 1972.

Supplements: From the Earliest Essays to "Being and Time" and Beyond. Ed. John van Buren. Albany: SUNY Press, 2002.

Towards the Definition of Philosophy. Trans. Ted Sandler. New York: Athlone, 2000.

What Is a Thing? Trans. W. B. Barton Jr. and Vera Deutsch. Chicago: Henry Regnery, 1967.

What Is Called Thinking? Trans. J. Glenn Gray. New York: Harper & Row, 1968.

What Is Philosophy? Trans. Jean T. Wilde and William Kluback. New Haven, CT: New College and University Press, 1956.

Zollikon Seminars: Protocols—Conversations—Letters. Trans. Franz Mayr and Richard Askay. Evanston, IL: Northwestern University Press, 2001.

Introduction

Lee Braver

It's a peculiar task, I realize, to write about a work unwritten, to create a book about a part of a book that is not. Then again, it's an extraordinary book. *Being and Time* is widely acknowledged as one of the great works of twentieth-century philosophy. A seamless blend of not just disparate, but what had previously seemed incompatible influences—phenomenology, existentialism, hermeneutics, transcendental philosophy—it is at the same time astonishing in its originality. Its immediate goal, as absurd as it is common, is to capture life as it really is, the way we live it instead of how we think it must be or how we've been taught it is or how it looks when we stop to look at it. Forget about bats—the real trick is to describe what it is like to be a human, a topic made difficult not by its inaccessibility or rarity but by its ubiquity. Perhaps the only thing more extraordinary than its ambition is its success, capturing human life as well as any book I know (except, perhaps, for *Nicomachean Ethics* or *One Hundred Years of Solitude*).

Nevertheless, our task here—to produce a secondary literature on a nonexistent primary work, a scholarship of *als ob*, if you will—is decidedly unusual, although not without precedent, at least among fictional works. The plot of Umberto Eco's *The Name of the Rose*, for example, centers on Aristotle's lost book on comedy. Thomas Carlyle's *Sartor Resartus* is a book-length review of an unreal book about reality written by an unreal German philosopher; he is a German Idealist, though, so the conceit isn't that much of a stretch. Stanisław Lem wrote a book of introductions to, and a book of reviews of, books that don't exist (*Imaginary Magnitude* and *A Perfect Vacuum*, respectively), and the latter opens, in quasi-Russellian fashion, with a review of itself (spoiler: he didn't particularly like it). In "Pierre Menard, Author of *Don Quixote*," Jorge Luis Borges reviews an imaginary book that (re)wrote a real book (*Don Quixote*, a book, it should be mentioned, in which many of the characters of the second volume have read and are reacting to the first volume), and in "Tlön, Uqbar, Orbis Tertius" a fake encyclopedia article gradually draws a fake world into reality. The imaginary *Necronomi-con* by the "Mad Arab" Abdul Alhazred threads its way through many of H. P. Lovecraft's works, as do Kilgore Trout's through Kurt Vonnegut's. *The Grasshopper Lies Heavy*, the reverse alternate history novel in Philip K. Dick's alternate history novel *The Man in the High Castle*, informs the characters of their status as characters within an alternate history novel, although both books were actually written by a third book, the *I Ching*. It turns out that there exists a considerable literature on nonexistent literature.

Heidegger himself undertook the project of writing on unwritten writings during his extensive study of Nietzsche in the late 1930s. At the time he became incapacitated, Nietzsche had been planning to present an overview of his thought as a whole under the title *The Will to Power*. Heidegger believed that studies of Nietzsche should focus on this "planned *magnum opus*, which, as we know, was not brought to fruition" (NI 7). The work Nietzsche did write "is so essential and rich" (NI 24) that we can reconstruct what he would have written, thereby committing commentary in the past subjunctive tense. "For every great thinker always *thinks* one jump more originally than he directly *speaks*. Our interpretation must therefore try to say what is unsaid by him" (NI 134; see also BT 448/396). Heidegger's 1929 book on Kant follows a similar method:

With any philosophical knowledge in general, what is said in uttered propositions must not be decisive. Instead, what must be decisive is what it sets before our eyes as still unsaid, in and through what has been said. Thus the fundamental intention of the present interpretation of the *Critique of Pure Reason* was to make visible in this way the decisive content of this work and thereby to bring out what Kant "had wanted to say" … in order to wring from what the words say, what it is they want to say. (KPM 140–141)

When he proposed this approach to Nietzsche and Kant, might Heidegger have considered its application to his own incomplete *magnum opus*?

Because one of the most important facts about *Being and Time* is that it *is* unfinished. The story goes like this: the dean at Marburg University wanted to promote Heidegger but the government balked over his lack of publications; even Heidegger faced publish or perish.[1] When the dean asked Heidegger if he had anything that could be published right away, Heidegger arranged to publish Division One in Husserl's journal. That wasn't enough, so he quickly completed Division Two, and together, the two satisfied the German government (oh, to have been a fly on the wall in that committee meeting!). But he never finished the Third Division of Part One, or at least he never published it; there are indications that he completed it but, unsatisfied, destroyed it.[2] The preface to the seventh edition in 1953 removed the designation "First Half," conceding that the book would never be completed, and referred the reader elsewhere (*Introduction to Metaphysics*) for "elucidation of this question" (BT 17).

Part Two of *Being and Time* was to have been a "phenomenological destruction of the history of ontology, with the problematic of Temporality as our clue" (BT 63/39). Inquiry, by its very nature, takes place within horizons inherited from the past, Heidegger argues, and this applies to his own inquiry into the meaning of being as much as to any other. We cannot escape preconceptions, but we can become aware of our own and correct for them when they don't match or illuminate experience, that is, when they are phenomenologically untrue. This process is what Heidegger is talking about when he says that our task is not to get out of the circle of inquiry, but rather to get into it in the right way (BT 195/153). Part Two was to take up time and being in Kant, Descartes and medieval ontology, and Aristotle, regressively peeling away the layers of sedimented tradition that had formed over the original experiences. Now this part was never written either, but its absence is not as problematic. For one thing, we have a pretty good idea of what it would have said. Brief discussions of Kant (BT 366–368/318–321), Descartes (BT 128–134/95–101), and Aristotle (BT 473–474/421) are to be found in Part One, and more extensive discussions appear in works from the 1920s such as *Plato's* Sophist, *The Basic Problems of Phenomenology*, *Phenomenological Interpretation of Kant's* Critique of Pure Reason, and *Kant and the Problem of Metaphysics*. Furthermore, at this point in his career, the historical approach to the question of being seems to be an optional addendum to Part One's account of Dasein, in contrast with his later work where Heidegger's thinking often cannot be cleanly separated from his dialogue with other thinkers.

Division Three of Part One, however, was no mere addendum but the point of the whole book. It was what the first two divisions were leading up to and what was to supply the guiding clue for Part Two. His general commitment to holism and the hermeneutic circle means that each part of a book affects how we understand all of it, but surely this must apply with special force to its conclusion. What one thinks Heidegger would have said there affects how one understands the book as a whole, and how one understands *Being and Time* determines a great deal about how one understands Heidegger in general, and how one understands Heidegger has vast implications for the entire history of continental philosophy. So much depends upon the Third Division.

It also has implications for what has come to be called Heidegger's "*Kehre*" or turning from his early work to his later, one of the central issues of his oeuvre. Why didn't he complete *Being and Time*? Did he become dissatisfied with it? If so, why? Was the reason he never finished the book the same reason he changed his general outlook and approach in the later work, if such a change in fact occurred (scholars disagree about the extent, nature, timing, and even the existence of a change from early to later Heidegger)? Furthermore, Division Three was where he was to turn to being itself after surveying Dasein's existence for the first two divisions. It might have been the best guide to what Heidegger means by being, his constant but constantly obscure theme. Herbert Spiegelberg's famous characterization of the book as an "astonishing torso" (Kisiel 1993, p. 489) isn't quite right, for a torso contains a body's vital organs, its heart. A more accurate metaphor might be that *Being and Time* is an astonishing pile of limbs.

Like most readers, I wondered what this concluding section would have contained when I first read *Being and Time*. And I wondered on every subsequent reading, too. I also wondered what experts on Heidegger thought it might have said and why he didn't write it. And then I realized that many others wondered the same things and would be interested in these reflections on the issues that concerned Heidegger the most by the people who know Heidegger the best. So I asked them. You hold the results in your hand: the work of a group of scholars in search of lost "Time and Being."

Being and Time is a book about being, and about time; more specifically, it is about the way being is experienced and understood in terms of time. Heidegger considers being the ultimate issue that is forever at issue, the first and last question of philosophy, the perpetual and perennial and continuous subject of all thought whatsoever.[3] After all, what do we ever encounter or think about except beings, which presupposes some sense of the fact and the way that they are just to be able to encounter or think about them as beings? Yet investigating being is so different from all the inquiries we normally engage in that it baffles utterly. How do we go about looking into this question? What objects should we study, where should we travel to, what observational instruments should we use—to study being? To put it in terms academics can recognize, what would we ask for if we were applying for a grant to study the meaning of being? It's not just that we don't know how to *answer* this question; we don't have a clue how to ask it.

The introduction to *Being and Time* supplies this clue. As it happens, there is a particular entity that possesses an understanding of being, so if we could locate this being and investigate its understanding, we could extract the meaning of being from it. That entity is us, what Heidegger calls "Dasein" to avoid the conceptual baggage accumulated by traditional terms such as "humanity" or "consciousness." "Dasein" denotes those aspects of us that allow us to understand being, to be aware of anything at all. This is why, in the formula that lays out the strategy of the book as we have it, "*fundamental ontology*, from which alone all other ontologies can take their rise, must be sought in the *existential analytic of Dasein*" (BT 34/13). The foundation or starting point of ontology is to be found, and founded, in the analysis of Dasein's distinctive way of being, which Heidegger terms "existence." The analysis of existence (Dasein's way of being) founds ontology (the study of being) because Dasein possesses an understanding of being. Or, better, we are in such a way that we embody an understanding of being, one that we are continuously enacting; it is built into our very being because it is our very being. We are such that we understand being,[4] so a thorough understanding of our being will encompass an understanding of being as a whole.

Of course, few of us possess a conscious, articulate definition of what it means to be, what Heidegger calls an ontological understanding.[5] But we all have a pre-ontological understanding, something like a know-how rather than a knowing-that, a skill for dealing with various types of beings that orients our comportments to them. We don't so much possess this understanding in our thoughts as enact it in our behavior. The fact that we interact appropriately with different sorts of beings—asking permission to take money from people but not from ATMs, say, or picking up a hammer and hammering versus staring at a slide in a microscope—shows that we understand that these different kinds of entities are different and *are* differently and so call for different forms of behavior from us.

To be a Dasein is to take a stand on our own being by trying to be someone, which we do by taking up roles and projects that give us definition. We become some*body* by doing some*thing*; we make a life and a self by making a living. These ways of living involve interacting with some *things*, (at least?) three different kinds of beings: ready-to-hand tools, present-at-hand objects, and existing Dasein (ourselves and others). To deal with them appropriately, we need a basic grasp of what it means to be a tool, an object, and a person, since understanding their being determines what is fitting and proper to do with them. Hence, being a Dasein requires a sophisticated understanding of several modes of being in a way that being a rock doesn't, even though we rarely think about them nor are we typically capable of articulating this understanding; just ask Socrates' poor flustered interlocutors. Recall Augustine's famous line about knowing perfectly well what time is until he is asked to explain it. For Heidegger, this not only indicates the *lack* of an ontological understanding of time but, just as importantly, it also shows the *presence* of a fully functioning pre-ontological understanding. The purpose of *Being and Time*—reminiscent of Platonic recollection, as Heidegger notes (BP 326)—is to take this pre-ontological understanding we all have and make it ontological, that is, to articulate it explicitly, and that will tell us what it means to be. This is why the analysis of Dasein, which is all that we have of the book, is not tangential to the question of being. At this point in his career, Heidegger seems to believe that the only way to get at being is by going through Dasein.[6]

There is a slightly different and perhaps even more important reason why we study Dasein in order to study being. Of the many influences on the book, none seems greater to me than that of Kant.[7] For Kant, science and math constitute the rules of phenomena, instruction manuals for the construction of the world that appears to us. Certain facts about us—the nature of our transcendental faculties—determine certain necessary and universal features of phenomena because, in order to be phenomena and thus objects of scientific or mathematical knowledge, experience of these objects must be compatible with the ways we experience anything. It is the nature of our minds, for example, to organize the world in terms of causal relationships, so everything we experience will necessarily have a cause. Features of the structures of thinking get transferred to all that gets structured as thinkable.

I believe that *Being and Time* follows this basic strategy: the nature of Dasein, existence, determines everything about us, including our understanding. What our understanding is like in turn determines what we can understand and how we understand it, and hence the understandability or meaning of anything we can ever become aware of. That which we understand is the meaning of being, and how we understand anything determines the meaning of everything.

Heidegger changes Kant's approach[8] in three important ways: (1) Kant contrasts phenomena or the world we experience with noumena, the world as it is in itself or independent of our experience of it, but Heidegger's phenomenological background leads him to dismiss the very coherence of noumena.[9] The only reality we can talk about as real is the one we can have access to in some way. (2) Whereas Kant focuses on scientific objects, Heidegger considers this just one mode of being, presence-at-hand, and a relatively rare and derivative one at that.[10] He is much more interested in the traditionally neglected kind of beings that we encounter in our daily activities, as well as the features of ourselves that emerge during existential crises. (3) Kant's transcendental organizing principles appeared to many of his successors like a semirandom grab bag of two forms of intuition, twelve concepts of understanding, and three ideas of reason. Like some of the German Idealists, Heidegger attempts to unify all these features by basing them on a single factor: "More than Kant, we attempted to render visible the unitary character of the original dimension, in order to let the essence of the categories spring from it" (PIK 273). He unifies them in the most basic or primordial level of our nature: time.[11] "If we have regard for the possible totality, unity, and development of those fundamental structures of Dasein which we have hitherto exhibited, these structures are all to be conceived as at bottom 'temporal' and as modes of the temporalizing of temporality."[12]

His overarching claim then is that

whenever Dasein tacitly understands and interprets something like Being, it does so with *time* as its standpoint. Time must be brought to light—and genuinely conceived—as the horizon for all understanding of Being and for any way of interpreting it. In order for us to discern this, *time* needs to be *explicated primordially as the horizon for the understanding of Being, and in terms of temporality as the Being of Dasein, which understands Being.* (BT 39/17)

The argument is that we are, at bottom, temporal beings; Heidegger even says at times that "*Dasein itself ...* is *time.*"[13] Because of this, everything about us will be temporal, with different forms of temporality accounting for the various features of our being. One of these features is our understanding of being, so it too must be temporal. Just as Kant's transcendental subject can only experience the world, for example, causally, so Dasein experiences and understands reality in temporal terms.

If temporality constitutes the meaning of the being of the human Dasein and if understanding of being belongs to the constitution of the Dasein's being, then this understanding of being, too, must be possible only on the basis of temporality. ... Time is the horizon from which something like being becomes at all intelligible. We interpret being by way of time.[14]

Since we are temporal, our understanding must be temporal as well. That means that being as we understand it must be temporal. But (1) above states that there is no being but being as we experience it. Hence being itself is temporal. Being can only be temporally.

Let me use an analogy. Let's say we wanted to investigate the visibility of being instead its meaning or understandability. Visibility is not a free-floating, objective fact about reality as it is in itself regardless of seeing beings. It is essentially a relational quality: what it means for things to be visible contains an inherent reference to possible ways of seeing which exist in seers.

In order to determine the visibility of the world, we would have to examine the visual system of potential seers—the anatomy of their eyeballs, optic nerves, the visual parts of the brain, and so on. Figuring out how seers see is what determines the most general facts about the "see-ability" of reality.

I think this maps onto *Being and Time*'s existential analysis. The very meaning of meaning is to mean something *to* a being that can grasp meaning, that is, that can understand. Therefore, to investigate the meaning of being, we have to study those beings that can understand meaning. We study Dasein's being to understand her understanding, which in turn sets the parameters for the understandability of anything at all. Dasein's being is, at bottom, temporal, so she understands in temporal terms. This means that the understandability of being must be temporal, or, put another way, time is the meaning of being. This is also why what might look like changes of topic from being, to the meaning of being, to the being that understands being, at the beginning of the book are not changes of topic at all, but rather a relatively straightforward way to pursue this very puzzling inquiry. We are talking about the meaningfulness of being, which can only be meaningful to and in an understanding of its meaning.[15] It is Dasein—the being that understands—that provides the clearing or horizon within which being can have meaning, and Dasein's being that enables this meaningfulness is time. The conclusion of the book is in the title: being *and* time.

Heidegger thinks that the questions we bring to a text partially determine how it responds, and our question here of why he did not complete his proposed project highlights certain details. One possible answer is that he realized that the very way he had framed the inquiry prevented its appropriate resolution. He frequently accuses other philosophers of unwittingly working within a horizon of inherited inadequate concepts; perhaps he realized that he too had been similarly enmeshed in the tradition, despite his attempts to escape. A few candidates for the conceptual obstacle stand out, although none is definitely the source of error; for every later passage criticizing his early work, one can find two where he excuses it, blames others for misinterpreting it, or reinterprets it to be more in line with his later views. Among Heidegger's strengths we do not find humble self-criticism (one rare concession of fault graciously admits that "the fundamental flaw of the book *Being and Time* is perhaps that I ventured forth too far too early" [OWL 7]). Here are four of the more likely suspects.

(1) Subjectivism. One of the key points of the book as we have it is that philosophers have consistently misconstrued the nature of our selves, usually as self-sufficient, self-enclosed subjects who emerge to come into contact

with external objects by acquiring knowledge of them. Heidegger calls this "the ontological perversion of making Dasein something present-at-hand" (BT 293/250), though we misunderstand ourselves in ready-to-hand ways as well (BT 36–37/15). *Being and Time*'s existential analytic is an attempt to describe Dasein on and in its own terms rather than with concepts borrowed from foreign ontological regions.

However, as innovative as his conception of Dasein is, it still resembles the traditional subject in a number of ways.[16] Startlingly, given his later attempts to escape subjectivity, Heidegger's early work argues for its inescapability.

The direction of the path [Kant] follows, by returning to the subject in its broadest sense, is the only one that is possible and correct. It is the direction of the interpretation of being, actuality, existence that was followed not just by modern philosophy since Descartes, by expressly orienting its philosophical problems to the subject … or toward what is basically meant by it, namely, our Dasein. … All philosophy, in whatever way it may view the "subject" and place it in the center of philosophical investigation, returns to the soul, mind, consciousness, subject, ego in clarifying the basic ontological phenomena. … Reversion to the ego, to the soul, to consciousness, to mind, and to the Dasein is necessary for specific and inherently pertinent reasons.[17]

Being and Time's transcendental phenomenological approach makes being Dasein-dependent and Dasein-centric. If he has indeed done away with noumena, then being is only in our awareness, like Kantian phenomena, which is why "only as long as Dasein *is* (that is, only as long as an understanding of Being is ontically possible), 'is there' Being."[18] We are the clearing in which being can manifest itself and so be, and it is our approach that determines the mode of being of the beings we interact with. Without Kant's contrast between reality as we form it and reality as it is independently of our interactions, the fact that we shape phenomena comes out most clearly in the change-over of ready-to-hand tools to present-at-hand objects. If we unthinkingly use them they remain ready-to-hand, whereas stopping to stare makes them present-at-hand. Instead of Kant's distinction between things-for-us and things-in-themselves indicating our influence, Heidegger relies on this change in their being that results from a change in the stance we take toward them. I take this change-over to be the smoking gun for the transcendental activist reading of *Being and Time*.

This view puts us in charge; as Deleuze once said of Kant, "it is we who are giving the orders."[19] Being cannot be without us, and being is to some extent the way it is because of our actions. Since we press into projects that employ tools, beings take on the modes of useful and useless; since we disengage and contemplate, they also become inert substances. There are enormous differences between traditional notions of the subject and Dasein, of course, but Dasein performs some of the functions traditionally assigned to the subject, as Heidegger admits. Although he argued early on that studying being as experienced via studying Dasein's ways of experiencing is the only path, did he come to find this approach too subjectivistic to say what he wanted to say in Division Three?[20] There are a number of places where he identifies the idea of a fundamental ontology[21] or the influence of Kant or transcendentalism[22] as features he needed to overcome. Division Three was to move from Dasein to being itself. Did he come to believe that starting with Dasein locked him into the view from being-there, such that he could not get to being itself? But is a phenomenologist even entitled to such a distinction?

(2) History. History plays a significant role in *Being and Time*. The entire second half of the book was to have recounted the history of philosophy in order to grasp the inquiry's own preconceptions (BT 41–42/20–21). And yet, the very fact that this account was to occupy a separate half indicates that it was considered separable from the first half's existential analytic, a distinct path of its own rather than an integral part of the question of being. History is important to Dasein: it furnishes us with our concepts and the for-the-sakes-of-which that organize our lives and our world. But this adoption of ideas and roles seems to take its place within an ahistorical framework of *existentialia*.[23] These appear to be the same for all Dasein, across time and cultures, meaning that history only goes so deep. Beneath a layer of variable *nomos* lies the universal *physis* of our inherent nature, unaffected by what transpires atop it.

In the later work history goes all the way down. Being itself acquires a history in that different eras have distinct understandings of being which guide and inform all the experiences and actions of that time. To study being now means to examine "the changing forms in which Being shows itself epochally and historically" (TB 52) rather than the three ways of being that structure all Dasein's worlds. On the Kantian model, the form of phenomenal being is due to our nature—including, for Heidegger, the stance we take up—and if we remain the same then so do these ways of being. A fifth-century Roman carpenter projects himself into roles that require the use of equipment, so he will experience much of the world as interconnected ready-to-hand tools in basically the same way that a twenty-first-century data entry clerk does. They differ ontically—different for-the-sakes-of-which, different tools—but agree ontologically—they experience themselves as existing, their tools as ready-to-hand, their peers as *das Man*.

This is why

one tries in vain to interpret this occurrence [the destiny of Being] in terms of what was said in *Being and Time* about the historicity of man (*Dasein*) (not of Being). By contrast, the only possible way to anticipate the latter thought on the destiny of Being from the perspective of *Being and Time* is to think through what was presented in *Being and Time* about the dismantling of the ontological doctrine of the Being of beings.[24]

In other words, only Part Two's destruction of the history of philosophy could have prepared the way for this central theme of his later work. However, this passage has interesting parallels to Division III of Part One since the move from "the historicity of man (*Dasein*)" to that of Being is just the kind of transition or "turning" that Division III was to have effected.

His later work does not allow a division like that between Parts One and Two of *Being and Time*.[25] In these works, Heidegger often thinks by carrying on a conversation with the canon, as in the works he specified as new versions of Division III (*The Basic Problems of Phenomenology* and *Introduction to Metaphysics*). At the end of his long career, he even said that his "entire work in lectures and exercises in the past thirty years was mainly just an interpretation of Western philosophy" (HR 328).

(3) Metaphysics or the Forgetfulness of Being. The history of philosophy that appears in many of Heidegger's later works takes a number of forms, but it is usually characterized as a history of metaphysics, often beginning with Plato's theory of Forms and culminating in Nietzsche's will-to-power. At times he simply equates philosophy with metaphysics (e.g., BW 265, 432). To understand philosophy, then, we must ask, to quote the title of one of his essays, what is metaphysics?

Heidegger's later work breaks the history of philosophy into epochs organized around different "understandings of being," that is, basic understandings of what it means to be that shape much of what that period thinks, experiences, and does. Metaphysics is the attempt to describe these understandings by studying "the totality of beings as such with an eye to their most universal traits" (PM 287); it tries "to find words for what a being *is* in the history of its Being" (NIV 7). Whereas most of us focus on beings while relying on a pre-ontological understanding of their way of being, metaphysicians look beyond (*meta*) the vast array of beings coming in and out of existence (*physis*) to their most basic and common features, what Heidegger sometimes refers to as "beingness" or "the being of beings." It is these qualities that qualify entities as real and, on some schemes, determine their degree of realness, by defining what it is to be for that time.

The story of philosophy is the story of the various ideas that have held this role. Briefly, for the pre-Socratics it was *physis*; for Plato it was participation in an unchanging Form (sometimes the Greek understanding in general is characterized as production); for the medievals to be was to be a creation of God; for moderns it was being a mathematically measurable substance; and for us it is to be a malleable resource maximally amenable to use.

These understandings are extraordinarily important since, as *Being and Time* showed us, what one understands an entity to be determines what kinds of actions, thoughts, and words are natural and appropriate for it: "We always conduct our activities in an understanding of Being" (BT 25/5). These understandings comprehensively shape a culture's entire way of acting, thinking, and speaking: "Always the destining of revealing holds complete sway over men."[26] Instead of focusing on ontic events, Heidegger seeks their ground, that which accounts for people taking the actions they did, so that "*actual history* ... always concerns the openness of Being—or nothing at all" (BW 304).

I find Heidegger somewhat ambivalent about the relationship among the epochal understandings. Sometimes he anticipates Kuhn by considering them incommensurable, characterizing the changes between them as "leaps." We cannot put the phases into an overarching coherent story since there can be no general explanation of the way one transitions into another; the very notion of what counts as a satisfactory explanation varies with the understanding of being.[27] This is how I understand the claim that being sends these understandings to us: it is utterly incomprehensible why one transitions into another, why those particular ones occurred and in that order. At other times, though, he does construct a narrative of the adventures of being as the story of an ever-growing obliviousness to being across millennia-long variations on the being–becoming and appearance–reality distinctions.[28]

Metaphysics is implicated in this forgetfulness of being by focusing on beingness or what it means to be, without wondering why we have the particular understanding we do or where they all come from. Now there can be no answer to this question since any explanation presupposes a system of intelligibility in which it makes sense, whereas the question seeks to account for this very intelligibility, for the fact that we can make sense of anything in any way. But asking the question does change our perspective, letting us see our understanding as *an* understanding instead of simply the way things are, and as one among many possible ways of making sense of the world. "If the answer could be given it would consist in a transformation of thinking, not in a propositional statement about a matter at stake" (BW 431).

The key is to appreciate the fact that we have an understanding at all, that we can become aware of anything in any way. This turns us from beingness to the source or emergence of understandings, which Heidegger continuously tries to find a way to express throughout his long career. He calls it variously being itself, the truth of being, the clearing, Seyn, the "it gives" ("Es gibt"), Ereignis (translated as "the event" or "appropriation"). The point is to move from the metaphysical level of the common traits of the real to the far simpler and even more elusive fact that there is reality at all, that we are aware of it in any way. Although "the truth of Being as the clearing itself remains concealed for metaphysics" (BW 235), "it is necessary for thinking to become explicitly aware of the matter here called clearing" (BW 442).

The great achievement of metaphysicians is to put their epoch's understanding into words;[29] their great failing is to stop there without asking why or how that understanding came about.[30] "In the beingness of beings, metaphysics thinks being, yet without being able to ponder the truth of being" (PM 232), which means that "all metaphysics leaves something essential unthought: its own ground and foundation."[31] While Being and Time deploys the ontological difference between beings and their being—what he later calls their beingness—it does not move up the next ontological step to their bestowal upon us. He even says that "from the perspective of Appropriation [Ereignis] it becomes necessary to free thinking from the ontological difference"[32] since staying at the levels of beings and beingness blocks our way to being itself. There are a few points where Heidegger criticizes his earlier work for either being metaphysical or employing the language of metaphysics, which opens it to the misinterpretation of it as metaphysical.[33]

(4) All of the Above. Holism is a constant theme throughout Heidegger's work. Being and Time, for example, depicts the facets of being-in-the-world as so deeply interrelated that none can be nor be understood apart from the others. The later work posits holisms among humanity and being, the elements of the fourfold, members of a society, and, as we have just seen, all aspects of a culture. One of the things that an epochal understanding of being does is uncover the underlying unity of what initially appears to be a haphazard collection of attitudes and actions. "The fundamental characteristic of all beings ... must, so to speak, be 'encountered' by the thinking of this thought in every region of beings: in nature, art, history, politics, in science and in knowledge in general."[34] This means that all the thoughts of

the modern era, including those which lead to Heidegger's failure to finish
Being and Time, should fit together into a coherent overall view. This certainly applies to the three factors listed above.

(2) History leads to (1) Subjectivity because it is only in the modern era's
understanding of being that the subject comes to hold such a central position, one that continues to some extent in *Being and Time*.

> The essence of humanity altogether transforms itself in that man becomes the sub-
> ject. … He becomes that being upon which every being, in its way of being and its
> truth, is founded. Man becomes the relational center of beings as such. But this is
> only possible when there is a transformation in the understanding of beings as a
> whole.[35]

This is the paradox at the heart of modern subjectivism and technology:
we think we gave ourselves this central position in reality with control over
nature, but we could never have even considered such matters had the ideas
not struck us. Thus the idea that everything is our creation and should be
under our control was itself not our creation or under our control. Nevertheless, the notion that Dasein's stance effects a change-over in the being
of equipment or objects contains an echo of this subject-centered ontology.

It works in the reverse direction too. The anchor that kept *Being and
Time* from fully immersing being into history was the ahistorical essence
of Dasein. It is our three constant understandings of being that keep being
in these three forms. Since our understandings form and enable all experience, as long as the former remain the same, so do the latter (there are
occasional glimmers of rejections of this, e.g., BP 22).

But Heidegger rejects all such ahistorical pretensions in the later work,
allowing humanity to change along with everything else when being sends
us new understandings. Dasein cannot serve as the foundation of ontology
because we receive these new structures along with everything else. Each
new epoch will "bestow on [man] the foundation of a new essence. This
need displaces man into the beginning of a foundation of his essence. I say
advisedly *a* foundation for we can never say that it is the absolute one."[36]
This change also leads to (3). As long as Dasein is responsible for the form
being takes, and Dasein's *existentialia* are fully explained, we need not wonder about the world's being intelligible. It could not be otherwise. By pursuing our projects, we *make* sense of the world. But if we change with the rest
of being, then these cannot be coming from us but rather must descend
upon us. This realization leads us to wonder about their source or emergence, which turns us from beingness to being itself, thereby beginning the
overcoming of metaphysics.

Now let us turn to the scholars who are trying to uncover the unsaid in Heidegger's work. I invite you onto their paths to and through Heidegger's greates- *Holzweg*.

Notes

1. TB 80; Safranski 1999, 143, 171; Kisiel 1993, 477–489.

2. Kisie- 1993, 486; M 366–367.

3. "We assert now that *being is the proper and sole theme of philosophy*. … Philosophy is the theoretical conceptual interpretation of being, of being's structure and its possibilities. Philosophy is ontological" (BP 11; see also BP 15, BT 35/15, 62/38).

4. "Its understanding of being is not one capacity among others, but the basic condition for the possibility of Dasein as such" (MFL 16; see also BT 176/137, 274/231, 383/33=, 402/350, 416/365).

5. Confusingly, "ontological" contrasts with "pre-ontological" when denoting an explicit understanding, and with "ontic" when distinguishing being from beings.

6. See BT 62/38, BP 73–75, 111, 116–117, 155, 166; although cf. BT 487/436.

7. "When some years ago I studied the *Critique of Pure Reason* anew and read it, as it were, against the background of Husserl's phenomenology, it opened my eyes; and Kant became for me a crucial confirmation of the accuracy of the path which I took in my search. … Kant has *the* immense significance in education for scientific, philosophical work" (PIK 292–293). For more on Kant's influence, see Braver 2007, 176–181, 187, 221–225, 273–275, 284, 502–504, 508, 532n9.

8. "We can also call the science of being, as critical science, *transcendental science*. In doing so we are not simply taking over unaltered the concept of the transcendental in Kant, although we are indeed adopting its original sense and its true tendency, perhaps still concealed from Kant" (BP 17).

9. "It is phenomenologically absurd to speak of the phenomenon as if it were something behind which there would be something else of which it would be a phenomenon in the sense of the appearance which represents and expresses [this something else]. . . What the phenomenon gives is precisely that something in itself" (HCT 86; see also HCT 82, BT 60/35–36, 193/152, 228/183, 251/207, 255–256/212, 269/226, 414/362; Braver 2007, chap. 5). Note: some scholars disagree with this reading. Graham Harman, for example, argues that "Heidegger turns out to be *the* philosopher of the noumenal" (2002, 160), while Julian Young holds that limiting being to our experience of it is the essence of the humanism that Heidegger is trying to overcome (private correspondence).

10. "If we radicalize the Kantian problem of ontological knowledge in the sense that we do not limit this problem to the ontological foundation of the positive sciences and if we do not take this problem as a problem of judgment but as the radical and fundamental question concerning the possibility of understanding being in general, then we shall arrive at the philosophically fundamental problematic of *Being and Time*" (PIK 289; see also PIK 48, 252, KPM 141–142).

11. One of the main theses of Heidegger's reading of Kant in the late 1920s is that Kant himself was heading in the direction of unifying intuition and understanding in temporality by means of the transcendental imagination, but he recoiled from this radical discovery in the second edition of the first *Critique*. "Even if Kant not infrequently strives toward this original dimension, i.e., toward the boundaries of subjectivity as the unity of time and the I-think, of receptivity and spontaneity, nevertheless Kant does not proceed from this dimension of the origin disclosed in advance in its unity" (PIK 273–274). One is reminded of Husserl's contention that Descartes' thought teetered on the brink of discovering phenomenology.

12. BT 352/304; see also BT 456–457/404. This holism is another *leitmotif* of Heidegger's thought: "The existential analytic of the Dasein ... must aim at bringing to light the ground of the basic structures of the Dasein in their unity and wholeness" (BP 227; see also BT 65/40, 78–79/53, 169–170/131–132, 226/181, 274–276/231–233, 279/236, 293/249, 309/264, 351/304, 370/323, PIK 291; Braver 2012, chap. 3).

13. HCT 197; see also HCT 319.

14. BP 16; see also BP 228, 274, 280, PS 439–440, BT 38–39/17.

Temporality is the basic constitution of human Dasein. On the basis of Dasein's original constitution it is possible for Dasein to have pure understanding of being and of determinations of being. Understanding of being in general is constituted on the basis of the temporality of Dasein. And only because something like this is possible can Dasein as an existing being comport itself toward beings that are not Dasein and simultaneously toward a being that Dasein itself is. Although Kant did not unfold the problem of ontological knowledge in such a fundamental way and did not push the possibility of a radical resolution this far, nevertheless he offers a hint at the problem. (PIK 288–289)

15. BT 62/37, 140/106, 193/152, 274/231, 292/248.

16. Derrida makes this point: "*Dasein* cannot be reduced to a subjectivity, certainly, but the existential analytic still retains the formal traits of every transcendental analytic," which leads to the fact that "in spite of everything it opens up and encourages us to think, to question, and to redistribute, *Dasein* still occupies a place analogous to that of the transcendental subject" (Derrida 1995, 258, 273; see also 267).

17. BP 73; see also BP 122, 299, 301, 312, BT 146/111.

18. BT 255/212; see also BT 228/183, 251/207, 269/226. There is considerable debate over how to understand these apparently idealistic or antirealist claims. See Braver 2007, 181–198, for a discussion of the issues and the secondary literature.

19. Deleuze 1984, 14.

20. "The reason for such noncomprehension lies in our habituation, entrenched and ineradicable, to the modern mode of thought: man is thought as subject. ... In struggling loose from it, it necessarily and continually refers back to the course of the past and even calls on it for assistance, in the effort to say something entirely different. Above all, however, the path taken terminates abruptly at a decisive point [Division III?—LB]. The reason for the disruption is that the attempt and the path it chose confront the danger of unwillingly becoming merely another entrenchment of subjectivity; that the attempt itself hinders the decisive steps" (NIV 141). "In *Being and Time*, Da-sein still has an appearance that is 'anthropological,' 'subjectivistic,' 'individualistic,' etc., and yet the opposite of all of this is in view here. It is admittedly not kept in view as what is primarily and uniquely focused on. Instead, this opposite is in view only as the *necessary consequence* of the decisive transformation of the 'question of being'" (CP 233/§172; see also CP 237/§176, 255/§199, FS 41, TB 31–32, BW 231). At other times Heidegger denies subjectivistic readings of *Being and Time*, blaming the misinterpretation on readers (see PR 86, CP 204/§138, TB 27, Zo 116, 191, BW 138, M 123, 188).

21. "What is fundamental in fundamental ontology is incompatible with any building on it. Instead, after the meaning of Being had been clarified, the whole analytic of Dasein was to be more originally repeated in a completely different way. Thus, since the foundation of fundamental ontology is no foundation upon which something could be built, no *fundamentum inconcussum*, but rather a *fundamentum concussum* .. whereas the word 'foundation' contradicts the preliminary character of the analytic, the term 'fundamental ontology' was dropped" (TB 32; see also CP 39/§19).

22. "At first, what was available, simply out of metaphysics, was—to name only this—the schema of the transcendental, such that this itself was immediately conceived, according to the basic position of *Being and Time*, in its own truth ('primordial temporality'). Yet thereby also resulted by necessity the fatal delivery of the step to metaphysics; it seemed that everything was only a modification of Kant's laying of a foundation for metaphysics" (E 120/§181; see also E 111–112/§176, TB 29, 44–46, CP 138/§88, 188/§122, 337/§259, 353/§262, Zo 194, IM 19–20).

23. Despite the fact that Heidegger denies this: "It must still have seemed that Being-in-the-world has the function of a rigid framework, within which Dasein's possible ways of comporting itself towards its world run their course without touching the 'framework' itself as regards its Being" (BT 221/176). That is indeed how it seems to me.

24. TB 9; see also EP 14–15, M 91, FS 78, E 75/§123.

25. "Philosophical cognition is essentially at the same time, in a certain sense, historical cognition. History of philosophy, as it is called, belongs to the concept of philosophy as science, to the concept of phenomenological investigation" (BP 23; see also BP 15, 19, CP 36/§16, 345/§259, 355/§262, M 367–368, IM 45, 97, EPM xix).

26. BW 330; see also BW 167–168, OBT 57, 79, NII 80, 131, NIV 7, 100, 205, WT 95–96, PR 55, 87, 94, ET 150, FS 61, WCT 66.

27. "In no way can it be seen that individual philosophies and epochs of philosophy have emerged from one another in the sense of the necessity of a dialectic process" (WIP 63; see also QT 39, M 17, 206, TB 52, BW 433, IM 30, FS 9, CP 171/§125, PR 108).

28. "The decline of the truth of beings occurs necessarily, and indeed as the completion of metaphysics" (EP 86; see also TB 9, PR 91). John D. Caputo distinguishes these two approaches to the history of philosophy as demythologized Heidegger and the myth of being, respectively (Caputo 1993).

29. M 300, 322–323, 375, TB 37.

30. EGT 60, 99, 122, QT 115, PM 287, NIV 7, 211–212, OBT 57, EP 90, BW 247, PM 278, 288, AM 8, 102.

31. WCT 100; see also PM 277, 318.

32. TB 37; see also EP 85.

33. BW 231, TB 29, CP 136/§85.

34. NIII 19; see also BW 294–295, PR 94, NIV 10, 48, 53.

35. OBT 66–67; see also QT 151, PR 76–77.

36. BQ 139; see also TB 35, 45, FS 47, Z 207, QT 128, 151, 153, DT 77–78, PM 285, 334, P 138, NIII 221.

References

Braver, Lee. 2007. *A Thing of This World: A History of Continental Anti-Realism.* Evanston, IL: Northwestern University Press.

Braver, Lee. 2012. *Groundless Grounds: A Study of Wittgenstein and Heidegger.* Cambridge, MA: MIT Press.

Caputo, John D. 1993. *Demythologizing Heidegger.* Bloomington: Indiana University Press.

Deleuze, Gilles. 1984. *Kant's Critical Philosophy.* Trans. Hugh Tomlinson and Barbara Habberjam. Minneapolis: University of Minnesota Press.

Derrida, Jacques. 1995. *Points ... Interviews, 1974–1994*. Trans. Peggy Kamuf et al. Stanford. Stanford University Press.

Harman, Graham. 2002. *Tool-Being: Heidegger and the Metaphysics of Objects*. Chicago: Open Ccurt.

Kisiel, Theodore. 1993. *The Genesis of Heidegger's Being and Time*. Berkeley: University of California Press.

Safransk., Rüdiger. 1999. *Martin Heidegger: Between Good and Evil*. Trans. Ewald Osers. Cambricge, MA: Harvard University Press.

1 Heidegger's Parmenides

Alain Badiou

So who is this Parmenides? We do not know much. Here we have someone practically reduced to his text. This is not for want of learned studies attesting to his date of birth—of which I will spare you the details—but they are so contorted that I do not believe that there is any sense in celebrating Parmenides' birthday. Well then, what do we know about him?

We know that he is at the boundary of the sixth and fifth centuries before the Common Era, so strictly speaking, before the Classical period of Greek philosophy. That he is thus stamped by the academies with the seal of pre-Socratic philosophy, belonging to the Greek sequence still called archaic or pre-Classical. This is what brings us incidentally to Heidegger, who, after citing a passage, says of the Parmenides fragments,

These few words stand there, like archaic Greek statues.[1]

The image of the "archaic Greek statue" appears here explicitly as a double metaphor. First, it indicates the precisely pre-Classical character of Parmenides, ascribing something originary and foundational, and also something aesthetic, whose mode of presence involves a riddle and is not immediately accessible to our perception. We also know that he is native to Elea in Magna Graecia, in a remote and eccentric colony of Athens. We can situate the city of Elea in what is now called southern Italy, just south of Naples. And because he was from Elea, the doctrinal movement of which Parmenides is the founder has been called "Eleatic," and his philosophy has been designated "Eleatic philosophy." But the question of knowing whether he was really its founder remains open. A troubling, double question: for once one has recognized a founder, an earlier always appears. And that would be Xenophanes of Colophon, meaning that Parmenides, being the second founder, would have to be the true one. It is always the second founder who founds, because the founder founds what the first unfounds, or has left unfounded—that is to say, the first founder initiates something that was not formerly founded or foundable. Such is the case for Xeno-phanes—but we do not know much about him because he is even more mysterious than Parmenides. This is a vast question that has opened and remains open to German philology—leaving the field open for scholars to reconstruct to the smallest detail both the philosophy of Parmenides and that of Xenophanes, for whom he would have been the audience, their con-nections, the direct influence of one on the other, and so on. In some sense, this is a paleontological task. The pre-Socratic period of Greek philosophy is one of reconstructions: we have a single line of writing, barely legible, and we rebuild the doctrine, the influences, the origin, and so on. Indeed, this is essentially what Heidegger does with a line from Anaximander.

Whether second or first founder, Parmenides is in fact the one who pro-vides the kernel of the Eleatic doctrine, by virtue of the texts, the real texts that he left us. From him there remain the fragments of what was once a *Poem*. Only fragments of a half-present whole to decipher, half-absent to construct. Some fairly extensive fragments, some debris too; but enough to reconstruct a differentiated whole and to give voice to the coherence and the logic of the work, despite the gaps. As far as the pre-Socratic epoch is concerned, nothing, or almost nothing, is authentic: by way of transmis-sion through all of antiquity, the entire constellation of texts and their interpretation arise from a practice, reinvented several times, of writing and of quotation, whose legitimacy remains to be proven. Indeed, it is often the very late authors of the Christian era who refer to some of these fragments. This is to say that each time, they have been filtered, and filtered accord-ing to principles or procedures that are difficult to rediscover. Is there, per-haps precisely because from a very early date Parmenides was such a fabled and legendary founding figure, a highly selective filtering in the system of his theses? And this we cannot recreate. The mode of expression that Par-menides chose is thus poetic. A *Poem*—sometimes in pieces, or even debris, reduced to a half-verse, and elsewhere the lengthy development of a unique work. This is in any case the dominant hypothesis of current scholarship that allows us to speak of "the" *Poem* of Parmenides. Its exceptional place among the pre-Socratic philosophers, those of ancient Greece, enshrines him as a truly legendary figure, and not, like others, as a person or, for his life, as in the case of the poetic mythical figure of Empedocles, tied to the hypothesis of his suicide. No, none of this for Parmenides: the tradition enshrines him as a properly philosophical legend. Very early on, from the Classical period of philosophy a scant century after his death, a conceptual legend places him in an originary position, as the father of philosophy and practically as the proper noun designating the emergence, the appearance, of philosophy as such. Why?

The earlier pre-Socratics, who were islanders, like the Thales of "All is water" fame, are referred to as physicians, still halfway between legendary cosmologies and rational apparatus developing this or that particular thesis, actually instituting a new regime of the functioning of discourse—which will, indeed, be called "philosophy" in the Classical period. There is no lack of evidence for this break, but the most significant evidence turns up in Plato, especially in the two dialogues *Sophist* and *Parmenides*, in which Plato's attitude toward Parmenides differs radically from that of all of his predecessors and rivals. This much is common knowledge. But I recall the operations to which the Parmenidean figure has been subjected. In the *Sophist* the metaphor of parricide appears explicitly, referring to the duty felt by Plato to criticize some of Parmenides' statements. To establish that non-being has a kind of being, he declares "a parricide" with respect to "our father Parmenides," thus inscribing a Parmenidean fixation into all of philosophy. And see how remarkable Plato's use of the term "parricide" is! Then, at the beginning of the *Parmenides*, the complex setting presents an encounter between the young Socrates and the old Parmenides—or on closer reflection, an encounter between the real father and the symbolic father, because the Plato–Socrates relationship is, so to speak, immediate, running throughout the work, whereas this other relationship, this reference to the old Parmenides that Socrates would have encountered, is an explicit name-of-the-father figure, a strictly symbolic paternity. So we have this astonishing dramatization, in which the immediate predecessor, to whom we constantly pay tribute, the main character of the dialogues, Socrates, encounters he who is in truth the general father, the universal father the father *qua* father, the very founder of philosophy itself. This is all the more striking as it is an encounter between a very young Socrates and a very old Parmenides. Socrates is so very young and Parmenides so very old that this encounter certainly never took place. Plato rigged the dates. It is truly a parable, a theatrical portrayal. Every reference to Parmenides, to his role as founding father, unfolds in its symbolic singularity, showing how, through these two dialogues, the conceptual Parmenidean legend has persisted since the time of the ancient Greeks. By *conceptual legend* I mean the following: Parmenides is the founder of a new regime of discourse on which all philosophers depend, regardless of tendency—even those who, like Plato in the *Sophist*, feel compelled to commit parricide.

This conceptual legend is then maintained or transmitted across the entire history of philosophy. I will punctuate it with two points of reference: one in Hegel, and the other in Heidegger.

At the very beginning of the *Logic*, when he deals with being, Hegel says this:

> The Eleatics were the first to give voice to the simple thought of pure being—notable among them Parmenides, who declared it to be the absolute and sole truth. In his surviving fragments, he did it with the pure enthusiasm of thought which for the first time apprehended itself in its absolute abstraction: *only being is, and nothing is not absolutely.*[2]

What do we find in this Hegelian tribute? That Parmenides has stated the simple thought of "pure being," and the idea of "pure enthusiasm of thought which for the first time apprehended itself in its absolute abstraction." The theme of "the first time" as such is, in a sense, revisited and questioned by Hegel.

Likewise, in his *Introduction to Metaphysics*, among other reverential eulogies to Parmenides, Heidegger writes,

> Anyone today who is acquainted with the standards of such a thinking discourse must lose all desire to write books.[3]

Heidegger recognizes not only the idea of the absolutely originary Parmenides, but also that of the unsurpassed character of Parmenidean procreation: *Anyone today who is acquainted with the standards of such a thinking discourse must lose all desire to write books.* It is as if, in a sense, the very existence of an originary Parmenides rendered the historical destiny of philosophy pointless. From this first procreation, from that very first time when being is proclaimed in its being, Parmenides appears, in the strict sense, as a hero—in the mythological sense of the word—a hero of philosophy: one who accomplishes the prodigious task of naming, for the first time, being in its being and, in the same act, invents philosophical discourse properly so called.

Still, we will have to revisit the aura surrounding Parmenides, at least in part. Not because it's inconsequential—quite the contrary. But he is one of those figures petrified by history not only in form, but also in what was said. For better or worse, because crafting such a thing is very difficult—history has given birth to a counterlegend of Parmenides, animated by a willingness to deconstruct him. Like any legend, that of Parmenides as symbolic Father is shadowed by a counterlegend. On this counterlegend, while Parmenides did indeed inaugurate thinking about being, he initiated an approach to this question more abstract than real. This is evidently

Nietzsche's thesis—as we might have expected. It opposes the abstract, cold immobility of Parmenides, which Nietzsche might call mechanical, to what he takes to be the dynamic vitality of Heraclitus. But let us leave Heraclitus aside for now. What is interesting is to see the great legendary figure of the founder of thinking about being opposed to the counterfigure who, instead of beginning by liberating thought, would have begun by immobilizing it, that is, would have fixed it from the start. On this countercurrent, Parmenides appears not as the founder of philosophy, but as the source of the danger of internal abstraction in philosophy itself, the founder of abstraction, or the founder of a regime of philosophy that disregards life. The Parmenidean figure is thus so saturated as to be saddled both with founding philosophical discourse and with awakening the menace that stalks this discourse.

I maintain that these two interpretations—that of Heidegger and that of Nietzsche, which Heidegger explicitly criticizes—are both inadequate. The trick is to find the precise point of inadequacy, which of course is the same in both. It is the same because neither reconnects Parmenides—what Parmenides said—to the "system" of his conditions. Not, of course, in the sense of his sociohistorical conditions: it is not a matter of telling you that at the moment when Parmenides declared immobility to be the best, the rising prices of ceramics in Sicily had paralyzed trade. It is the "system" of the conditions of *enunciation* of the Parmenidean dictum—to speak like Heidegger—the system of those conditions that establish him as founder, but not immediately, not only, because he pronounces himself on being. What must be apprehended—to do justice to Parmenides, so that he is neither the Heideggerian legend nor the Nietzschean counterlegend—is the regime of *conceptual* conditions that he obeys. There is, certainly, something of the founder in Parmenides. If not in Parmenides, then in Xenophanes, who, it turns out, is nothing more than his projected shadow. But the system of conditions for this founding is part of the foundation itself. This is the inadequacy of the Heideggerian and Nietzschean interpretations.

It must also be said that the tone Parmenides himself uses has contributed greatly to the dramatization of his conceptual legend. In the *Poem*, the tone is at once imperative and sacral. It is imperative because it is in a very pronounced regime of prescriptive certitude: it proclaims and forbids. It is sacral because it presents itself in a regime of inspiration, of pronouncement for which Parmenides does not present himself as the immediate source, but rather as though dictated to him by an inspiration whose image is a goddess. This subtle mix of imperative and sacral form gives the *Poem* an exceptional loftiness, an absolutely singular abruptness and grandeur that has always fascinated.

Three passages from the *Poem* let you hear the founder's tone. Here is the first:

The steeds that bear me carried me as far as ever my heart
desired, to abundant discoveries, crossing all cities,
since they brought me and set me on the road of the goddess,
who conducts the man who knows. On this road was I borne
along; for on it the wise steeds carried me, drew my chariot,
and maidens showed the way.[4]

This is the beginning, such as we have it. It is both the fiction of an initiatory voyage to the celestial dwelling place of the divinity about to speak and, at the same time, the pride of he who knows.

The second fragment attests to the elevated, imperative character:

Come now, I will tell you—listen to my words
and carry them away—I will tell you the only two paths
of inquiry which are for thinking: the first—how it is and that it is
not possible that it is not—is the path to trust—for it attends upon the Truth;
second, to know that it is not, and that non-being is necessary,
this path, I declare to you, is only a path on which we find absolutely nothing to
trust. For one cannot know what is not—
there is no possible through-road—nor [can one] state it in speech.[5]

And now the seventh fragment:

We will never bend being to the diversity of that which is not;
divert then your thinking of this path of inquiry, and do not let habit,
rich in experience, compel you along this path:
where an eye tries its utmost not to see, an ear fills with noise,
and directs a tongue, but by reason, decide by the arguments and in midst of controversy
what my words disclose for you.[6]

This is the language Parmenides has devised to make himself heard. It is a poetic language, a language of proclamation, a language of inspiration, of certitude. And the idea of a "first time"—here I again insist—has contributed to staging the legend, evoking the enthusiasm of the first time, as Hegel called it, but also the idea of inspiration. All the while, he knows that what he has to say is unheard of.

What, at bottom, is this about? What is inscribed in his opening? In his *Introduction to Metaphysics*, Heidegger proposes an analysis that is sufficiently precise and persuasive in its proximity to the text: what Parmenides is supposed to have stated for the first time in perfect clarity is the connection of two irreconcilable differences. The first is the difference between being and nonbeing; as we all know, faced with a choice between two paths, we must choose one. The second is the difference between being and seeming. The insight is that the two delimited differences—being and nonbeing, being and seeming—are strictly speaking constitutive of philosophy, for it is they that began philosophy. Heidegger's entire aim is to show how the delimitation of these differences—being/nonbeing and being/seeming—is the originary condition of philosophical discourse. It is not that this discourse can be reduced; rather, this discourse is possible only within the regime of the delimitation of these differences. From this he deduces that poetry offers three ways of thought—here, he reprises the same metaphor as Parmenides—three roads, three paths, three tracks, whose properties differ. There is the way of being, which Parmenides considers necessary; there is the way of nonbeing, which is impracticable, which leads nowhere; and there is finally the way of seeming—or seeming-opinion. The Greek word for this is *doxa*—the way of opinion, always accessible, always practical, in some sense the easy path, what Parmenides would call the path of "men," but nonetheless a path we can avoid, for we are not required to take it.

Let us review: the first path is necessary, the second inaccessible, and the third can be avoided—it can be avoided in the sense in which, normally, it is the one that is always practical. What Heidegger demonstrates—I believe correctly—is that Parmenides' great power, in light of this trifurcation of possible paths for thought, is that of establishing philosophy as a decision. Heidegger would be willing to say that Parmenides' tone—the loftiness of Parmenides' tone—is that of decision and not of argumentation. So, on this interpretation, it is not quite fair to say that Parmenides is the first philosopher. Parmenides is less philosopher than the one who *decides* philosophy. After which, there are philosophers, but there are philosophers because philosophy has been *decided*. And as far as philosophy is concerned, Parmenides is not *a* philosopher, not even the first. He is more than that, because he is the one who *decides* philosophy. He decides it because he delineates its paths, and consequently the metaphor of the crossroads is pivotal for him. The metaphor of the chariot drawn by horses to the crossroads is essential, because it designates the *place* of the decision. We are conducted to the crossroads, where it is at once prescribed and possible to decide philosophy. But in order to decide it, there naturally must first be a representable compresence of paths. It is for this reason that Parmenides does not say: there is but one way. That, for Heidegger, would be philosophy losing its way. Philosophy will be lost precisely when it begins to pretend that there is only one path. But even more essential for Parmenides: there are in fact, two paths, and thus three—that of being, that of nonbeing, and that of seeming—and philosophy must *on this point* be decided. The es ence of Parmenides, Heidegger went on, is then to think *at the place* where paths diverge, that is, to think "at the place of a decision," and to be the one who thinks the path of nothingness at the same time as that of being. The greatness of Parmenides—on this point I agree with Heidegger—is not to have said "being is," but to have decided philosophy at the cross oads of two paths, at which the being of being and the nonbeing of nonbeing are both thought at the same time, and to have represented this point as the strategic crossroads of philosophical decision.

Heidegger summarizes it as follows:

The [Parmenides] fragment at the same time gives us the most ancient document that shows that, together with the path of Being, the path of Nothing must expressly be *thought*.[7]

If we must expressly think the path of nothing at the same time as the path of being, it is because the essence of that which is at play, there, is the decision. This is not because one should forge a synthesis of them, or think them at the same time. It is rather that, if the decision is to decide philosophy, we must naturally think the paths of this decision concurrently. This interpretation is one of the most powerful hypotheses on the originary character of Parmenidean thought.

What should we make of this? In the sentence, "the most ancien document that shows that, together with the path of Being, the path of Nothing must expressly be *thought*," everything turns on *philosophy*. Everything turns on it on grounds of a first complexity, which is: to what extent does "to decide philosophy" constitute a philosophical document, a document *of* philosophy? This is the first question. The second question, much more important in my opinion, appears because in this sentence, Heidegger acts as if the explanation of the two paths and of the decision between them— the explanation of the path of being and that of nonbeing, the metaphor of the crossroads and the associated decision imperative—described the origin of philosophy, or was the original decision of philosophy. The question is whether it is true that Parmenides decides philosophy, because he implies that the path of being and that of nonbeing are the place of decision. Is it he who decides philosophy, or better, is it philosophy that he decides, in the act, and only in the act of making explicit what I call "the crossroads of the decision," the critical imperative of decision where the path of being meets that of nonbeing? Is it fair to say that it is philosophy that has been decided at this point? Because plainly what Heidegger will call "philosophy" is precisely what was decided there: the doctrine of the necessity of concurrently thinking the path of being and that of nothingness. His interpretive method consists in saying, at the same time, first, that philosophy was decided there, and second, that philosophy must be that which this decision constitutes. This is to say that the interpretation delivers both senses simultaneously. But what is the problem? If philosophy were to decide on this point and this point alone—to think at the same time the path of being and that of nothingness, and thereby institute a decision regime—and if so doing was absolutely originary to the existence of its discursive apparatus, then we must declare, as indeed I do, that philosophy has been decided well in advance.

I turn now to an Egyptian text dating to three or four centuries before Parmenides, the Bremner-Rhind Papyrus.[8] Its structure is also metaphorical and poetic—as in the *Poem* of Parmenides, it is being who speaks, the "divinity."

The text reads:

When I came into existence, existence existed.
I came into existence under the form of the existing
that had come into existence as the first time.
Having come into existence under the mode of the existence of the existing, I will exist.
And this is how existence came into existence.[9]

This is the Egyptian text. Now let us place ourselves in Heidegger's position. What would he have said if he was dealing not with Parmenides but with this Egyptian text? For that matter, what should we say? We might say: here is the original proclamation of the ontic–ontological difference, fully present in this text. What was this unknown Egyptian telling us? That there is a dialectic of "existing" and "existence," of "beings" and "being" in the face of the uncertainty over what this word means. It means "existence," it means "having come to be," it means "birth," it means "transformation," "being." This is the dialectic of existing and existence, that of beings and being. And what the text tells us is that existence has come to itself, and that this coming to be is mediated within existing, in a kind of self-founding primordiality: *Having come into existence under the mode of the existence of the existing, I will exist. And this is how existence came into existence.* This is being that is thought of as birth—that is to say, thought as the originary birth giving birth to itself, the birth in which being comes to itself, at the same time depositing, as an indication of self, existing, which is both its principle of mediation and its efficacy. Of course, all this presupposes a high degree of metaphysical and ontological speculation in that era. But might it instead be claimed that the mythologizing *corpus* of the text, of the textual fragment, is mythology only—an account of the birth of the world, and not a philosophical decision? By itself this is unpersuasive, because the opening of Parmenides' *Poem* also deploys maidens, Goddesses, a chariot with silver wheels, and so on. All of the usual referential mythological ornamentation contributes to the mode of proclamation. Thus one might perfectly well assert that if philosophy decides itself at the place where the question of being and nonbeing is represented, if philosophy decides itself when the question of being and of nonbeing is constituted or represented, then there is every reason to think it is of Egyptian origin. This is all the more true, given that what has come down to us is in a fragmentary state. The Parmenidean *Poem*, or the few bits of it that remain to us, details on the one side such elements as "the ethereal fire of the flame," "the very lightness of favorable light" that resembles itself, and on the other, "the night without light," "without structure." Such considerations also belong to primitive descriptive cosmology. It is therefore not true that Parmenides' text is a text of pure ontology. It also has a cosmological purpose, ultimately claiming to describe the protocol of the framework of elements, of the distribution of "hot" and "dry," of "wet," of "earth," of "heaven," and so on. The same sprinkling of abstract dialectic and pure ontology in cosmological arrangements that we find, partially, in the Parmenidean text, we also see, more robustly, in the Egyptian text. But why is it so incomplete in the former? It is because it was filtered by the subsequent philosophical tradition. It is because this was where the operational regime of philosophy properly so called was discovered, that the material that would ultimately be retained within philosophy was progressively distilled from the work of the founding father, while residual mythology and cosmology were somewhat sanitized. Still, philosophy *was not founded* in Egypt. Why no? How did this come to pass? The Egyptian text has come to us amid a jumbled flood, spilling out among cosmological, mythological, and religious texts: sacred texts. Had the Parmenidean text survived completely unfiltered by the foundation of a particular regime of discourse, philosophical discourse, it would convey, in my view, very much the same feeling. What we can say is that we cannot identify the philosophical act by virtue of the mere presence of speculations on being and non-being, even when the logic of their implication is clearly articulated.

Let us now turn to Indian texts, beginning with the *Hymns of the Veda*. The most recent of these predate Parmenides by four centuries, the oldest by ten. Let us consider a text from the second period—around three or four centuries before Parmenides:

Neither non-Being existed then, nor Being.
There neither existed the realm of space nor the firmament beyond.
What stirred powerfully? Where? Under the care of whom?
Was it water, unfathomably deep?

There existed at that time neither death, nor immortality;
there was no distinctive sign for the night or the day.
The One breathed its own momentum, without breath.
Apart from This, there existed nothing else.

In the beginning, darkness was hidden by darkness.
This universe was only an indistinct wave.
Then, by the power of intense heat, the One was born,
out of void and covered with emptiness.

Desire was in the original development,
(desire) which was the first seed of Consciousness.
Investigating themselves, the Poets were able to discover
by their reflection the connection of Being with nonbeing.[10]

Our second, later text, comes from the Upanishads, a century before Parmenides. It reads:

Initially being alone existed.
Being only and without a second.
Some say that in the beginning, nonbeing alone existed.
Non-being, only nonbeing, without a second.

And from this nonbeing, being will proceed.
But in truth where could it be so?
How could being proceed from nonbeing?
One must think that being alone exists, being only and without a second.[11]

We might also find Chinese texts, or Tibetan texts. Why the Eastern detour? The question is: why is it not possible to retain the Egyptian, Indian, or other such proclamations, as philosophical documents, in Heidegger's sense? With respect to their own tension, they are absolutely similar, and it is not poetry that distinguishes them. Heidegger himself said: *The thought of Parmenides is still poetic.* He even added: *The thought of Parmenides is still poetic, that is to say, here, philosophical and unscientific.* Let us leave aside for the moment "philosophical and unscientific," instead focusing on the claim that the thinking is poetic, that is, that there is a metaphorical cloaking of the discourse. We can find plenty in Parmenides to irk the commentators, such as the claim that being is a sphere confined within limits. The metaphorical cloaking is obvious. But either we take these claims literally, in which case they are genuine cosmological images, or we think of them as inaugurating philosophy, and must decipher them, ascribing to them another meaning beyond their immediate imagery. So it is not the poetry that sets this text apart, any more than the immediate challenge of its thought. In both cases, the challenge consists not only in proclaiming being, but in finding the form of dialectical delimitation between being and nonbeing. And obviously these texts refer, as does Parmenides, to an entire polemical context on the question of knowing whether it is tenable for nonbeing to be. In the last text that I quoted, from the Upanishads, the logic of refutation is the same as that of Parmenides: if we suppose the being of nonbeing, we cannot see in what sense being can be, what being of being is tenable if, indeed, there is a being of nonbeing. Or, in the words of the first of our Indian texts, with regard to poets, it's a question of knowing "the connection of being with nonbeing," or how the questions of being and nonbeing are bound up in themselves. So the challenge is formally comparable, the tension is the same, and they are distinguished neither by poetry nor by cosmological context.

In light of this situation, we have two possibilities. The first is to say: yes, it is not true that philosophy was unequivocally decided in Greece by Parmenides. We retain the Heideggerian thesis that it is by this decision that philosophy begins—on the question of delimitation of differences and of the dialectic of being and nonbeing—but we add that the version or which it was decided only in Greece is limited, and ultimately Western-centric. We retain therefore the discriminating kernel of the point of view of being and of nonbeing, along with the criterion of philosophical foundation, while abandoning the "originally Greek" essence of philosophy.

By a curious turn of events, this hypothesis, though not on the foundation but on philosophy itself, is shared by Lardreau and Jambet I cite Jambet's *The Logic of Orientals,* and Lardreau's *Philosophical Speeches and Spiritual Discourse.*[12] These two works have in common the substantive claim that current philosophical topology is fallacious. We must renounce an occidental vision of philosophical discursivity and philosophical rationality, reworking their entire history by expressly including what I call the "Eastern dimension." Once again, this does not exactly address the foundation, but rather looks at the general regime of philosophical discourse.

Jambet thinks, for example, that the great philosophers and theologians of Islam, and especially Shia Islam, are in fact an organic part of the philosophical apparatus, that is, they are part of the historicity of philosophical thought, not only in the sense of an "add-on," but in the sense in which, by failing to take them into account, we obscure even our understanding of Western philosophers, leaving a historicity of philosophy incapable of recognizing Islam as such. Jambet's thesis is that all philosophical apparatus involves an Eastern dimension. Eastern and Western dimensions will become internal concepts in the evaluation of all philosophical thought. Consequently, to neglect the Eastern dimension of the great founders—of the thread that constitutes the unique material of the great speculations linked to Shia Islam—is ignorance pure and simple, and must be redressed. Jambet proposes that we refound the history of philosophy as a whole—not just augment it, but refound it.

As for Lardreau's book, in which he focuses on the work of Philoxenus of Mabbug, a Syriac monk of the fifth century, its goal is different: it is about the Christian space, not Islam. What Lardreau maintains is that the substructure of decision can be clarified only by examining discourse other than philosophical discourse properly so called, such as it is received in the West. The substructure of the decision can be elucidated only by considering another type of discourse, which he calls "spiritual discourse," and thereby once again refounding the history of philosophy. We must refound it because we are blind to its regime of decision, and thus fail to see that fundamental decisions regarding philosophy, decisions that would determine the future of philosophy itself, decisions about decision, were taken within a regime of discourse other than the philosophical. Lardreau's fundamental thesis is that the philosophical subject, that is, the subject who decides philosophically may do so only in a place of a prephilosophical spirituality, whose mode of articulation is absolutely different, where the regime of belief of the decision maker requires, as operator, concept, and historical referent, the examination of spiritual discourse, of which he takes Christian spirituality as an example, though not one he takes to be unique.

These two attempts, which I take to be post-Heideggerian, have the novelty of asserting that the history of philosophy, and thus philosophical thought itself, can and must be refounded through the incorporation and examination of decisions and statements external to Western philosophy and its Greek origin. Eastern dimension for Jambet; spiritual discourse for Lardreau. Of course, this exteriority in their endeavor was in truth an unnoticed interiority. It was not an addition, but the unnoticed, unknown to philosophical discourse itself. As they are Lacanians, their regime of thought sets out from interpretation, attempting to show how the unknown of philosophical and intellectual discourse, the hidden dimension of Western philosophy, is an Eastern discourse. The case must be made by recourse to a specific corpus of knowledge, that of Shia Islam or archaic Christian spirituality, which serves as the argument's point of departure. O course, we might further broaden this spectrum of possibilities, as I did by aiming my sling at Egypt and India. Each instance undermines the Heideggerian thesis of a specifically Greek foundation of philosophy.

This is the first path. The second possibility is to declare that speculation and decision on being and nonbeing are not the foundation of philosophy. What problems ensue?

The problems are numerous, because there are subsidiary hypotheses. It even might be said that at bottom Parmenides founds nothing at all, because he is still Egyptian—a refined Egyptian, simplified, in par decosmologized, but all the same, an Egyptian. In what sense? In the sense that he did not institute a new regime of discursivity, for this regime of discursivity, speculating on being, nonbeing, and so on, existed previously, elsewhere, and was perfectly compatible with religious regimes, political regimes, and the like, absolutely foreign to those of Greece.

But here a difficulty presents itself: if we go so far as to entertain the hypothesis that there was never any establishment of the regime of philosophy on the question of being and nonbeing, if Parmenides was not a founder, then when was philosophy founded? When, and on what? We might simply go back to asserting that philosophy is founded in the Socrates–Plato apparatus, to which we might add Aristotle—because, of course, Aristotle and Plato are present at the birth of philosophy. But here I object that Plato says otherwise: he says that to his eyes, philosophy was well and truly established by Parmenides, his paternity indisputable.

The thesis I maintain is as follows. First, I think, like Heidegger, that there is a Greek foundation of philosophy, and it is, indeed, a regime of Western discourse. So I will expose myself in a considered way to the charge of Western-centrism. A corollary of this thesis is that there are regimes of discourse and of thought, even some concerning being and nonbeing, that are not philosophical. This in no way detracts from their greatness and dignity: they are simply something else. This leads to the second major claim: strictly speaking, the philosophical decision *does not exhaust* the proclamation on being and nonbeing, since in some regimes this decision is not taken as philosophical. The third claim follows: a supplementary condition is required. Philosophy is conditional on something other than the decision regarding the path of being and of nonbeing. Fourth and last, I maintain that Parmenides is in fact the founder of philosophy, but not for the reasons that led Heidegger to assign him this role.

What we seek in Parmenides' text and its interpretation is the trace of this supplemental condition: what supplemental condition must a discourse obey to be historically described as philosophical, beyond the fact that it decides on the question of being *qua* being, and of nonbeing? More generally, where, indeed, does the notion that there is something originally Greek in philosophy come from? Further, what is the unknown in the discourse of Heidegger himself? What is missing such that Heidegger did not actually designate the difference of philosophical discourse? I believe that he was not, in the end, in a position to establish the thesis of the originally Greek character of philosophy, to capture it with his strict apparatus. He could do so only by extremely complex distortions, which have constantly caused the already established character of philosophy to retroact on the theme of its foundation. It is this that allows him to decide that Parmenides is founder; it is Plato and Aristotle, because it is from the perspective of the loss of foundation that they decided the founder. The problem is one of circularity: in proclaiming the founding, we stand on the foundation, but this does not authorize us to say that the founding criteria are those thus announced, because these criteria as such are not previously differentiated. I understand that the retroactive method works, but it founders on this point that the criteria it broadcasts as foundational do not discriminate radically enough. There is a supplemental condition—and that is what we seek.

Acknowledgments

This chapter was adapted from the lecture transcript of the October 29, 1985, session of a seminar on Parmenides. This text was transcribed by Véronique Pineau and translated by Megan Flocken and Javiera Perez-Gomez. With respect to the text's translation, immeasurable thanks go to Alex Levine for his support and guidance on this project, and gracious appreciation to Lee Braver for giving us the opportunity to translate this work.

Notes

1. Martin Heidegger, *Introduction to Metaphysics*, trans. Gregory Fried and Richard Polt (New Haven: Yale University Press, 2014), §73, p. 106.

2. Georg Wilhelm Friedrich Hegel, *The Science of Logic*, trans. George Di Giovanni (Cambridge: Cambridge University Press, 2010), §136, 21:70, p. 60. This passage itself carries a footnote to Aristotle, *Metaphysics*, 986b, pp. 28–29.

3. Heidegger, *Introduction to Metaphysics*, §74, p. 106.

4. Parmenides, fragment 1: 28B1. [Badiou uses Beaufret's French translation, without modification. The following three passages from Parmenides' *Poem* are from Jean Beaufret, *Le Poème de Parménide*, Coll. Epiméthée, Essais philosophiques (Paris: Presses Universitaires de France, 1955).

Les cavales qui m'emportent m'ont conduit aussi loin
que mon cœur pouvait le désirer, puisqu'elles m'ont entraîné
sur la route abondante en révélations de la divinité, qui,
franchissant toutes cités, porte l'homme qui sait. C'est par cette route
que j'ai été porté ; car c'est sur elle que m'ont conduit les très prudentes
cavales qui tiraient mon char, et des jeunes filles montraient la route.

We are indebted to the John Burnet translation, http://philoctete.free.fr/parmenidesunicode.htm. After comparing the many extant English versions Burnet seems to capture most closely what Badiou emphasizes from this first passage—Trans.]

5. Parmenides, fragment 2: B2. [Beaufret's translation:

Eh bien donc, je vais parler—toi, écoute mes paroles
et retiens-les—je vais te dire quelles sont les deux seules voies
de recherche à concevoir: la première—comment il est et qu'il n'est
pas possible qu'il ne soit pas—est le chemin auquel se fier—car il suit la Vérité ;
la seconde, à savoir qu'il n'est pas et que le non-être est nécessaire,
cette voie, je te le dis, n'est qu'un sentier où ne se trouve absolument
rien à quoi se fier. Car on ne peut connaître ce qui n'est pas—
il n'y a pas là d'issue possible—, ni l'énoncer en une parole.

Compare McKirahan and Curd's English translation:

But come now, I will tell you—and you, when you have
heard the story, bring it safely apath—which are the only routes
of inquiry that are for thinking:
the one, that is and that it is not possible for it not to be,
is the path of Persuasion (for it attends upon Truth),
the other, that it is not and that it is right that it not be,
this indeed I declare to you to be a path entirely unable to be investigated:
For neither can you know what is not (for it is not to be accomplished)
nor can you declare it.

Cited from Proclus, "Commentary on Plato's *Timaeus* 1.345.18"; lines 3–8: Simplicius, "Commentary on Aristotle's *Physics* 116.28"; both in *A Presocratics Reader: Selected Fragments and Testimonia*, 2nd ed., trans. Richard D. McKirahan and Patricia Curd (Indianapolis: Hackett, , 2011), pp. 57–58.—Trans.]

6. Parmenides, fragment 7: B7. [Beaufret's translation:

On n'arrivera jamais à plier l'être à la diversité de ce qui n'est pas;
écarte donc ta pensée de cette voie de recherche, et que l'habitude
à la riche expérience ne t'entraîne pas de force sur cette voie:
celle où s'évertuent un œil pour ne pas voir, une oreille remplie de bruit,
une langue, mais d'entendement, décide de la thèse sans cesse controversée
que te révèle ma parole.

For our translation, we are again indebted to the version cited from: lines 1–2: Plato, *Sophist* 242a; lines 2–6: Sextus Empiricus, *Against the Mathematicians* 7.114; translations by Richard D. McKirahan, modified by Patricia Cura, in *A Presocratics Reader*, p. 59.—Trans.]

7. Heidegger, *Introduction to Metaphysics*, H85, p. 117; translation emended to read "thought" in place of "considered." [There is some ambiguity in Badiou's quotation of this Heidegger passage. His quotation modifies Heidegger's text, so that it reads: "...the path of non-Being must be thought at the same time as the path of Being." Our translation has restored it to its original sense.—Trans.]

8. The Bremner-Rhind Papyrus (British Museum No. 10188). [Badiou appears to cite this text from a French source: S. Sauneron and J. Yoyotte, "La Naissance du monde dans Eygypte ancienne," in *La Naissance du Monde, sources orientales*, vol. 1 (Paris: Seuil, 1959), pp. 49–50. For more on this text, see R. O. Faulkner, "The Bremner-Rhind Papyrus: I. A. The Songs of Isis and Nephthys," *Journal of Egyptian Archaeology* 22, no. 2 (Dec. 1936): 121–140, and also an article by Sir Ernest Alfred Wallis Budge in *Archaeologia*, vol. 52, London, 1891. The ancient hieratic text is at the British Museum: http://www.britishmuseum.org/research/collection/collection_online/collection_object_details.aspx?objectId=113969&partId=1.—Trans.]

9. [The translation that Badiou uses:

Quanc je me fus manifesté à l'existence, l'existence exista.
Je vins à l'existence sous la forme de l'existant
qui es venu à l'existence comme première fois.
Venu à l'existence sous le mode d'existence de l'existant, j'existai.
Et c'est ainsi que l'existence vint à l'existence.

—Trans.]

10. [Badiou appears to have taken the exact text from Louis Renou's translation of the Rig Veda, Book X, §129, *Études védiques et pāṇinéennes* (Paris: Boccard, 1955). Here is the French:

Ni le non-Être n'existait alors, ni l'Être.
Il n'existait l'espace aérien, ni le firmament au-delà.

Qu'est-ce qui se mouvait puissamment? Où ? Sous la garde de qui?
Était-ce l'eau, insondablement profonde ?
Il n'existait en ce temps ni mort, ni non-mort ;
il n'y avait de signe distinctif pour la nuit ou le jour.
L'Un respirait de son propre élan, sans qu'il y ait de souffle.
En dehors de Cela, il n'existait rien d'autre.
À l'origine les ténèbres étaient cachées par les ténèbres.
Cet univers n'était qu'onde indistincte.
Alors, par la puissance de l'Ardeur, l'Un prit naissance,
(principe) vide et recouvert de vacuité.
Le Désir en fut le développement original,
(désir) qui a été la semence première de la Conscience.
Enquêtant en eux-mêmes, les Poètes surent découvrir
par leur réflexion le lien de l'Être dans le non-Être.

For the English translation, we have relied heavily on Wendy Doniger O'Flaherty's translation of the Rig Veda, Book X, §129, from *The Rig Veda: An Anthology of One Hundred Eight Hymns*, pp. 25–26. In deciding which translation to use, we found Dominic Goodall's *Hindu Scriptures* incredibly helpful.—Trans.]

11. [From the Chandogya Upanishad, Part 6, Chapter 2. We could not find a popular French edition that aligns with Badiou's translation. The French text:

Au commencement l'être seul existait.
L'être unique et sans second.
Certains prétendent qu'au commencement, le non-être seul existait.
Le non-être, le non-être unique, sans second.
Et de ce non-être l'être procèdera.
Mais en vérité d'où en pourrait-il être ainsi?
Comment du non-être pouvait-il procéder?
Il faut penser que l'être seul existe, l'être unique et sans second.

For our English translation, we consulted *The Upanishads: A New Translation* by Swami Nikhilananda in four volumes (New York: Ramakrishna Vivekanada Center, 1986).—Trans.]

12. Christian Jambet, *La logique des orientaux: Henry Corbin et la science des formes* (Paris: Editions du Seuil, 1983); Guy Lardreau, *Discours philosophique et discours spirituel: Autour de la philosophie spirituelle de Philoxene de Mabboug (L'Ordre philosophique)* (Paris: Editions du Seuil, 1985).

2 Metaphysics without Metaphysics

Alain Badiou

In Heidegger's work, the question of being is wholly structured by its becoming historical, namely, by the becoming of metaphysics, which unfolds between the original oblivion inscribed by Plato on the regime of being as an Idea, and contemporary nihilism. In this text, my goal is to clarify this structure, starting from a line opposed to that of Heidegger—a line that proposes neither a "return" nor a "turning point," but, simply, a continuation: a continuation of metaphysics.

Our point of departure can be simply stated: What does "metaphysics" name, in any philosophical discourse that announces, at the very least, a crisis of metaphysics, and at worst, as for Heidegger and his students, its end, or its fundamental non-sense? To which tendency of thought does this word "metaphysics" refer—for all those who claim to criticize or reform its admitted effects?

Let us recall that the pattern, be it one of obsolescence or of a necessary radical transformation, persists without interruption under the name "metaphysics" from Kant through to the present. It is certainly useful to review these maxims. It is beneficial to bring to mind a compendium of the modern, antimetaphysical mindset, if only to be astonished that nothing other than the interminable and uncertain history of its perpetual reconstitution responds to such negative certainty.

The opera of the end of metaphysics, in a number of extraordinarily varied productions, has remained in the repertoire for nearly three centuries. The main plot twists of the libretto are of great interest.

We will divide their assertions into four main groups:

- That of the interruption and of the judicative limitation of metaphysical ambitions. Let us call this the *critical trial of all dogmatic metaphysics*. Here, Kant is the canonical figure.

- That of the exhaustion, not only intellectual, but also historical and political, of the supposed virtues of metaphysics, which are finally replaced by the rational positivity whose paradigm the empirical sciences set forth. Let us call this the *positivist trial of any imaginary metaphysics*. Here, we might follow Auguste Comte, as well as early Wittgenstein or Carnap.
- That for which metaphysics is but a mutilation of all thought, which assumes the becoming concrete and alive of contradictions against unilateral entities and fixed categories, where metaphysics makes something like a submission to death prosper. Let us call this the *dialectical trial of any metaphysical immobilism or eternityism*. In this trial Hegel serves as witness for the prosecution, but also Marx and Nietzsche, and even Freud and Lacan.
- Finally, that which discerns under the name of metaphysics, the nihilistic disposition of the entire history of the West. "Metaphysics" is then the prescription that the history of being be such that, in longing for return, it must commit itself to interminable hermeneutic postponement. Let us call this the *historial trial of metaphysics*, which in the end cannot oppose its technical proliferation save by the discretion of the poet, or by announcing the return of the dead gods. This time Heidegger is the necessary hero.

So, antimetaphysics indicts itself four times: as critique, as positivism, as dialectic, and as hermeneutics. Insofar as, in opposition to the vacuity of the metaphysical concept, it initiates a discipline of limitation, it is the essence of critique; initiating a discipline of mathematized experimentation, it is positivism; initiating the supersession of its founding identity principle, it is the dialectic; and finally, insofar as it initiates the deciphering of the history of being, culminating in an epochal diagnosis, it is hermeneutics.

In all four cases, it is not enough to say that the violence of these assertions is symptomatic. One might say they are flung at philosophy in the mode of a scream, insult, or venomous mockery. Let us listen to them one last time:

1. Let us begin with critique. Who would expect from the reasonable Kant such peremptory and contemptuous statements as, for example, those referring to the irresponsibility of the metaphysician? Thus, in the *Prolegomena*, §52b, he asserts that "One can tinker around with metaphysics in sundry ways without even suspecting that one might be venturing into untruth."[1] We can see that the metaphor is not far from the denunciation of the common metaphysician as a craftsman in search of a swindle. For Kant, the metaphysician always remains a swindler if he imagines he can

offer us something new. For example, Kant does not hesitate to state, in the very last section of the same prolegomena, concerning the concept of substance and thus the very heart of classical metaphysics, that "through all this analysis nothing has been achieved, nothing created and advanced, and after so much bustle and clatter, science is still where it was in Aristotle's time."[2] We might wonder all the same if, by his somewhat emphatic style, Kant does not in fact add to the bustle and clatter.[3] This despite the fact that he proclaims, with a self-confidence that also calls for commentary, that all the bustle in question has once and for all been disrupted. This is, in any case, the injunction that opens the *Prolegomena*, and which must be quoted intact, because such pride is quite rare: "My intention is to convince all those who find it worthwhile to occupy themselves with metaphysics that it is unavoidably necessary to suspend their work for the present, to consider all that has happened until now as if it had not happened, and before all else to pose the question: 'whether such a thing as metaphysics is even possible at all.'"[4]

As we have seen, the introduction to critical metaphysics, which is the exposition of the transcendental as such, is performed according to a line of antidogmatic violence whose necessity it is important to question.

2. The positivists are no less acrimonious, even when, like Auguste Comte, they take metaphysics for a state of thought, useful in its time but since then obsolete. While Kant likes the image of metaphysics as interminable and vain battle, conceptual sparring for hot air, Auguste Comte introduces the image of metaphysics as mental illness. So, in *A Discourse on the Positive Spirit*, he claims that "we can finally envisage the metaphysical state as a sort of chronic illness naturally inherent to our mental evolution, individual or collective."[5] To date, this propensity to pathologize metaphysics, and to offer a brutal therapy for its acute cases, continues to be profitable. The number of eager physicians at the bedside of the man sick from metaphysics, or sick from whatever metaphysics itself is sick of, is now beyond count.

It is true for Auguste Comte that the metaphysical state is not only a mental disposition—but was it so different for Kant or Wittgenstein, or even Heidegger? The metaphysical state is also that which an entire intellectual group, one with great power in society, claims for itself. In fact, if the critique of metaphysics is so quick to turn violent, it is because political decisions are in play. For Auguste Comte, there is a metaphysical party he has every reason to fear, as he clearly explains in the surprising text of his "Personal Preface" to *The Course in Positive Philosophy*. There, comparing the perils that the clerical party pose for him to those threatened by the metaphysicians, he writes, "Towards the metaphysical party, whether ruling or aspiring, my unavoidable position—though related to a less pronounced collision—is, fundamentally, even more dangerous for me."[6] And his reason, which in my opinion has lost none of its value, is that "More enlightened and more flexible, this equivocal party ... is no less concerned today than the purely theological ambitions to prevent, at any cost, the social installation of true modern philosophy."

That is where we are. One of the common meanings of the term "metaphysics" is to designate, beyond the discursive apparatus of the reigning philosophy, a formidable power whose space is more vast than the University, a conservative power that blocks a strategic crossing: the crossing between philosophy and social order. This is a power that, as Auguste Comte argues, attempts to prevent by any means "the social installation" of critical, or positive, or dialectical, or hermeneutic philosophy.

Digressing from my planned course, allow me to say that it is indeed just such a power that, in a different register, even an opposing register, Heidegger diagnoses under the name of metaphysics. Be it the tenacious and sterile irresponsibility targeted by Kant, or the equivocal, devastating pathological power named by Comte, Heidegger is more inclined to raise than call. It is only at this price that he can include Nietzsche himself and, ultimately, Nietzsche above all, within metaphysics. For it is precisely Nietzsche who has given the prevalence of a metaphysical disposition with regard to being the name that it ultimately deserves: the will to power. In response, Heidegger brandishes words every bit as violently as his predecessors. In the fourth part of his *Nietzsche*, Heidegger does not hesitate to brand as "machination" the hegemony of Being within the metaphysical structure. And he adds, "When meaninglessness comes to power by dint of machination, the suppression of meaning and thus of all inquiry into the truth of Being must be replaced by machination's erection of goals' (values)."[7]

In response to the conspiracy of the metaphysical party denounced by Comte, ontological machination arises, establishing the criminal reign of the absurd.

Admittedly, the conspiracy of the metaphysical party, for Comte, went only so far as his exclusion from the École polytechnique, whereas for Heidegger, metaphysics unleashed as machination, as technical nihilism's power of enframing, produces the devastation of the Earth. On the one hand, a civil servant denied a professorship; on the other, the planetary reign of technology, with a little touch of what I would like to call ontological ecology. It is, let us say, a Franco-German difference. This difference should not prevent us from discerning, a century apart and in opposing conceptual contexts, the continued pursuit under the name of "metaphysics" of the identification of a corrosive power bent on maintaining the dominance of a history as profound as it is off course, bent on posing an obstacle, by any means, to that which must come to save us, be it the expected remaking of the Greek gods, for the German, or an equally expected professor of physics at one of the *grandes écoles*, doubling as a founder of the subversive political faction.

At a more immediately philosophical level, the determination of the essence of metaphysics as power, or as party, as Comte and Heidegger bear witness, always refers to how metaphysics leaves undetermined the true nature of what is. This is a crucial point in any critical acceptance of the term "metaphysics": what is formidable about it is precisely the apparent deficiency of its content. For it is precisely in the vagueness, or the undecided of metaphysical determinations that their usage and deployment as power reside.

What renders metaphysics formidable is that it sets aside the work of the true questions in favor of an indeterminate, where it makes no difference which significance of mastery comes to take up residence. What is formicable in metaphysics, beneath the mask of the search for truth, is a cold and argumentative indifference to the question of truth. Heidegger states this particularly clearly in his notes *Metaphysics as the History of Being*, which forms section 9 of *Nietzsche*, in the translation by Klossowski: "All the events of the history of Being, which is metaphysics, have their beginning and their ground in this, namely that metaphysics leaves and must necessarily leave undecided the essence of Being, insofar as to appreciate 'what is worthy of question,' what is problematic, in order to rescue its very own essence, is from the beginning indifferent to metaphysics, and that of the indifference from not-knowing."[8]

Kant already recognized this indifference in his assessment of the fruitless struggle and conceptual immobility in place since Aristotle. He recognized that speculative dialectic constantly feeds on its inability to know. He identified what Heidegger would call "the indifference of not-knowing." Nevertheless, without a doubt, he did not recognize that, far from being a decisive objection, to identify the indifference of metaphysics is to identify the source of its power. "Metaphysics" means: the reign of the essential indeterminate. It is convenient for metaphysics, *qua* history of thought as power, that the essence of Being remain undecided. But this is what Auguste Comte glimpsed when he attested to what he sometimes calls the

"vagueness" or "ambiguity" of metaphysical entities, as an obligatory characteristic. And in writing, also in the *Discourse*, that "it was precisely their
equivocal character which made these [metaphysical] entities so useful in
the past," then, just like Heidegger, he tied the theme of the historical, or
destined power of metaphysics to the abstract nondifferentiation of problems.[9] For Heidegger, metaphysics conceals the question of Being beneath
that of the Supreme Being, then forgets even this forgetful configuration
to welcome, under the name of overman, the technological absoluteness
of the nihilist man. In this sense, metaphysics is a simplified and abstract
religion, dependent on these indecisive entities. But Auguste Comte had
already articulated, in his own language, what would become the thesis of
an ontotheological identity of metaphysics: "Metaphysics," he writes, "is
nothing but a sort of ennervated theology losing something of its vigour at
each successive simplification."[10]

Indifference, simplification, abstraction, separation, dissolution: these
are the operations by which the power of neutral thought, of pointless
argument, establishes itself by the conventional name of metaphysics. This
is the power of the undecided and of the indeterminate as such.

It is in complete agreement with this identification that contemporary
positivists—the adherents of linguistic empiricism—assert that what gives
power to metaphysics is the same thing that orders us to dismiss it, namely
its lack of meaning. Toward that end we must follow Wittgenstein's sinuous
steps all the way through aphorisms 6.40 to 6.50 of the *Tractatus*. There metaphysics is identified, just as in Carnap, with statements devoid of meaning.
Aphorism 6.53 explains that "one must say nothing but what can be said,
i.e., propositions of natural science." And he adds: "whenever someone else
wanted to say something metaphysical ... demonstrate to him that he had
failed to give meaning to certain signs in his propositions."[11]

Once again, metaphysics signifies: indeterminateness, devoid of attribut-
able meaning. For Wittgenstein, metaphysics denotes the void in signification, just as for Heidegger it denotes the void surrounding the problematic
or the question, and for Comte the void surrounding scientific denotation.
When all is said and done, Comte is quite close to the beginning of the *Tractatus* when he asserts, "As a fundamental law, that any proposition which is
not strictly reducible to the simple statements of fact, whether particular or
general, cannot offer any real or intelligible meaning."[12]

Sure—but in human experience there are not only thinkable facts, not
even for Comte, who, faced with the excessively singular fact of his desire
for Clotilde de Vaux, would one day proclaim what he would call "the characteristic verdict": "One cannot always think, but one can always love."[13]

Nevertheless, by this fact, something of the metaphysical power returns to support the indeterminate. And even for Wittgenstein, there is not only what can be said; there are also "things that cannot be put into words. They *make themselves manifest*. They are what is mystical."[14] But then, what distinguishes the mystically inarticulate from the metaphysically indeterminate? What, for Comte, distinguishes the social religion binding the alliance of women with the proletariat, from some vague and equivocal metaphysical entity? The whole problem of metaphysics as power, the capacity to invest the entire zone of the unsayable with the suprasensible, to overdetermine the indeterminate, slips into the gap between the mystical element and metaphysical non-sense, between the positive sciences and positivist religion. And even in Heidegger's valediction that only a god can save us, the question of knowing what this "god" names, and in what sense it is not merely the last appeal, in nihilistic extremity, to the metaphysically indeterminate, is posed with acuity.

At bottom, for critique, hermeneutics, and positivism, metaphysics is identified as a dogmatic elevation of the indeterminate, false consciousness of essence, and this is where its power lies. But to ward this off, we must appeal to a superior indeterminacy, or, more precisely, we must declare that the indeterminate remains indeterminate, the unknowable remains unknowable where metaphysics—and this is its rational ruse—inserts the indeterminate into the discursive visibility of a determination.

We shall therefore hold that critique, hermeneutics, and positivism, if they correctly diagnose metaphysics, in fact only substitute that which we will call an *archi-metaphysics*, that is, the suspension of the meaning of an indeterminate that is simply left to the historical contingency of its arrival. Archi-metaphysics is the replacement of a necessary indeterminate by a contingent indeterminate; it challenges the well-established power of the unknown master with the poetry or prophecy of he who comes. He reveals himself in Wittgenstein's mystical element, just like Heidegger's metaphorical God, or Comte's positivist church.

This, above all, is what we must first discern in Kant's replacement of knowledge with belief: the regulatory idea of God, God as postulated by pure practical reason, the God of religion within the limits of reason alone, much more essentially indeterminate and unknowable, and in this sense, more metaphysical than the God proved by Leibniz or Descartes. His justification of His own indeterminacy is progress in appearance only. For where Reason approaches its limit, it is suddenly common morality that evokes the arrival of its formless God, which we call Man, or something indistinct that must protect us against malice.

Archi-metaphysics, in its positivist, critical, or hermeneutic registers, always culminates in an indistinct promise, the ethical reversal of the order that it purports to impose. Philosophy of the day in various costumes, archi-metaphysics ineluctably activates all the possible decompositions of the concept.

In truth, we must recognize, as Hegel did, the native superiority of dogmatic metaphysics over critical archi-metaphysics. This superiority rests on postulates of rationality that, in dogmatic metaphysics, institute indeterminacy and subject transcendence to a rational control more rigorous than could be expected of positivist humanity, Kant's moral subject, or the poet of the hermeneuticists. Dogmatic metaphysics restricts the rights of the indeterminate to the bounds of a prior thesis maintaining that thought and the thinkable are mutually homogeneous. As Hegel writes in the introduction to the *Science of Logic*, "The older metaphysics had in this respect a higher concept of thinking than now passes as the accepted opinion. ... This metaphysics thus held that thinking and the determination of thinking are not something alien to the subject matters, but are rather their essence, [and] that thinking in its immanent determinations, and the true nature of things, are one and the same content."[15]

Let us say that traditional metaphysics assumed the role of the indeterminate in the Parmenidean maxim: that of the identity of thought and being. This is why it authorizes us to proceed, regarding the very concept of metaphysics, in a dogmatic rather than critical fashion.

We will say that a being, made philosophically accessible under a name, is *essentially indeterminate* if among the predicates that allow for its definition we explicitly find that this being exceeds, in its very essence, any predicative determination accessible to an understanding like ours.

It will be common, although not required, for the understanding that serves as measure to be declared finite, and for the essential excess of being under any determination to be called its infinity.

We will call *metaphysical* the discursive tendency that states that an indeterminate being, in the sense we have just explained—hence a being such that its determination exceeds our cognitive power—is required to complete the structure of rational knowledge. Traditionally, this indeterminacy receives the name of God, but metaphysics has lasted far past this name. For metaphysics to have power, it is enough for it to insert a point of indeterminacy in a discursive framework open to all, an argumentative framework and not a revealed one, thus a rational framework, such that it can henceforth accommodate any possible meaning of mastery.

It will be noted that this definition of metaphysics is compatible with the one commonly attributed to Aristotle, on which it is the science of being *qua* being, whose existence as a science is recognized in *Metaphysics* Γ. This immediately introduces the indeterminate, or what Auguste Comte called the equivocal. For being is said in many ways. But this also introduces the determinate framework of this indeterminacy. For being is said to be "προς εν," toward the One. This is the subtle balance of metaphysics, which must either determine, in the ledger of the One, what was elsewhere indeterminate, or pose as an excess of determination.

In its most concise definition, metaphysics is what makes a predicate of the impredicable.

In this reading, we must go back further than Aristotle, to Plato, to *Republic* VI, where Socrates simultaneously poses the requirement of the Good as radical transcendence, and the absolute conceptual indeterminacy of this Good. What is a determination for Plato? It is a Form, an Idea, an intelligible slice. And what is the Good? It is that which is not an Idea, that which Socrates says, far exceeds any idea in its prestige and in power.

Let us say that the existence of the Good is necessary, but its complete determination impossible. That we can prove an existence without thereby determining what exists is the heart of metaphysics as power.

Metaphysics is classical, or dogmatic, when it ascribes the rationality of its existence to the indeterminate point of its apparatus.

This consideration is crucial. What classical metaphysics has borrowed from mathematics ever since Plato is proof of existence starting from a single concept. Metaphysics is at bottom the recognition of pure existence, in the sense that this existence, which is not empirically verifiable, and whose being or content exceeds the compass of our knowledge, is nevertheless rationally demonstrable.

The power of classical metaphysics is mathematical, in the sense that it originates from an existence demonstrated as existing without the "what exists" having to conform to this demonstration. This is the case, for example, when we demonstrate the existence of an uncountable infinity of transcendental numbers, despite the continued difficulty of producing any, or when we maintain that there exists an infinite family of nonprincipal ultrafilters, though it is impossible to construct even a single one.

It is therefore true, as Kant saw, that the proofs of the existence of God are the hard core of classical metaphysics, as they already complete both Aristotle's *Physics* and *Metaphysics*. However, it would take a great deal for a refutation or dialectization of these proofs to be capable of uprooting the doctrine at issue, namely the confirmed existence of an essential indeterminacy. In truth, to subtract this existence from the regime of proof is only to shift from classical metaphysics to modern archi-metaphysics. For the function of the proof was not to prove. It was to analogically establish the mathematicity of existence, and thus the rational consistency of the indeterminate with the proposed regime of determination. In giving a proof of the existence of the indeterminate, or the infinity, or, more precisely, in asserting within discourse itself that the existence of the essential indeterminate rests on proof, you show that whether or not this proof is convincing to all minds, you must in any case maintain that existence is rationally divided between indeterminate and the determinate, between infinite and finite.

Descartes adds the finishing touch to this when he asserts that at least the will, or freedom, is in fact pure and naked existence, and admits of no distinction or hierarchy between God and Man.

Classical metaphysics owes its rational greatness to this transition from finite to infinite. This is what I call the mathematized regime of existence, to which Spinoza entrusted the entire structure of his thought.

In the end, nothing is more corrosive for philosophy than to part with this regime, which creates the reality of a simple possible outside the realm of the verifiable, and arranges thought only by that which counts, and which is the absolute identity of thought with the being that thought thinks.

This is to say that critique, in Kant's sense, lacks what was essential in dogmatic metaphysics, a way of subsuming the existential under the rational, whose paradigm was mathematics. This is what Plato saw, then Descartes, Spinoza, and Leibniz. And this is what Hegel will revisit, even if he believes that he can order the passage from the real to the rational by the artifice of speculative dialectic alone, and even though he proceeds to the damaging debasement of mathematics. In this respect, I am prepared to risk claiming that these thinkers were and remain of a caliber to which Kant cannot aspire.

Let us consider a variation on this thesis. What dogmatic metaphysics offers is a rational treatment of the existence of the infinite. In this sense, it balances empirical finitude and the inevitability of death with radical excess, whose existence proofs constitute its effective discourse. Critique, along with positivism and hermeneutics, takes us back to finitude, whereas it was the task of dogmatic metaphysics to return us there only to illuminate the horizon of the rational and the mathematical school, by which finitude is surpassed.

Let us say that antimetaphysics, as much as it uncouples the infinite from rational capacities and renounces the paradigm of infinite, demonstrable existence, merely restores an empirical finitude that Plato would unfailingly have seen as purely and simply prior to all philosophy.

For philosophy is devoted not to the care of limits, but to the care of the unlimited.

It is, moreover, on this point that ultimate justice must be rendered to Kant. For he did much more than glimpse that the true question of metaphysics was less one of its results than one of its existence. How else can we explain that to this day the repetitive vacuity of results has not discouraged anyone from returning? Metaphysics is similar to the situation of life, as Rimbaud described it in two aphorisms: "One does not leave."[16] And "I am there, I am always there."[17]

On this point, Kant sketches a doctrine consonant with the perception of metaphysics as power. When he writes, for example, that metaphysics is "the darling child of reason," and that "its germination is not to be attributed to a fortuitous accident, but to an original germ which it finds wisely organized in aim of great ends," it is clear that the biological, finalist metaphor treats metaphysics not as a determinate or natural object of knowledge, nor as within the subjective categories of such knowledge, which leaves nature and its ends beyond our reach.[18] Insofar as he considers it "a problem worthy of investigation to discover the ends of nature that can well apply this provision of our reason to transcendent concepts," we may say that Kant is, in the end, very near to absorbing the appearance of a critique of dogmatic metaphysics into an equally dogmatic metaphysics of the nature of thought, and of the ultimate significance of the contradiction between the transcendental organization of the understanding and reason's drive toward transcendence.

Nevertheless, considering that, in his own estimation, this is a delicate project, on which he has offered only conjectures, Kant devotes his rational efforts to the consolidation of the critique, and to the exposition of the transcendental.

But in the process, he increases the element of indeterminacy, rather than reducing it, and consequently fuels the recurrent possibility of true metaphysical obscurantism.

This is why, according to Hegel, the dialecticians thought that, unless we proceed to the real determination of the indeterminate that gives metaphysics its power, the mere critique of metaphysics paves the way for its archi-metaphysical repetition—that is, unless we respond to the question whose dogmatic response accounts for all the anti-obscurantist power of metaphysics and asks: what has the power to infinitize the finite? Let us say that the dialectic—whether Hegelian, Marxist, or Freudian, regardless of their differences—tries to break away from the transcendent indeterminacy where metaphysics prospers, without falling into the promises or moralisms of archi-metaphysical finitude, particularly in its transcendental, positivist, or hermeneutic forms.

A good negative definition of what ought to be called dialectical metaphysics would be that it restores to philosophy everything that is neither Kantian, nor empirical-positivist, nor phenomenological-hermeneutic.

We recognize in passing that this is a strong intuition of Lenin's, to have discerned the main philosophical enemy under the nominal guise of empirio-criticism. Against archi-metaphysics, this was to kill two birds with one stone.

Still, we remain grateful to Lacan, after Freud, for finding, despite all the philosophies of consciousness, the dialectical genius of the great Empedocles, or the Hegelian theory of a negativity that preserves, or even transforms, in its deceptive power, the very thing it denies, thus bringing the appearance of indeterminacy to the relentless repetitive determination of the symptom.

For this dialectic metaphysics of the unconscious, we refer to Freud's fundamental text on negation, written in 1925, and to the commentaries on it presented in the February 10, 1954 dialogue between Jacques Lacan and the great Hegelian Jean Hyppolite. This memorable encounter is reproduced in Lacan's *Ecrits*. It is certainly remarkable, given what I have proposed on the definition of metaphysics, that Hyppolite's commentary focuses on the real origin of the judgment of existence. Even more remarkable is Lacan's response, speaking of the symbolic guarantee demanded by all reality, including perceptual reality: "Nothing exists except insofar as it does not exist."[19]

This immediately brings us back to Hegel.

It is not that the antimetaphysical remarks of Hegel are more immediately congenial than Kant's. Hegel has no compunction in writing (in the preface to the *Logic*), "That which, prior to this period [the critical period], was called metaphysics has been, so to speak, extirpated root and branch and has vanished from the ranks of the sciences."[20]

It is rather that, at bottom, Hegel recognizes, after Kant, that "pure forms of thought,"[21] which are the very subject of metaphysics, were formerly applied uncritically to particular substrates, like the soul, the word, or God. Uncritically means—this time citing Hegel in the introduction to the

Science of Logic—that classical metaphysics "employed these forms *uncritically* without a preliminary investigation as to whether and how they are capable of being determinations of the thing-in-itself, to use the Kantian expression—or rather of the Rational."[22]

Otherwise how, for Hegel, could we verify that one or another form of pure thought is a determination not of the understanding but of the thing itself? Quite simply by following the deployment, the becoming effective, of the life of the object.

The dialectical critique of classical metaphysics consists entirely in that which the categories of metaphysics apply from the outside to the supposition of an indeterminate being. The dialectic shows that these categories, which metaphysics uses to arrange and demonstrate the essential indeterminacy, are in reality the names of the becoming of the determination of this purported indeterminacy. Each category—being, nothingness, becoming, quality, quantity, causality, and so on—is ultimately defined by this determination, if we have the patience to follow the intrinsic movement of transformation by which each occurs sequentially as the externalization and dialectical truth of those preceding it. This is what Hegel calls the replacement of the dialectic by logic, which as he graciously notes was first sketched by Kant. As he writes: "Critical philosophy had already turned metaphysics into logic."[23] "Logic" means: a regulated process of determination, whereby the absolute indeterminacy (e.g., being, being as such) calls forth the integral singularity as ultimate immanent specification of itself. Here, logic is the logic of determination, which leaves nothing indeterminate in its wake, and which, in this sense, abolishes metaphysics.

But more essentially, the point is the abolition of critical archimetaphysics.

To be sure, Kant was right to maintain, against a certain image of classical metaphysics, that one should not begin from a philosophy of special objects, like the soul, the world, or God, but from the exposition of categories. For otherwise the objects will remain as arbitrary indeterminates. But Kant pushed what Hegel nicely calls "the fear of the object"[24] so far that he felt obliged to give an essentially subjective meaning to the categories. In doing so, he created an indeterminacy even more radical than the one he denounced in classical metaphysics. The categorical determinations, as Hegel writes with his usual precise equanimity, "remained affected by the very object they avoided, and were left with the residue of a thing-in-itself, an infinite obstacle, as a beyond."[25] It is this step that creates a radical unknowable, allowing us to locate all of the signifiers of the moralizing oppression and conformity in a suprasensible beyond. This is what I have called archi-metaphysics, and what Hegel calls "a timid and incomplete standpoint."[26]

We note in passing that facing up to metaphysical power enlists the courage of thought, the same courage that Plato originally made the crux of philosophy, and of which, in the eyes of Hegel, Kant was too destitute. From this juncture, prudent archi-metaphysics further increases the space of indeterminacy by which dogmatic metaphysics organized the subjugation of wisdom.

The dialectical argument, being a courageous argument, tries simultaneously to cancel both the objectivity of the indeterminate in classical metaphysics and the subjective finitude confronting absolute indeterminacy in archi-metaphysical critique. The dialectical argument essentially suggests that a category of thought can count as such only if it exhausts without remainder what is thought in thinking via this category. If the category is a form of absolute thought, then, to quote Hegel, there cannot remain a surplus "*thing-in-itself*, something alien and external to thinking."[27] Once and for all, the argument "demands the account of the forms-of-thought as they are, in-itself and for-itself, without any such limitation and reference, i.e., as logic, as pure reason."[28]

In brief, we say that the dialectical metaphysical thesis asserts:

- Against classical metaphysics, that all indeterminacy leads to determination. Or alternatively, that any initial gap between the finite and the infinite must be regarded as the place where thought takes place, as the distance it crosses, and not as its obstacle. This is the sense in which everything real is rational. This means two things. First, insofar as the thinkable is thought, it is thought *absolutely*. On this point, Hegel follows Plato, Descartes, Spinoza, and Leibniz. Second, everything is thinkable, admitting if necessary the lack of time, or what our dearly departed Gérard Lebrun called, with Hegel, the patience of the Concept.
- Against archi-metaphysical critique, that categorical determinations are not unilaterally subjective. This does not mean, as in a return to classical metaphysics, that they are objective, or attached to particular objects, such as the world or God. Rather, this means that, deploying the contents of thought to which they are adequate, categorical determinations are simultaneously subjective and objective, which means, in terms henceforth accepted, that they are *conceptual*, that is, absolute. This is now the sense of "everything rational is real"—which again means two things. First, there is no category of the thinkable inadequate to any determinate content. On this point, Hegel follows Kant, and the thesis

of an indissoluble link between concept and experience. Second, that the becoming of concepts exhaust reality. Or, as a thinker best handled with tongs, Mao Tse-tung once said, "we will come to know all that we did not know before."

It is not only that, contrary to Hamlet, there is nothing on earth that is not dreamt of in our philosophies; there is also not anything in our power to philosophize that cannot happen in the real world.

It is this practical coextensivity of conceptual invention with the effect of reality that we name the absolute, the sole concern of philosophy.

It is a question of the definitive opposition of the absoluteness of the concept to the transcendental subjectivity of the categories. The recent linguistic transformation of the transcendental does not change much on this score. It is rather an issue of reinforcement, by way of a synthesis of criticism with positivism, and soon, via cognitivism, with intentional hermeneutics, of all that has arisen in two centuries of archi-metaphysics.

The point of departure for a response, as we have understood it, was always to be found in the dialectic, that is, in a singular conjunction, already articulated by Plato in the *Sophist*, between the absoluteness of the concept and the creative freedom of negation.

Will this point of departure suffice in the present day? This discussion would lead us too far afield. It would in any case call for a repeated examination of the axioms of classical metaphysics, in order to ferret out, within the mathematical paradigm, the secret of the tangled relationship between finitude, infinity, and existence—which Hegel himself underestimates. No doubt we would learn in the process what Descartes glimpsed: that in light of contemporary mathematics, and especially the Cantorian treatment of infinity, it is possible to begin with infinity, pure and simple.

We shall say that a contemporary metaphysics deserves the name of metaphysics insofar as, rejecting the archi-metaphysical critique, it maintains, in the Hegelian style, the absoluteness of the concept. However, it will not deserve this name insofar as, clarifying from the start the infinity of being as mathematizable multiplicity, it leaves no place for postulating the indeterminate.

And no doubt it would not be a metaphysical dialectic, in the strict sense if it truly does not have to resort to the motif of the historical self-determination of the indeterminate. Rather, it would affirm, in a Platonic, therefore metaphysical, style—but with all hyperbolic transcendence of the Good banished from metaphysics—that there exists an idea of anything thinkable, and that to bind thought, it suffices to select the appropriate axioms.

This is why we might well advance such a project under the paradoxical name of metaphysics without metaphysics. Its task would be, as Mallarmé requested, to send a "summons to the world on par with its obsession with rich quantitative predicates."[29]

Notes

Translated by Megan Flocken and Javiera Perez-Gomez, with the inestimable aid of Alex Levine. This essay initially appeared in English as Alain Badiou, "Metaphysics and the Critique of Metaphysics," trans. Alberto Toscano, *Pli* 10 (2000): 174–190.

1. Immanuel Kant, *Prolegomena to Any Future Metaphysics*, Ed. and trans. Gary Hatfield (Cambridge: Cambridge University Press, 2004), p. 92.

2. Ibid., "Solution to the General Question of the Prologomena," p. 119.

3. "Au tumulte et au tapage" is a notable phrase, used in the correspondence of Leon Gambetta when he declared the French Republic on September 4, 1370. See Léon Gambetta, *Discours et plaidoyers politiques de M. Gambetta (Volume 1: Speeches and political advocacy: Nov. 14 1868–Sep. 4 1870)*, ed. Joseph Reinach (Paris: G. Charpentier, 1881), p. 415.

4. Kant, "Preface," in *Prolegomena*, p. 5.

5. August Comte, *A Discourse on the Positive Spirit*, trans. Edward Spencer Beasley (London: William Reeves, 1903), p. 17: "The metaphysical state then may be regarded as a sort of chronic distemper naturally supervening in the mental evolution, whether of the individual or the race."

6. Auguste Comte, *Cours de philosophie positive*, "Préface personnelle" (Paris: Bachelier, 1842), xix, http://gallica.bnf.fr/ark:/12148/bpt6k762728.r=.langEN.swf.

7. Martin Heidegger, *Nietzsche*, vol. 3: *The Will to Power as Knowledge and Metaphysics*, ed. David Farrell Krell, trans. Joan Stambaugh, David Ferrell Krell, and Frank A. Capuzzi (New York: Harper & Row, 1987), p. 175.

8. [These notes do not appear in Krell's English translation of Heidegger's *Nietzsche* lectures. They can be found in the second volume of *Nietzsche* in the *Gesamtausgabe*. Martin Heidegger, *Nietzsche: Zweiter Band (Gesamtausgabe Band 6.2)*. We are indebted to Alberto Toscano for this citation (Alain Badiou, "Metaphysics and the Critique of Metaphysics," trans. Alberto Toscano, *Pli* 10 [2000]: 174–190, at p. 179). Badiou quotes Klossowski's French translation, which reads:

Tous les événements de l'histoire de l'Être, laquelle est la métaphysique, ont leur début et leur fondement en ceci, à savoir que la métaphysique laisse et doit nécessairement laisser indécise l'essence de l'Être, pour autant qu'apprécier "ce qui est digne de question," soit ce qui est problématique, en faveur du sauvetage de sa propre essence, est indifférent à la métaphysique depuis

le commencement, et cela dans l'indifférence du non-connaître. (Martin Heidegger, *Nietzsche*, trans. Pierre Klossowski [Paris: Gallimard, 1971])
—Trans.]

9. Auguste Comte, "Épistémologie," §9 of *Discours Sur L'esprit Positif* (Paris: Société positiviste, 1898), p. 13; Auguste Comte, *A Discourse on the Positive Spirit*, trans. Edward Spencer Beesly (London: William Reeves, 1903), pp. 13–14.

10. Comte, "Épistémologie," §10 of *Discours Sur L'esprit Positif*, p. 15; Comte, *A Discourse on the Positive Spirit*, p. 16.

11. Ludwig Wittgenstein, *Tractatus Logico-Philosophicus*, trans. D. F. Pears and B. F. McGuinness (London: Routledge & Kegan Paul, 1974), §6.53, p. 89.

12. Comte, *Discours Sur L'esprit Positif*, §12, p. 19. [For our English translation, we are indebted to *The Positive Philosophy of Auguste Comte*, vol. 2: *The Nature of Method*, trans. Harriet Martineau (Cambridge: Kegan Paul, Trench, Trübner, 1893), p. 425: "No proposition that is not finally reducible to the enunciation of a fact, particular or general, can offer any real and intelligible meaning."—Trans.]

13. *Testament d'Auguste Comte avec les documents qui s'y rapportent: Pièces justifcatives, prières quotidiennes, confessions annuelles,correspondance avec Mme. de Vaux* (Paris, 1896 ed.), p. 146, cited in Mary Pickering, *Auguste Comte*, vol. 2: *An Intellectual Biography* (Cambridge: Cambridge University Press, 2009), p. 144.

14. Wittgenstein, *Tractatus*, §6.522, p. 89.

15. G. W. F. Hegel, *The Science of Logic*, trans. George Di Giovanni (Cambridge: Cambridge University Press, 2010), §21.29, p. 25.

16. "On ne part pas." Arthur Rimbaud, "Mauvais sang," in *Rimbaud Complete*, trans. Wyatt Mason (New York: Random House, 2013), p. 487.

17. "J'y suis, j'y suis toujours." Arthur Rimbaud, "Qu'est-ce pour nous, mon coeur...?" in *The Drunken Boat: And Other Poems*, ed. and trans. Robert Scholten (Bloomington, IN: Xlibris, 2012), p. 210.

18. Cf. Immanuel Kant, *Prolegomena*, §57.

19. "Rien n'existe qu'en tant qu'il n'existe pas." Jacques Lacan, "Response to Jean Hyppolite's Commentary on Freud's 'Verneinung,'" in *Ecrits: The First and Complete Edition in English*, trans. Bruce Fink (New York: W. W. Norton, 2006), §392, p. 327.

20. Hegel, *The Science of Logic*, preface to "The Objective Logic: Book One: The Doctrine of Being," p. 7.

21. Ibid., §21.49, p. 42.

22. Ibid.

23. Ibid., §57.

24. Ibid.

25. Ibid., §21.35, p. 30.

26. Ibid.

27. Ibid., §21.47, p. 41.

28. Ibid., §57.

29. Stéphane Mallarmé, *Œuvres complètes*, vol. 2, ed. Bertrand Marchal (Paris: Gallimard, Bibliothèque de la Pléiade, 2003), p. 481.

3 Turning from a Given Horizon to the Givenness of Horizons

Lee Braver

Being and Time is, at bottom, a work of transcendental phenomenology. Yes, there's a healthy dose of Kierkegaardian existentialism, especially in I.iv[1] and the first half of the Second Division, some Diltheyan hermeneutics in I.v and II.v, a dash of Hegelian collective subjectivity and history in I.iv and I.v—but it all takes place within a framework consisting largely of a fusion of Kant and Husserl.[2] Perhaps the main point that Kant's first *Critique* and Husserl's many writings make is that despite how it appears, we don't just open up our eyes to find reality laid out before us, imprinting itself on our perception simply by being in the vicinity of our sensory organs. No, a great deal goes into the having of an experience on the part of consciousness. For Kant, to perceive an object the transcendental ego must use the forms of intuition and the concepts of the understanding to organize sensory data, giving it certain qualities such as time, space, causality, and objectivity. For Husserl, transcendental subjectivity stitches together an array of adumbrations or perspectives into a unified entity, thus conferring upon it the status of a single, persistent, independently existing object (we discover that we are the ones who issued this status when we revoke it via the epoché). We see many-sided objects instead of just discrete sides—indeed, we see them as *sides* in the first place—because we fused them together, like squeezing used slivers into a single transcendental bar of soap. For both, what seems to lie before us as a gift is largely a product of our own unconscious labor.

Now, with important differences (some of which I discuss in this book's introduction), *Being and Time* follows this basic approach. Beings can appear in the clearing—Heidegger's word for our awareness of anything—because we have cleared a space for them, and the way that we do this determines the ways that beings can be there for us. We set the conditions for experiencing anything, and everything we experience takes on the properties of these conditions.

One of the main points of the First Division is that we are primarily and for the most part engaged, active doers rather than contemplators. Because of this, beings first and mostly manifest themselves to us as ready-to-be-used for our projects; this is what the world is for Heidegger—a totality of beings organized in terms of our activities. Because we can disengage and disinterestedly observe as well, beings can also be inert present-at-hand objects. The point is that it is our pro-jecting ahead toward goals and reaching back for roles and taking up of tools at-hand that stretches open the clearing within which we can encounter and comport ourselves toward anything and anyone. Ex-tending ourselves in these three directions sets the contours of the clearing, which in turn determines what can come into it and so present itself to us: equipment, objects, world, other Dasein, history, occupations, nature. I have elsewhere called this move the Law of Transcendental Transitivity since features of our "transcendental' understanding get transferred to that which we understand. It is basically an adaptation of Kant's "highest principle of all synthetic judgments ... that the conditions of the *possibility of experience* in general are likewise conditions of the *possibility of the objects of experience*."[3] I'm not sure if Heidegger intends his account to be universal, such that any being who can become aware must do so this way, or if this is just our particular way of doing so, which may differ fundamentally from others, just as I am uncertain about Kant's position on this question.[4] Phenomenology, I think, can only substantiate the latter, weaker claim. It's up to bats and Martians to say what their worlds are like; we can only describe our own.[5]

In any case, this Law is why the book's first page immediately turns from asking about being to asking about the meaning of being, which can only be investigated by examining that being who understands and thus for whom meaning can be—Dasein. Accordingly, *Being and Time* asks the question of being via fundamental ontology: the examination of being or ontology is built on the foundation of an analysis of our way of being, the existential analytic (BT 34/13). It's not that meaning is often found hovering around this particular being so that if we stick close to her, we're likely to run into it. Dasein isn't where meaning just happens to be located; Dasein *generates* meaning. We *make* sense by living meaning-ful lives. When Heidegger says that Dasein *understands* being, the verb should be understood not as a passive registering of facts pressing upon us, but as an active productive process, as with Kant and Husserl.[6] We project the horizons within which anything can come to experience, so what we learn about the way we project these horizons also tells us about what can appear within those horizons, that is, being.[7] We can learn about rainbows by studying the shape of the prism that splays light out or, in the analogy I use in this book's introduction, we understand visibility by studying the eye. But, in the question that this book presses upon us, what happened? Why didn't Heidegger finish it?

One possible answer is that he did finish it; it's just hard to see because it was rushed. The structure of the book follows what I call the hermeneutic spiral, where Heidegger lays out certain ideas and then goes back over them—or rather under them—to show what enables them to be, the conditions for their possibility in Kantian terms.[8] Beginning with the introduction's claim that Dasein is an issue for herself (BT 32/12), we then find out that this feature is based on her being-in-the-world since one can only attempt to settle the issue of one's being by taking up self-defining roles that employ worldly equipment. Division I's conclusion is that we only try to settle this issue and so are-in-the-world if we care about our selves; care is thus the condition of the possibility of being-in-the-world. Division II gives the spiral its final spin to rest on temporality as our bottom-most level ("the ecstatical unity of temporality … is the condition for the possibility that there can be an entity which exists as its 'there'" [BT 401/350]), which determines the nature of all existentialia resting upon it. All features of our existence are actually forms of temporality,[9] including our understanding,[10] which by the Law of Transcendental Transitivity, makes all understood or meaningful beings temporal.[11] Hence, the meaning of being is time, as the very first page, even the title of the book tells us (BT 19/1).

What's odd is that the book doesn't quite follow this neat line of reasoning. Division II breaks into two distinct pieces: the first three chapters up to §64 constitute a deepening and existential darkening of Division I's examination of Dasein. Death and anxiety give us Dasein's being as a whole and in its authenticity, as attested by conscience, which completes the existential analysis. The middle of II.iii, at §65, represents the crux of the Second Division where the hermeneutic spiral takes its final turn to reveal temporality as the level beneath care, the bottom layer of existence. Then §66 promises to go back over the other aspects covered in Division I—everydayness, being-in-the-world, readiness-to-hand and presence-at-hand spatiality, history, and community—to show their temporal underpinnings as well, which the rest of the book partially fulfills. Although I didn't notice this break at first, every rereading since has made it more prominent, like the orchestral clouding over of "Strawberry Fields Forever" at around the one-minute mark (two different versions of the song were stitched together). I tentatively propose the hypothesis that II.i through

II.iii.§64 is a compressed draft of what was originally going to be the entirety of Division II. Where Division I focuses on worldly, busy Dasein, Division II was to show how this inauthentic way of life covers over the existential self that faces death, lives anxiously, listens to conscience resolutely and authentically, and chooses deliberately.

Division I lays out the three ways of being: readiness-to-hand, presence-at-hand, and an initial portrait of existence. According to the present hypothesis—let's call it the Overstuffed Division Theory—Division II would have fleshed out the third of these ways, existence, since the account in Division I was limited to inauthenticity. Then Division III would have concentrated on time's different modes as the temporal underpinnings of the ontological modes: authentic temporality enables being-in-the-world, now-time lets things be present-at-hand, world-time is the condition for ready-to-hand equipment and the world, history is what allows us to be-with others.[12] These all emerge out of fundamental ontology's foundational discovery of time as the bottom layer of Dasein and, by the Law of Transcendental Transitivity, the meaning of being: "By casting light upon temporality as the primordial condition for the possibility of *care*, we have reached the primordial Interpretation of Dasein which we require" (BT 424/372). This is why "the most primordial and basic existential truth, for which the problematic of fundamental ontology strives in preparing the question of Being in general, is the *disclosedness of the meaning of the Being of care*" (BT 364/316).

The two divisions got stuffed into one when Heidegger rushed Division II to press in order to secure a promotion at Marburg University.[13] He had a good idea of where the book was going, but in his hurry he crammed what was meant to be two separate divisions into one, which now splits down the middle. From this perspective, the last quarter of the book (II.iii.§65–II. vi) looks like a jumbled-up, highly compressed attempt to reconceive the modes of being already discussed as forms of temporalizing, which is precisely what the book was supposed to show.[14] Heidegger describes the content of Part One as "the Interpretation of Dasein in terms of temporality, and the explication of time as the transcendental horizon for the question of Being" (63/39). II.iii.§65 represents the culmination of the first part of this sentence—interpreting Dasein in terms of temporality—while II. ii.§66 corresponds to the "and," where we move from the temporality of Dasein's existence to that of all modes of being, from Dasein's *Zeitlichkeit* to being's *Temporalität*, in Heidegger's terminology. The question of why Heidegger didn't finish *Being and Time* would thus receive the answer that he did, just in a rushed, disorganized way that's hard to recognize.

Being and Time writes "a genealogy of the different possible ways of Being" (31/11) by tracing them back to their common progenitor: time. The book gives us an account of these ways of being and how they emerge from different ways of temporalizing, which is what "time is the meaning of being" means (BT 370–371/324). Furthermore, it builds this foundation of ontology atop the existential analytic, as promised: it is because Dasein is at bottom time that being is temporal. Our temporality determines everything about us, thus giving the clearing a temporal shape, which sets the being of all the beings that can appear there, in the *Da* that we are.

The Basic Problems of Phenomenology, one of the two works Heidegger refers us to for the missing Division III,[15] reaffirms a strong commitment to fundamental ontology:

We must keep a firm hold methodically on what makes something like being accessible to us: the understanding of being that belongs to the Dasein. So far as understanding of being belongs to the Dasein's existence, this understanding and the being that is understood and meant in it become all the more suitably and originally accessible, the more originally and comprehensively the *constitution of the Dasein's being itself* and the *possibility of the understanding of being* are brought to light. ... It is requisite that the Dasein be subjected to a *preparatory ontological investigation* which would provide the foundation for all further inquiry, which includes the question of the being of beings and the being of the different regions of being. We therefore call the preparatory ontological analytic of the Dasein *fundamental ontology*. ... It *alone first leads to the illumination of the meaning of being* and of *the horizon of the understanding of being*. ... After the exposition of the meaning of being and the horizon of ontology, it has to be repeated at a higher level. (BP 223–224)

Being can only be meaningful—and thus meaning can only be—for an understanding, and an understanding is understood in terms of the understander's constitution. Once this is reached in II.iii.§65 with Dasein's temporality, we turn the hermeneutic spiral once more to see how all modes of being, not just existence, are really forms of temporalization, so that "the exposition of the meaning of being and the horizon of ontology" gets "repeated at a higher level." Thus, "the center of development of ontological inquiry in general lies in the exposition of the Dasein's temporality" (BP 327).

Although the very end of *Being and Time* suggests that "our way of exhibiting the constitution of Dasein's Being remains only *one way* which we may take ... to work out the question of Being in general," *Basic Problems* repeatedly insists that "the direction of the path [Kant] follows, by returning to the subject in its broadest sense, is *the only one* that is possible and correct."[16] *Basic Problems'* study of the history of philosophy reaches two conclusions: first, all great philosophers turn to some form of subjectivity to explain the world;[17] second, none has done so correctly. Not only have all previous philosophers misconceived Dasein (generally as a present-at-hand substance), but they have not used these analyses the right way.

Philosophy for Heidegger asks what is being like, and why is it like that? Philosophers have botched both questions. They have answered the first question incorrectly, traditionally focusing exclusively on presence-at-hand (this critique becomes more complex in his later work). On the other hand, they have missed the very significance of the second question, answering it by appealing to particular beings such as God or Forms, a mistake Heidegger comes to call ontotheology. The problem with these answers is that they only push the inquiry back a step to why *these* entities are the way they are. Each explanans takes its turn as an explanandum in an infinite regress of explanation. Throughout his career, he accuses philosophical doctrines of employing distinctions or concepts in order to explain certain phenomena, while leaving those explanatory ideas themselves unaccounted for. "The basic concepts are not themselves given an express and explicit foundation but are simply there, one knows not how."[18] To actually explain the world we must explain the explanation as well. Why are *these* particular concepts applicable to the world? We need what Kant called a transcendental deduction that would justify the use of these specific notions.

And, Heidegger thinks at this point in his career, we must do this the same way that Kant did, only better. When Hume argued that there's no reason why reality must be causal, Kant responded that there is a very good reason: us. Our transcendental faculties make the world causal so everything we ever experience will be linked deterministically. The early Heidegger considers this an enormous step forward, the point at which philosophy finds its proper *telos*.

The critical discussion of the Kantian thesis leads to the necessity of an explicit ontology of the Dasein. For it is only on the basis of the exposition of the basic ontological constitution of the Dasein that we put ourselves in a position to understand adequately the phenomenon correlated with the idea of being, the understanding of being which lies at the basis of all comportment to beings and guides it. ... The ontology of the Dasein represents the latent goal and constant and more or less evident demand of the whole development of Western philosophy.[19]

As Kant grounded the disciplines of math and science in our transcendental faculties, as Husserl named the study of consciousness the science of all sciences because consciousness' activities account for the basic features of experience studied by all other disciplines, so Heidegger makes the study of Dasein's being (the existential analytic) the foundation of ontology. Of course, there are enormous differences among these thinkers, especially in their conceptions of consciousness as opposed to Dasein, but they all agree that this is the way to explain why the world we experience is the way it is. Interestingly, like Hegel's,[20] this narrative makes the modern turn to subjectivity the key to progress instead of decay, the essence of true philosophy instead of its betrayal and degeneration, as Heidegger will later describe it. Kant first hit upon the strategy, but, as the German Idealists complained, he simply picked up concepts he found around him without accounting for why we have these particular ones.[21]

Heidegger wants to take up Kant's project and do it right. Not only will he give us a better account of Dasein, but he will show how all of our *existentialia* emerge from our ultimate being of temporality, thereby unifying and explaining the loose group that Kant dogmatically presupposed.

The primordial phenomenon of temporality will be held secure by demonstrating that if we have regard for the possible totality, unity, and development of those fundamental structures of Dasein which we have hitherto exhibited, these structures are all to be conceived as at bottom "temporal" and as modes of the temporalizing of temporality. Thus, when temporality has been laid bare, there arises for the existential analytic the task of *repeating* our analysis of Dasein in the sense of Interpreting its essential structures with regard to their temporality.[22]

We step back from the various phenomena we experience to the *existentialia* that account for why phenomena are the way they are, and then one more step to Dasein's temporality to account for why we have the *existentialia* that we do, and that would constitute a full explanation of the meaning of being.

Heidegger might have run into a minor problem here. As *Being and Time* makes readily apparent, he is quite enamored of neat architectonics at this point in his career. Everything in the book comes in threes because everything is ultimately based on time's three tenses. So Division III's full explication of the temporality of the three modes of being presumably would have lined them up with the three tenses. Presence-at-hand nicely matches the present and existence correlates with the future (BT 376/327, 385/336), but readiness-to-hand also seems primarily futural. Equipment has a past in its material (hinted at on BP 115, PM 370, n. 59) and a present in its immediate use, but it is fundamentally teleological, which makes it future-oriented: a hammer is in-order-to accomplish a goal that lies ahead of me.[23] In fact, these modes of being are asymmetrical in relation to Dasein in general. Dasein must be-in-a-world of equipment first and for the most part, whereas presence-at-hand emerges only occasionally, during breakdowns or disengaged examination. Indeed, it seems coherent to imagine a thought experiment where the world never breaks down and hence never allows the emergence of presence-at-hand, a bit like Hume's perfectly satiating world in which questions of justice do not arise.[24] This is why "worldhood itself is an *existentiale*. … Ontologically, 'world' is not a way of characterizing those entities which Dasein essentially is *not*; it is rather a characteristic of Dasein itself" (BT 92/64). Even more strongly, "Dasein *is* its world" (BT 416/364), leaving presence-at-hand out in the cold as an atypical and, strictly speaking, unnecessary form of being. Heidegger's (relative) privileging of readiness-to-hand seems to unbalance the architectonic he was building.

Now, there are three more significant problems with the Overstuffed Division Theory. First, Heidegger often says that we need an understanding of being itself before we can fully comprehend Dasein's being (even though fundamental ontology requires us to understand Dasein's being in order to understand being; this is the (virtuously) circular nature of all inquiry for Heidegger).[25] This implies that the three modes of being aren't enough to answer his question; we need a sense of being that is above and beyond these ways of being, which means that being isn't just these three modes. Indeed, one can argue that this sense is necessary just to recognize them *as* ways of being.[26] This means that Division III would have given us something that isn't contained within the first two divisions' analyses of the three modes of being: being itself.

Second, *Being and Time*'s definitive explanation of the basic features of phenomena by means of Dasein's *existentialia* only works as long as Dasein retains these particular structures. Kant secured the universality and necessity of math and science by assuming that all humans organize experience the same way, thus ensuring intersubjective agreement, which he calls, somewhat paradoxically, universal validity for us.[27] However, as Hegel immediately pointed out, we cannot prove that all humans have the same transcendental faculties. Indeed, evidence from history—a discipline overlooked by Kant's focus on math and science—strongly suggests the opposite, that people have experienced the world in profoundly different ways across cultures and times. Insisting that they all had the same form of phenomena while their scientific theories radically departed from it forces us to convict our predecessors of a kind of transcendental stupidity that seems both implausible and rather obnoxious.

Now, Heidegger does make Dasein historical in *Being and Time*, but only so much. While he never explicitly states it, the book strongly suggests that all Dasein everywhere and at all times are-in-the-world in the same basic way, encountering the same modes of being.[28] Particular ontic entities vary, sure, but not their ontological types. Today we drive cars instead of chariots or stagecoaches, but presumably all three vehicles are in-order-to travel distances quickly, and all withdraw inconspicuously during smooth usage in basically the same way. Individual for-the-sakes-of-which have changed, but we today take up professions such as accountant or software developer just as our ancestors defined themselves as centurions or samurai or spice merchants.

One of the changes in his later work is that history goes all the way down, so that we transform along with the beings around us at epochal shifts. This change makes *Being and Time*'s fundamental ontology untenable:

What is fundamental in fundamental ontology is incompatible with any building on it. Instead, after the meaning of Being had been clarified, the whole analytic of Dasein was to be more originally repeated in a completely different way. Thus, since the foundation of fundamental ontology is no foundation upon which something could be built, no *fundamentum inconcussum*, but rather a *fundamentum concussum* … whereas the word "foundation" contradicts the preliminary character of the analytic, the term "fundamental ontology" was dropped.[29]

We cannot build a permanent system of a single set of modes of being on the new shifting sands of Dasein's historically altering being. Hegel was able to incorporate historical change while still founding ontology on the subject, but only because he contained all the possible forms of subjectivity and reality within a completed totality as tightly systematic as Kant's single group of forms and concepts. Heidegger doesn't think that history can be tamed like this by being fit into an overall pattern or logic (although his suggestions that Nietzsche exhausted all possible variations on the being-becoming distinction that started with Plato, and that the history of being is one of progressive corruption and forgetfulness, come close).[30] In general, he thinks that there is no way to corral the permutations of humanity and being into an overarching systematic explanation since any such analysis would itself only make sense within a particular epochal understanding.

This new emphasis on history is supported by the fact that the two works Heidegger refers to as reconceptions of Division III, *The Basic Problems of Phenomenology* and *Introduction to Metaphysics*, both focus explicitly on history. While the entire second half of *Being and Time* was to have dealt with the history of philosophy, the very separation between Part One's fundamental ontology and Part Two's historical approach shows the latter to be external to and, perhaps, unnecessary for the question of being, a distinction he later seems to disavow.[31] Because Dasein's being changes along with everything else, the existential analytic can no longer serve as foundation. Each new epoch will "bestow on [man] the foundation of a new essence. This need displaces man into the beginning of a foundation of his essence. I say advisedly *a* foundation for we can never say that it is the absolute one."[32]

Third, as we saw, the movement of *Being and Time* was one of progressively stepping back or digging deeper. We start, as Aristotle says, with what is most obvious in the order of knowing but least essential in the order of being, and end with what is least obvious but most essential.[33] In Heidegger's thought, this means that we start with beings and move to their being, or from phenomena to what makes those phenomena possible.

What we are now to be directed toward is nearer to us than what is ordinarily and "at first" the closest, and therefore it is correspondingly more difficult to see. Thus in the zeal of the ordinary seeing of sense perception, we overlook what holds good and serves under visible things and between them and our vision, the closest of all, namely brightness and its own proper transparency, through which the impatience of our seeing hurries and must hurry. To experience the closest is the most difficult. In the course of our dealings and occupations it is passed over precisely as the easiest. … We see first, strictly speaking, never the closest but always what is next closest. The obtrusiveness and imperativeness of the next closest drives the closest and its closeness out of the domain of experience.[34]

First we describe tools and then move back to their readiness-to-hand, then to our understanding of their readiness-to-hand, then to what makes this understanding possible—the fact that we care to settle the issue of our being by taking up roles that require equipment—and finally to time as what makes any understanding/appearance of being possible. The conclusion is that since we are the clearing, our temporal nature makes readiness-to-hand—and being in general—temporal.

Now Kant was the first to appeal to the subject to account for legitimate features of reality (philosophers have blamed subjectivity for illusory or deceptive contributions as far back as Parmenides' path of error, Heraclitus' sleepers who don't perceive the *logos*, and the atomists' phenomenal qualities beyond atoms and void). As we have seen, Heidegger's critique of Kant's solution was that he didn't adequately accomplish his own project by failing to unify or justify the selection of just these concepts, leaving their specific constitution a brute fact, as Kant himself occasionally admitted.[35] Early Heidegger solves this by showing how all three modes of being emerge from Dasein's care, which itself comes from her temporality, thus demonstrating *why* we have these particular ones.[36]

However, it is readily apparent that this answer merely pushes the question back a step. We experience these kinds of phenomena because we have these *existentialia*, and we have them because we are temporal in the specific way that we are. This is interesting and enlightening, but the question reappears in relation to our temporality—why are we temporal, and why in this particular way? Heidegger has no answer to this, and even if he did, the question would pop up once more behind *that* answer, infinitely regressing into the unexplained.[37] His later works often criticize ontotheological attempts to answer the question of being by appealing to a particular being—traditionally God—because God is just one more being who would also need to be accounted for. Perhaps *Being and Time* commits a variation of that mistake, with Dasein in place of God—an ontoanthropology, if you will, as long as we're careful not to think of it as traditional anthropology.[38]

What we find here, in a strikingly Humean and Wittgensteinian vein,[39] is the inescapable end of explanation. No matter how far back we go, we will always reach a point that is itself unexplained. The problem is not that *Being and Time* gives a bad answer but, as Wittgenstein says of Moore's response to skepticism, that it gives an answer at all, that is, an "ultimate" explanation for the fact and way that beings show up for us.[40] What Heidegger realizes in the later work is that in principle there can be no such final explanation. Whatever it is about our existence that accounts for our clearing cannot account for itself, so any explanation would necessarily leave a last step unexplained. "All metaphysics leaves something essential unthought: its own ground and foundation."[41] This is what he means by the expression "groundless grounds": we can find grounds, but these must themselves remain groundless. Heidegger replaces Dasein as the foundational ground of ontology with groundless being.

He now sees that at the bottom of any kind of transcendental activity lies a necessary, ineliminable point of passive receptivity.[42] In the terms of the early work, thrownness swallows up projection: even if we are Kantian-style projectors, we must have been thrown into these particular ways of projecting, limiting their explanatory power. This, I think, is what Heidegger means when he says that being sends us our clearing and our epochal understanding of being. It is not something we could have made ourselves without already having a clearing, which itself we could not have made. As Wittgenstein argues, explanation must end somewhere.[43]

One might read this turn as a change in Heidegger's position relative to Kant and Hegel. Initially he sides with Hegel's objection to Kant's ungrounded grab bag of forms and concepts as ununified and unjustified.[44] *Being and Time* tried to solve that problem by tracing all *existentialia* to time, which explains why we experience the world the way we do. His later work, on the other hand, appreciates the depth of Kant's lack of answer, now siding with him against Hegel's demand for final explanations.[45] Some of the works from the late 1920s describe temporality as the deepest instance of facticity, the ultimate mystery instead of the final answer: "The primal fact … is that there is anything like temporality at all."[46] This connects problem 2 above, deep historicality, with problem 3, the demand for final answers. If our nature is liable to change, then we can never come to a definitive determination of our being that could ground all else. One way Heidegger shows this is by questioning the final result of his early fundamental ontology, namely, that Dasein is at bottom time.[47] Heidegger frequently insists on the utter inexplicability of being in the later work.[48] This deliberate nonanswer reminds one a little of Nietzsche's praise of the Greeks for knowing "to stop courageously at the surface … to adore appearance. … Those Greeks were superficial—*out of profundity*" (1974, 38).

Whereas in the early work, Dasein opened the clearing, agency and initiative now move to being: "That Being itself and how Being itself concerns our thinking does not depend upon our thinking alone. That Being itself, and the manner in which Being itself, strikes a particular thinking, lets such thinking spring forth in springing from Being itself in such a way as to respond to Being as such."[49] Our thoughts are but responses to the way things strike us; our actions, reactions. And being's provocations cannot be explained, thus ruining *any* kind of fundamental ontology, any attempt to understand why being is and why it is the way it is. "Being offers us no ground and no basis—as beings do—to which we can turn, on which we can build, and to which we can cling. Being is the rejection of the role of such grounding: it renounces all grounding, is abyssal [*ab-gründig*]."[50]

Here the third problem with the Overstuffed Division Theory—ultimate intelligibility—joins with the first—the need for an explication of being itself. Heidegger's early work introduces the ontological difference between the various (ontic) beings we encounter and their (ontological) being, which means roughly the way they are—ready-to-hand, present-at-hand, or existing. His later work makes a particular way of being, now called beingness or the being of beings, common to things in a particular epoch. The Greeks, for example, experienced beings as *physis* whereas medievals found themselves amid *entia creata*. Heidegger also adds a third level to this distinction—being itself. This historical diversity of ways of being should lead us to wonder where they all came from. Why have people experienced things so differently? They could not come from our innovations, for where did *these* come from? A medieval person could not have created the modern outlook, because the only thoughts she had to work with were medieval; even the idea of tinkering with one's thinking process to make it more efficient or fruitful was not particularly sensible before Descartes. This is one reason Heidegger rejects our ability to overcome the contemporary technological understanding of being by ourselves, why we must wait for a god to save us. "By itself and on its own, no human calculation and *design* can bring forth a turning in the world's present condition. Especially not, because human design is already formed by this very condition of the world. ... How then could it [human design] still gain control over it [the world's condition]?"[51] We must wait for being to send us a new understanding of being, which I take to mean that we cannot make one ourselves, nor point to any particular entities or events or individuals' efforts to explain these transitions. They are *fundamentally* mysterious.

This answer to the question of why being is, and why it is the way it is, is intentionally a nonanswer, like Silenus' rose blooming because it blooms in *The Principle of Reason*. The fact that being manifests itself differently at different times is the ultimate brute fact, the fact *that* there is, that there is a "there is," that a *there* is. It could not be explained without appealing to beings that are and employing ways of thinking that are given to us which, belonging as they do to specific epochs, cannot account for epochality itself. Heidegger calls this third level being itself, beyng (*Seyn*), *Ereignis*—the event (that being happens), the clearing, or truth. To be is to be manifest for a being who can become aware of it. While Heidegger retains *Being and Time*'s mutual interdependence of being and Dasein[52] (now called humanity), the explanatory valence has been reversed: being's epochal appearance now accounts for why we are the way we are instead of our being the way we are explaining why being is the way it is.

Heidegger planned to turn to being itself in Division III, making its absence particularly painful, but the published text does touch on the topic in two places: §7 and §§43–44. A good hermeneutic principle is to pay special attention to what doesn't fit; that's what such prominent hermeneuticists as Jacques Derrida and Sherlock Holmes do. And one of the worst-fitting parts of the book is §§43–44, at the end of Division I. Ignoring §42's odd myth of *cura*, I.vi.§41 marks the natural conclusion of Division I, its triumphant climax even. The preliminary definitions of Dasein are laid out in the introduction and Chapter I, then Chapters II through V analyze the three facets of being-in-the-world, finishing in Chapter VI with care as what underlies being-in-the-world as a whole. Division II picks up in §45 precisely where §41 leaves off—care as the "structural whole" of being-in-the-world—by asking whether this truly captures the whole of Dasein in its totality and unity as it claims to (BT 274–275/231–232), preparing the way for the analysis of authenticity in the next three chapters.

But a discussion of reality and truth intrudes in the middle of this analysis with no obvious connection to the paragraphs before or after, paragraphs that connect smoothly with each other as if §§43–44 simply weren't there (I leave these sections until the end when I teach the book and it reads more smoothly). Why did he insert a large non sequitur here, and on such important topics?

Here's my guess: these were part of the explication of being itself that Heidegger was planning for Division III, or at least a preparation for them. When he decided not to publish it, he stuck the parts of it he was reasonably happy with between the divisions. What we learn in these sections is that reality and truth require us in order to be, and that truth is unconcealment or appearing to us, basically the same as the definition of being in §7. It's no accident that truth forms the dominant topic of the next decade of Heidegger's writings and lectures—1930's "The Essence of Truth," 1931–32's "Plato's Doctrine of Truth," and the extensive lectures on Nietzsche throughout the late 1930s. The point that emerges over and over again is that being means the same[53] as truth ("Being and truth 'are' equiprimordially" [BT 272/230]): emerging from concealment into the clearing. Heidegger frequently rereads, and in my opinion reinterprets, core aspects of *Being and Time* in terms of truth,[54] making this a further turn of the hermeneutic spiral. Reflecting on his "Pathway Hitherto" in 1939, he says that "the inquiry into Da-sein must be made anew and begun more originarily, but at the same time in explicit relation to the truth of be-ing" (M 367).

Now this definition of being does a number of things. First, it cuts off explanation, renouncing the quest for ultimate answers, thus solving problem 3. We cannot account for the source of all appearing without appealing to apparent entities, which unhelpfully presupposes appearance. As with the big bang—which could only be explained by entities that it itself, as the origin of all that is, is supposed to explain (if causes preceded it, then it isn't truly the *big* bang)—all explanations come too late.

We can only name it, because it will deign no discussion. For it is the place that encompasses all locales and time-play-spaces. ... Propriating dispenses the open space of the clearing into which what is present can enter for a while. ... What the propriating yields through the saying is never the effect of a cause, nor the consequence of a reason. ... What propriates is propriation itself—and nothing besides. ... There is nothing else to which propriation reverts, nothing in terms of which it might even be explained. Propriation is not an outcome of a result of something else, it is the bestowal whose giving reaches out in order to grant for the first time something like a "There is."[55]

To explain the source of the explicable is to make a kind of category mistake. That is why Heidegger praises Parmenides: "the primal mystery for all thinking is concealed in" Parmenides' phrase "for there is Being" (BW 238). What else can we say about being than that it is? That beings manifest themselves to us as perceptible and thinkable? This is the miracle we must never take for granted; it is the gift of all gifts, for it is the gift that enables us to receive what is given (WCT 142).

Second, it frees us to accept being as it appears instead of imposing presupposed restrictions on what it must be like, thereby solving problem 2: history. In particular, we can acknowledge the flux of experience—whether in the form of the dynamism of equipment and world as opposed to the inert stasis of presence-at-hand in the early work,[56] or the historical variety of ways of being in the later.[57] We can truly think being *and* time instead of just spinning out further variations on the Platonic "or." I think this radical openness to what shows up is what Heidegger means when he credits Husserl with teaching us "genuine philosophical empiricism" (BT 490, n. x), even though Husserl did not live up to the promise of his own discovery (neither did the empiricists, for that matter [BW 151–152]).

Third, this helps us appreciate the deep significance of phenomenology. On this reading, §§43–44 represent the turning of the hermeneutic spiral on §7's initial explication of phenomenology. Where §7 introduces the method of phenomenology, §§43–44 show its ontological underpinnings, the conditions for its possibility, inevitability even. After all, how can one say that *"only as phenomenology, is ontology possible"* (BT 60/36)? Traditionally reality does—and for many, must—contrast with how it appears to us, which is what phenomenology captures. This appearance–reality dichotomy (extensively discussed in *Introduction to Metaphysics*) is neatly solved if we adopt the definition of being in §7 and §§43–44, and which receives a fuller account in §9 of *History of the Concept of Time* (a very important passage for understanding early Heidegger, in my view). Beings are the phenomena or what appears, since to be is to appear, in all its myriad forms. The question of a reality itself behind or below or in some way separated from what we experience would render phenomena "mere" appearance, a word Heidegger says has caused more "havoc and confusion in philosophy" than any other (HCT 81). Instead, studying the way we experience the world *is* studying reality in-itself, a phrase Heidegger doesn't hesitate to use once we have rid ourselves of the invidious contrast with another realm.[58]

The full analysis of this idea would serve as a kind of Transcendental Deduction, justifying the application of the concepts of being as found in our experience to being full stop.[59]

This account of truth also overcomes whatever subjectivism remains in *Being and Time* by removing Dasein's influence over the existence and form of the clearing. Instead of *our* projecting open the clearing, being opens itself up, drawing us into the event of its occurrence, the happening of happening itself.

What is inappropriate in this formulation of the question is that it makes it all too possible to understand the "project" as a human performance. Accordingly, project is then only taken to be a structure of subjectivity. ... In order to counter this mistaken conception and to retain the meaning of "project" as it is to be taken (that of the opening disclosure), the thinking after *Being and Time* replaced the expression 'meaning of being' with 'truth of being.'[60]

He had wanted to turn from Dasein to being itself in the Third Division. It's rather difficult to see how such a change could be effected within the framework of that book: being was viewed there as experienced by Dasein, which, I have argued, is largely determined by Dasein's nature.[61] Indeed, he denies that being or truth can be without us.[62] One of the challenges of his later work is to maintain this mutual interdependence of being and humanity without putting us in charge. "What is needed now is the *great inversion* ... in which beings are not grounded on the human being, but humanness on being" (CP 145/§91). Although he still insists that being needs us in order to be—manifestation needs someone to be manifest to, appearance must appear *to* someone[63]—he now reverses the initiative and control.

Within the transcendental framework of *Being and Time*, we autonomically create the clearing much the way Kant's transcendental subject does. There is a constant emphasis there on Dasein as initiating, laying out the conditions for the possibility of experiencing particular kinds of beings that cannot be had simply by passively receiving experience. This, I argued in the opening of this essay, is his legacy from Kant and Husserl. Perhaps the most frequently repeated point Heidegger makes about awareness in *Being and Time* is that it is made possible and conditioned by our understanding. "All ontical experience of entities ... is based upon projections of the Being of the corresponding entities."[64] No amount of studying a hammer, for example, could ever teach us its equipmentality unless we already possessed an equip-mentality—knowing what it is to use something to achieve a purpose, that is, unless we understood readiness-to-hand.[65] Heidegger makes this point again and again throughout the book, both generally and with regard to specific kinds of beings: we only find facts by adopting a present-at-hand perspective (BT 251/207, 414/362–363); we encounter others because we start with an understanding of the being of other Dasein; and so on.[66] Indeed, we open up a clearing at all by caring about ourselves (BT 401–402/350–351).

In *Being and Time*, it is because we are the kinds of creatures that we are and because we do the kinds of things that we do that beings show up for us at all and in the specific ways that they do. It is our use that structures tools as ready-to-hand; they change over to presence-at-hand when we stop to study them. The later work turns this formulation around: it is because beings show up for us and in the specific ways that they do that we are the kinds of creatures that we are and do the kinds of things that we do. In 1929 he argued that "world is brought before Dasein through Dasein itself. ... This projection of world ... first makes it possible for beings as such to manifest themselves."[67] This means that "the transcendence of Dasein assumes the role of making possible the manifestation of beings in themselves. ... Only in the illumination granted by our understanding of being can beings become manifest in themselves" (PM 129–130). The later work reverses this: "The field of vision is something open, but its openness is not due to our looking" (DT 64). Being is something that happens to us rather than something we do, even autonomically, and its particular form provokes us to act the way we do rather than the other way around. This, along with the dynamic connotation, is why he comes to use the term *Ereignis*: being manifesting itself is not an act we perform but an event in which we are caught up. "Thinking accomplishes the relation of Being to the essence of man. It does not make or cause the relation. Thinking brings the relation to Being solely as something handed over to it from Being."[68]

This understanding of being solves all three of the Overstuffed Division's problems. Obviously, it supplies an explication of being itself, one that turns the hermeneutic spiral by deepening and developing the conception in §§7, 43–44. It overcomes transcendental metaphysics that stops at the level of beingness without inquiring why we have these particular ways of experiencing beings. It overcomes subjectivity by removing initiative and control from Dasein. It brings in a deep historicity by acknowledging the variety of forms of beingness that have issued from/in the *Ereignis* to descend upon us and the rest of beings. This turns us from a particular given horizon—Dasein's *existentialia*—to the givenness of horizonality—to the very fact that we have a horizon that allows us to be aware of anything. We move to the horizon of givenness, of the gift, gratitude for which is the fulfillment of thinking.

This reading also makes sense of another poorly fitting portion of the text: I.iii.§17 on signs. There we learn that whereas most tools withdraw inconspicuously when functioning properly, signs work by drawing attention to themselves. They shine light on the web-work of the world's instrumental relations, illuminating them without knocking us out of our engagement with them the way breakdowns do; think of the signs in a bus airport directing you to its various areas, each with its own *Umwelt* of equipment. Although it never reappears, this topic is actually rather important, in particular for the question of the possibility of the book itself. For the study of tool use as described in I.ii–iii faces a dilemma: while functioning, tools are inconspicuous and so elude direct examination. When studied, on the other hand, they change over to present-at-hand things, once again avoiding direct inspection. So how can we, how did Heidegger, study tools properly, that is, as ready-to-hand?

Whereas "The Origin of the Work of Art" points to artworks to solve this problem, perhaps §17 was meant to foreshadow Division III's discussion of phenomenology as a solution. Perhaps Heidegger thought of the book *Being and Time* as possessing the mode of being of a sign—a tool (the paper and ink of the sheaf of papers withdraw as we read) that lights up without committing the kind of interruption that transforms and thus distorts the subject (one of the main problems with Husserl's epoché). This would make Division III, "Time and Being," what Heidegger calls humanity in *What Is Called Thinking*: an unread sign pointing to withdrawing being.[69]

Notes

1. I cite *Being and Time* by division number as a capital Roman numeral, followed by chapter number in lowercase Roman numeral, and, when appropriate, paragraph number with the "§" symbol, separated by periods. "I.iv.§25," for example, denotes Chapter IV of Division I, Paragraph 25.

2. I discuss this Kantian framework and show where it can be found in the primary and secondary literature in Braver 2007, 176–181, 187, 221–225, 273–275, 284, 502–504, 508, 532n9. Heidegger calls the book transcendental a number of times (BT 63/39, 251/208, 401/350, 424/372, IM 19–20, TB 29, PM 123n. b, 371n. 66, BP 17, 323, CP 197/§132, 214/§184–185).

3. Kant 1965, A158/B197; see also Kant 1950, 44, Ak. 296; 53, Ak. 306; 55–66, Ak. 319; Braver 2014, 18.

4. As far as I can tell, Kant vacillates on this; see Braver 2007, 49–57, 498–501; 2012, 196.

5. See BT 140/106, 193/152. Much hangs on this issue, in particular the question of whether any intelligence must be like ours or if we could build a very different AI, or recognize and communicate with a deeply alien mind. Discussions of AI in the work of figures such as Dreyfus, Haugeland, Clark, and others have been perhaps the main way Heidegger's ideas have penetrated beyond continental philosophy. See Braver 2011 for details.

6. From 1929: "Our understanding of being ... as an unveiling projecting of being— is the primordial activity of human existence" (PM 124).

7. "All our efforts in the existential analytic serve the one aim of finding a possibility of answering the question of the *meaning of Being* in general. To work out this *question,* we need to delimit that very phenomenon in which something like Being becomes accessible—the phenomenon of the *understanding of Being.* But this phenomenon is one that belongs to Dasein's state of Being. Only after this entity has been Interpreted in a way which is sufficiently primordial, can we have a conception of the understanding of Being, which is included in its very state of Being; only on this basis can we formulate the question of the Being which is understood in this understanding" (BT 424/372; see also BT 274/231). We study our being (existence) in order to understand our understanding, so that we can understand what can be understood—the meaning of being.

8. BT 31/11, 34/13, 62/37, 117/85, 120–121/87, 184/145, 237/193, 269/226; Braver 2014, 12.

9. "All Dasein's behavior is to be Interpreted in terms of its Being—that is, in terms of temporality" (BT 456–457/404–405).

10. "The function of time is to make possible the understanding of being" (BP 303).

11. "We project being ... upon Temporality. ... Temporal projection makes possible an objectification of being. ... All the propositions of ontology are Temporal propositions. ... *Time is the primary horizon of transcendental science,* of *ontology,* or, in short, it is the *transcendental horizon*" (BP 323).

12. "Let us once more take note of the whole context of the problem and the direction of our inquiry. What we are seeking is the *condition of the possibility of that understanding-of-being which understands beings of the type of the handy and the at-hand.* ... This commerce with the beings we most immediately encounter is, as existent comportment of the Dasein toward beings, founded in the basic constitution of existence, n being-in-the-world. ... Since Dasein is being-in-the-world and the basic constitution of the Dasein lies in temporality, *commerce with intraworldly beings is grounded in a specific temporality of being-in-the-world*" (BP 291). The lecture course of 1927, *The Basic Problems of Phenomenology,* which he calls "a new elaboration of

division 3 of part 1 of *Being and Time*" (BP 1), offers an account of the temporality of equipment (BP 293, 303, 309).

13. TB 80; Safranski 1999, 143, 171; Kisiel 1993, 477–489.

14. Heidegger said that he decided not to publish Division III when discussions with Jaspers made him despair over the intelligibility of portions of the text that he identified as Division III (Kisiel 1993, 486; M 366–367), but which Bill Blattner argues are actually II.iii and II.iv (Blattner 1999, 2, n. 2). I am arguing that these two portions of the book were not fully distinct.

15. He calls it "a new elaboration of division 3 of part 1 of *Being and Time*' (BP 1, n. 1; see also PM 105, n. b). The other work is *Introduction to Metaphysics*, mentioned in the preface to the 7th edition (BT 17).

16. BT 487/436, BP 73 (italics added to BP); see also BP 74–75, 111, 116–117, 155, 166, KPM 198, 202. "The necessity of such a reversion to the Dasein's comportments is generally an indication that the Dasein itself has a distinctive function or making possible an adequately founded ontological inquiry in general. This implies that the investigation of the Dasein's specific mode of being and ontological con titution is unavoidable. Furthermore, we stressed repeatedly that all ontology, even the most primitive, necessarily looks back to the Dasein. Wherever philosophy awakens, this entity already stands in the sphere of vision" (BP 122).

17. BP 73, 104, 110–111, 122, 154–155, 223, 312; see also BT 34/14, PM 125, MFL 15–16.

18. BP 111; see also BP 117, IM 27, 56, 193, WT 39–40, OBT 178. See his criticism of Sartre's famous definition of existentialism in "Letter of Humanism" fo a particularly clear example of this objection (BW 232).

19. BP 74–75; see also BP 110, 122, 154, 223, 312. See also from 1929: "Kant, in and through his *transcendental* way of questioning, was able to accomplish the first decisive step since Plato and Aristotle toward *explicitly* laying the ground for ontology" (PM 368, n. 17; see also CP 200/§134, 249/§193, 337/§259).

20. Hegel says of Descartes's turn to subjectivity in lieu of reliance on external authority: "Here, we may say, we are at home, and like the mariner after a long voyage in a tempestuous sea, we may now hail the sight of land" (Hegel 1995, 217; see also 549). Heidegger cites this passage at OBT 97, and refers to it and Husserl's making consciousness foundational at BW 438.

21. For Hegel's objection, see Hegel 1975, 142–143, §235; 68–69, §42; 76, §121R; Hegel 1995, 436–439, 456; Braver 2007, 93–95.

22. BT 352/304; see also BT 384/335, 456–457/404–405, BP 111, 116–11⁻, 294, 312.

23. Note that in BP Heidegger bases readiness-to-hand on "praesens" (BP 305, 308–309, 323), which is a form of the present, but its goal-orientation makes it essential

futural to me, whereas it is presence-at-hand that actually has an affinity with the present.

24. Hume 1975, 183–184/145.

25. BT 33/13, 227/183, 272/230, 362/314, 382/333, 418/366, 423/371–372, 487/436, BP 280.

26. See BT 227/183, 285/241.

27. "We cannot judge in regard to the intuitions of other thinking beings, whether they are bound by the same conditions as those which limit our intuition and which for us are universally valid" (Kant 1965, A27/B43).

28. He comes close to stating it at times, such as here: "In this everydayness there are certain structures which we shall exhibit—not just any accidental structures, but essential ones which, in every kind of Being that factical Dasein may possess, persist as determinative for the character of its Being" (BT 38/17). Note that while he later uses the word "essence" in an innovative sense, here it appears to retain the traditional meaning of that which is common to all beings of a certain sort by making them that sort of being. This is, after all, what the existential analytic tries to capture. He also calls being-in-the-world "necessary *a priori*" (BT 79/53). A tantalizing but undeveloped and rare exception to this ahistorical universality appears at BP 22.

29. TB 32; see also CP 357/§263.

30. TB 52, BW 433, IM 19–20, 30, BQ 147.

31. BP 15, 19, 23, CP 36/§16, 345/§259, 355/§262, M 367–368, TB 9, IM 45, 97, KPM xix.

32. BQ 139; see also TB 35, 45, Z 207, QT 128, 151, 153, DT 77–78, PM 285, 334, P 138, N II: 221, IM 149, CP 386/§271. "This determining of philosophy on the basis of the human being never intends 'the' human being as such but the historical human being" (CP 347–348/§259).

33. Heidegger employs this distinction in another context at BP 65; see also WCT 110, where, quoting Aristotle, he complicates matters by arguing that what is least conspicuous is so precisely because it is most obvious.

34. P 135; see also BQ 127–128, 159, 178.

35. Kant 1965, B145–146; 1950, 65, Ak. 318; 1993, 48/46–47. At other times, he seems to insist on the necessity of at least the concepts of the understanding; see note 3 above.

36. Heidegger opens the final chapter of *Being and Time* as we have it by saying that his "previous characterization of temporality is incomplete" and defective because it hadn't shown how the form of temporality under discussion, world-time, "belongs to temporality itself. We must come to understand how this is possible and why it is

necessary" (BT 457/405; see also KPM 198, 207)—a nice description of his project in general.

37. I think there may be a better way—though it is not Heidegger's way—if we start from finitude rather than temporality. The fact that we aren't everything at once is what accounts for time—time is the discrepancy between what we are and what we are not, what we have and what we lack, spread out along three dimensions. This also grounds care as the drive to be accomplished (authenticity is the recognition that this cannot be a constitutive goal). This then presents the world as the array of tools, and history as the repertoire of roles, that we take up to settle the issue of our being, to gather up our existential dispersion into the world, among others, into the past and future. We still start with a brute fact but here it is finitude, a much more basic trait to me than temporality, and the topic he focuses on in the late 1920s (see, e.g., KPM 160–161, 192, 197). Note also the interesting connections with Sartre's early philosophy, perhaps a strike against this reading for some. An adequate discussion of this would require an essay of its own.

38. For his many rejections of anthropological readings (which is how Husserl read the book), see, e.g., BT §10, KPM 199, PM 371, n. 66, E 94/§154, C 55/§31, 233/§172, 237/§176, 386/§271, IM 149.

39. For more on the connection between Hume and Heidegger, see Braver 2012, 211–221; for Heidegger and Wittgenstein, see Braver 2012, passim, esp. chap. 5 and the conclusion.

40. Of course, there are contrary notes to this theme in the book, especially gathered around the themes of facticity and thrownness that bring Dasein "before the 'that-it-is' of its 'there,' which, as such, stares it in the face with the inexorability of an enigma" (BT 175/136; see also 271/228, 321/276, 390/340). Ultimately, however, I find that projection ends up overcoming and defanging thrownness, making it overly exorable; see, e.g., BT 436/384–385, PM 128.

41. WCT 100; see also PM 277, 318.

42. Note that Heidegger rejects the terminology of activity versus passivity (see BQ 151, DT 61, BW 217, 330). As long as we realize that he is offering an innovative conception of action or agency, I think it is safe to use these terms, especially to orient ourselves to his highly original ideas. For more, see Braver 2007, 308–325.

43. See Wittgenstein 2009, §§201, 211, 217, 219.

44. "We can say that Fichte and Hegel are looking for a ground where for Kant there could only be an abyss. ... Speculation becomes autonomous. This unveils a power of speculation that was impossible for Kant" (FS 18). "In attempting to lay the ground for Metaphysics, Kant was pressed in a way that makes the proper foundation into an abyss" (KPM 202; see also KPM 15, 151–152, 160–162, 166, 207, STF 41, LQT 224, 234, 243,256, 312, 322, 325–327, BT 271/228, 330/284, NIII 179, PR 65,

HPS 105; AM 27; Kant 1950, 65, §36; 1965, B145–146). Kant then shrank from this abyss in the second edition of the first *Critique* and in the second *Critique*, according to Heidegger. He raises the same objection to Nietzsche's three forms of history (BT 448/396).

45. "For Hegel, there rules in history necessity. … For Heidegger, on the other hand, one cannot speak of a 'why.' Only the 'that'—that the history of Being is in such a way—can be said" (TB 52; see also BW 433, IM 30, FS 9, CP 171/§125, M 17, 206, PR 91, 108, WIP 63, QT 39).

46. MFL 209. He sometimes talks about temporality in terms reminiscent of how he will discuss the mysteriousness of being later on: "*Time is earlier than any possible earlier* of whatever sort, because it is the basic condition for an earlier as such" (BP 325). Compare that with: "Man in his very nature belongs to that-which-regions. … Not occasionally, but—how shall we say it—prior to everything. … The prior, of which we really can not think … because the nature of thinking begins there" (DT 82–83; see also WCT 98).

47. Whereas at BP 308 Heidegger assures us that the series of nesting layers built up through the hermeneutic spiral "has its end at the horizon of the ecstatic unity of temporality," he later rejects the very idea that this inquiry could have a final answer "Time, which is addressed as the meaning of Being in *Being and Time*, is itself not an answer, not a last prop for questioning, but rather itself the naming of a question" (TB 28); or: "1. The determination of the essence of the human being is *never* an answer, but is essentially a question. 2. The asking of this question and its decision are historical" (IM 149). This later historical nonfinality is foreshadowed in his 1925–26 lectures: "According to the state of our present philosophical possibilities, being can be singularly understood in terms of time. I do not want to be so entirely dogmatic as to say that being can be [understood] *only* in terms of time. It may well be that tomorrow someone will discover a new possibility" (LQT 222; see also LQT 232, MFL 210, BP 22).

48. EHP 43, EGT 64, BW 135–136, 172, 415, PT 47, 55–56, BQ 147, OTB 9, 52, NIII 181. This argument, which I call the Framework Argument and discuss in Braver 2012, also finds a precedent in Kant's refusal to use our concepts to explain themselves (Kant 1950, 65).

49. PM 279; see also BW 217, 384, IM 166–167, PLT 171. "The unconcealment itself, within which ordering unfolds, is never a human handiwork. … The unconcealment of the unconcealed has already propriated whenever it calls man forth into the modes of revealing allotted to him. When man, in his way, from within unconcealment reveals that which presences, he merely responds to the call of unconcealment" (BW 324).

50. NIV 193; see also NIII 90, PR 68, 94, BQ 53, PM 232, BaT 204.

51. Zo 266; see also TB 78; Young 2002, 23, 83.

52. BT 193/152, 255/212, 272/230.

53. I know he often says that "the same" means that they belong together rather than that they are identical, but he describes them almost the same way over and over again.

54. BT 408/357, PM 123, n. a, 132, 249, 283, 286, HR 303, TB 28, CP 11/§, 55/§31, 355/§262, M 367, EGT 64, E 94/§154, 108/§174, 111–112/§176, 131/§184, 240/§304, 244/§312, HR 303.

55. BW 415; see also DT 67.

56. "It is precisely when we see the 'world' unsteadily and fitfully in accordance with our moods, that the ready-to-hand shows itself in its specific worldhood, which is never the same from day to day" (BT 177/138).

57. "There is Being only in this or that particular historical character: φύσς, Λόγος, Έν, Ἰδέα, Ενέργεια, Substantiality, Objectivity, Subjectivity, the Will, the Will to Power, the Will to Will. … The manner in which it, Being, gives itself, is itself determined by the way in which it clears itself. This way, however, is a historic always epochal character" (ID 66–67).

58. See, e.g., BT 101/71; Braver 2007, 181–186.

59. *"The problem of the transcendental deduction … is basically what we call a fundamental ontological interpretation of Dasein"* (PIK 252; see also PIK 260–261). Heidegger suggests at BT 408/357 that Division III would have developed §7's preliminary description of phenomenology and his analysis of truth (see also HR 301).

60. FS 40–41; see also FS 47, PM 361, IM 19–20, 148–149, 181, 186–187, 219

61. "Our investigation … asks about Being itself insofar as Being enters into the intelligibility of Dasein" (BT 193/152, see also 140/106).

62. BT 228/183, 255/212, 269/226–227.

63. M 133, ID 31–33, PM 308–310, BW 228–229, 235, MHC 40, WCT 79, 106, 144, PR 70, 94, PM 283, TB 12, 38, NIII 49, NIV 216, QT 130–131, DT 84, Zo 176–180, EGT 96. See Braver 2007, 273–279 for a fuller discussion of what I call there Mutual Interdependence.

64. BT 371/324. "It is to the human Dasein that there belongs the understanding of being which first of all makes possible every comportment toward beings" (BP 16; see also BP 10–11, 52, 72, 75, 114–115, 171, 208, 217, 275, BT 27–28/8, 31/1, 190–191/150, 363/315, 414/362, HCT 299, MFL 16). For more on this, see my "Heidegger, Foucault, and Clocks: An Impure Genealogy of Time," unpublished.

65. "Whether we consider and describe the window as a utilitarian thing, an instrument, or as a pure natural thing, we already understand in a certain way what it means to say 'instrument' and 'thing.' In our natural commerce with the instrument

... we understand something like *instrumentality,* and in confrontation with material things we understand something like *thingliness"* (BP 68; see also BP 293, 299, BT 117/85, 403–404/352–353, 415/364).

66. "Because Dasein's Being is Being-with, its understanding of Being already implies the understanding of Others. This understanding, like any understanding, is not an acquaintance derived from knowledge about them, but a primordially existential kind of Being, which, more than anything else, makes such knowledge and acquaintance possible" (BT 161/123; see also 157/121, HCT 239). Examples can be multiplied: historical entities (BT 446/394), moods (BT 176–177/137, 391/341), broken tools (BT 176/137, 253/210, 406–407/354–355).

67. PM 122–123. In the margins, he later reflects that this idea has been "contorted into phenomenological-existential and transcendental 'research'" (PM 123, n. b).

68. BW 217; see also BW 237, 240, 256, 416, P 76–77, HH 91. "We today, and many generations before us, have long forgotten the realm of the unconcealment of beings, although we continually take it for granted. We actually think that a being becomes accessible when an 'I' as subject represents an object. As if the open region within whose openness something is made accessible *as* object *for* a subject, and accessibility itself, which can be penetrated and experienced, did not already have to reign here as well!" (NIV 93; see also NIII 240, NIV 89, 108, 139, 218, PLT 111, 127, PR 80, WT 97). "The opening up of the essential occurrence of beyng manifests that Da-sein does not accomplish anything" (CP 188/§122).

69. WCT 9–10, 18, 149.

References

Blattner, William D. 1999. *Heidegger's Temporal Idealism.* Cambridge: Cambridge University Press.

Braver, Lee. 2007. *A Thing of This World: A History of Continental Anti-Realism.* Evanston, IL: Northwestern University Press.

Braver, Lee. 2011. Analyzing Heidegger: A history of analytic reactions to Heidegger. In *Interpreting Heidegger,* ed. Daniel Dahlstrom. Cambridge: Cambridge University Press.

Braver, Lee. 2012. *Groundless Grounds: A Study of Wittgenstein and Heidegger.* Cambridge, MA: MIT Press.

Braver, Lee. 2014. *Heidegger: Thinking of Being.* Cambridge: Polity Press.

Braver, Lee. Unpublished. Heidegger, Foucault, and clocks: An impure genealogy of time.

Hegel, G. W. F. 1995. *Lectures on the History of Philosophy vol. 3: Medieval and Modern Philosophy*. Trans. E. S. Haldane and Frances H. Simson. Lincoln: University of Nebraska Press.

Hegel, G. W. F. 1977. *Phenomenology of Spirit*. Trans. A. V. Miller. Oxford: Oxford University Press.

Hegel, G. W. F. 1975. *Hegel's Logic*. Trans. William Wallace. Oxford: Clarendon.

Hume, David. 1975. *Enquiries*. 3rd ed. Ed. P. H. Nidditch. Oxford: Clarendon.

Kant, Immanuel. 1950. *Prolegomena to Any Future Metaphysics*. Trans. Lewis White Beck. New York: Library of Liberal Arts.

Kant, Immanuel. 1965. *Critique of Pure Reason*. Trans. Norman Kemp Smith London: St. Martin's Press.

Kant, Immanuel. 1993. *Critique of Practical Reason*. 3rd ed. Trans. Lewis White Beck. New York: Library of Liberal Arts.

Kisiel, Theodore. 1993. *The Genesis of Heidegger's Being and Time*. Berkeley: University of California Press.

Nietzsche, Friedrich. 1974. *The Gay Science*. Trans. Walter Kaufmann. New York: Vintage Books.

Safranski, Rüdiger. 1999. *Martin Heidegger: Between Good and Evil*. Trans. Ewald Osers. Cambridge, MA: Harvard University Press.

Wittgenstein, Ludwig. 2009. *Philosophical Investigations*, 4th ed., rev. trans. Trans. G. E. M. Anscombe, P. M. S. Hacker, and Joachim Schulte. Oxford: Blackwell.

Young, Julian. 2002. *Heidegger's Later Philosophy*. Cambridge: Cambridge University Press.

4 The End of Fundamental Ontology

Daniel Dahlstrom

If one radicalizes the Kantian problem of ontological knowledge, in the sense that one does not limit it only to the ontological founding of the positive sciences and, further, does not construe it as a problem of judgment but instead as the radical and fundamental question of the possibility of understanding being at all, then the result is the fundamental set of philosophical problems of *Being and Time*.[1]

The story of the immediate genesis of the published version of *Being and Time* is by now familiar. Under pressure from the Prussian Ministry to produce a substantial publication as a condition of his appointment to a chair in Marburg's philosophy department, Heidegger begins the process of getting *Being and Time* into print. In the work, Heidegger sets for himself ontology's "fundamental task," namely, the clarification of the sense of being in general by way of an analysis of the entity with a disposition toward and understanding of being. Thus, the aim of *Being and Time* is a fundamental ontology rooted in the analysis of what it means for us to be here, that is, the existential analysis of being-here (*Da-sein*). After a year of submitting parts of the manuscript and correcting galleys, *Being and Time* appears as part of Husserl's *Yearbook for Philosophy and Phenomenological Research* in late April of 1927.[2]

The published version, however, delivers only part of the planned work. In the introduction, Heidegger announces that the complete work is to have two parts, each of which is to comprise three divisions. The title of the first part, "The Interpretation of Being-Here on the Basis of Timeliness [*Zeitlichkeit*] and the Explication of Time as the Transcendental Horizon of the Question of Being," signals its theme (SZ 39/BT 63).[3] But the published work contains, following the introduction, only the first two divisions, with an "interpretation of being-here," that is,

Part One, Division I: "The Preparatory Fundamental Analysis of Being-Here" and

Part One, Division II: "Being-Here and Timeliness"

While parts of Part One, Division II can be read as initiating the "explication of time" flagged in the title of the first part, Heidegger no doubt intended to leave the explication largely to the Third Division, i.e., Part One, Division III: "Time and Being" (a heading and theme to which Heidegger returns thirty-five years later in the 1962 essay with that same title). Presumably, this Third Division was to furnish the end of fundamental ontology, completing its task as "the basic grounding of ontology in general."[4]

In later years Heidegger relates how, by early January of 1927, thanks to friendly disputes with Jaspers over the galleys of *Being and Time*, he came to realize that "the elaboration that he had managed up to this point of this most important section [Part One, Division III] would necessarily be unintelligible" (GA49 39–40). At the time he thought that, in the course of the year (1927), it would be possible to say everything more clearly, though that, he adds, was a "delusion." Part of his original confidence in his ability to revise Division III effectively may have been due to the fact that he conceived his next lecture course, *Basic Problems of Phenomenology*, as "a new elaboration" of Division III.[5] Yet, even though he continues, as late as 1929, to allude to its eventual publication, he never delivers on Division III. By 1931 he abandons the project of finishing it.[6]

Hence, readers of *Being and Time* are left to ponder what precisely he intended for the concluding and, by his own account, "most important" division of the first part, particularly in the wake of the powerful existential analyses of the first two divisions. What did he have in mind as the contents of Division III? It seems likely that we shall never know for sure, given the lack of archival material. That is apparently how Heidegger wanted it, as he acknowledges that he had destroyed the manuscript containing Division III before embarking on a new version in the lectures of the summer semester of 1927.[7] Heidegger notes how the size of the *Yearbook* in 1927 had "fortunately" grown too large to include that section, of whose "inadequacy" he was all too aware. "In retrospect," Heidegger questions his decision to refrain from publishing Division III, since, with all its warts, it might have nonetheless hampered the widespread misconstrual of *Being and Time* as a mere "ontology of human beings" and the rampant misinterpretation of "fundamental ontology." He adds:

Precisely because the inquiry into the *sense of being* ... is different from that of all previous metaphysics, this questioning ... would still have been able to show what it accomplishes, for what was insufficient about the part held back [i.e., Division III] was not an insecurity about the direction of the question and its realm, but only that of the correct elaboration. (GA66 414/M 367)

Following this rueful admission, Heidegger finds solace in the thought that the difficulties of getting a handle on the question are not the sort that are affected by a single treatment, presumably like that of Division III. Instead they require renewed questioning from the ground up, including, preeminently, the question of the entire stance toward the history of philosophy (and Christendom)—that is, the sort of transition in questioning, Heidegger adds, that his thinking undertakes in the 1930s (GA66 414–415/M 367–368).

Nonetheless, the passage cited in the preceding paragraph is particularly intriguing since, made in 1938, it suggests that, despite shifts in his thinking, he regards the destroyed version of Division III, like the published part, as anything but a failure. Or rather, if it falls short, as *Being and Time* does in his eyes, it has as much to do with his readers as it does with his writing. Read in the right way, even the published version of *Being and Time* manages to articulate something that he is concerned to say, despite the metaphysical language that admittedly impairs its message (GA9 327–328/P 249–250).

The following essay ventures a reconstruction of the main theme of Division III as the end of fundamental ontology.[8] The "end" here signifies both the aim and the termination of the project of fundamental ontology. In other words, I reconstruct this section with a view to determining what Heidegger initially intended as the culmination of that project, and quickly came to see as its demise, a reason for terminating it. The two published divisions of *Being and Time* demonstrate the timeliness of being-here that underlies its pre-ontological understanding, that is to say, the temporal character of its worldly understanding of being. Completing the project consists in making the transition from the demonstration of this timeliness inherent in being-here to the demonstration of the temporality of being. Heidegger gives up the effort, no doubt because he sees how it founders on several levels, not least the pretension of tying the senses of being to temporality in general and to a temporality derived from the timely character of being-here in particular.[9] In a concluding section I suggest briefly how, nonetheless, the contents of Division III anticipate dimensions of his later thinking.

The Tasks of Fundamental Ontology, Its Different Horizons, and Timeliness

Typically drafted when a work is completed or near completion, introductions to books frequently serve the purpose of laying out and defending the entire undertaking, its rationale or aim, as well as the steps to accomplishing it. The introduction to *Being and Time* is no exception and, as regards the contents of Division II, it provides important information, in addition to the already cited announcement of the three divisions of the first part. The task of the ontological analytic of Dasein (as Heidegger puts it in that introduction) is to free up or lay open (*freilegen*) the horizon for an interpretation of the sense of being as such. The implication is that the horizon has been obscured and then forgotten (hence, too, the other task of dismantling the history of ontology). A further implication is that, while distinct from one another, the sense is drawn from the horizon, depending upon it (just as we can make out a figure and determine the sense of it, only against a background).[10] The fundamental ontology pursued in *Being and Time* is supposed to show that time forms the horizon for the ways we implicitly and explicitly understand being. "This [i.e., time] has to be brought to light and genuinely conceived as the horizon for every understanding of being and every interpretation of being. In order for this to be patently discernible, what is needed is an *original explication of time as the horizon of the understanding of being on the basis of timeliness as the being of the Dasein that understands being*" (SZ 17/BT 39).

The term "timeliness" is a key word of art for Heidegger, signifying (a) the ontological sense of being-here (a certain timeliness constitutes who we are, our ways of being); (b) the basis for other senses of time, including the ordinary or vulgar understanding of time as a sequence of distinct now's; and (c) the platform for the understanding of being in general—the theme of the aborted Division III. He accordingly stresses the need to set this timeliness off from the ordinary or vulgar understanding of time, the sort of understanding that has figured in the traditional concept of time maintained from Aristotle to Bergson. Heidegger already pursues this project in the sixth chapter of Part One, Division II, and continues it in the summer semester of 1927.[11] The aim is not to dismiss the ordinary concept of time but to derive it from timeliness. While that ordinary concept has served as a criterion for demarcating regions of being, what needs to be shown, Heidegger notes, is "that and how the central problem of all ontology are rooted in the rightly understood and rightly explicated phenomenon of time."[12]

Given the baggage of the term *zeitlich* ("time-related," "passing"), Heidegger introduces the Latin term *temporale* to characterize how time determines the basic sense of being. "The fundamental ontological task of the interpretation of being as such thus encompasses in itself the elaboration of the *temporality of being*. In the exposition of the problematic of temporality, the concrete answer to the question of the sense of being is first given."[13] This characterization corresponds to the "explication of time as the transcendental horizon of the question of being" (SZ 39/BT 63) in terms of which Heidegger introduces the unpublished Division III—as noted above. Thus, the task of fundamental ontology by no means ends with the published version of *Being and Time*. Though fundamental ontology must find its bearings in existential analysis, that is to say, in demonstrating how timeliness provides the sense of being-here (i.e., the sense of its being), it only succeeds by showing how temporality forms the horizon for determining the sense(s) of being as such.

In the summer semester of 1927, Heidegger explicitly turns to this task.

To what extent is time as timeliness the horizon for the explicit understanding of being as such, insofar as it is supposed to be the theme of the science of ontology, i.e., scientific philosophy? To the extent that timeliness functions as the condition of the possibility of the pre-ontological as well as ontological understanding of being, we call it *temporality*. (GA24 388/BP 274)

Thus, on this account, far from being something different from timeliness, temporality is timeliness insofar as it provides the horizon for understanding not being-here (*Da-sein*) but being (*Sein*).

In the just cited text, as in Heidegger's allusions to the contents of Division III in the introduction to *Being and Time*, he relies on the metaphor of a horizon. Though the term ordinarily designates a place, one with defining yet orienting limits (e.g., the meeting place of earth and sky, a corresponding visual perimeter), he also employs it, like Husserl, to characterize time. Just as a horizon defines something's place, making its place possible at all, so time is the horizon for the understanding of being, the condition for the possibility of understanding it. Heidegger also employs the metaphor to designate a limiting, yet orienting part of the timeliness of being-here, from which ordinary meanings of "time" are derived. In this latter usage, he combines it with another metaphor, one that normally designates a position or positioning, namely, *ecstasis*, meaning "standing out" within or in the direction of a horizon. (More on this below.) Though, as we shall see below, these different uses of "horizon" are related, they are formally distinct. The way in which time forms the horizon for the question of being is not the[13] same as the way in which a horizon enters, jointly with an *ecstasis*, into the constitution of time. Nevertheless, the project of fundamental ontology relies on the significance of both metaphorical uses of "horizon."[14]

Since timeliness is the key to the explication of temporality as the horizon for the understanding of being, I begin with a brief review of Heidegger's account of timeliness. His account follows the preparatory analysis of being-here given in Division I, as he turns in Division II to the question of the underlying sense of Dasein's thrownness and projection, its facticity and existence. Being-here, we are always already ahead of ourselves; our very being, our being-in-the-world, consists in projecting possibilities from the world of possibilities into which we have been thrown. These possibilities range from the prethematic, such as breathing and fearing, to the thematic, planning an event or being resolute. These possibilities do not come in isolation, but as a package, a package that has everything to do with (a) the state of the world we've been thrown into; (b) the immediate situation we find ourselves in, that is, the situation we are dealing with; and (c) our aims, hopes, and dreams. This tripartite structure, informing the ways we are—the ways we relate to our possibilities—betrays the fundamental timeliness of being-here, its past, present, and future.

This structure is evident in the most mundane activities. Suppose that you are going out the door of a building, grabbing the knob, turning it, pulling it with some force, and swinging it behind you as you stride out the door. As you do these things, you are attending to this complex of implements (even if you do not pay close attention to any one of them) in a way that makes certain possibilities present. So, too, as you reach out to the door knob and pull the door toward you, you do so by holding onto (retaining) certain possibilities—for example, that the door is hinged, that you are able to move around it as it pivots, and so on. Moreover, you do so with the expectation that the door can open and you are able to pass through it. That process of attending to (*gegenwärtigen*) the complex in using it is the original sense of the present; holding onto (*behalten*) and expecting (*gewärtigen*) possibilities of the complex are original senses of the past and future. Timeliness is the unity of these three sorts of processes that together make up being-here, construed in a purely formal, existential manner, setting aside the concrete details.[15] At the same time (no pun intended), they provide the basis for ordinary senses of time. For example, if you happen to say to yourself that you are *now* opening the door, this use of "now" presupposes that you are attending to the complex of implements, rendering them and their possibilities present as such. Timing such an event, locating it in a public time, or comparing its movement or a part of its movement with some other movement, such as the hands of a dial, to designate that you are now opening the door—all of these time-determinations suppose the original *present* of attending to something (as they do the original past of retaining something and the original future of expecting something).[16]

As a means of characterizing what is generic to each of these original, Dasein-constituting modes of time, Heidegger exploits the metaphor of an *ecstasis.* The expression literally signifies standing out or standing forth, typically implicating a place, a direction, and thus a potential relation. The borrowed meaning applies not to a specific location (here or there), but to the indexical process of being here (*da*, taken metaphorically) by way of attending to entities' possibilities while retaining or holding onto and expecting the same or other possibilities. What is common to each of these original modes of time is a way of being outside itself (again, "ec-centric," to borrow Plessner's term) in relation to certain possibilities. In the threefold process of relating to possibilities coming *toward* it, of coming *back to* the same or other possibilities, and of allowing the encounter *of* entities' possibilities (i.e., of being amid them), being-here is inherently "outside itself" (SZ 329/BT 377).

Ecstases, however, like projections, are not free-standing; they do not merely stand out from something, they also stand both within a specific space and in a certain direction. Thus, with every *ecstasis*, there is a distinct horizon (in the second sense discussed above). "The horizon is the *open expanse* into which the displacement [*Entrückung* inherent to the *ecstasis*] is, as such, outside itself. The displacement opens this horizon and holds it open" (GA24 378/BP 267; SZ 365/BT 377). Horizons in the ordinary sense are a constant, even if they are constantly changing. Even as they delimit and circumscribe our line of vision and action, they also open up vistas and possibilities for us. Yet we do not experience horizons without moving into some and away from others, that is, without projecting possibilities upon them. All these meanings of "horizon"—in conjunction with the corresponding meanings of "*ecstasis*"—have their metaphorical counterparts in Heidegger's use of the term to designate timeliness. The ordinary spatial significance of the term gives way, as it does for Husserl before him, to a temporal significance, indeed, to the determination of the most basic meaning of "time."[17]

The horizonality of timeliness is disclosed in and with the various *ecstases*, the various ways we stand out, projecting some possibilities out of a range of possibilities, onto their respective horizons. As noted earlier, this ecstatic-horizonal character, the most basic sense of time, constitutes the very sense of being-here (*Da-sein*).[18] This insight is key to Heidegger's attempt to radicalize the notion of subjectivity, construing it as the site of the disclosure (truth) of being. Subjectivity is being-here in the radical sense that, at its root, it exists by standing out in a horizon distinct from it, of projecting possibilities onto a horizon that cannot be collapsed into the projection. Conceived in this radical sense, subjectivity exists by and as being-in-the-world, projecting certain possibilities and discarding others in the world into which it has been thrown.

The Basic Argument of Division III

Understanding, as a basic determination of being-in-the-world, encompassing every sort of comportment toward entities (theoretical as well a practical and technical), entails an understanding of its distinctive being ("being in the sense of existence"). Thus it projects, it understands itself a being. The same holds for other entities. Codisclosed (projected, understood) with it, by virtue of being-in-the-world, are the existence of others and the manners of being of other innerworldly entities. To be sure, while all these different manners of being are understood, they are not explicitly conceived. Still, the base line for an analysis is given: "*In it* [being-in-the-world] *lies an understanding* that, *as a projection*, not only understands these beings in terms of their being but also, insofar as being itself is understood. *has in some way projected being as such*" (GA24 396/BP 280).

Just as we understand entities, including ourselves, *as* being (projecting them onto the horizon of being), so we understand being *as* something or other, that is, we project it onto some horizon.[19] This parallel leads to the question of the horizon for the understanding of being, that i , what we project being *as*, and whether this line reasoning leads to a regress.[20] If we understand beings in terms of a conception of their being and we understand being in terms of a conception of time, what prevents us from asking what conception makes possible our understanding of time? While the details need to be filled in, we know from the preceding analyses that for Heidegger the horizon—and the end of the analysis, at least in one direction—must be time. The following formulation of his basic argument (an implicit modus ponens) presents the rationale for Division III.

If being-here contains in itself an understanding of being but timeliness makes being-here possible in terms of the constitution of its being, then *timeliness* must also be the *condition of the possibility* of the *understanding of being* and, with it, *of the projection of being onto time*. (GA24 397/BP 280)

Heidegger makes a similar claim on the final page of *Being and Time*, arguing that since the constitution of being-here, in its totality, is grounded in
timeliness, the latter "must" itself enable "the ecstatic projection of being
in general" (SZ 437/BT 488). However, in the 1927 lectures, he importantly
adds that this condition is necessary but not sufficient. So, too, a (pre-ontological, unthematized, nonobjectified) understanding of being is necessary
for the (ontic) experience of entities and the positive sciences concerned
with them, just as it is for ontology proper which consists in making that
understanding explicit, but neither that experience nor ontology is entailed
by that understanding (GA24 398–399, 456/BP 281–282, 321). Though Heidegger later eschews any talk of conditions of possibility, the remark raises
intriguing questions not only about what else is necessary and what would
be sufficient for ontology, but also about the implications of such considerations for the pretension to a *fundamental* ontology.

The quoted conditional and the implicit modus ponens signaled by it
turn on the twin supposition of (a) the basic timeliness of being-here and
(b) the fact that an understanding-of-being is inherent in being-here. Given
these suppositions, the consequent clearly follows, that is, it is necessary
to understand being in terms of time. But note that this conclusion does
not formally entail that being is temporal. For that conclusion to follow, it
must be shown or at least assumed that being is identical to or subsumed
by the understanding of being. Heidegger undoubtedly struggles with this
assumption and its warrant.

On the one hand, the very fact that he projects Division III to demonstrate the temporality of the sense of being indicates that the demonstration
of the timeliness of being-here does not suffice for that purpose. Moreover,
the sense of being is not the same as the meaning of "being," something
that we mean or presume to mean when we use the word. Rather, the sense
is that upon which we project possibilities and, to the extent that "projecting" and "understanding" are metonyms, that sense is not of our doing.
Indeed, the ordinary sense of a horizon suggests something irreducible
to where we stand relative to it or to what we project upon it. Moreover,
one of the horizons within timeliness (and thus part of all its horizons)
corresponds to the thrownness of being-here—something that we do not
project. In this sense, horizons are presupposed and underdetermined by
projections onto them. Apparently playing on this sense, Heidegger explicitly eschews a "subjective idealism that first sets up a subject that then in
some way fashions for itself an object"; to the contrary, the very meaning
of being-in-the-world entails that it is with others and with innerworldly
things *originally*.[21]

On the other hand, the slippage between talk of being and talk of the understanding-of-being in his accounts[22] reveals fundamental ontology's basic affinities with Kant's transcendental philosophy—an affinity Heidegger repeatedly affirms. Like Kant, Heidegger eschews centering philosophy in something objectively transcendent and looks instead to conditions constitutive of the "subject."[23] For Heidegger, "the genuine ontological sense of transcendence" is not something beyond or other-worldly but the process of passing through and beyond oneself, something that can only be said of being-here, of being-in-the-world. Being ahead of ourselves, projecting possibilities, enables us to relate (comport ourselves) to different entities, to come back to them as such, "such that the foregoing understanding of being is grounded in our being-here" (GA24 426/BP 300).

Whether or not the tension depicted in the last two paragraphs is resolved (it is hard to see how it could be, particularly when phenomenology is the method of ontology[24]), the foregoing sketch of the line of investigation in the summer semester of 1927 iterates the steps of fundamental ontology given in the introduction to *Being and Time*, that is, the move from analyses of being-here and its timeliness (Division I and Division II) to the way that timeliness serves as the horizon for the understanding of being (Division III). Not surprisingly, many of the analyses in those lectures (e.g., the analysis of the timeliness of authentic and inauthentic understanding) are familiar to readers of *Being and Time*. However, what is new—and likely part of the new elaboration of Division III—is the explicit consideration of the temporality of modes of being other than being-here, namely, being handy (ready-to-hand) and on hand (present-at-hand). Taking the latter together, Heidegger speaks of attempting to clarify the understanding of being of the entities we immediately encounter, the entities that are also there when we are not dealing with them.[25]

Iterating the account given in *Being and Time*, Heidegger focuses on the encounter where we use a complex of implements. This encounter consists in *attending to* a complex of implements—or, to put it more abstractly, standing out (*ekstasis*) toward a set of possibilities (*horizon*)—such that the implements are handy (*zuhanden*) or not, perhaps even to the point of slipping or being "out of our hands" (*abhanden*). How we attend to the complex depends upon what possibilities of it we *retain or hold on to* and—above all—*expect* in the process. As noted earlier with the example of the door (and the complex of implements involved in using it), the process of attending to its possibilities is the original sense of the present, while holding onto and expecting possibilities of it are original senses of the past and future. But in the summer of 1927 he stresses that these original senses of the determinations of time also make up the foregoing, pre-ontological understanding that we have of the door's manner of being. In this way the sense of being handy or, equivalently, the understanding of the being of what is handy, is grounded in a specific timeliness of being-in-the-world, "the original ecstatic-horizonal unity of timeliness" (GA24 413, 429, 433/ BP 291, 302, 305). "Understanding the handiness of the handy has *already projected this being onto time*" (GA24 430/BP 302–303).

The Now, the Present, and the Presence in the "New Elaboration" of Division III

Heidegger's new elaboration of Division III in the 1927 lectures turns on distinguishing various time-determinations. If we take something handy to be now (*jetzt*), in the sense that it is "in" or "within" time (*innerzeitig*), occupying one of a series of present moments, we are already presupposing that it is. Hence, this ordinary time-determination is useless when it comes to determining the entity's manner of being. More precisely, time-determinations in the ordinary sense cannot explain the foregoing, pre-ontological understanding of the implement's manner of being, its being handy. The ordinary temporal determination of entities is ontic, since the entities involved, like time itself, are taken for granted and their manner of being not questioned.

Heidegger accordingly distinguishes ontic uses of "now" (designating what is within-time) from his transcendental use of "present" (*Gegenwart*) to signify the ecstatic character of being-here, "attending to" entities, "rendering them present" (*gegenwärtigen*), that is part of the original phenomenon of time. Demonstrating this transcendental use coincides with the aim of Division II, namely, demonstrating the timeliness that constitutes being-here, including its understanding of being in general and its foregoing understanding of the handiness (the manner of being) of what is handy. However, Heidegger further distinguishes this use of the "present" from the ontological use of "presence" to signify the horizon onto which the process of attending to entities projects them.

Heidegger takes the possibilities of being handy or not-handy as variations on a basic phenomenon that he characterizes formally as "presentness" and "absentness," and generally as *presence* (*Praesenz*), modifiable as *absence* (*Absenz*).[26] He reserves this Latin-based term, as he does *Temporalität*, for the temporal interpretation of being, in contrast to the Germanic terms that he uses to designate other time-determinations, for example, the timeliness (*Zeitlichkeit*) of being-here, the present (*Gegenwart*).

The following table illustrates the aforementioned three different determinations of time:

Time-Determinations	Corresponding Term	Concept of Time
Ontic: entities (*Seiendes*)	"now" (*jetzt*)	ordinary (*vulgär*)
Transcendental: being-here (*Da-sein*)	"present" (*Gegenwart*)	timeliness (*Zeitlichkeit*)
Ontological: being (*Sein*)	"presence" (*Praesenz*)	temporality (*Temporalität*)

The present is part of the timeliness of being-here; presence is a form of temporality that makes up the sense of being. While Heidegger elaborated the timeliness of being-here in Division II, he left it to Division III to demonstrate how temporality makes up the sense of being. Heidegger confines the end of his 1927 lectures—the so-called "new elaboration," it must be recalled, of Division III—to demonstrating how presence, as a mode of temporality, determines one sense of being, namely, what it means to "be handy" (*zuhanden sein*).[27] Note, however, that this determination—the ontological determination—piggybacks on the transcendental determination, that is, the determination of the ecstatic-horizonal character of timeliness that is the sense (horizon) of being-here.

As indicated above, Heidegger distinguishes *the present* of timeliness from *the presence* of temporality, even as he insists on their complementarity. To appreciate what he is driving at in this respect, let us return to our example of using a door. The present consists originally (i.e., as a condition for any use of "now") in my attending to the door and its possibilities, and in that sense making them present. The door's presence is precisely the horizon or set of possibilities (their possible presence or absence) onto which I project the door in using it. Its presence, in other words, comprises the possibilities in terms of which I understand it or, equivalently, know how to use it. Precisely this presence, the temporal determination of the door's manner of being, insofar as it is present for me in attending to it, constitutes its manner of being as something handy. The demonstration of this last sentence exemplifies the general project of Division III.

The transcendental and ontological determinations of time (exemplified by the present and the presence respectively) are in fact complementary precisely in the way that every instance of being "outside oneself" (*ecstasis*) or projecting has a horizon and vice versa. If we understand the original time-determinations as projections, then each has its horizon that is determined *in some sense* by the projection. Just as Heidegger's account of the original senses of time (those that determine our being-here) is tied to this trope, so, too, is his "new elaboration" of Division III as the final stage of fundamental ontology.

The attending to, whether authentic ... or inauthentic, *projects what it attends to and thus makes present*, the very thing that can possibly be encountered in and for a present, *onto something like presence*. The *ecstasis* of the present is, as such, the condition of the possibility of a specific [way of being] "beyond itself," of transcendence, the projection onto a presence. As the condition of the possibility of [being] "beyond itself," it has in itself a *schematic preconfiguration* of *where* this "beyond itself" is. What lies beyond the *ecstasis* as such, on the basis of its character of moving away, and is determined by it as beyond it, more precisely, what determines at all the *where-to of the "beyond itself"* as such, is the *presence as horizon*. (GA24 435/BP 306)

In this way Heidegger distinguishes the present and the presence as complementary, necessary components. Thus, he characterizes presence as the "basic determination of the horizonal schema of this *ecstasis*," filling out the complete time structure of the present. The schema indicates and pre-configures the horizon for the *ecstasis*, enabling it to be "beyond itself." He adds—albeit with no explanation—that something analogous holds for the two other *ecstases*, the future and the having-been (GA24 435/BP 306).

With this account of presence, Heidegger is now ready to take the first step toward answering the question that motivates *Being and Time* in general and the originally destroyed Division III ("Time and Being") in particular: what is the sense of being?

We understand being on the basis of the original, horizonal schema of the ecstasies of timeliness. (GA24 436/BP 307)

Though *ecstasis* and horizon remain indissoluble, the horizonal schemata, taken by themselves as conditions of the possibility of the understanding of being, make up the content of the general concept of temporality.

Heidegger takes pains, as indicated above, to stress the complementarity of *ecstasis* and horizon as well as, by extension, that of timeliness and temporality. Yet his account of their relation leaves much unexplained. Consider his remark that the projection (*Ekstase*) "determines" the horizon and that the horizon "completes" the projection (GA24 435/BP 306). The remark leaves room for different and, indeed, inconsistent interpretations and his further deliberations do not resolve or reconcile them. Does the projection completely determine the horizon or only partially—as talk of its "schematic preconfiguration" might suggest? Is the projection the determining factor or one determining factor? In what sense does the horizon complete the projection? Does it add something not preconfigured by the projection?

Earlier I used the term "piggyback" to characterize the way the determination of the temporal sense of being (Division III) rests on the determination of the timeliness of being-here (Division II). This characterization may
well be tendentious, given a robust account of the complementarity of the
two determinations, that is, the horizon and the projection. Nevertheless,
there is no gainsaying the fact that Heidegger ties the determination of the
horizon to the projection, grounding temporality (the determination of the
sense or understanding of being) in the timeliness of being-here. Timeliness
is the fundamental condition of the possibility of all understanding that is
grounded in the transcending inherent to being-here. However hidden it
may be, "above all in regard to its temporality," this timeliness dominates
being-here and its everyday dealings with things, as Heidegger puts it, even
more basically than daylight does (GA24 437/BP 307). As the possessive in
the just cited phrase suggests, temporality belongs to timeliness. Though
his talk of horizons (much like his talk of a clearing) suggests a center of
gravity other than being-here, Heidegger's plan for Division III amounts
to deriving the sense of being (temporality) from the sense of being-here
(timeliness). This plan may give transcendental philosophy its most radical
formulation (entailing an ontology!), and it may fashion the most radical
account of subjectivity, but it continues to center the sense of being in our
way of being-here.[28]

Heidegger himself recognizes the limitations of this account. He reveals
one such limitation while glossing the experience of missing something.
To miss something is anything but a failure to attend to it; it cannot be
equated with something that we do not attend to. If the door is missing a
knob, we may not be able to use it. The missing knob captures our attention, but it does so precisely as crucial to the use of the door complex. This
modification of the presence of that complex, its negation, is not nothing,
but a relevant absence that is tied to the way that attending to the complex
is combined with holding onto certain possibilities and expecting others.

Yet whence this negation, this modification of the presence? The foregoing account of the missing implement raises "a fundamental but difficult
problem regarding the extent to which precisely an inherent negative feature is constituted in the structure of this being, i.e., the handiness" (GA24
442/BP 311). Heidegger questions the extent to which "a negative, a not"
resides in temporality and, at the same time, in timeliness. The question,
he notes, might even be: "To what extent is time itself the condition of the
possibility of nullity altogether?" (GA24 443/BP 311). He is convinced that,
on closer consideration, it will be apparent that this nullity—and, with
it, the interplay of presence and absence—can only be interpreted on the

basis of time.[29] He remarks, too, that Hegel was on the right track when he claimed that being and nothing belong together, inviting "the more radical question" of what makes this most original union possible. Yet in the 1927 lecture he ends this discussion peremptorily with the observation: "We are not sufficiently prepared to penetrate into these dark depths" (GA24 443/ BP 312). Perhaps this "we" refers to the seminar setting and not the royal We, but it may also reveal Heidegger's sense of the limitations of Division III as planned. If the contents of Division III, as he envisioned them and tried to elaborate them, were unable to explain how time makes nullity possible, then they cannot accomplish the task assigned to them, the task that constitutes the end (the completion) of fundamental ontology, namely, articulating the sense of being.

Conclusions

Heidegger's 1927 account of temporality, reviewed above, sketches how it provides the horizon for the understanding (projection) of a mode of being, namely, being-handy (ready-to-hand). Yet, as we have seen, a sketch is not an argument. If we take our bearings from the timeliness of being-here and ask about the horizons onto which, in being-here, we project possibilities, then it follows that the sense of being of what we encounter by virtue of those horizons must have a character in keeping with that timeliness. However, Heidegger himself tells us that the latter is only a necessary condition of the possibility of encountering them as being handy. But then it hardly follows that temporality is the sense of being as such or even that it determines our understanding of what it means to be handy or on hand.

The "end" of fundamental ontology in the sense of its final act, announced in Being and Time and pursued in the lectures of 1927, coincides with talk of horizonal schemata. The use of a notion fundamental to Kant's theoretical philosophy is hardly accidental, as we know from Heidegger's work from the next few years. As an aside, it may be helpful to draw attention to a parallel with Kant's doctrine of schematisms.[30] In Kant's Critique of Pure Reason, the aim of the transcendental deduction is to demonstrate that the categories apply to experience as conditions of its possibility, albeit only in combination with time as the form of all sensoriness (outer as well as inner). Having demonstrated in the deduction that the categories must be synthesized with time, Kant introduces the doctrine of schematism to demonstrate how they are temporally synthesized. In a similar way, the published portion of Being and Time (especially Division II) corresponds to the transcendental deduction, demonstrating that the sense of being in general must be temporal, given the timeliness of the transcendence inherent in being-here. The aim of Division III was to demonstrate, analogous to the role of the doctrine of schematisms in the *Critique of Pure Reason*, how temporality provides the senses of being.

However, there is also an instructive disanalogy. Kant restricts schemata to things as they appear, that is, things for us, leaving open the possibility that things in themselves do not coincide with how they are for us. By contrast, Heidegger's horizonal schemata are supposed to provide the sense of being in general.[31] From this vantage point, while both appeals to schemata cement their respective idealisms, fundamental ontology alone makes that idealism complete.

Heidegger recognizes as much, and his subsequent rejection of all idealisms—along with any ontology or appeal to transcendence, any transcendental rubric or talk of "conditions of the possibility"[32]—fittingly coincides with the "end" of fundamental ontology, understood this time as its demise. So, too, in *The Country Path* (1944–45) Heidegger discusses the inherent limitedness of talk of horizons and transcendence, their inability of yielding the expanse that, surrounding them, originally opens them up.[33] In broad strokes, this opening up continues the inversion that makes up the theme of Division III (i.e., from "being and time" to "time and being"), but it is no longer time as temporality, the time that derives from timeliness of being-here, but time as a marker of the origin of ways and conceptions of being as such.

Acknowledgments

I am grateful to James Kinkaid for helpful comments on an earlier version of this essay.

Notes

1. GA25 426/PIK 289. All translations are my own.

2. Theodore Kisiel, *The Genesis of Heidegger's* Being and Time (Berkeley: University of California Press, 1993), pp. 480–487.

3. "Timeliness" translates *Zeitlichkeit* in contrast to *Temporalität*, which I translate as "temporality." *Zeitlichkeit* is a word of art for Heidegger, signifying a condition for the possibility of what is by virtue of being timely or not. Heidegger deploys *Temporalität* in a way that—drawing on the significance of timeliness in Part One, Division II—proves essential to the contents of I, 3. "It [temporality] designates timeliness

insofar as it is itself made into the theme as condition of the possibility of the understanding-of-being and of ontology as such" (GA24 324/BP 228).

4. In the summer semester of 1928, Heidegger distinguishes three parts of fundamental ontology as "the basic grounding of ontology in general": (1) "the interpretation of Dasein as timeliness," (2) "the temporal exposition of the problem of being," and (3) "the development of the self-understanding of this problematic, its task, and limits—turning around [*Umschlag*]" (GA26 196/MFL 154). Fundamental ontology encompasses the entire enterprise of founding and developing ontology, including the analyses of existence and the temporality of being (GA26 201/MFL 158). These texts offset other references to fundamental ontology that seem to identify it either with the published divisions (see, e.g., SZ 14/BT 35) or with the unpublished division of SZ (see, e.g., SZ 183, 403/BT 227, 455).

5. GA24 1, 319/BP 1–2, 224; GA66 413–414/M 366–367. The task of fundamental ontology also informs his Leibniz lectures in 1928 (see n. 4 above) and his interpretations of Kant, both in lectures in 1927–28 and in his book, *Kant und das Problem der Metaphysik*.

6. Ted Kisiel, "The Demise of *Being and Time*," in *Heidegger's* Being and Time: *Critical Essays*, ed. Richard Polt (Lanham, MD: Rowman & Littlefield, 2005), pp. 208–209. Boyce Gibson relates how, in the fall of 1928, Heidegger tells him that it will take just a little while longer, probably not in time for the next issue of Husserl's *Jahrbuch*, for the rest of SZ to appear; see W. R. Boyce Gibson, "From Husserl to Heidegger: Excerpts from a 1928 Freiburg Diary," *Journal of the British Society for Phenomenology* 2 (1971): 72.

7. GA25 582.

8. The reconstruction is based mainly on two resources: (1) the introduction to SZ and (2) the final sections of the summer lectures of 1927 (GA24/BP). I leave aside closer consideration of publications from 1927 through 1930. Also omitted is any speculation on the particular contents suggested by a pair of footnotes in SZ. After contending that only the timeliness of discourse, i.e., of being-here, can explain the genesis of meaning and make the possibility of concept-formation ontologically intelligible, Heidegger adds the footnote (suppressed in later issues): "Compare Section III, Chapter Two of this treatise" (SZ 349n/BT 401n). In the immediately following §69 Heidegger characterizes thematization in science as an exceptional way of attending to (*gegenwärtigen*) things. The verb here, "attending to," used by Husserl to characterize sensory perception, signifies for Heidegger an original sense of the present. After noting that the intentional analysis of perception necessarily suggested this temporal characterization of the phenomenon, Heidegger observes: "The following section [i.e., Division III] will show that and how the intentionality of 'consciousness' is *grounded* in the ecstatic temporality of Dasein" (SZ 363n1/BT 414n).

9. The failure can be traced to Heidegger's overreaching attempt to combine, in a fundamental ontology, the two traditional meanings of "transcendental": medieval and modern, i.e., Scotistic and Kantian meanings, respectively.

10. On the opening page of the text, he advises that its aim is "the concrete elaboration of the question of the sense of 'being,'" while "the interpretation of time as the possible horizon of any understanding of being at all is its provisional goal" (SZ 1/BT 19). A few pages later, while observing that an average and vague understanding of being is a fact, he remarks: "We are not even familiar with the horizon from which we should take and fix the sense [of being]" (SZ 5/BT 25). A bit later in the introduction he iterates the idea that the analysis of being-here is provisional, picking out its being without giving an interpretation of its sense. "Rather it is supposed to prepare the freeing-up of the horizon for the most basic interpretation of being" (SZ 17/ BT 38).

11. See GA24, §19, 324–388/BP 229–274.

12. SZ 18/BT 40. The key historical precedent in this regard is the Greek determination of the sense of being as a presence, a sense that ultimately derives from the basic timeliness of attending to things (gegenwärtigen) that, while distinctive of being-here, gives rise to the original sense of the present (Gegenwart). Unbeknownst to the Greeks (who conceived time as one entity among others), time in that basic sense has a fundamental ontological function (SZ 25–26/BT 47–48).

13. SZ 19/BT 40. In the introduction to SZ Heidegger also employs Temporalität and temporal to characterize the dimension and problematic that informs his dismantling of the history of ontology (SZ 23–26, 40/BT 44–49, 64). Only once—a reference to the pending "temporal interpretation of being" (SZ 148/BT 189)—does one of the terms surface again in SZ.

14. Thus, Heidegger sometimes uses "horizon" as a metonym of "sense" in talking about the "sense of being"; other times it signifies a constitutive feature (together with ecstases) of the timeliness that makes up that sense. The metonymy is evident from Heidegger's explicit treatment of "sense" as something that, properly speaking, can only be attributed to being-here (SZ 151–152/BT 193). We understand beings or being in terms of some sense, i.e., the horizon upon which we (usually tacitly) project this or that, thereby rendering it intelligible as such and such. For example, I understand a strikeout in baseball because I have a sense of baseball, which is to say that I project a particular movement or event onto that horizon which makes it intelligible as a strikeout. We can say, in an extended manner, that baseball makes sense but only because we have a sense of it, i.e., because it makes sense to us. When Heidegger speaks of timeliness as the horizon from which the senses of being are taken, he is presumably using "sense' in that extended sense.

15. See Der Begriff der Zeit, 26/CT 51: "Dasein ist ... Zeitlichkeit."

16. Missing in this gloss in English is the cognate character of the words in German that Heidegger uses for "attending to" (*gegenwärtigen*) and the present (*Gegenwart*).

17. Ecstatic-horizonal timeliness is the generic concept for the way that different modes of time in the most basic sense, despite their differences, are ways of standing out or projecting onto a horizon, from which the ordinary senses of past, present, and future are derived. Heidegger seems to use the metaphorical projection in two senses that are not always disambiguated: (1) the projection of a horizon or schema, in terms of which entities are understood (namely, as being) and (2) the projection of possibilities onto the horizon.

18. "Being-here," like "horizon," is a word of art for Heidegger, obviously removed from its traditional philosophical significance, interchangeable with a generic sense of "existence," or from the ordinary spatial or topological significance of *da* (i.e., "here" or "there"), though his use of *Dasein* and *Horizont* as metaphors continues to trade on their ordinary and related meanings.

19. Tying the "as-structure" of understanding and interpreting to the phenomenon of projection (i.e., understanding *x* as *F* by virtue of projecting it onto *F-ness*), Heidegger contends that this "as-structure" is grounded in the "ecstatic-horizonal unity of timeliness" (SZ 360/BT 411).

20. Heidegger notes the Platonic character of the question of what lies beyond beings and makes them intelligible as such; see GA24 400–405/BP 282–286.

21. GA24 421/BP 296–297. One might also enlist Heidegger's contention that entities, unlike being, are not dependent upon our understanding of being (SZ 212/BT 255).

22. For an example of this slippage, see Heidegger's remark: "What interests us now is solely this type of being of the implement, namely, the *handiness* of the same, *with respect to its temporal possibility*, that is to say, with respect to how we understand handiness as such temporally" (GA 24: 433/BP 305). Here he moves, perhaps all too nimbly, from *Seinsart* to *Seinsverständnis*. For similar examples, see GA3 8, 225/KPM 5, 157; GA24 23, 423, 431, 445–452/BP 17, 298, 303, 313–318; GA25 69–70/PIK 48.

23. GA24 427/BP 301: "Das Dasein selbst als 'Subjekt-sein' transzendiert." Elsewhere Heidegger characterizes Dasein as a "subject," albeit always in scare quotes; see GA24 422–427/BP 297–301; see, too, the remark that philosophical inquiry necessarily depends upon an adequate clarification of the "subject" (GA24 444/BP 312).

24. GA24 466–467/BP 328.

25. GA24 412–413/BP 291. When we encounter entities that are unfamiliar and thus simply on hand, that unfamiliarity trades on some foregoing familiarity with what is handy (GA24 432/BP 304). The important point, however, is not simply that our original familiarity with entities depends upon using them in the relevant way, but that our use itself is constituted in a timely fashion.

26. The term *Praesenz* derives from the Latin *praesentia*, which can signify a presence as in "presence of mind" (Caesar: *praesentia animi*) or the temporal present as in "for the present" (Caesar: *in praesentia*). Notably, the noun derives from *praesens*, which is the participial form of *praeesse*, meaning "to be before or over, to take the lead." Heidegger sometimes uses *Anwesenheit* in apposition to *Praesenz*, perhaps indicating not their interchangeability but their interdependence; see GA24 439–443 BP 309–312.

27. Unaddressed are other senses of being, e.g., that of others (*Mitdasein*) or nature, though, as in SZ, he flags how the sense of being on hand emerges when the use of implements is *disturbed* (GA24 439–440/BP 309). Also unaddressed are horizons for the other ecstasies of timeliness, e.g., retaining and expecting as the original senses of past and future, though there are clear hints to their makeup, given their unity with the original sense of the present. It should be noted, however, that, following his account of the temporality of the handy (*Zuhandenes*), which he distinguishes from the on hand (*Vorhandenes*), Heidegger begins §21b with an observation to the effect that the exposition of the being of the on hand is now finished, perhaps suggesting that the difference between them is somewhat fluid (GA24 440, 445/ BP 309, 313).

28. It may be possible to have recourse to the *ordo exhibitendi* (order of presentation) or *ordo cognoscendi* (order of knowing), since Heidegger does speak of the necessity of redoing the existential analysis in the wake of Division III. But the closest thing that we have to Division III—the admittedly truncated account in GA24—does not inspire confidence that a transcendental ontology is more than an oxymoron. For Heidegger's conception of ontology as a transcendental science, see GA24 23, 466/ BP 17, 327; SZ 38/BT 62.

29. One recalls his account of nullity in the chapter on conscience in *Being and Time* and his gloss of the experience of things "slipping away" to capture the experience of nothingness in "What Is Metaphysics?"

30. D. O. Dahlstrom, "Transzendentale Schemata, Kategorien und Erkenntnisarten," *Kant-Studien* 75, no. 1 (1984): 38–54.

31. The difference is, in Heidegger's view, that Kant remains focused on beings or beingness (*Seiendheit*) and not being (*Seyn*) as such; see GA65 253–254/CP 200. For a useful comparison and contrast with Kant's doctrine of schematisms, see Dietmar Köhler, *Martin Heidegger: Die Schematisierung des Seinssinnes als Thematik des dritten Abschnittes von "Sein und Zeit"* (Bonn: Bouvier, 1993), p. 115.

32. GA65 206/CP 162; GA40 44/IM 60; for further references and Heidegger's struggles with the idealist and transcendental aspects of his thinking, early and late, see my essays "Heidegger's Transcendentalism," *Research in Phenomenology* 35 (September 2005): 29–54, and "Heidegger and the Impact of Idealism," in *The Impact of*

Idealism, vol. 1: *Philosophy and Natural Sciences*, ed. Karl Ameriks, Nicholas Boyle, and Liz Disley (Cambridge: Cambridge University Press, 2013), pp. 225–245.

33. GA77 111–112/CPC 72–73. Compare, too, the following note by Heidegger in the margins of §8 of his cabin copy of *Being and Time*: "The difference in terms of transcendence, the overturning of the horizon as such, the turn-around [or inversion: *Umkehr*] into the origin, coming to be present out of this origin" (GA2 53n). In Ted Kisiel's estimation, the note stems from the late 1930s; see Ted Kisiel, "The Paradigm Shifts of Hermeneutic Phenomenology: From Breakthrough to the Meaning-Giving Source," *Gatherings* 4 (2014): 1–13.

5   The Place of Division III in Heidegger's Plan for *Being and Time*: Part One as Discovering a "Clue" and Part Two as Giving the Answer

Charles Guignon

Most astute readers of *Being and Time* have noted that, despite its aura of being a systematic work in the grand style of German philosophy, there is a way in which different voices and orientations may be detected throughout this massive tome. In his seminal work, *The Genesis of Heidegger's "Being and Time"* (1993), Theodore Kisiel traces the development of Heidegger's thought from his early phenomenological and hermeneutic beginnings through his engagement with the ontological tradition to the final drafts of *Being and Time* in the mid-1920s lecture courses.[1] Given this wide range of influences, it is amazing that there is as much stylistic and substantive coherence as there is in *Being and Time*. Herman Philipse's masterful work, *Heidegger's Philosophy of Being: A Critical Interpretation* (1998), analyzes the work in order to show how, throughout the book, different voices or frames of reference emerge and then fade into the background.[2] John Richardson's *Heidegger* (2012) traces how movements such as phenomenology, pragmatism, and existentialism provided frames for different parts of Heidegger's early work.[3] And Denis MacManus's *Heidegger and the Measure of Truth* (2012) shows how important it is to recognize that different sections of *Being and Time* are products of different ways of framing ideas, with the result that apparent conflicts in the work can be understood in terms of the frames in effect at particular points.[4]

The introductions to *Being and Time*, almost certainly written after the main body of the work was composed,[5] provide a showcase for the different frames Heidegger had tried out in the years preceding the completed draft from the summer of 1926. The opening sections revive the ancient "question of being," the question posed by the branch of metaphysics that asks "What is it *to be*?" (the German noun for "being," *Sein*, is taken from the infinitive, unlike our English word "being," which comes from the gerund). Heidegger then turns to neo-Kantian reflections about the philosophy of science, attempting to motivate an inquiry into "ontology taken in its widest sense," as well as the more fundamental questioning of the *meaning* (*Sinn*) or context of intelligibility for any understanding of being (BT 11/31). The next section introduces the existentialist motif that Heidegger had only recently adopted: the question about the being of the entity that asks about, and already has some understanding of, the meaning of being, namely, the existing individual, or Dasein. The following sections of the introductions examine issues raised by the Historical School in Germany, traditional reflections on time and temporality, the nature of phenomenology, the role of hermeneutics, and the ideals of philosophy in general.

The final section of the introductions, titled "Design of the Treatise," is supposed to lay out Heidegger's overall plan for *Being and Time* as a whole. This short prospectus (less than a page in German) has proved baffling to readers because, at the end of his short account of the "design," Heidegger suggests that this book will be quite large. It will have, we are told, two major "parts," each of which will have three "divisions" (BT 39–40/63–64). What is disconcerting about this claim is that the work that comes down to us in fact has only one part, and of that one part there are in fact only two divisions. What we have, in other words, is an "astonishing torso,"[6] a rump of a book that covers less than half of what is promised in the introductions. The question therefore arises: What did Heidegger have in mind for the rest of the book? Although very little of what was promised seems to have been preserved, he never modified the claim in the preface that the published parts of the book are only a "path" (*Weg*) one must traverse "if our Dasein is to be stirred by the question of being" (BT v/17). It remains a necessary path, though it never reaches its supposed destination.

What is most puzzling about the overall plan for *Being and Time*, of course, is the question of what Heidegger proposed to say in the projected Division III of the first "part" of the work. There is plenty of room for speculation about this, given Heidegger's occasional comments over the years on the missing division. Yet it is unlikely we will ever have any part of the division that was to be called "Time and Being." As to other sources, neither the material on time and being in the Second Division of the *History of the Concept of Time: Prolegomena*,[7] nor sections 20–22 of *The Basic Problems of Phenomenology* (1927), nor the account of the temporality of being-in-the-world in section 69 of *Being and Time*, provide an adequate basis for reconstructing what was planned for Division III. Even Heidegger's lectures from the early 1920s, including the course *The Concept of Time* (1924), as well as the lecture of the same title prepared that year for the Marburg Theological Faculty, provide little help.[8] Among secondary sources available in English, there are three excellent works focusing in part on the plan for

Division III: William D. Blattner's *Heidegger's Temporal Idealism*, Karin de Boer's *Thinking in the Light of Time: Heidegger's Encounter with Hegel*, and Françoise Dastur's *Heidegger and the Question of Time*.[9] But these works remain speculative insofar as Heidegger's actual plan remains uncertain.

Instead of trying to guess what Heidegger would have said about time and being if he had completed the first half of his *opus magnus*, I want to clarify the role of the missing Division III of Part One by making explicit what Heidegger actually says about his vision for the undertaking as a whole. The best answer available is found in the second introduction, titled "The Twofold Task in Working Out the Question of Being: Method and Design of Our Investigation" (BT 36/15). Heidegger had already shown in the first introduction that his leading concern is to address the question of being—in other words, to get clear about what it is to be not just for the entities that make up the subject matters of the regional sciences, but for anything of which we can say "it is." This is the concern of "ontology taken in the widest sense" (BT 11/31).

Before addressing this question, however, Heidegger says that we must address the question of what the "to be" *means* when we are considering entities or what-is (*das Seiende*). The technical term *meaning* (*Sinn*) in nineteenth- and twentieth-century German logic referred to the underlying, generally unnoticed ordering principles that provide a frame of reference or conditions of intelligibility in terms of which anything can *count* for us or *matter* in some comprehensible way or other. The *meaning* of *x*, then, is the place *x* occupies in what Wittgenstein called "logical space" insofar as we have some understanding of what is.[10] This use of the term *meaning* is in line with its use in the tradition extending from Kant's notion of "transcendental logic" through Hegel to Husserl's *Formal and Transcendental Logic*, where we find such statements as the following:

True logic, [which is] a logic that, as transcendental logic, lights the way for the sciences with the light of a deepest self-cognition of cognition, ... does not intend to be a mere pure and formal logic. ... [It] intends even less to be a merely empirical technology for a sort of intellectual production having the greatest practical utility. ... [Rather,] it intends to bring to light the system of transcendental principles that gives to sciences the possible sense [*Sinn*] of genuine science.[11]

Given this conception of "meaning," the question asked in *Being and Time* is the question of the *meaning of being*, the question that asks about the "horizon" of intelligibility in terms of which anything can show up for us as the kind of thing it is.

Heidegger assumes that this concern with meaning implies that fundamental ontology must start by giving a full account of the entity for whom
anything whatsoever can be intelligible or accessible. As he says,

What we are *seeking* is the answer to the question about the meaning of being in
general, and, prior to that, the possibility of working out in a radical manner this
basic question of all ontology. But to lay bare the horizon within which something
like being in general becomes intelligible, is tantamount to clarifying the possibility
of having any understanding of being at all—an understanding which belongs to the
constitution of the entity called Dasein. (BT 231/274)

In other words, we can understand *what it is to be* only if we understand the
meaning or *horizon of intelligibility* in which the "to be" emerges and makes
sense, and we can grasp this horizon only if we first work out the being
of *the entity that is capable of having some understanding of what is*, namely,
ourselves (Dasein).

The "twofold task in working out the question of being" therefore begins
with an "ontological analytic of Dasein as laying bare the horizon for an
interpretation of the meaning of being in general" (§5). This interpretation
of Dasein is "preliminary" and "provisional" in the sense that its aim is only
to lay out the "horizon"—that is, the framework of intelligibility—in terms
of which Dasein itself can be understood (BT 17/38). This "laying bare the
horizon" is only a first step on the way to addressing the question of being,
for it still focuses on the being of one entity—namely, Dasein—and so does
not yet reveal "being in general." Moreover, as becomes apparent through
the course of Divisions I and II, working out the meaning of Dasein's being
itself requires two stages. Insofar as it begins with a description Dasein's
"average everydayness," it initially leaves out the potential wholeness and
fullness of Dasein's being. This wholeness can be included in the description of Dasein only by grasping our potentiality-for-being authentic.

The first two divisions reveal that the meaning of Dasein's being (identified as "care") is *time* (*Zeit*). As an unfolding *happening* (*Geschehen*) or *movement* (*Bewegtheit*), Dasein has a tripartite temporal structure that underlies
and makes possible our being as care. This temporal structure has three
ex-stases or ways of "being outside" itself. We exist as beings who are futural
(*zukunftig*), being "out there" toward the fulfillment of our potentiality-for-
being. In this forward-directedness, we draw on what has been in the formation of our lives, our *Gewesenheit* or beenness, the enduring resources for
our agency. And as thrown projections, we "make present" (*gegenwärtigen*)
what we encounter in our comportments with what shows up in the world.
These temporal structures, tied together in a sequential order by our ways of

being *stretched out* or *stretching ourselves out* over a life course, make up our being as temporality. The structure of Dasein's being as "temporalizing" (the German *sich zeitigen*, translated by this English neologism, literally means "coming-to-fruition" or "bringing-to-maturity") has the consequence that the being of anything accessible to us is going to be encountered as having a temporal structure. Because we can only gain access to entities through our own modes of access, the meaning of being of entities in general will be shaped by temporality (e.g., numbers as eternal, tools as ready-to-hand, historical events as somehow in the past, imaginary beings as not being in time, and so forth).

Divisions I and II of Part One carry out the first step in developing the horizon of intelligibility, the frame of reference by virtue of which we can apprehend entities *as* such and such, that is to say, insofar as they count or matter to us in some way. But these two divisions are said to be only "preparatory" in the overall task of Part One, which is titled the "Explication of Time as the Transcendental Horizon for the Question of Being" (BT 39/63). What we need at the end of Division II is a way to move beyond the temporality (*Zeitlichkeit*) of Dasein to *time itself*, which Heidegger designates with the Latinate term *Temporalität*. In particular, Heidegger's goal is to interpret time in such a way that it does not cast a subjectivistic or anthropocentric shadow onto what there is in the course of disclosing "being in general." This final stage of Part One was to have been accomplished in Division III, a division titled "Time and Being." As we have seen, this division is not extant, and presumably was never put in writing in a form Heidegger found satisfactory.

Instead of trying to reconstruct Heidegger's intentions for Division III, we might take a close look at what role this division was projected to have according to the plan for the book as a whole. We know that Division III of Part One was supposed to complete the first "task" of the work as a whole, "the explication of time as the transcendental horizon for the question of being" (BT 39/63). The second "task" of *Being and Time* was to be accomplished in Part Two of the work. According to the "Design of the Treatise," Part Two was supposed to provide the "basic features of a phenomenological destruction of the history of ontology, with the problematic of Temporality as our clue." The "Design" specifies that this second part will, like the first part, contain three divisions:

1. Kant's doctrine of schematism and time, as a preliminary stage in a problematic of Temporality;

2. the ontological foundation of Descartes's *cogito sum*, and how the medieval ontology has been taken over into the problematic of the *res cogitans*;

3. Aristotle's essay on time, as providing a way of discriminating the phenomenal basis and the limits of ancient ontology. (BT 40/64)

As should be apparent, Part Two consists of a historical regression or "destructuring" that traces back key developments in the history of Western philosophy, using *time* as the "clue" or "leading thread" (*Leitfaden*) for reading the historical course of events. It is a "destruction" in the sense that it peels off the layers of a "hardened tradition"—the seemingly self-evident viewpoint that has come down to us—in order to uncover the "primordial experiences in which we achieved our first ways of determining the nature of being—the ways which have guided us ever since" (BT 22/44). Time provides a *clue* to this retrieval or repetition of the ontological tradition by indicating the underlying core of meaning of the entire historical story.

The historical Part Two of the overall project of disclosing the being of entities is a "destructuring" in a double sense. On the one hand, it diagnoses and helps us see what is wrong with the tradition. On the other hand, it retrieves from forgetfulness the concealed origins of our diverse ways of understanding what it is to be. Although Part Two of *Being and Time* was never undertaken, a number of works reveal the sorts of things Heidegger planned for this part. *Kant and the Problem of Metaphysics* (winter semester, 1925–26) shows how he planned to give an account, both critical and appreciative, of Kant's use of time in the first *Critique*. Heidegger's frequent references to Descartes give us a hint of how he would have worked out what has been called the "metaphysics of presence" as it appears in the immediate presence of self to self of the *cogito*. And *The Essence of Human Freedom* (summer semester, 1930), together with other works on Aristotle, makes clear how Aristotle's conception of *ousía* as possessions and estate gives primacy to what is present for Dasein.

Through these stages, the historical part of *Being and Time*, would have exposed the way that *presence* (and the concealment of absence) constitutes the unifying understanding for all conceptions of being throughout Western thought. It is because the unifying and most original meaning of being is found only in such a historical recovery that Heidegger says that "the question of being does not achieve its true concreteness until we have carried through the process of destroying the ontological tradition" (BT 26/49). What this means is that the leading question of *Being and Time* is only answered by the historical part of the project. On this view of *Being and Time*, the definitive role of the discussion of temporality and Temporality is to provide a *clue* for carrying out these historical investigations into origins. What Heidegger calls the "transcendental" part of the overall work has as its sole function the goal of indicating what we should look for in the historical destruction. But it is in the Part Two destruction that the question of being is first actually addressed.

As we noted earlier, in the years after completing *Being and* Time Heidegger offered a variety of comments on why the Third Division of Part One never appeared, and on why the overarching project of *Being and Time* was never carried out in the form originally conceived for it. One of his later comments on this topic is a passage in the 1949 "Letter on Humanism" where Heidegger discusses the "turn" or "reversal" that was to occur in (or through?) the third division of *Being and Time*, a division that, he says here, was "held back" (WM327–28/PM249–250). According to the "Humanism" letter, the 1930 lecture "On the Essence of Truth" shows that the turning from "Being and Time" to "Time and Being" is "not a change of standpoint" from the question of being that is posed in *Being and Time*. Rather, it is a change (*Änderung*) in the thinking aimed at arriving at the locality from which *Being and Time* was first experienced, namely, in the "forgetfulness of being" (ibid.). This comment, none too perspicuous in itself, has been discussed at length by a number of commentators.[12] For my purposes here, I will follow de Boer in setting this quote against the background of some remarks (equally obscure, perhaps) in Heidegger's *Contributions to Philosophy* of 1936–1938.

The problem, as described in *Contributions*, is that what Heidegger was seeking is inexpressible not only in the language of metaphysics, but in any language as this word is commonly understood. The missing Division of *Being and Time* was the keystone of the overarching project of "expos[ing] 'time' as the domain of projection for beyng" (GA65 451/CP 355). But, as Heidegger suggests, there is something wrong with this project itself. For it tends to lead to an attempted "objectification" of being, inclining us to think of being as, despite all contestations to the contrary, an object that can be represented, and thus as something set over against the human subject. Avoiding this is possible only by "*withholding* the 'temporal' interpretation of beyng [and at the same time] attempting to make the truth of being 'visible' independently of that interpretation" (ibid.).[13] What this is saying, as I understand it, is that the need to withhold the temporal interpretation is not rooted in anything incorrect about the temporal interpretation itself—indeed, many of Heidegger's later writings can be understood as different ways of trying to think of being in terms of temporality. On the contrary, the problem arises from the fact that any attempt to *give an interpretation* (*Auslegung*) of being, where "interpretation" means something like arriving at a correct representation, inevitably tempts us to see being as an *object* of some sort. What Heidegger is looking for is a way to make the truth of being "visible" in some way other than a transcendental phenomenology that tries to get a correct interpretation of being. Heidegger has come to see that the problem lies in the very idea of interpretation itself.

The writings from the 1930s constantly emphasize the need to free ourselves from the illusion of the human mastery of all that is, and to experience and act in the light of an awareness of the human *need* for beyng. In a typical passage, Heidegger writes,

To grasp the abyss [*Abgrund*] of the neededness of beyng means to be transposed into the necessity of grounding the truth for beyng and not to resist the essential consequences of this necessity but, instead, to think toward them and thereby to know, without playing into the hands of the claim to "absoluteness," that that necessity withdraws all thinking of beyng from every merely human contrivance. (GA65 439/ CP 346)

The proper relation of the human to being, as now conceived, is one that grasps (the absence of ground of) beyng and recognizes the need for humans to provide the site or "there" for the realization of beyng.[14] And it is also to see that beyng is not the product of human contrivance (as antirealists typically presume), while at the same time avoiding any ontotheological positing of being as an "absolute" that has no need whatsoever for humans. The underlying conception of being as more an agent than a product of human constituting activity is not easy to understand for thinkers raised in the age of anthropocentrism (though it might be familiar to panentheists with their idea of humans as cocreators with the Creator).[15] Its mysterious nature notwithstanding, it is clearly what Heidegger is trying to articulate in these post–*Being and Time* writings.

In *Contributions*, Heidegger seeks a nonobjectfying way of thinking of beyng that liberates the traditional question of being from the idea of inquiry as a matter of arriving at a correct representation of an "object." This new way of approaching the question involves, Heidegger says, "a multiple leap (*vielfache Sprung*) into the essence of beyng itself" (GA65 451/CP 355), an approach that examines what things look like from many different frames of reference. One consequence of this approach is that being can no longer be thought of as an "object" set over against and represented by a "subject." As Heidegger puts it in another context, "human being is placed back into the essence of being and is released from the fetters of 'anthropology'" (GA65 84/CP 67). When the subjectivism and the "anthropological sleep"[16] of modern humanism is extracted from the inquiry, and human being achieves a new correlate of a more original relation to being, the question of being escapes from the distorting influence of the subject–object model. Seen in this light, our being as humans is carried along by beyng.

A second consequence of this radical shift in approach is that it displaces the linear and goal-directed conception of questioning still dominant in *Being and Time*. *Being and Time* was a "*path*," a "*way*," Heidegger reminds us—and he adds: assuming that constantly "stumbling and getting up again can be called a path" (GA65 84/CP 67). In other words, the "way" of the question of being can no longer be thought of as a straight, orderly route comparable to logical deduction or idealized scientific reasoning. Approached in this way, "the positions of the questioning are constantly different" (ibid.). As a result, there can be "no gradual 'development' here," no discovering the later in the earlier (ibid.). We must constantly approach the topic from new points of view, changing our frame of reference at almost every step. These alternatives and changes are "so essential that their scale can be determined only if in each case the *one* question is pervasively asked out of its own site of questioning" (and, Heidegger adds, frameworks of questioning "arise from the widening abyss [*Abgründigkeit*] of the question of being itself") (GA65 84/CP 68).[17] "For the task is not to bring to cognition new representations of beings but rather to ground the *being* of the human being in the truth of being and to prepare this grounding in the inventive thinking [*Erdenken*] of being and of Da-sein [i.e., being the *there* as the site in which being is what it is]" (GA65 86/CP 68).

A third consequence of this transformed way of questioning (and of *being* human as a philosopher) is that "thinking becomes ever more historical" (GA65 451/CP 355). The "multiple leap into the essence of being" has the consequence that there must be a "more original binding into [*Einfügung*] history" (ibid.). Though Heidegger had always thought of history as crucial to the question of being, this transformed approach of multiple perspectives and frameworks lights up the thinking of the beginning (*Angang*). In the transition from *Being and Time* to the writings of 1936–1938, "the thinking became ever more historical; i.e., the distinction between a historiological and a systematic consideration became ever more untenable" (ibid.). As the idea of a step-by-step procedure is replaced by multiple frames, the basic bonds between the frames and historical epochs become more prominent and exigent. What was only hinted at in the last pages of *Being and Time*— that starting from Dasein and moving by means of a sort of transcendental argument is "only *one path* which we may take" (BT 436/487)—now becomes the recognition that the path taken in *Being and Time* is merely one among innumerable possible paths one could take, with none having a privileged status in relation to the others (GA65 436/CP 487).

At the end of the *Contributions*, Heidegger makes a remark that seems both frustrating and promising. He observes that, "seen with respect to the question-*worth*iness of being and its essential unfolding," the first clarification of the "wholly other asking of the question of being" is "something like a first tentative step on a very long springboard. With this step hardly anything is detected of the demand which, at the end of the springboard, is necessary for making the leap" (GA65 468/CP 368). It should be obvious that this trope is deeply ambiguous. On the one hand, it suggests that a definitive, final answer to Heidegger's lifelong project—clarifying once and for all "what it is *to be*"—is not something we are likely to arrive at through ordinary sorts of linear thinking. Yet, on the other hand, it suggests that the questioning is not a fool's errand, and that there is the promise of getting closer to an insight (or a collection of insights) into what it is to be. From this perspective, Division III's exposition of the relation of being to time would have been an important early step. But it would have been only one step, and not yet the needed "leap."

Notes

1. Theodore Kisiel, *The Genesis of Heidegger's "Being and Time"* (Berkeley: University of California Press, 1993).

2. Herman Philipse, *Heidegger's Philosophy of Being: A Critical Interpretation* (Princeton: Princeton University Press, 1998).

3. John Richardson, *Heidegger* (London: Routledge, 2012).

4. Denis MacManus, *Heidegger and the Measure of Truth: Themes from His Early Philosophy* (Oxford: Oxford University Press, 2012).

5. Alfred Denker, pers. comm.

6. See Kisiel, *Genesis*, p. 489.

7. GA20 (1979); *History of the Concept of Time: Prolegomena*, trans. Theodore Kisiel (Bloomington: Indiana University Press, 1985).

8. GA64, *The Concept of Time*, trans. Ingo Farrin and Alex Skinner (New York: Continuum, 2011), and the lecture to the Marburg Theological Faculty of July 1924, *Der Begriff der Zeit: Vortrag vor der Marburger Theologenschaft Juli 1924* (Tübingen: Max Niemeyer, 1989), translated as *The Concept of Time* by William McNeill (Oxford: Blackwell, 1992).

9. William D. Blattner, *Heidegger's Temporal Idealism* (Cambridge: Cambridge University Press, 1999); Karin de Boer, *Thinking in the Light of Time: Heidegger's Encounter with Hegel* (Albany: SUNY Press, 2000); and Françoise Dastur, *Heidegger and the Question of Time*, trans. François Raffoul and David Pettigrew (Highlands, NJ: Humanities, 1998).

10. See my "Wittgenstein, Heidegger, and the Question of Phenomenology," in *Wittgenstein and Heidegger*, ed. D. Egan, S. Reynolds and A. J. Wendland (New York: Routledge, 2013), pp. 82–98.

11. Edmund Husserl, *Formal and Transcendental Logic*, trans. Dorian Cairns (The Hague: Martinus Nijhoff, 1969), p. 16.

12. See, *inter alia*, de Boer, *Thinking in the Light of Time*, pp. 131–133.

13. Heidegger uses the archaic German word *Seyn* (translated here as "beyng") in part to distinguish his new way of "enthinking" *being* from that of earlier ways of thinking about the *to be*, including that of traditional metaphysics. More can be said about the distinction between "beyng" and "being," but for my purposes in this context the two terms can be used interchangeably. For a full clarification of this distinction, see Richard Polt, *The Emergency of Being: On Heidegger's "Contributions to Philosophy"* (Ithaca, NY: Cornell University Press, 2006), pp. 54–63.

14. Translating the German word *Abgrund* as "abyss" is ingenious and commonplace, but it conceals the relation of this word to the German word for "ground" (*Grund*) Heidegger's wordplay suggests that, where traditional philosophy seeks a ground in the sense of what lifts up and supports, the need that beyng has for humans is more like an opening that sucks humans in so that they may play a crucial role (i.e., fill the need for a site or space-time of freeplay, a *Da*) in which beyng can come to be appropriated and realized as what it is.

15. See Charles Hartshorne and William L. Reese, *Philosophers Speak of God*, 2nd ed. (Amherst, NY: Humanity Press, 2000).

16. The term is from Michel Foucault, *The Order of Things: An Archaeology of the Human Sciences* (New York: Vintage, 1994).

17. See n. 14.

6   The Beings of Being: On the Failure of Heidegger's Ontico-Ontological Priority

Graham Harman

In Search of *Being and Time*, Part One, Division Three

It was not long ago that Heidegger's *Being and Time* was still routinely described as an "unfinished" work. This description remains perfectly warranted, since the outline found in the book's introduction announces two parts with three divisions apiece, though only the first two divisions of Part One ever appeared.[1] Heidegger's most direct explanation can be found in his famous preface to the seventh German Edition of 1953: "While the previous editions have borne the designation 'First Half,' this has now been deleted. After a quarter of a century, the second half could no longer be added unless the first were to be presented anew" (BT 17). But not only the "second half" of the book is at issue, assuming that this phrase refers to the unpublished Part Two. Also missing is Division III of Part One, provisionally entitled "Time and Being." In a sense, the absence of Division III is more mysterious than that of the bulkier phantom known as Part Two. It has often been observed that the historical discussions announced for Part Two (on Kant, Descartes, and Aristotle) can either be found in other volumes of Heidegger's Complete Edition, or are easy to imagine on the basis of those volumes. For instance, it is hard to conceive of Heidegger giving a better treatment of "Kant's doctrine of schematism and time, as a preliminary stage in a problematic of Temporality" (BT 64) than can already be found in his widely respected *Kant and the Problem of Metaphysics*.[2] The real stumbling block in the completion of *Being and Time* seems to be Division III of Part One, "Time and Being." Division III cannot plausibly be replaced with the similarly entitled *On Time and Being*: this latter work dates to 1962, or nearly a decade after the project of *Being and Time* was publicly abandoned, and is a most comically different in tone from Heidegger's 1927 *magnum opus*.[3] By contrast with the easily reconstructed Part Two of *Being and Time*, the missing Division III is a truly puzzling omission that may provide a key to understanding the noncompletion of *Being and Time*. By the same stroke, this topic could teach us a more general lesson about the difference between the finished and unfinished business of Heidegger's thought, and thus of twentieth-century philosophy as a whole.

Biographical reasons appear to shed a certain light on the uncompleted state of the book. In Heidegger's touching retrospective essay "My Way to Phenomenology," we read the following well-known anecdote:

> "Professor Heidegger—you have got to publish something now. Do you have a manuscript?" With these words the dean of the philosophical faculty in Marburg came into my study one day in the Winter Semester of 1925–26. "Certainly," I answered. Then the dean said "But it must be printed quickly." The faculty proposed me *unico loco* as Nicolai Hartmann's successor for the chief philosophical chair. Meanwhile, the ministry in Berlin had rejected the proposal with the explanation that I had not published anything in the last ten years. Now I had to submit my closely protected work to the public.[4]

The professional hurry surrounding the appearance of *Being and Time* may explain the initial omission of the noncompleted Division III. Yet it cannot explain the continued nonappearance of the pages in question between 1927 and 1953, when Heidegger finally ended all public expectation that the rest of the book would ever appear. Though there may be some merit in Heidegger's claim that "After a quarter of a century, the second half could no longer be added unless the first were to be presented anew," there are at least three problems with this brief excuse. First, it dodges the question of the missing portion of the *first* half, which ought to have followed naturally from the first two divisions. Second, it is not even true that one cannot complete a major philosophical work after the passage of many years. A good counterexample can be found in a living thinker, Alain Badiou, who published his major work *Being and Event* in 1988 but did not release its second volume, *Logics of Worlds*, until the spring of 2006.[5] Though some critics still doubt whether Badiou's two volumes work well together, the problems they cite have less to do with the passage of eighteen years than with a possible ambiguity in the heart of Badiouian philosophy itself.[6] Likewise, if Heidegger decided not to complete *Being and Time*, this cannot be because the work was dated by the mere passage of time, but because Heidegger was somehow unable to rise to the challenge of Division III. Third and finally, there is no use saying that Heidegger could not complete the work owing to the much-discussed "turn" (*Kehre*) in his thinking, dated variously by different commentators, but invariably placed somewhere between *Being and Time* in 1927 and the remarks in the preface of 1953. The reason is that the causal relation between the *Kehre* (if it occurred at all) and the noncompletion of Division III may be the reverse of what we expect. That is to say perhaps the nonappearance of Division III was itself the deadlock that *generated* the apparent turn in his thinking. After all, it took Heidegger twenty-six years to throw in the towel on *Being and Time* (at least publicly), suggesting that he planned for at least most of those years to get back to his great book sooner or later.

The Threefold via Hegel, Husserl, and Heidegger

The strategy of this essay will be to link Heidegger's incomplete three divisions of *Being and Time*, Part One with some completed threefold elsewhere in the book that somehow alludes to the content of the missing Third Division. For it is no random accident of planning that Part One of *Being and Time* was to have had precisely *three* divisions, rather than two, four, five, or some other number. Triple structures dominate Heidegger's philosophy.[7] We encounter one such triple structure in the thrownness, projection, and thrown projection of Dasein, which overlaps with the *temporal* structure of Being as past, future, and present. There is the threefold structure of questioning in the form of *das Gefragte*, *das Erfragte*, and *das Befragte*. In Heidegger's relatively neglected gem "On the Essence of Ground," written on the crucial occasion of a *Festschrift* for Edmund Husserl, there is the pivotal threefold of *Weltbezug*, *Haltung*, and *Einbruch* (world-relation, attitude, and irruption).[8] Even in the celebrated 1929–30 Freiburg Lecture Course,[9] the subtitle contains the trio of world, finitude, solitude, and though the third of these is never fully developed, it would not be hard to show that these three terms are another variant of the always triplicate temporal structure of Dasein and correlatively of Being itself.[10]

If there is a more famous thinker of threes than Heidegger, it is surely G. W. F. Hegel. It will be worth our while to draw a clear contrast between their respective methods of using threes, even if this requires a somewhat lengthy detour. Though the textbook Hegelian triad of thesis, antithesis, and synthesis (found in many histories of philosophy and many comprehensive exam responses) has long been ridiculed by Hegel scholars, the threefold character of Hegel's thought clearly survives the ridicule unblemished, if in more sophisticated form. The Hegelian dialectic is an overt three-step movement that begins with some apparently simple shape of consciousness (in the *Phenomenology of Spirit*) or apparently simple logical idea (in the *Science of Logic*).[11] This simplicity is then negated, and eventually the negation is negated. Negativity, including the culminating negation

of the negation, is the engine of the dialectic. Indeed, the basic threefold
organization of Hegel's *Science of Logic* (being, essence, concept) forms
the backbone of most Hegelian responses to realist critiques that Hegel is
trapped in a dialectics of thought that wrongly recuperates all excess into
the movement of thought.[12] To posit something essential outside thought,
Hegelians tell us, is to remain trapped in the Logic of Essence, rather than
continuing on with its proper sublation into the Logic of the Concept.
What Heidegger calls "Being," that which withdraws into concealment and
never comes fully to presence, would be dismissed as "Essence" under the
Hegelian terminology. In reciprocal fashion, Hegelian "Being" (the simply
given shape of a moment of spirit or logic) would be dismissed by Heidegger as sheer *Vorhandenheit*, or presence-at-hand. Hegel is by no means
one of the heroes of Heidegger's history of being, however great His respect
for Hegel. But notice as well that Heidegger is not one of the heroes of contemporary Hegel-inspired thinkers such as Badiou or Slavoj Žižek, despite
their intermittent rhetorical homage to Heidegger. A basic deadlock persists
between present-day Hegelians (including Marxists and *Frankfurter Schüler*)
and Heideggerians, and this deadlock can be located precisely in their dif-
fering interpretations of the threefold structure of reality. For philosophy
of a Heideggerian inspiration, one term of the threefold necessarily resists
recuperation by dialectical movement, while for the heirs of Hegel this
claim is merely a retrograde pre-Hegelian maneuver that remains obsessed
with Kant's supposed tragic flaw: the inaccessible thing-in-itself. Neither
Hegelian philosophy nor its latter-day heirs could ever permit the veiling,
concealment, or withdrawal that are the *sine qua non* of Heideggerianism.
    The missing link between Hegel and Heidegger is surely Edmund Hus-
serl, founder of phenomenology, who has been excessively eclipsed by the
tacit ongoing duel between the other two great "Capital H" thinkers. To
my knowledge there has never been a convincing account of the relation
between Hegel, Husserl, and Heidegger. Viewed from a Heideggerian perspective, Husserl might seem closer to Hegel: both talk like idealists, and
both use the word "phenomenology," suggesting that the phenomenal
level is where philosophy must unfold. But from a Hegelian perspective,
Husserl can only seem closer to Heidegger: not only chronologically and
in terms of teacher-student relations, but because Husserl's phenomenology also seems obsessed with "essences" that, at least initially, are hidden
behind the surface appearances of things. For Husserl unlike for Heidegger,
these essences are capable of being exhaustively known given sufficiently
rational procedures, but this knowledge will always be direct and intuitive

rather than mediated through the long labor of the negative as Hegelian knowing must be.

Now, it seems to me that both the Heideggerian and Hegelian views of Husserl miss the point, though the limits of this essay enforce more brevity on the topic than the case deserves. Hegel and Husserl are certainly united in their idealism, even if we try to defend Hegel by calling him an "objective idealist" or defend Husserl by saying that consciousness is "always already outside itself" in intending objects in the world. For both philosophers it would be an absurdity to defend a Kantian thing-in-itself, or indeed any notion of something that might exist without (at least in principle) being presentable to consciousness. This is obviously not the case for Kant and is just as little the case for Heidegger, for whom Being simply *cannot* become directly present, despite Jacques Derrida's misleading claim that for Heidegger Being exists only in its various temporal manifestations (true for Derrida but not for Heidegger).[13] Heidegger's critique of presence is not the same as Derrida's. For Heidegger, the reason that Being does not become present is because it is a real surplus that reveals itself only partially in any given manifestation. It can never be directly intuited as in Husserl's categorial intuition, but for Heidegger this is not because it only *exists* in its diverse manifestations. For Derrida, by contrast, the reason there is no presence is simply because there are no *privileged* manifestations: all are contaminated, disseminated, interwoven with other manifestations. But in Derrida's world there is no withdrawn Heideggerian surplus, inaccessible to view. Stated differently, Heidegger undercuts presence from below and Derrida undercuts it from above. While it is true that Heidegger resembles Husserl in heaping frequent scorn on the problem of the reality of the external world, as in both *Being and Time* (246–252) and his brilliant 1925 Marburg Lecture Course account of phenomenology,[14] Heidegger's question of the meaning of Being makes sense only insofar as he *rejects* Husserl's doctrine of being. While for Husserl the "is" of every phenomenon is simply the deepest layer of categorial intuition, Heidegger's Being is not something that can be intuited at all, since it is precisely what is concealed from any intuition. Also too frequently ignored are the closing words of *Kant and the Problem of Metaphysics*, where Heidegger takes sides with Kant *against* German Idealism, whose war on the things-in-themselves is interpreted as a war against one of Heidegger's pet concepts and one of Hegel's most despised enemies: finitude.

We must now turn to the relation between Husserl and Hegel, which is seldom considered at all. The key to Hegel's threefold is the process of sublation (*Aufhebung*), where what seems at first to be a relation of otherness between thing and thought collapses into something like a simultaneous internality of thing and externality of thought. There is no object merely standing over against thought, since the very relation between them is sublated into a sort of thing–thought composite whose negativity is internal to the composite itself. In any case, subject and object are not two different things; they are dialectically interwoven. Yet this is precisely where Husserl differs most crucially from Hegel, whatever their shared idealist commitments. It is well known that Husserl's teacher Franz Brentano revived the notion of intentionality or "immanent objectivity," by which he distinguished mental life from mere physical interaction.[15] The scattered present-day disciples of Brentano still sometimes claim that Husserl stole his teacher's ideas and took credit for them. Yet there is a crucial difference between these two thinkers. This has less to do with Brentano's relative silence about an unknowable external world and Husserl's idealist denial of it than with their pivotal difference on the nature of intentional objects.[16] For Brentano, there is obviously a difference between intentional acts and the objects at which they aim, yet there is no clear difference *within* these objects. By treating presentation as the basic mode of intentionality, all of the content an intentional object presents is placed on the same level; there cannot be any difference between "essential" and "accidental" presentations, since all presentations are equal *qua* presentation. Yet the *denial* of this principle is what made Husserl the thinker he is. Namely, the key dispute of Husserl's *Logical Investigations* with Brentano is that for Husserl it is *object-giving acts* that are primary rather than presentations of experienced contents.[17] For Husserl, not all content is equal. When an object is present to us, it is present as an adumbration (*Abschattung*) showing countless specific qualities, most of them utterly dispensable as we subtract them step by step in search of a thing's *essence*. If Brentano tacitly follows British Empiricism in treating intentional objects as bundles of qualities, Husserl distinguishes between something like essential and accidental qualities in the intentional objects, though the essential ones are not "hidden" in the way that Heideggerian Being is hidden.

Husserl's primary difference from Hegel should now be clear as well. For the Hegelian dialectic, the otherness of the object is sublated; the object maintains no autonomy and is thus of no especial interest. By contrast, Husserlian phenomenology is deeply interested in concrete perceptual details such as how a coffee mug can show vastly different features at different times while remaining essentially the same object. This Husserlian rift *within* the object has no place in Hegel's philosophy, where the sole gap to be addressed (and overcome) is the familiar opposition between thought and its object. Neither Hegel nor Brentano see the fissures in the objects that Husserl sees and that his heirs explore in even greater detail. Emmanuel Levinas and Maurice Merleau-Ponty spend many pages describing the perceptual vicissitudes of flames, smoke, bread, cigarettes, and sports cars, which makes a great deal of sense when working in a phenomenological idiom. It would make no sense at all in the school of Hegel, where negativity unfolds only in what Hegel presents as an artificial gap *between* subject and object, never within the object itself, where for Husserl the essential and the adumbrational are in constant tension. Furthermore, there is no threefold structure in Husserl, since he halts the *Aufhebung* in its tracks. For Husserl there is a certain density and opacity to the various objects of perception that cannot be sublated. Intentional objects even taunt us with a certain perplexity, though Husserl thinks these riddles can eventually be solved through an adequate intuition of essences. The old anecdote about Husserl having his students spend a semester analyzing a mailbox still makes us chuckle because it sounds like "typical Husserl." In no way could it ever be "typical Hegel": what could Hegel possibly teach his students to see in an apparently mute object such as a mailbox?

The lack of sublation in Heidegger's philosophy is clear enough. His Being is not some transient Hegelian essence posited behind the immediate appearance of a thing but later overcome in a sophisticated doctrine of the Concept. Heidegger's Being is not sublatable, but haunts all rational conception as a dark and inassimilable residue. Yet Heidegger's difference from Husserl should be just as obvious. One index of this difference is the fact that for Heidegger, unlike for Husserl, there can be no final intuition of the essence (or rather, "Being") of a thing. Heidegger's as-structure, the seeing of a thing *as* such and such, can only be a hermeneutic or interpretative operation haunted by an unglimpsed background, not a direct access to reality *in propria persona*. This is why Heidegger retrieves a threefold structure that was simply not to be found in Husserl's twofold duel between an intentional object and its various profiles. For Heidegger, reality is necessarily three: we have the dark background into which we are thrown, the interpretative projection of this background that takes on a specific but always inadequate configuration, and the semi-shadowy middle ground in which these first two moments intersect. What we now need to do is show how the first two divisions of *Being and Time* relate to this threefold schema. That having been done, we should be able to detect the missing third term of Heidegger's book, and perhaps be in a position to speculate as to why he was unable to finish it.

Three Priorities for the Question of Being

The introduction to *Being and Time* already mentions a number of three-fold structures. We might ask which of them corresponds sufficiently to the topic of the three divisions of Part One that it can help pinpoint the missing content of the proposed Division III. The first threefold list of *Being and Time* targets the presuppositions that seem to render the question of Being impossible: "First, it has been maintained that 'Being' is the 'most universal concept.' ... It has been maintained secondly that the concept of 'Being' is indefinable. ... Thirdly, it is held that 'Being' is of all concepts the one that is self-evident" (BT 22–23). Though I suspect that even this list sprouts from Heidegger's threefold structure of temporality, it has no clear connection with how *Being and Time* is organized, and hence cannot provide the clue we are seeking. The second threefold list of *Being and Time* is Heidegger's classic distinction, seemingly so pedantic, between the three moments of all questioning: "Any inquiry, as an inquiry about something, has *that which is asked about* [sein *Gefragtes*]. ... In addition to what is asked about, an inquiry has that which is *interrogated* [ein *Befragtes*]. ... Further-more, in what is asked about there lies also *that which is to be found out by the asking* [das *Erfragte*]" (BT 24). Heidegger's usual temporal structure here is clear enough, since we confront something already before us (*das Gefragte*, or past), and we ask about it in order to reveal it *as* what it is (*das Erfragte*, or future), with these two moments intertwined in the question itself (*das Befragte*, or present). Heidegger identifies these three moments for us more explicitly as follows: *das Befragte*, or that which is interrogated in the question, is entities; *das Erfragte*, or that which is to be found by the asking, is the meaning of being; *das Gefragte*, or that which is asked about 'is Being—that which determines entities as entities, that on the basis of which enti-ties are already understood, however we may discuss them in detail" (BT 25–26). But despite the intimate link between the threefold structure of questioning and Heidegger's temporal model of Being, this second three-fold structure is also not the clue we are seeking. For it has no clear link to the three divisions of *Being and Time*, nor does the threefold structure of the question "fail" in any sense that would explain the missing Division III. Rather, the threefold question succeeds in setting up the structure of the question of being from the outset, and has nothing of the unfinished symphony about it.

Appropriately enough, it is only the *third* threefold structure in *Being and Time* that makes an effective link with the proposed (and failed) organiza-tion of the book. I speak of the three types of priority of the question of being: the ontological, the ontical, and the ontico-ontological (BT 28–35). As readers of Heidegger are aware, "ontological" refers to Being and "ontic" to beings, with the latter often used disparagingly—as when speaking of "a mere ontic fact" that tells us nothing about Being itself. But "ontico-ontological" is a rare adjective in Heidegger, and if memory serves it appears nowhere in his collected works besides the introduction to *Being and Time*. If the ontic and ontological priorities of the question of Being correspond to Divisions I and II, as I propose, then the phrase "ontico-ontological" should refer to the missing subject matter that would have made up Division III. If the ontico-ontological refers to a theme that Heidegger was never able to master, this would also explain the disappearance of this 1927 compound adjective from Heidegger's lexicon, just as the briefly promising 1928 word "metontology" also disappeared. In fact, I will shortly claim that the "ontico-ontological" and the "metontological" cover the same terrain for Heidegger.

Let's look briefly at how Heidegger defines each of these three priorities of the question of Being. The ontological priority of the question is explained by Heidegger in terms of the priority of ontology over the various positive sciences, in what is perhaps his trademark defense of the autonomous importance of philosophy. As he puts it, "The real 'movement' of the sciences takes place when their basic concepts undergo a more or less radical revision which is transparent to itself. The level which a science has reached is determined by how far it is *capable* of a crisis in its basic concepts" (BT 29). Heralding a later idea of the media theorist Marshall McLuhan, Heidegger holds that we are driven to inquire into the basic concepts of each science "mostly by reacting against … [their] increase in information" (BT 29).[18] Numerous fields of inquiry seemed to be in crisis in Heidegger's time. His own famous list includes mathematics, physics, biology, the historiological humanities, and even theology (BT 29–30). Research into the foundations of these disciplines "must run ahead of the positive sciences, and it *can*. Here the work of Plato and Aristotle is evidence enough" (BT 30). Yet all such regional ontology, so crucial for resolving the crises of the various disciplines, "remains blind and perverted from its ownmost aim, if it has not first adequately clarified the meaning of Being, and conceived this clarification as its fundamental task" (BT 31; emphasis removed).

This brings us to the second or "ontic" priority of the question of Being. Though all the various sciences have the world as their topic, it is also the case that "as ways in which man behaves, sciences have the manner of Being which this entity—man himself—possesses. This entity we denote by the term *'Dasein'*" (BT 32). And further: "Dasein … is ontically distinguished by the fact that, in its very Being, that Being is an *issue* for it. ... Dasein is ontically distinctive in that it *is* ontological" (BT 32). In short, "Sciences are ways of Being in which Dasein comports itself towards entities which it need not be itself. ... So whenever an ontology takes for its theme entities whose character of Being is other than that of Dasein, it has its own foundation and motivation in Dasein's own ontical structure, in which a pre-ontological understanding of Being is comprised as a definite characteristic" (BT 33). It is not surprising to see Dasein take center stage in the ontic priority of the question of Being. I have said that Heidegger's threefold structures inevitably mirror the threefold temporality of Being that lies at the heart of his philosophy, and it Dasein (as the "projector" of the "thrownness" that is handed to it) which always occupies the futural portion of the threefold temporal structure, just as Being itself always embodies the forgotten immemorial past.

Before moving on to the third, "ontico-ontological" priority of the question of Being, we pause to note what is most surprising about the ontological and ontic priorities just discussed. Not long after *Being and Time*, Heidegger introduced his term the *ontological difference*, or the difference between Being and beings.[19] It has long seemed to me that two completely different senses of this term are conflated, sometimes even by Heidegger himself. In the first sense, we have Heidegger's recurrent "temporal" difference between absence and presence, withdrawal and clearing, veiling and unveiling, or whatever such pair of terms one prefers (different but analogous terms do this work in *Being and Time*). Whereas beings seem to be directly accessible to us, Being itself is that which can never possibly come to direct presence through any perception, concept, or other more exotic means. Yet there is another sense of the ontological difference that is too often lumped together with the first. This is the difference between the *unity* of Being and the *plurality* of the various beings. For on the one hand the question of Being does not merely ask about the many possible meanings of "is," but seeks the underlying unity of Being in all its different modes. As the young Heidegger wordlessly wondered when confronted with Brentano's thesis on the multiple meanings of being in Aristotle, "The following question concerned me in quite a vague manner: If being is predicated in multiple meanings, then what is its leading fundamental meaning?"[20] And on the other hand, the sheer multiplicity of individual entities is often greeted by Heidegger with instant scorn: "ink-stand, paper, blotting pad, table, lamp, furniture, windows, door, room. These 'Things' never show themselves proximally as they are for themselves, so as to add up to a sum of *realia* and fill up a room" (BT 97–98). Passages of the latter sort often lead Heideggerians to downplay the significance of individual beings in his philosophy, as if only the primal correlate of Being and Dasein were of any importance, with everything else reduced to role players in the Heideggerian universe. But now notice that when Being is (predictably) assigned to the *ontological* priority of the question of Being, and human Dasein (perhaps surprisingly) to the *ontic* side, nonhuman entities are placed on the side of the *ontological* priority of the question—not the ontic side as we might have expected. After all, "Being is always the Being *of an entity*" (BT 29; emphasis added), and cannot be reified as something outside individual entities.

We now return to the ontico-ontological priority. Heidegger provides us with his missing third term by informing us that "with equal primoridality Dasein also possesses—as constitutive of its understanding of existence—an understanding of the Being of the entities *of a character other than its own.* Dasein has therefore a third priority as providing the ontico-ontological condition for the possibility of any ontologies" (BT 34; emphasis added). In this passage Heidegger slips from speaking of the three priorities of the question of *Being* (as the section headings announce) to speaking of three priorities of *Dasein*, a maneuver not quite justified by anything in the text itself. But more importantly for our purposes, this ontico-ontological priority involves the intersection of Dasein and "entities of a character other than its own." And we may be surprised to find that Dasein provides the "ontico-" half of the new compound word while "other entities" fill up the ontological side.

Moreover, Heidegger views this new third term not just as a flashy innovation of his own, but as one of the classical topics of philosophy:

Dasein's ontico-ontological priority was seen quite early, though Dasein itself was not grasped in its genuine ontological structure, and did not even become a problem in which this structure was sought. Aristotle says ... "Man's soul is, in a certain way, entities " The "soul" which makes up the Being of man ... discovers all entities, both in the fact *that* they are, and in their Being *as* they are—that is, always in their Being. (BT 34)

It is not just that *Dasein* was "not grasped in its genuine ontological structure." The same holds true for the *thing* in the sense of entities not of the character of Dasein. As Heidegger states in his postwar debut in Bremen in 1949: "Plato, who represented the presence of what is present on the basis of outward appearance, thought the essence of things as little as Aristotle and all subsequent thinkers."[21] In other words, things *other* than Dasein were also not seen with sufficient clarity by the greatest Greek philosophers and their later heirs.

But we now need to see how the three priorities of the question of Being link up with the proposed three divisions of Part One of *Being and Time*, only two of them ever completed. Though I am generally not in agreement with the prevailing view that Division I presents the ontic characteristics of Dasein in its everydayness while Division II considers the problem on a "deeper" level by considering it in terms of temporality, this does seem to be Heidegger's own understanding of how the book works. For after spending several pages at the outset of Division II letting us know that Division I was an insufficiently fundamental account, he turns toward the explicitly temporal theme of Division II: "Within the horizon of time the projection of a meaning of Being in general can be accomplished" (BT 278).

Thus, Heidegger's plan for *Being and Time* seems to conceive of Part One as the "ontic" approach to the meaning of Being and Part Two as the "onto-logical" approach. His hesitation and eventual incapacity with respect to the "ontico-ontological" approach seems prefigured by his rushed three-paragraph overview of this third term, hastily clipped to a section whose title evokes the second term ("ontic priority"), following an entire section devoted to the first ("ontological priority"). To summarize, Heidegger was unable to deliver a completed Division III because he was unable to formulate a satisfactory theory of "the Being of the entities of a character other than [Dasein's] own." The completion of Division III of *Being and Time* would have required a presentation of the question of Being not through the factical everyday life of Dasein (completed in Division I) or the structure of Dasein's temporality (available in Division II), but in terms of "all entities, both in the fact *that* they are, and in their Being *as* they are." Division III would have focused on neither of the dual Heideggerian monarchs Dasein and Being, topics already covered in the first two divisions. Instead, a finished Division Three would have given us a new theory of *beings*: the beings of Being, if you will, rather than the Being of beings. It is surely no accident that the central concept of the postwar Heidegger is neither language nor technology. His reflections on these topics depend on one that is even more fundamental for him from 1949 onward: *the thing*.

Additional Remarks in the Form of an Appendix

The pre–World War II Heidegger by no means avoids the topic of beings other than Dasein. I have often argued for the crucial role of the tool-analysis in *Being and Time*, against frequent efforts to treat it as a transient stepping-stone toward the question of Dasein.[22] There is also Heidegger's noteworthy failure in the 1929–30 Freiburg Lecture Course, which feels like a premonition of the eventual failure to appear of Division III. In 1929–30 Heidegger announces a new way of distinguishing between humans, animals, and stones, yet he ultimately divides them according to nothing more than a terminological version of everyday common sense: humans are *world-forming*, animals are *poor in world*, and stones are *worldless*.[23] The ostensible novelty of human "world-forming" and animal "world-poverty" never materializes as anything ontologically useful, memorable, or even clearly discernible. Perhaps more important is the fleeting reference to "metontology" in the 1928 Marburg Lecture Course on Leibniz. As Heidegger tells us there, in high ontico-ontological fashion: "We need a special problematic which has for its proper theme beings as a whole. This new investigation resides in the essence of ontology itself and is the result of its overturning. ... I designate this set of questions *metontology*."[24] Metontology would not be "about" ontology in the sense that metaethics is a preliminary discussion "about" the possibility of ethics. Instead, the prefix "meta-" refers in this context to the Greek *metabole*, an overturning or turnabout. (The hint at Heidegger's own eventual "turn" [*Kehre*] is unmistakable.) But though Heidegger gives only two examples of possible metontological topics (ethics and sexual difference), the never-completed discipline would also have dealt with every possible sort of entity "of a character other than Dasein." As he puts it in the 1928 course:

Metontology is possible only on the basis and in the perspective of the radical ontological problematic and is possible conjointly with it. To think being as the being of beings and to conceive the being problem radically and universally means, at the same time, to make beings thematic in their totality in the light of ontology.[25]

In the second section of this essay ("The Threefold via Hegel, Husserl, and Heidegger"), we reviewed the importance for Husserl of *intentional objects*. In keeping with Husserl's idealism, these objects were not impenetrable to the gaze of knowledge, but could be adequately known in their essence as long as proper phenomenological procedures were followed. Nonetheless, such objects remained external to thought; there was no sublation of the difference between thought and thing, and no commandeering of essence in the name of a more encompassing logic of the concept. Essence for Husserl is certainly not outside all possible knowledge, but is outside thought in a way that (however seemingly contradictory in ontological terms) gives Husserl definitely more of a "realist" flavor than Hegel ever has.

Heidegger's beings retain the non-Hegelian autonomous life found in Husserl's intentional objects. But Heidegger pushes it a step further by placing things outside all possibility of adequate knowledge, whether through the long labor of the negative or the direct but painstaking intuition of essences. Indeed, Heidegger's things are no longer intentional objects of the Husserlian sort, since the jug (for example) need not be the correlate of an intentional act in order to continue holding the wine. In other words, Heidegger's things are even more external and more unsublatable than Husserl's intentional objects. In this respect Heidegger harks back to Kant's too quickly discredited model of the *Ding an sich*. Rather than a phenomenology, Heidegger in Division III could have given us something more like a *noumenology* of things.

Whenever attempts are made to date the "turn" in Heidegger's thinking or to identify his "second *magnum opus*," attention is usually focused on the post-Rectorate 1930s. A far more likely candidate year for the turn, however, would be 1949. There is biographical support for this view, given that 1949 was Heidegger's first postwar appearance following his denazification and borderline nervous breakdown. But there is ample conceptual support as well, given the way in which "Insight Into that Which Is," delivered in Bremen in early December of that year, sounds the keynote for all the great Heideggerian themes of the 1950s: technology, language, distance, and nearness—and especially *the thing*, the central concept in Bremen. I have argued that the thing would also have been the topic of the missing Division III of *Being and Time*, presenting "entities of a character other than Dasein" in an unsublated threefold structure, in keeping with the ontico-ontological priority of being. But of course, the thing in 1949 and later years is portrayed in terms of a *fourfold* structure. Perhaps this is why the Heidegger of 1953 told us as follows: "While the previous editions have borne the designation 'First Half,' this has now been deleted. After a quarter of a century, the second half could no longer be added unless the first were to be presented anew." The threefold of *Being and Time* would need to be rewritten in terms of the fourfold of Bremen. But this would take us beyond the question of the missing *Being and Time*, Part One, Division III.

Notes

1. Martin Heidegger, *Being and Time*, trans. J. Macquarrie and E. Robinson (San Francisco: Harper, 1962), p. 64. All further references to this book will appear in the text in parentheses, preceded by BT.

2. Martin Heidegger, *Kant and the Problem of Metaphysics*, 5th ed., enlarged, trans. R. Taft (Bloomington: Indiana University Press, 1997).

3. Martin Heidegger, *On Time and Being*, trans. J. Stambaugh (New York: Harper-Collins, 1972).

4. Ibid., p. 80.

5. Alain Badiou, *Being and Event*, trans. O. Feltham (London: Continuum, 2005); Alain Badiou, *Being and Event*, vol. 2: *Logics of Worlds*, trans. A. Toscano (London: Continuum, 2009).

6. See, e.g., Markus Gabriel, *Fields of Sense: A New Realist Ontology* (Edinburgh: Edinburgh University Press, forthcoming).

7. See Graham Harman, *Heidegger Explained: From Phenomenon to Thing* (Chicago: Open Court, 2007), p. 181.

8. Martin Heidegger, "On the Essence of Ground," in *Pathmarks*, trans. W. McNeill (Cambridge: Cambridge University Press, 1998).

9. Martin Heidegger, *The Fundamental Concepts of Metaphysics: World, Finitude, Solitude*, trans. W. McNeill and N. Walker (Bloomington: Indiana University Press, 2001).

10. Here Gadamer is right to say that Heidegger's point is not that time is the "horizon" of Being, but that Being itself *is* time. See Hans-Georg Gadamer, *Truth and Method*, trans. J. Weinsheimer and D. Marshall (London: Bloomsbury, 2013), p. 248.

11. G. W. F. Hegel, *Phenomenology of Spirit* (New York: Oxford University Press, 1976); G. W. F. Hegel, *Science of Logic*, trans. A. V. Miller (Amherst, NY: Humanity Books, 1969).

12. For a fine example of a realist response from one of Heidegger's most important students, see Xavier Zubíri, *On Essence*, trans. A. R. Caponigri (Washington, DC: Catholic University Press, 1983).

13. Jacques Derrida, *Of Grammatology*, trans. G. Spivak (Baltimore: The Johns Hopkins University Press, 1998).

14. Martin Heidegger, *History of the Concept of Time: Prolegomena*, trans. T. Kisiel (Bloomington: Indiana University Press, 1985).

15. Franz Brentano, *Psychology from an Empirical Standpoint*, trans. A. Rancurello, D. B. Terrell, and L. McAlister (London: Routledge, 1995).

16. For a fuller summary, see Graham Harman, *The Quadruple Object* (Winchester: Zero Books, 2011).

17. Edmund Husserl, *Logical Investigations*, 2 vols., ed. D. Moran, trans. J. N. Findlay (Oxon: Routledge, 2001).

18. See also the fascinating discussion of the reversal of overheated media in Marshall McLuhan and Eric McLuhan, *Laws of Media: The New Science* (Toronto: University of Toronto Press, 1992).

19. Martin Heidegger, *The Basic Problems of Phenomenology*, trans. A. Hofstadter (Bloomington: Indiana University Press, 1988).

20. Heidegger, *On Time and Being*, p. 74.

21. Heidegger, *Bremen and Freiburg Lectures: Insight into That Which Is and Basic Principles of Thinking*, trans. A. Mitchell (Bloomington: Indiana University Press, 2012), p. 7.

22. Graham Harman, *Tool-Being: Heidegger and the Metaphysics of Objects* (Chicago: Open Court, 2002).

23. Heidegger, *Fundamental Concepts of Metaphysics*.

24. Martin Heidegger, *The Metaphysical Foundations of Logic*, trans. M. Heim (Bloomington: Indiana University Press, 1992), p. 157.

26. Ibid.

7 The Antinomy of Being and the End of Philosophy

Karsten Harries

This essay is an all too brief response to what the editor of this volume calls "one of the most tantalizing questions of Heidegger scholarship, indeed of twentieth-century continental philosophy: What would the Third Division of *Being and Time* have said and why didn't Heidegger ever publish it?" (Braver, pers. comm.). But just what makes these questions so tantalizing? Has Heidegger himself not answered both, or, if not answered, at least suggested where we must look for the answer?

A first answer to the second question is thus hinted at already by Heidegger's introduction to *Being and Time*: That the book we have is only a fragment of the work envisioned at the time is made clear in paragraph 8, which presents us with a sketch of the "Design of the Treatise" (GA2 55/BT 63–64)—with its rushed publication, Heidegger responded to pressure by the dean of the philosophical faculty at Marburg, which had chosen him to succeed Nicolai Hartmann, but he was informed by the ministry in Berlin that a major publication was needed (GA14 99).[1] That "Design" not only tells us that the book we now have contains only the first two divisions of Part One, that is to say roughly one-third of the envisioned two-part work, but also gives us an idea of what the envisioned third section of Part One was supposed to accomplish. As Heidegger explains the overall design of the envisioned work: "If we are to arrive at the basic concept of 'Being' and to outline the ontological conceptions which it requires and the variations which it necessarily undergoes, we need a clue which is concrete. We shall proceed towards the concept of Being by way of an Interpretation of a certain special entity, Dasein, in which we shall arrive at the horizon for the understanding of Being and for the possibility of interpreting it; the universality of the concept of Being is not belied by the relatively 'special' characteristic of our investigation. But this very entity, Dasein, is in itself 'historical,' so its ownmost ontological elucidation necessarily becomes an 'historiological' [*historischen*] Interpretation" (GA2 52–53/BT 63). This tells us that the projected Third Division of Part One, which is here under consideration, would have returned to the task of determining the concept of Being, after an analysis of the temporality of Dasein had provided the necessary horizon. Heidegger's "design" also suggests that such a determination could still only have been provisional in that an adequate determination of the concept of Being is said to call for the three-step destruction of the history of philosophy that Part Two of *Being and Time* was supposed to accomplish, a destruction that would have led the reader back to the origin of Greek ontology and thus to the limit of philosophy as we know it, and with it to a more original understanding of time and Being than allowed for by the phenomenological-transcendental approach adopted in *Being and Time*. Such a "destruction" has to call into question the phenomenological method for which Heidegger thanks his mentor Edmund Husserl in a footnote (GA2 52), a method that remains rooted in the tradition to be "destroyed." Already here then we get a premonition of the collision between the claim of phenomenology to lay firm foundations and an ever growing awareness of the historical embeddedness of thought, a collision that dooms any attempt to arrive at the promised adequate determination of the concept of Being. That impossibility becomes explicit in subsequent works: there is indeed tension already in the very expression "concept of Being" in that Being resists being assigned its place in logical or linguistic space.

Much of the destruction of the history of philosophy promised for the projected Part Two is now available in one form or another, both in Heidegger's lectures and in his published essays. But what about the Third Division of Part One of *Being and Time*? Paragraph 8 gives only its title "Time and Being." What strikes the reader immediately is the reversal that has taken place: instead of journeying from Being to time we now are to return from time to Being, raising the question of whether the much-discussed *Kehre* in Heidegger's path of thinking, supposed to have taken place several years after the publication of *Being and Time*, had in fact already been anticipated in the original projection of the work.

In his *Hüttenexemplar* Heidegger glossed the heading of the Third Division of Part One with this rather cryptic remark:

Die transzendenzhafte Differenz
Die Überwindung des Horizontes als solchen
Die Umkehr in die Herkunft
Das Anwesen aus dieser Herkunft

(GA2 53)

The quasi-transcendent [neither "transcendental" nor "transcendent" seems right]
difference
The surpassing of the horizon as such
The turn back into the origin
Presencing [thought] from this origin

To speak of a *transzendenzhafte Differenz* is to hint that any attempt to
adequately think the relationship of time and Being will demand a fundamental rethinking of the ontological difference as thought in *Being and
Time*. In that book Heidegger still would seem to follow a fundamentally
transcendental approach, inquiring into Being as the presupposition of the
possibility of our experience of beings. But if Being so understood determines *how* beings present themselves, *that* just these beings present themselves must have another source. Must an adequate concept of Being not
do justice to both: the *how* and the *that*? *Transzendenzhaft* hints that any
attempt to think the difference between beings and Being more adequately
will confront us with the need to confront something like the transcendence of Being in a way for which the approach initially taken by *Being
and Time* leaves no room. In his prefatory remark Heidegger had stated his
"provisional aim" as "the Interpretation of time as the possible horizon for
any understanding whatsoever of Being" (GA2 19/BT 21). With this gloss
Heidegger seems to suggest that the thinking that dictated the progress of
Being and Time must give way to a clarification of the origin of that horizon.
The Third Division of Part One was to provide such clarification.

Too much here remains unsaid to give us more than hints of how Heidegger came to think of the issue of "Time and Being," where the much
later lecture of that title and the seminar that followed, in which he recon-
siders what *Being and Time* had left unsaid, demand special attention. This
much, however, is clear: by the time Heidegger wrote the above gloss, he
had come to recognize the insufficiency of what he had envisioned when
beginning work on *Being and Time*, an insufficiency that, having completed
his analytic of Dasein, forced him to abandon the project. But this leaves
the question: How might Division III of Part One of *Being and Time* have
looked as Heidegger initially envisioned it?

Heidegger himself answered this question. He had indeed worked out in
great detail much of what was to be covered in this section. In a later marginal note to the second part of the title of Part One, "The Explication of
Time as the Transcendental Horizon for the Question of Being," he thus
refers us to GA24 (GA2 55), that is, *The Basic Problems of Phenomenology*.
In the beginning of that lecture we find a note, calling it a working out of

Division III of Part One of *Being and Time* (GA24 1) and much ater in that
lecture he reaffirms that interpretation (GA24 460–461). So the question,
what would the Third Division of Part One of *Being and Time* have said,
would seem to receive here its answer: It would have included much of
the material now found in *The Basic Problems of Phenomenology* especially
in its second part. As Friedrich-Wilhelm von Herrmann suggested in his
postscript: "For the thematic of 'Time and Being' the first chapter of Part
Two is decisive. The text published here allows, even given its incompleteness, an understanding of the systematic design (*Grundriss*) of the question
of Being, as it presented itself to Heidegger, given the point that he had
reached at the time on his path of thinking" (GA24 473). Heidegger here
sums up the result of the existential analytic presented in *Being and Time*:
"*The constitution of the Being of Dasein is founded in temporality (Zeitlichkeit).*
… As such temporality (Zeitlichkeit) also *makes possible the thematic interpretation of Being and its articulation and many modes*, i.e. makes possible ontology. Out of this grows a distinct problematic, related to *Zeitlichkeit*. We call
it *Temporalität*. The term '*Temporalität*' is not synonymous with *Zeitlichkeit*,
although it is only its translation. It means temporality, in as much as it
has been thematized as the condition of the understanding of Being and
of ontology as such" (GA24 323–324). The thematization developed in this
chapter remains thus very much within the orbit of the still fundamentally
transcendental approach of *Being and Time*. The essential temporality of
Dasein is analyzed and said to make possible any understanding of Being
(GA24 429). And so Heidegger can claim that "all ontological propositions
are, because assertions about Being, in light of time rightly understood,
a priori propositions" (GA24 461). A priori, he explains, refers to what is
prior. Given our ordinary, that is, as Heidegger puts it, vulgar concept of
time, such a claim makes little sense: first of all and most of the time we
encounter beings, not their Being. That is said to have misled philosophers
again and again. "Because one fails to recognize the extent to which the
interpretation of Being necessarily takes place in the horizon of time, one
has to attempt to explain away the temporal determination of the a priori.
One goes so far as to claim that the a priori, the essences, that is the determination of beings in their Being, was the extra-temporal, what is beyond
time, the timeless" (GA24 462). But such an understanding of the a priori
is said to be misled by the vulgar understanding of time. To gain a more
adequate understanding of the a priori we have to recognize that the vulgar understanding of time descends from and presupposes "original time
(ursprüngliche Zeit) in which the constitution of the Being of Dasein has
its ground. Only the temporality of the understanding of Being allows one

to clarify why the ontological determinations of Being have the character of a priority" (GA24 462). Key here is the concept of possibility. Referring to Kant, Heidegger states: "A priori means what makes beings as beings in *how* and *what* they are possible" (GA24 461), that is, a priori means their Being. But the very origin of possibility, Heidegger insists, is original time.

But in what sense can original time account for things being *what* they are? To be sure, first of all and most of the time we are preoccupied with things, paying no heed to the fact that Being has always already been understood. "This, what is prior, factically existing Dasein has forgotten. If, then the Being, which as 'prior' has always already been understood even though forgotten, is to become the object, the objectification of this prior, of this forgetting, must have the character of a coming back to what was already and in advance understood" (GA24 463). What Heidegger says here, summing up the preceding discussion, may be read as a possible abstract for the missing Third Division of Part One of *Being and Time*, as originally envisioned: "A twofold possibility of the objectification of the pregiven lies essentially in the essence of Dasein. Factically the possibility of two basic kinds of science is given with the existence of Dasein: the objectification of beings as positive science, and the objectification of science as temporal, i.e. transcendental science, ontology, philosophy" (GA24 466). What Heidegger here calls phenomenology is the effort to gain step by step "access to Being as such and to work out its structures" (GA24 466). The key to phenomenology so understood is said to be the step back to original time. But Heidegger also warns us not to expect results that would allow us to say that we had finally arrived at our goal: "The only thing that is truly new in science and in philosophy is genuine questioning and the battle with things that serves them" (GA24 467).

Far from having led Heidegger to some sort of foundation, the question of Being was rendered more questionable by his attempt to ground it in the constitution of Dasein and that in turn in original time. In *The Basic Problems of Phenomenology* this difficulty shows itself in the paragraph just preceding its second part. Heidegger here takes up the problem of truth in a way that remains close to the parallel discussion in *Being and Time*. "The problem concentrates itself in the question: how does the existence of truth relate to Being and the way and manner in which Being is?" (GA24 318). There is no truth, Heidegger had shown, without Dasein (GA24 316). And so he asks: "Is there Being only, when truth exists, i.e. when Dasein exists? Does whether there is Being or not depend on the existence of Dasein?" (GA24 317). Heidegger's fundamental ontology would seem to demand that we answer this question affirmatively. But does this mean that there was no Being before human beings came into existence? His answer invites questioning: "The kind and manner, in which Being is and alone can be, prejudges nothing concerning whether and how beings can be as beings" (GA24 317). Earlier he had explained: "Before their discovery Newton's laws were neither true nor false. That cannot mean that the beings that are uncovered with the revealed laws before that were not so, as they showed themselves after their uncovering, and, as showing themselves thus, are. The discovering, i.e. the truth reveals beings precisely as what they already were, without regard to their being discovered or not" (GA24 314). To be what it is, Heidegger rightly insists, nature does not need to disclose itself to human beings, that is, does not need truth. But do we not want to say then that nature transcends Dasein and thus also truth and that primordial time which Heidegger's fundamental ontology ties inseparably to Dasein? And if we have to think nature in this way, do we not also think of Being as transcending the Dasein-dependent Being to which *Being and Time* sought to lead us? And does this not also hold for time? Must what Heidegger here calls original time not have its origin in something still more primordial?

The discussion of truth in *The Basic Problems of Phenomenology*, and more especially the cited Newton passage, tracks and expands on the parallel discussion in paragraphs 43 and 44 of *Being and Time*. There already Heidegger faces the need to take a step beyond an understanding of Being that makes it dependent on Dasein and thus beyond his own existential analysis. To be sure, no more than in the *Basic Problems* does Heidegger recognize at this point a deep challenge to his project:

But the fact that Reality is ontologically grounded in the Being of Dasein does not signify that only when Dasein exists and as long as Dasein exists, can the Real be as that which in itself it is.

Of course only as long as Dasein is (that is only as long as an understanding of Being is ontically possible), "is there" Being. When Dasein does not exist, "independence" "is" not either, nor "is" the "in-itself." In such a case this sort of thing can be neither understood nor not understood. In such a case even entities within-the world can neither be discovered nor lie hidden. In such a case it cannot be said that entities are, nor can it be said that they are not. But now, as long as there is an understanding of Being and therefore an understanding of presence-at-hand, it can indeed be said that in this case entities will still continue to be. (GA2 211–212/BT 255)

Like the Newton passage cited above, this would seem to force us to think "beings" as transcending "Being." But to think them in that way, must we not attribute to them some sort of transcendent Being? But if so, Heidegger warns us, such Being cannot be understood. The attempt to grasp the essence of Being here suffers shipwreck. Key to that shipwreck is what elsewhere ¯ have called the *antinomy of Being*, which forces us, on one hand, to think Being relative to Dasein, and on the other, as transcending Dasein. I developed that antinomy in an essay with that title that appeared in *The Cambridge Companion to Existentialism*,[2] and much more fully in a book I just published in German with the title *Wahrheit: Die Architektur der Welt*.[3] Heidegger had to confront this antinomy in *Being and Time*, in his attempt to think the ontological difference. When we approach that difference from the perspective of his transcendental phenomenology, we will want to say: Being is constitutive of and in this sense transcends beings. Beings can present themselves only to a being that is such as we are, a being that, embodied and dwelling in language, is open to a world in which beings have to take their place and present themselves if they are "to be" at all. And so Heidegger came to call language the house of Being. The way beings present themselves is always mediated by the body, by language, by history, and founded in the being of Dasein as care. In the *Letter on Humanism*, Heidegger will repeat thus the sentence: "Only as long as Dasein is, is there [*gibt es*] Being" (GA9 336/216).

But Heidegger qualifies this when he speaks in paragraph 43 of *Being and Time* of the dependence of Being, but not of beings, of reality, but not of the real, on care, that is, on the always understanding and caring being of human beings (GA2 281/BT 255). In "The Letter on Humanism" this qualification becomes: "But the fact that the Da, the lighting as the truth of Being itself, comes to pass is the dispensation of Being itself" (GA9 336). There is therefore a sense in which beings and the real can be said to transcend that Being (Sein) which is said to be relative to Dasein. To be sure, these beings could not "be" in the first sense without human beings. Only human consciousness provides the open space, the clearing that allows things to be perceived, understood, and cared for. That space is a presupposition of the accessibility of things, of their Being. But this is not to say that we in any sense create these beings. They are given to us. Our experience of the reality of the real is thus an experience of beings as transcending Being so understood. This invites a distinction between two senses of Being: the first a transcendental sense relative to Dasein and in this sense inescapably historical, and the second a transcendent sense, gesturing toward the ground or origin of Dasein's historical being and thus also of Being understood transcendentally. Transcendent Being dispenses "the Da, the lighting as the truth of Being." But any attempt to lay hold of that originating ground threatens to transform it into a being, such as God, and must inevitably fail. Here our thinking bumps against the limits of

language. Being refuses to be imprisoned in the house of language. And yet
this ground is somehow present itself to us, calls us, if in silence opening a
window to transcendence in our world, a world shaped for us by the progress of philosophy, that is, of metaphysics. The evolution of Heidegger's
thought since *Being and Time* can thus be described as supplementing the
silent call of conscience with the silent call of transcendent Being (gestured
toward by his understanding of "earth"[4]), where there is a suggestion that
only as a response to the latter can there be authentic speech that would
seem to be inseparable from authentic dwelling. To speak here of a *Kehre*, as
Heidegger himself does for the first time in print in the "Letter on Humanism" (GA9 328), is misleading, in that it suggests a reversal. But, as Heidegger points out, "there has been no change of standpoint." The question
of Being remains central. The so-called *Kehre* is thus better understood, as
Heidegger himself here describes it, not as a philosophical advance, but as a
more thoughtful attempt to attend to the matter to be thought (GA9 343).
What makes it necessary is the antinomial essence of Being, which denies
the thinker a foundation. The antinomy of Being shows us why we cannot
dispense with something like the Kantian understanding of the thing-in-
itself as the ground of phenomena.

In his brief postscript to *The Basic Problems of Phenomenology* von Herrmann
reminds us that Heidegger's thinking must be understood as essentially
underway. This has of course been recognized. Thus it has become custom-
ary to contrast *Being and Time* and the immediately following published
works, *The Essence of Reasons, Kant and the Problem of Metaphysics,* and *What
is Metaphysics?*—and we can now add to these *The Basic Problems of Phenomenology* and other lectures—with the later works, beginning with the *Introduction to Metaphysics* and *The Origin of the Work of Art* (1935). Pöggeler and
von Herrmann have celebrated the posthumously published *Beiträge zur
Philosophie (Vom Ereignis)* (1936–38), *Contributions to Philosophy,* published
as GA65, as Heidegger's second main work, which is said to make the turn
from a Dasein-centered explication of the problem of time as horizon of the
question of Being to a restatement of this question in terms of the history
of Being.[5] *The Beiträge* can thus be understood as the most worked out, certainly the most ambitious attempt to meet the promise made for Division
III of Part One of *Being and Time*. But to speak here of a *Kehre* can be misleading, in that it may lead us to overlook the way in which such a turning
is demanded already by the progress of Heidegger's thinking in *Being and
Time,* by his growing awareness of the temporal situatedness of Dasein and
its implications for the project "to arrive at the basic concept of 'Being.'"

That suffices to explain why Heidegger left *Being and Time* a torso, choosing not to gather the many pages he had amassed to finish the book as originally envisioned. Being refuses to be imprisoned in the house of language.

Did the so-called *Kehre* allow Heidegger to advance beyond the position at which he had arrived in *Being and Time*? Or does the question of Being as developed in *Being and Time* present itself as a limit where philosophy reaches some sort of end? In the *Letter on Humanism* Heidegger suggests just this: "It is everywhere supposed that the attempt in *Being and Time* ended in a blind alley [*Sackgasse*]" (GA9 343/222). Heidegger leaves that supposition standing, hinting that not only his philosophy but perhaps all philosophy understood as metaphysics had reached here something like a dead end. "The thinking that hazards a few steps in *Being and Time* has even today not advanced beyond that publication. But perhaps in the meantime it has in one respect penetrated further into its own matter" (GA9 343/222).

This further movement led Heidegger to redescribe the path of his thinking, not as a *Sackgasse*, but as a *Holzweg* (GA13 91). And so he gave the most important collection of essays he published the title *Holzwege* (GA5). But what is the difference? Do not *Sackgasse* and *Holzweg* both suggest a path that lets us miss the intended goal? The transcendental path Heidegger followed in *Being and Time* indeed did not lead him to the intended goal. But if *Sackgasse* lets us think of some urban cul-de-sac that invites us to retrace our steps, *Holzweg* has a very different connotation. As Heidegger explains in the very beginning of *Holzwege*:

Holz lautet ein alter Name für Wald. Im Holz sind Wege, die meist verwachsen jäh im Unbegangenen aufhören,
Sie heißen Holzwege.
Jeder verläuft gesondert, aber im selben Wald. Oft scheint es, als gleiche einer dem anderen. Doch es scheint nur so.
Holzmacher und Waldhüter kennen die Wege. Sie wissen, was es heißt, auf einem Holzweg zu sein.

(GA5, iii)

Holz is an old name for a wood. In such a wood are paths that suddenly stop in the untrodden.
They are called *Holzwege* (woodpaths).
Everyone takes its separate course, but in the same wood. Often it seems as if one were the same as another. But it only seems that way.
Wood cutters and foresters know these paths. They know what it means to be on a *Holzweg*.

(My trans.)

Holzweg names a path that is cut into the forest to enable loggers to bring out the trees they have cut. This meaning should be kept in mind. A *Holzweg* is thus a path that does not lead where those who wanted to get somewhere were expecting to go. Such a path leads nowhere and suddenly stops. Because *Holzwege* are not commonly used, they tend to be overgrown and difficult to walk. Often such a *Holzweg* will lead to an open place in the forest where some trees have been cut down, that is, into a clearing. But clearing, *Lichtung*, is a key metaphor Heidegger uses to describe the Being of Dasein, where this choice of metaphor, which joins light and an open place, provides a good example of the point of Heidegger's metaphorical speaking. (Consider in this connection Descartes's understanding of the "open space" that separates subject and object and of the need for a *lumen naturale*.)

The expression *auf einem Holzweg sein* is used in German to suggest that we have lost our way, precisely that condition which Wittgenstein took to describe the form of a genuinely philosophical problem. Greek philosophy spoke of *aporia*. To be on a *Holzweg* usually means that you have taken a wrong turn. And traveling with Heidegger you may well find yourself disappointed. Significant questions go unanswered. In an important sense, Heidegger's path leads nowhere. And yet, leading nowhere, it leads us back to ourselves.

One last thing: a *Holzweg* begins in a familiar landscape, as Heidegger's path of thinking begins in the (to many philosophers) still familiar landscapes of neo-Kantianism and transcendental phenomenology, only to end in the bewildering and unfamiliar.

Heidegger's late essay "Zeit und Sein" ("Time and Being," 1962) presents itself to us as such a *Holzweg*. The title may suggest that after thirty-five years, Heidegger had decided to complete, in the only way he then still thought possible, what he had left unfinished for so long, thus giving his belated version of Division III of Part One of *Being and Time*. Instead, the essay casts further light on why Division III had to remain unwritten and the project of *Being and Time* unfinished. Especially illuminating with respect to the relationship of the essay to the unwritten Third Division of *Being and Time* is Alfredo Guzzoni's "Protokoll zu einem Seminar über den Vortrag 'Zeit und Sein'" ("Summary of a Seminar on the Lecture 'Time and Being'") that Heidegger chose to include in the original edition of *Zur Sache des Denkens* (1969). The very project of a fundamental ontology, that is, the entire project of *Being and Time*, is here called into question: "The decisive matter that here must be considered is the relationship of fundamental ontology to the one question in search of the meaning of Being for which *Being and Time* is the preparation. According to *Being and Time* fundamental ontology is the ontological analytic of Dasein. 'Hence *fundamental ontology*, from which alone all others can arise, must be sought in the *existential analytic of Dasein*' (GA2 18)." Accordingly, it appears as if fundamental ontology were the foundation for the still missing ontology itself, which is to be raised on this foundation. (GA14 39). But this is a misleading impression. This supposedly fundamental ontology is unable to provide us with a *fundamentum inconcussum* on which we might then raise our philosophical edifice; rather, it provides us with a *fundamentum concussum* (GA14 40). What shakes this supposed foundation is what I called above the antinomy of Being; that antinomy is inseparable from the temporality of Dasein.

In *Being and Time*, as I suggested, this antinomy announces itself in the questions raised by Heidegger's claim that, while Being cannot be without Dasein, that cannot be said of beings. And of course, there were countless things before there were human beings. But how is this "were" to be understood? And what about the locution "Being cannot be without Dasein"? Is that to be understood as a tautology? In Heidegger's transcendental sense, these beings that were before human beings indeed had no Being. But Heidegger does not deny that they were.

In "Time and Being" this antinomy shows itself throughout the text in the difficulty Heidegger has saying what is to be thought, a difficulty of which he himself reminds us with his closing sentence, which calls attention to the way assertions, with which such a lecture cannot dispense, must fail us when trying to answer the question of Being (GA14 30). Thinking here bumps against the limits of language.

Consider the following paragraph:

Die Zeit ist nicht. Es gibt Zeit. Das Geben, das Zeit gibt, bestimmt sich aus der verweigernd-vorenthaltenen Nähe. Sie gewährt das Offene des Zeit-Raumes und verwahrt, was im Gewesenen verweigert, was in der Ankunft vorenthalten bleibt. Wir nennen das Geben, das die eigentliche Zeit gibt, das lichtend-verbergende Reichen. Insofern das Reichen selber ein Geben ist, verbirgt sich in der eigentlichen Zeit das Geben eines Gebens. (GA14 20)

Time *is* not. There is, It gives time. The giving that gives time is determined by denying and withholding nearness. It grants the openness of time-space and preserves what remains denied in what has been, what is withheld in approach. We call the giving which gives true time an extending which opens and conceals. As extending is itself a giving, the giving of a giving is concealed in true time. (Trans., 16)

The first two sentences draw us into the antinomy of Being. At first reading we seem to be presented with a contradiction. The German *es gibt x* is often used simply to state that *x* exists. So understood "Es gibt Zeit" would appear to contradict "Die Zeit ist nicht," "Time is not." To guard against such a reading the translator, Joan Stambaugh, italicizes "is" to remind us that in the sense in which entities are, time is indeed not, no more than Being is. Her translation of "Es gibt Zeit" as "There is, It gives time" demands that "is" now has to be understood differently. But just what is the difference? The first formulation reminds us that time is no thing; it is in this sense nothing. But it is nevertheless present in the presencing of things, present even in our thoughts of what is no longer and in our expectation of what is to come. As thus presupposed, it was to provide the key to an understanding of Being. How then is the Being of time to be understood? The second formulation invites us to link this Being to a giving. Giving suggests a giver. But how are we to understand this "It" that is said to give time and with it that time-space in which everything that can be must take its place? We may be tempted to invoke God and understand time, too, with the Marschallin in Hugo von Hofmannsthal's *Rosenkavalier* as a divine gift. But any such appeal is ruled out by Heidegger's insistence that ontological inquiry not blur the ontological difference by appealing to some being as the ground of the Being of beings. But had not *Being and Time* done just that when asserting that only as long as Dasein exists is there Being? Heidegger now insists that his Being be understood not just as being present (to Dasein) but as being given. But again: how then are we to think this giving without both a giver and a recipient?

Already in *Being and Time* what is fundamentally the same question is posed by Heidegger's understanding of Dasein as *geworfen*, as essentially cast or thrown into the world of things. What or who is here the thrower? There are obvious ontic answers in terms of the past that has made us who we are, but all such answers already presuppose that this past has disclosed itself, presuppose the finite Being of Dasein. And so Heidegger could write: "If what the term 'idealism' says amounts to the understanding that Being can never be explained by entities but is already that which is 'transcendental' for every entity, then idealism affords the only correct possibility for a philosophical problematic. If so Aristotle was no less an idealist than Kant" (GA2 275/251). But this does not mean that the realist is not right to insist that the existence of other entities does not depend on the existence of the entity that I am. Cast into the world Dasein essentially finds itself in the midst of what is given. But again the question arises: who or what is the giver of that gift? There is the obvious answer that the very question fails to recognize the ontological difference. We are left with an understanding of Being as the presencing of things. A deeper understanding of time was to help us to reach a more adequate understanding of the mode or modes of their presencing, of their Being. But such presencing must be understood as a being given and time itself, Heidegger now insists, is part of the gift. Being and time are so intimately joined that they cannot be untangled.

Has "Time and Being" progressed beyond *Being and Time*? In terms of *Being and Time* the question "What gives time?" could only be answered with: "Dasein's essentially temporal being in-the-world." In the passage cited above, Heidegger answers this question by invoking "denying and withholding nearness," "verweigernd-vorenthaltene Nähe" (GA14, 21). This *Nähe* Heidegger understands as "true time," "Die eigentliche Zeit": "True time is the nearness of presencing out of present, past and future— the nearness that unifies time's threefold opening transcending" (GA14 21/16). This is to say that what is no longer present or not yet present, while not present in one sense, is yet somehow present in its absence. Heidegger glossed "eigentlich" with "'eigentlich' + zum Ereignis gehörend/von der ekstatischen/Zeitlichkeit des Da-seins/Zum Eigenen der Zeit" (GA14 21). Ever since 1936 *Ereignis* is, according to Heidegger himself (GA9 316), the key word in his thinking.[6] In ordinary German, *Ereignis* means first of all simply "event" or "happening"; with Heidegger it means the happening of Dasein. Heidegger's translators have struggled with the word, which Stambaugh translates as "appropriation"—misleading, but preferable to the unbearably tortured "enownment." Here *Ereignis* names "What determines both, time and Being, in their own, that is, in their belonging together" (GA14 24/19). But this names nothing other than the Being of Dasein, underscoring, however, that this Being is in its essence historical and as such determines the way we experience persons and things, their Being. As far as responsible thinking can reach, that destiny is essentially groundless. The recourse to original time cannot provide ontology with the foundation that Heidegger once had promised.

As Heidegger pointed out in the *Letter on Humanism*, since *Being and Time* there had been no real progress in his thinking, but he had explored more deeply the question of Being. Such exploration had opened up an abyss into which responsible thinking cannot descend. And in the process, it has become clear that no determination of the Being of things can claim to provide philosophical thinking with a definitive foundation. There is indeed a sense in which with *Being and Time*, not only Heidegger's thinking but philosophy had come to an end. And so it seems fitting that Heidegger chose to include in the volume *Zur Sache des Denkens*, together with "Time and Being" "The End of Philosophy and the Task of Thinking" 1964). Why does any of this matter? What task remains for thinking after the end of philosophy as understood by Heidegger? Heidegger h nts at the answer with this remark: "The effect proves the correctness of technological scientific rationalization. But is the manifest character of what-is exhausted by the demonstrable? Doesn't the insistence on what is demonstrable block the way to what is?" (GA14 89/72). At stake is the legitimacy of the world we live in, a world shaped by our science and technology. This is also to say: at stake is our humanity.

Notes

1. References in the text are to the following volumes of the Martin Heidegger's *Gesamtausgabe* (Frankfurt am Main: Vittorio Klostermann), listed below. When I use a translation, the page reference follows that to the German original.

GA2   *Sein und Zeit* (1927)
        Being and Time, trans. John Macquarrie and Edward Robinson (New York: Harper & Row, 1962)
GA5   *Holzwege* (1935–46)
GA9   *Wegmarken* (1919–1958)
        "Letter on Humanism," trans. Frank A. Capuzzi and J. Glenn Gray, *Basic Writings*, ed. David Farrell Krell (New York: Harper & Row, 1977)
GA14   *Zur Saches des Denkens* (1969)
        On Time and Being, trans. Joan Stambaugh (New York: Harper & Row, 1972)
GA24   *Die Grundprobleme der Phanomenologie* (1927)

2. Karsten Harries, "The Antinomy of Being: Heidegger's Critique of Humanism," in *The Cambridge Companion to Existentialism*, ed. Steven Crowell (Cambridge: Cambridge University Press, 2012), pp. 178–198.

3. Karsten Harries, *Wahrheit: Die Architektur der Welt* (Paderborn: Wilhelm Fink, 2012).

4. See Karsten Harries, *Art Matters: A Critical Commentary on Heidegger's* The Origin of the Work of Art (New York: Springer, 2009), pp. 109–123, nn. 7–8.

5. Cf. Friedrich-Wilhelm von Herrmann, "Technology, Politics, and Art in Heidegger's *Beiträge zur Philosophie*," trans. Karsten Harries and Parvis Emad, in *Martin Heidegger: Politics, Art, and Technology*, ed. Karsten Harries and Christoph Jamme (New York: Holmes & Meier, 1994), pp. 55–70.

6. See Günter Seuboldt and Thomas Schmaus, "Ereignis: Was immer schon geschehen ist, bevor wir etws tun," in *Heidegger-Handbuch: Leben-Werk-Wirkung*, ed. Dieter Thomä (Stuttgart, Weimar: Metzler, 2003), pp. 302–336.

8   The Drafts of "Time and Being": Division III of Part One of *Being and Time* and Beyond

Theodore Kisiel

The first volume of *Being and Time* was drafted in the course of 1926 under publish-or-perish conditions and appeared in print in April 1927 under the title "Being and Time, First Half," both as a separate edition and together with only one other lengthy article (Oskar Becker's "Mathematische Existenz") in Husserl's *Jahrbuch für Philosophie und phänomenologische Forschung*. The decision to divide his opus magnum into two volumes was made in the first days of January 1927, as Heidegger relates it in retrospect, during a visit to Karl Jaspers in Heidelberg, "on the day that the news of Rilke's death reached us" (GA49 40). The purpose of the visit was to discuss the page proofs of *Sein und Zeit* (SZ) that Heidegger had been forwarding to Jaspers. During the course of this visit, it became clear to Heidegger that his elaboration up to that point of the pivotal Third Division of *Being and Time*, entitled "Time and Being," would have been incomprehensible to keen minds like Jaspers and Rilke. The published portion thus contains only the first two divisions of the systematic Part One of *Being and Time*. "Moreover, external circumstances (the excessive length of the *Jahrbuch* volume) fortunately prevented the publication of this division [I.3]" (GA66 413/M 366). Its first elaboration "was 'destroyed,' but a new start was made, on a more historical path, in the lecture course of Summer Semester 1927" (GA66 413–414/M 366–367). Combined historical-systematic attempts seeking a lucid elaboration of various aspects of this crucial Third Division continued into 1930. Heidegger's still unpublished file of notes entitled "Supplements to *Being and Time*"[1] contains the draft of a preface to the third edition of the book, handwritten in the middle of 1930, which announces a completely new reworking of the published first half of *Being and Time* and a second half that would embody only the Third Division of Part One, sufficiently surcharged historically. But in 1931, the third edition of *Being and Time, First Half* appeared unchanged. The book project entitled *Being and Time* had now finally come to a dead end (*Holzweg*), although Heidegger communicated his decision to abandon this path through *Being and Time* in personal letters to only a few confidants. For example, on September 18, 1932, he writes to Elisabeth Blochmann: "People think that I am writing SZ II, and are even talking about it. That's OK with me. SZ I was once a path that led me somewhere, but this path is now no longer trodden and has become overgrown. That is why I can no longer write SZ II. I am not writing any book."[2] Even earlier, on November 14, 1931, Heidegger writes to Rudolf Bultmann about new directions in his work now being carried out behind "the mask of someone who 'is writing his second volume.'"[3]

We begin with an attempt to reconstruct Heidegger's various efforts toward drafting the Third Division immediately after the completion of the "First Half" of *Being and Time*, starting with the "unintelligible" version that was therefore "destroyed" (*vernichtet*).

References to the Very First Draft of the Third Division

Textual references. In the earliest editions of *Being and Time* (until the seventh edition) one finds a footnote to §68d on "The Temporality of Discourse" (SZ 349) that provides an insight into the thematic structure of the very first draft of the Third Division—that is, the "systematic" draft that was said to be completely incomprehensible to intellects like Rilke and Jaspers. The footnote reads, "Cf. Division Three, Chapter II of this treatise" and is attached to the following hermeneutically charged sentence: "It is only out of the temporality of discourse, i.e., of Dasein as such, that the 'emergence' of 'meaning' can be clarified and the possibility of any concept formation be made ontologically intelligible" (SZ 349). This section also refers to problems that in part are already indicated in §69 as substantive themes to be treated in Division III, such as the development of the problem of the connection in principle between being and truth on the basis of the problematic of temporality. But in §68d the elaboration of this basic problem of phenomenology now becomes the presupposition for "the analytic of the temporal constitution of discourse and the explication of the temporal characteristics of language-structures" (SZ 349). Central to an ontological explication of discourse is the widely dispersed grammar of the verb "to be" in the classification of the variations of its conjugation. For discourse does not primarily temporalize itself in one particular ecstasis. The verb is grounded in the whole of the ecstatic unity of temporality. Furthermore, the three tenses are mingled with "the other temporal phenomena of language—'aspects' ['*Aktionsarten*'] and 'temporal stages' ['*Zeitstufen*']." In particular, contemporary linguistics, which is obliged to carry out its analyses with the help of the common concept of time, cannot even pose the "problem of [the] existential-temporal structure" of aspects (SZ 349).

Verbal action is grammatically divided into three basic types: (1) momentaneous, instantaneous, iterative; (2) continuous, ongoing, lasting, imperfect; and (3) perfect, complete, perfecting. This grammatical division of verbal action ("aspects") will find an experiential variant in the phenomenological division of three types of boredom in the winter semester (WS) 1929–30, which are based accordingly on a wavering fleeting time, a limited constant time, and the time of Dasein as a whole, which is spellbound by a horizon. For horizonal time as Temporality is an ontological, transcendental, or a priori perfect that "characterizes the kind of being belonging to Dasein itself" (SZ 85). "Each ecstasis as such has a horizon that is determined by it and that first of all completes that ecstasis' own structure." The open horizon where each ecstasis ends is a perfective sign of the finitude of temporality, for "this end is nothing but the beginning and starting point for the possibility of all projecting." The enabling of the transcendental perfect has the character of a prior letting-be (*Seinlassen*) (SZ 85), where the perfective suffix is both active and passive, in the ambiguity of the middle voice: it means both already-having-let-be-in-each-case and letting-be. Thus we have a series of perfective existentials in *Being and Time*: thrown*ness*, disposed*ness*, disclosed*ness*, fallen*ness*, resolute*ness*, and so on. The perfect expresses an action that has somehow become definitive and that is always still in the further process of becoming. The perfect is used only when the effect of earlier activity is still at work. Heidegger comments, for example, that in perception, understood in terms of intentionality, what is central is neither perceiving nor the perceived; instead, perceivedness is the enabling center of the intentionality of perception, the sense of its intentional direction, which is neither subjective nor objective and which, as what makes perception possible, can ultimately be understood only on the basis of the essence of time.

Archival reference. Included with Heidegger's manuscript of the lecture course of WS 1925–26 in the Heidegger Archives in Marbach, there is a file of some 200 pages wrapped in a sheet marked "I.3." A selection of 30 pages from this text has been published, but these include none of the many pages—and an entire file—that are marked with the number "69." The entire folder is a collection of notes that refer to the themes, and even to particular chapters, of the unpublished Division III, probably written in the course of 1926. A summary of the classification of the notes suggests a division into about six chapters of Division III. Chapter 1 would have probably borne a title such as "Phenomenology and the Positive Sciences" and would have treated the method of ontological (as opposed to ontical) thematization. "Temporality (*Zeitlichkeit*) and Worldliness" is he explicit title of Chapter 4, which would have taken its themes primarily from §69c of *Being and Time*, which bears the title "The Temporal Problem of the Transcendence of the World." One also finds remarks, expressions, and turns of phrase throughout this text that do not appear in Heidegger's known lectures and publications: for example, the division of awaiting into "expectative—presentative—perfective"; "moments of existence" such as "the formally futural" and "the formally perfect"; and the claim that "time is a self-projection upon itself (its horizonal [self-projection], its ecstatic [self-projection])." A thorough study of the entire file can deepen our knowledge of the direction and goals of the missing Division III, and enrich the attempt to reconstruct it.

Summer Semester 1927: *The Basic Problems of Phenomenology*

Propaedeutic. "That the intentionality of 'consciousness' is grounded in the ecstatical unity of Dasein, and how this is the case, will be shown in the following division" (SZ 363n.). The markers that project the contents of the Third Division that would have concluded the systematic Part One of *Being and Time* are clustered around the pivotal §69. Section 69 refers not only to the "idea of phenomenology, as distinguished from the preliminary conception of it which we indicated by way of introduction [§7]," but also to the corresponding "existential conception of science" and its understanding "of the ontological genesis of the theoretical attitude." "Yet a fully adequate existential interpretation of science cannot be carried out until the *meaning of being and the 'connection' ['Zusammenhang'] between being and truth* have been *clarified* in terms of the temporality of existence" (SZ 357). And this clarification is the "central problematic" (SZ 357) of Division III. As a preparation for these tasks of the following division, §69c (SZ 364–366) develops "the temporal problem of the transcendence of the world," that is, the problem of how the world temporalizes itself as the toward-which of the temporal ecstases into a horizonal unity in accordance with the "horizonal schemata"—the respective "whithers" of the ecstases. The temporal transcendence of the world is thereby founded ecstatically-horizonally. The ecstatical unity of temporality is also designated at the start of §9 as the cleared clearing of Dasein, which grounds the disclosedness of the there (cf. SZ 350–351). The clarification of the connection between being and truth thus begins with Dasein, whose fundamental characteristic is the understanding of being. In turn, the understanding of being is made possible by disclosedness, that is, disposed understanding—dynamically understood as thrown projecting (cf. §44c, SZ 230). The thrown projection that is Dasein in its ek-sistence is ultimately—and so finitely—grounded in ecstatical temporality, in the cleared clearing of the there. In this way time is used as the "preliminary name" for truth, which is now understood as disclosedness, clearing, and unconcealment. "Being [projected as time] and truth 'are' equiprimordially" (SZ 230).

Summer semester 1927. Heidegger's older students like Karl Löwith knew in advance that the lecture course of summer semester (SS) 1927 was to be a "new elaboration of Division 3 of Part One of *Being and Time*" (GA24 1/BP 1) by way of a more historical path. But because of the long historical detour that it takes through the "destruction" of four traditional theses about being in order to come to four basic problems of phenomenological ontology, the course covers only a part of the path projected in §69 toward establishing the correlation of being and truth in terms of temporality, before it had to be broken off for lack of time.

The "first and last and basic problem" of a phenomenological science of being is: "How is the understanding of being at all possible?" (GA24 19/BP 15). More explicitly, "Whence—that is, from which antecedently given horizon—do we understand the like of being?" (GA24 21/BP 16). The already developed analytic of Dasein gives a first answer: "Time is the horizon from which something like being becomes understandable at all. We interpret being by way of time (*tempus*). The interpretation is a Temporal [*temporale*] one. The fundamental subject of research in ontology ... is Temporality [*Temporalität*]" (GA24 22/BP 17). Ontology is not only a critical and transcendental science (cf. GA24 23/BP 17), but also a Temporal one (cf. GA24 324/BP 228), which is hence quite different from all other, so-called positive sciences. But it is like the positive sciences in one way. A positive science must objectify the entities that lie before it upon the latent horizon of their particular being, upon the whither of the "projection of the ontological constitution of a region of beings" (GA24 457/BP 321). Similarly, ontology must objectify being itself "upon the horizon of its understandability" (GA24 459/BP 322)—that is, upon Temporality. Ontology becomes a Temporal science "because Temporal projection makes possible an objectification [*Vergegenständlichung*] of being and assures conceptualizability, and thereby constitutes ontology in general as a science" (GA24 459–460/BP 323). "It is in the objectification of being as such that the ground act constituting ontology as a science is performed" (GA24 398/BP 281). This basic act has "the function of *explicitly* projecting what is antecedently given upon that toward which it has *already* been projected [and unveiled] in pre-scientific experience or [preconceptual] understanding" (GA24 399/BP 282; transl. modified). The explicit objectification "thematizes" (GA24 398/BP 281), and "thematization objectifies" (S. 363). This explicit articulation of the basic concepts of a science, or explicit interpretation of its guiding understanding of being, determines the distinctive conceptual structure of the science, the possibility of truth that pertains to it, and its manner of communicating its true propositions (SZ 362–363). The true propositions of scientific ontology are a priori, transcendental, and Temporal (GA24 460–461/BP 323–324). The phenomenological language of being as such is the language of Temporality, which is properly "the transcendental horizon for the question of being" (GA24 461/BP 324). With this, the announced goal of Division III, "the explication of time" as just such an interrogative horizon, has been reached (SZ 39). Thus, Temporality is the transcendental horizon of the understanding of being especially in its more question-worthy moments in the radical questioning "of" being.

Temporality (*Temporalität*) is the temporality (*Zeitlichkeit*) already laid out in the existential analytic of Da-sein but now thematized in its function as condition of possibility of the pre-ontological and ontological understanding of being, and thus of ontology as such (GA24 324/BP 228, 388/274). In this function, Temporality is "the most originative temporalizing of temporality as such" (GA24 429/BP 302). As the most original temporality, it is the most radical—the temporality that is fundamentally factical down to its abyssal ground, that is, the "propriating event" (*Er-eignis*), if we may here use the later Heidegger's favorite word for be-ing. But in 1927 Heidegger hesitates to plunge into the concealed depths of temporality, "above all with regard to its Temporality," and to enter "the problem of the finitude of time" (GA24 437/BP 307–308).

One reason for this hesitation lies in the incompleteness of the analyses of Temporality as a whole as "temporality with regard to the unity of the horizonal schemata belonging to it" (GA24 436/BP 307). The horizon of ecstatic temporality is understood more precisely as the horizonal schema of the corresponding ecstasis. For every ecstasis, as a removal-unto, also has in it an anticipation of the formal structure of the "whither" of the remotion, which is never an indefinite removal into nothingness. This anticipated whither of the ecstasis is the horizonal schema that belongs to it (GA24 428–429/BP 302). In *Being and Time* (SZ 365), the horizonal schemata are expressed prepositionally, that is, in a meaninglike way, following the model of meaning as the prestructured toward-which (SZ 151): the for-the-sake-of (the ecstasis of the future as coming-toward), the from-which of thrownness or the to-which of abandonment (past as having-been,

Gewesenhei), the in-order-to (present). But in SS 1927, Heidegger proposes to designate the horizonal schemata with the Latin expressions for the "tenses" (*Tempora*) of time. "Here, in the dimension of the interpretation of being via time, we are purposely making use of Latinate expressions for all the determinations of time, in order to keep them distinct in the terminology itself from the time-determinations in the previously described sense" (GA24 433/BP 305). *Praesens* is used instead of "present" (*Gegenwart*), where *praesens* now means the horizonal schema of the present. More precisely, *praesens* (instead of the in-order-to) is supposed explicitly to "constitute the condition of possibility of understanding handiness as such" (GA24 434/ BP 305).

But Heidegger treats only the ecstasis of the present in regard to *praesens*, and says nothing at all about the other ecstases in regard to their presumably Latinized tenses and schemata, the *futurum* and *praeteritum*. Yet *praesens* in particular is not independent; it stands in an inner Temporal connection with the other Temporal schemata. "In each instance the inner Temporal interconnections of the horizonal schemata of time vary also according to the mode of temporalizing of temporality, which always temporalizes itself in the unity of its ecstases in such a way that the precedence of one ecstasis always modifies the others along with it" (GA24 436/ BP 307). In a summary of the prepositional nexus already laid out in *Being and Time*, Heidegger had already emphasized that the relations of the in-order-to can be understood only "if the Dasein understands something of the nature of the for-the-sake-of-itself" (GA24 418/BP 295). An in-order-to (present) can be revealed only insofar as the for-the-sake-of (future) that belongs to a can-be is understood.

But the *futurum*, as the condition of possibility of understanding the self of Dasein, does not come under consideration at all, not even in its inner connection to *praesens*. With his exclusive treatment of *praesens*, Heidegger appears to yield to the domination of the traditional metaphysics of constant presence, which understands the being of beings only "in the horizon of productive-intuitive comportment" (GA24 165/BP 117) and would soon find its epochal denouement in the contemporary age of technology. In this way the most brilliant insights of the analytic of Dasein—for example insights into the existential priority of the future and into the historicity of Dasein—are not pursued any further and silhouetted upon the fundamental horizon of the most radical temporality. Heidegger's break with Plato's anamnesis-thesis had already been projected in his transformation of Pindar's saying, "become what you [always already] are," into "become what you are to be"; in *Being and Time* the directive is "be what you will be" (see SZ 145), "become what you yourself are not yet at all" (see SZ 243), or "become what you can be" (see the statements on "resoluteness," SZ 305–306). But this transformation is not taken further, into the uttermost Temporal horizon and into its abyssal implications. The levels of Dasein's historicity—for example, how, in the resolute "repetition" of a communal destiny in the "natural" course of a change of generations, the past perfect of precedented Dasein assumes the form of the future perfect of a community—remain uninvestigated in the Temporality of their modes of being. For example, the practical historical science of Christian theology, which takes as its object the historically transmitted and repeated happening of revelation for the community of faith, is corrected only in a formally indicative way by philosophical concepts and not comprehended in a philosophically scientific way, that is, Temporally ("Phenomenology and Theology" [1927–28], GA9 45–77/BP 39–61). With the renunciation of the language game of Temporality, the dream of philosophy as a Temporal science—that is, the objectification of being itself upon the horizon of time—comes to an end. The thought that philosophy cannot be a science at all then becomes the central theme of *Introduction to Philosophy*, the lecture course of WS 1928–29.

Transcendence—Horizon—Temporality

Nevertheless, the conceptual pair "transcendence—horizon" persists in the next lecture courses, although *Temporalität* virtually disappears from Heidegger's vocabulary and henceforth appears only "in brackets." The course of SS 1928, *The Metaphysical Foundations of Logic*, renews the elaboration of ecstatic-horizonal temporality without any reference to Temporality. In contrast to the previous year's emphasis on the horizon of *praesens*, originary temporality is now focused on the ecstatic being-toward-itself in the mode of the for-the-sake-of-itself (GA26 276/MFL 213). "This approaching oneself in advance, from one's own possibility, is the primary ecstatic concept of the future" (GA26 266/MFL 206). The for-the-sake-of is the distinctive mark of the Dasein that is in each instance mine (yours, ours), "that it is concerned with this being, in its being, in a particular way. Dasein exists *for the sake of* Dasein's being and its can-be. ... It belongs to Dasein's essence to be concerned *in its being about its very being*" (GA26 239/MFL 186; my emphasis). The for-the-sake-of-itself thus formally determines an ontological circuit from being to being that transcends beings—the "circle" (GA26 278/MFL 215) of self-understanding, of freedom, of selfhood and its binding obligations in being. "Freedom gives itself to understand, freedom

is the primal understanding, i.e., the primal projection of that which freedom itself makes possible" (GA26 247/MFL 192). But what does freedom
make possible? The meaningful context of the world, "the wholeness of
beings in the totality of their possibilities" (GA26 231/MFL 180), which
gets its specifically transcendental form of organization from the particular
for-the-sake-of in each instantiation (see GA26 238/MFL 185). The world
temporalizes itself primarily from the for-the-sake-of, from the ecstasis of
the future, and is grounded in the ecstatic unity and wholeness of the tem-
poralized horizon (GA26 275, 273/MFL 211–212). Heidegger now speaks of
an "ecstematic" unity of the *horizon*, that is, a systematic unity that is tem-
poralized by the unity of the ecstases (GA26 269/MFL 208). This horizonal
unity directed toward the future is the "temporal condition for the possibility of world" (GA26 269/MFL 208). Because this horizon is not an entity,
it can nowhere be localized. It shows itself only in and with the ecstases as
their organized ecstema. Its horizon is "not at all primarily related to looking and intuiting, but by itself means simply that which delimits, encloses,
the enclosure. ... It 'is' not as such, rather it temporalizes itself" (269/208).
Or better: It's worlding! (*Es weltet*)—to use an expression that Heidegger
now revives (GA26 219–221/MFL 170–173), after having coined it in 1919.
With this formulation, Heidegger seeks to indicate that the world is not
an entity, but rather a temporal how of be-ing. The world, the unity of the
temporal horizon, is "nothing that is and yet 'it gives.' The 'it' that gives
this non-entity is itself not entitative, but rather is the temporality that
temporalizes itself. And what the latter, as ecstatic unity, temporalizes is
the unity of its horizon, the world ... that which simply arises in and with
temporalization. We therefore call it the *nihil originarium*" (GA26 272/MFL
210).

It's worlding, it's giving, it's temporalizing: these are the impersonals of
the sheer dynamism of facticity. "The primal fact, in the metaphysical sense,
is that there is anything like temporality at all" (GA26 270/MFL 209). Sheer
facticity is the *nihil originarium*, and the product of the "peculiar productiv-
ity intrinsic to temporality" is "precisely a peculiar nothing, the world"
(GA26 272/MFL 210), the historical world. Thus the primal fact of temporality is no *factum brutum*, but rather "primal history pure and simple" (GA26
270/MFL 209), "the primal event of propriation [*Urereignis*]" (GA26 274/
MFL 212). The impersonal sentence "it's propriating itself [*es er-eignet sich*]"
already makes an appearance in 1919 as the *principium individuationis*, that
is, the principle of facticity as such (GA26 270/MFL 209; cf. GA56/57 75/
TDP 63–64). But in this course, Heidegger emphasizes the ontic upshot of
the "historical happening of transcendence," in which "beings are already

discovered as well" (GA26 281/MFL 217). The metaphysical primal history of Dasein as temporality also documents the completely "enigmatic" tendency to understand beings as intratemporal, extratemporal, and supratemporal (GA26 274/MFL 212). Of course, "the event of the world-entry of beings" happens only as long as historical Dasein exists, which as being-in-the-world gives beings the opportunity to enter the world. "And only when [being-in-the-world] is existent, have extant things too already entered world, i.e. become intraworldly" (GA26 251/MFL 194). "There is time, in the common sense, only with the temporalization of temporality, with the happening of world-entry. And there are also intratemporal beings that transpire 'in time' only insofar as world-entry happens and intraworldly beings become manifest for Dasein" (GA26 272/MFL 210). The thorough elaboration of world-entry here is in part Heidegger's answer to the basic metaphysical problem of the ontological relation between realism and idealism (SZ §§43, 44c) in his confrontation with Max Scheler (GA26 164–169/MFL 131–134), which he inserts into this lecture course on the occasion of Scheler's death. Intraworldliness and intratemporality do not belong to the essence of the extant in itself, which remains the same entity that it is and as which it is "even if it does not become intraworldly, even if world-entry does not happen to it" (GA26 251/MFL 194). The happening of the world-entry of beings is only the transcendental condition of possibility for the fact that extant entities reveal themselves in their in-itself, and thus "for [extant] things announcing themselves in their not requiring world-entry regarding their own being" (GA26 251/MFL 195; cf. GA26 194–195/153). The fact that we are called to let beings be what and how they are is another sign of the facticity and thrownness of temporal Dasein, whose powerlessness in the face of beings is disclosed in transcendence and in world-entry (cf. GA26 279/MFL 215). The freedom of transcendence is at the same time the binding character of the ground. To sum up what has been said in sheer temporal terms: "The ecstematic in its expansive sweep temporalizes itself as a worlding. World entry happens only insofar as something like ecstatic sweep [Schwingung] temporalizes itself as a particular temporality. ... The entrance into the world by beings is primal history pure and simple" (GA26 270/MFL 209).

The next lecture courses, delivered upon Heidegger's return to Freiburg as Husserl's successor, document the first signs of the gradual and often halting and even silent abandonment of the conceptual constellation "transcendence—horizon—Temporality," which had formed the original core of the projected third division. In "On the Essence of Ground" (his article for the Husserl Festschrift composed in October 1928 and published in 1929) Heidegger speaks, without explicitly mentioning Division III, of *Being and Time*'s "*sole* guiding intention ..., the entire thrust, and the goal of the development of the problem": "what has been published so far of the investigations on 'Being and Time' has no other task than that of ... attaining the '*transcendental* horizon of the *question* of being'" (GA9 162n./ PM 371n.66). But he also notes that "in the present investigation, the Temporal interpretation of transcendence is intentionally set aside throughout" (GA9 166n./PM 371n.67). Yet Heidegger's personal copy of the 1929 edition contains two handwritten marginalia that still recognize Temporality as the condition of possibility of temporality: "the essence of the 'happening'— temporalizing of Temporality as a first name for the truth of be-ing [*Seyn*]" (GA9 159/PM 123, n. a; GA9 171/PM 132, n. a). In the *Contributions to Philosophy* (1936–38), Temporality or "the originary unity of the self-clearing and self-concealing transporting [that] provides the immediate ground for the grounding of Da-sein" (GA65 234/CP 184) is understood as the first beginning's transition to the grounding of the temporal playing field (*Zeit-Spiel-Raum*) of the site of the moment (cf. GA65 18/CP 16, GA65 29/CP 25, GA65 294–295/CP 232). To complete this passage of transition, it was necessary "above all to avoid any objectification of be-ing, both by *withholding* the 'Temporal' interpretation of be-ing and by attempting to make the truth of be-ing 'visible' independently of this interpretation (freedom toward ground in 'On the Essence of Ground'; especially the first part of that treatise still adheres strictly to the ontic-ontological schema)" (GA65 451/CP 355). Thus, in the course of SS 1930, freedom and not the unitary horizon of Temporality is designated as "the condition of the possibility of the manifestness of the being of beings, of the understanding of being" (GA31 303/ EF 205). Nevertheless, one could always still "identify" freedom and temporality by way of mediating concepts like "possibility." The displacement of Temporality by freedom is in fact already in full swing in SS 1928, where freedom is already related to the "play" and "leeway" (*Spielraum*) offered by the particular possibilities of the historical world into which we happen to find ourselves thrown. Freedom is thus actualized by transcendence to the world disclosed as the "temporal playing field" (*Zeit-Spiel-Raum*) of historically transmitted possibilities. World becomes the historical playing field where we play out our most fundamental freedom of transcendence. "'World is the name of the game that transcendence plays" (GA27 312; cf. 300, 305–317). Freedom here is not a property possessed by humans but is rather the happening that possesses or "properizes" the unique human being into ex-sisting its historically particular being-in-the-world. It is this freedom that serves to re-place horizon-schematizing Temporality with "time-play-space," or "time-space" (*Zeit-Raum*: from 1934) for short, of the later works (GA66 424/M 375).

The very idea of a "horizon of time" comes under intense critical scrutiny in a litany of questions (GA29–30 219–220/FCM 145–146) in WS 1929–30, in the context of a phenomenological interpretation of the essence of radical or "deep" boredom. It has long become a commonplace, Heidegger notes, to invoke a single yet threefold horizon of time when we wish to gather all beings together simultaneously in all three *perspectives* of time—with *respect* to the present, in *retrospect* of the past, and in *prospect* of the future, "the perspectives of all action and inaction of Dasein" (GA29–30 219/FCM 145). But the complete indifference induced by total boredom—"being bored with it all"—empties this temporal horizon of beings as a whole in all respects and turns this horizon into an empty expanse "not at all actually articulated and delimited according to the past and future" (GA29–30 222/ FCM 148). The lengthening of the while of Dasein that characterizes boredom (= *Langeweile* = "long while") only accentuates this hollowed expansion into the full expanse of the temporality of Dasein (GA29–30 229/FCM 153). In such total boredom, Dasein as a whole, left empty and oppressed by the indeterminacy of the long while of total boredom, with a sense of being everywhere and yet nowhere, in fact becomes captivated, spellbound, entranced by its temporal horizon.

This spell of time is broken by the moment of holistic insight into the unique situation of action of being-here, Da-sein, which is in each instantiation mine (yours, ours). Since this proper possibility is intimated in the entrancement in the temporal horizon, the two apparently juxtaposed aspects of temporality belong together in a "single unitary phenomenon, in which ... the Dasein in us swings [*schwingt*] out into the expanse of the temporal horizon of its temporality and only in this way is able to swing into the moment of essential action" (GA29–30 227/FCM 151). The inactivity induced by profound boredom is thus dispelled. The mood of radical boredom is precisely this swinging between the empty expanse of the temporal horizon and the peak experience of the moment of insight (*Augenblick*). The moment is the keen vision of Dasein's resolute openness toward being-here, which in each instance, as existing, is in the comprehensively grasped situation of action, as this particular, singular, and unique being-here (GA29–30 251/FCM 169, GA29–30 224/FCM 149). "The moment of holistic insight breaches the binding spell of time, and is able to breach it insofar as it is itself a specific possibility of time. It is not some now-point ... but is the look of Dasein in the three perspectival directions" (GA29–30 227/FCM 151). The entrancement of time is broken, and can be broken only by time itself, by the "breakthrough"—often characterized as a sudden insight—of transcendence into the peak experience of the holistic moment. Thereby time itself has now become still more enigmatic for us, "when we think of the horizon of time, its expanse, its horizonal function—among other things as spellbinding—and finally when we think of the way in which this horizon is connected to what we call the moment of holistic insight" (GA29–30 228/FCM 152).

Whence the necessity of this relation between "expanse" and "peak"—horizon and holistic moment of insight—world and individuation, and why does it arise? What kind of "arc" is it that links these terms? Why must that expanse of the spellbinding horizon ultimately be breached by the moment of insight? And why can it be broken only by this moment of insight, so that Da-sein attains its existence proper precisely in this breach? Is the essence of the unity and structural linking of both terms ultimately a *breach*? What is the meaning of this *brokenness of Da-sein in itself*? We call this the finitude of Da-sein and ask: *What does finitude mean?* (GA29–30 252/ FCM 170)

The finitude of the world, the finitude of the moment of individuation, the finitude of Dasein in the insecurity of its basic questioning: these intercalated questions of world, individuation, and finitude reach in their origin back to the question of the essence of time (GA29–30 252/FCM 171, 256/173), and the groundlessness and fundamental concealment of its finitude (GA29–30 306/FCM 209). Is the horizon of time a confining enclosure or a defining limit that is at once an opening of finite possibilities?

In the *Contributions of Philosophy* (1936–38), *Horizont* becomes a recessive term (GA65 200–201/FCM 157–158), being replaced on the one hand by the more incipiently "being-historical" term, time-(play)-space, and on the other hand by its metaphysical German synonym, *Gesichtskreis*, literally "circle of vision," which thus irredeemably ties it to two millennia of the Occidental metaphysics of sight and light (GA65 250/FCM 197, 270/213, 376/297, 444/350, 450/355, 502/395; GA66 300–303/M 268–270). A note from the same time period (probably later), written by Heidegger in the copy of *Being and Time* that he kept in his mountain cabin, in the section on the "Outline of the Treatise" (SZ 39), provides the Third Division on "Time and Being" with a new direction. This note lists three tasks that must be carried out in "the transcendental difference": "The overcoming of the horizon as such. The turn-around into the source. Meaningful presence out of this source" (GA2 53 n.). The note charts a course that will lead to the very last draft of "Time and Being," so definitive that it found its way into print.

Philosophy: Not a Science but a Formally Indicative Protreptic

Since 1919, when Heidegger first characterized philosophy as the pretheoretical primal science of original life, he repeatedly vacillated on the question of whether phenomenological philosophy is a primal science, or even
a science at all. For philosophy as primal science is unlike any other science, since it aims to be a *supra*theoretical or *pre*theoretical—thus a non-
theoretical—science, which appears to be a contradiction in terms, like a
"square circle." Already in WS 1919–20 Heidegger remarks that philosophy,
as "originary science," is not a science at all "in the true and proper sense"
(GA58 230/BP [1919–20] 174), since every philosophy presumes to do more
than mere science. And in the next semester he traces this "more" back to
the original motive of philosophizing, that is, to the radically disquieting
character of life itself.

This pretheoretical "more" is thematized again in WS 1928–29, at the
end of the phenomenological decade of Heidegger's development (1919–
1929). As Husserl's successor, Heidegger returns again to the theme of the
scientificity of philosophy in this first of the later Freiburg lecture courses,
which bears the title *Introduction to Philosophy*. Philosophy is not a science
among others, but is more originary than any science. "Philosophy is indeed
the *origin* of science, but for this very reason it is not science—not even
a primal science" (GA27 18). Because it gives science its possibility, philosophy is something more, something else, something higher and more
originary. This "something else" is philosophy's power of transcendence, of
which science as such is incapable. In exercising this transcending power,
this "freedom toward ground," philosophizing is "an existing out of the
essential ground of Dasein, becoming essential in transcendence" (GA27
218; cf. GA26 285/MFL 221). It is not a science at all, not out of lack but
out of excess, because through its overt dwelling in the understanding-of-
being (*Seinsverständnis*) it is always in a bond of intimate friendship (*philia*;
GA27 22) with the *evidential* "things themselves," thus truer to the matters
at stake and thereby "more scientific than any science can ever be" (GA27
219). Therefore the expression "scientific philosophy" is not only superflu-
ous, like the term "round circle," but also a misleading misunderstanding
(GA27 16, 219, 221).

Philosophizing as explicit transcending, as explicitly letting transcendence happen, is grounded in the "primal fact" (GA27 223, 205) of the
understanding-of-being, the thrown projection of being. Transcending is,
first, the surpassing of beings, which happens in science on the basis of the
prior, nonobjective, background projection of the ontological constitution

of beings. On this basis, beings in themselves come to appear and can be articulated as openly lying before us (*positum*). "Against the background of the being that is projected in the projection, the entity that is thus defined first comes into relief" (GA27 196). But in this projection of the fundamental positive concepts of the sciences, being itself remains unconceived and, at first, even inconceivable. Nevertheless, the understanding-of-being is "nothing other than the possibility of carrying out the distinction between beings and being—in short, the possibility of the ontological difference" (GA27 223). There remains the radical possibility of developing the understanding-of-being into a conceiving of being, that is, into a question about what being itself is, and how such matters as the understanding-of-being and transcendence become possible. This self-articulating transition from the preconceptual understanding-of-being to the interrogative will to conceive being is philosophy as explicit transcending.

Philosophy is now sharply delimited from science, which is the cognition of beings as *positum* in a demarcated domain. "Neither being as such nor beings as a whole and as such, nor the inner connection between being and beings is ever accessible ... to a science" (GA27 224). "Transcendence is nothing that could lie before us like an object of science" (GA27 395). Being itself is no *positum*, but is like a nothing, and is close to the nonentities of world and freedom. What, then, is the language of being, *onto-logos* (GA27 200–201) if it is not scientific language? For the propositional truth of science is founded "on something more originary that does not have the character of an assertion" (GA27 68). Philosophy as onto-logy, "the thematic grasping and conceiving of being itself" (GA27 200), in essence becomes a problem that can be solved only when we "unveil the full, inner direction of the essence of philosophizing" (GA27 217).

Significant in the edition of this 1928–29 lecture course is a single paragraph on time as the transcendental horizon of the question of being, that is, on the schematic-phenomenological *construction* of the concept of being by way of time at the heart of Division III. This paragraph, as the editors inform us, was not read aloud in the lecture course (GA27 218n.).[4] Even the discussion of the "*Konstruktion* of the problem of being" or the "*Konstruktion* of transcendence" (cf. GA27 394, 396, 400), which occasionally surfaces in Heidegger's lecture-manuscript, is not to be found in the more extensive student transcripts of the course. Instead, philosophizing as questing and questioning of the comprehensive concept of being becomes an everlasting inexhaustible deconstructive task—a task that "leads us again and again into situations from which there seems to be no exit" (GA27 216). And the question of being, which "leads us anew into abysses" (GA27 205), is only one path to philosophy, the path via science. To make the full concept of philosophy intelligible, this path must be supplemented by two further paths: via worldview and via history.

A goal common to both paths is important for our purposes. *Being and Time* had already articulated the transcendence of being-in-the-world and thereby the transcendence of the world (cf. SZ §69c). "If transcending means being-in-the-world, and if this in each instantiation is a way of comporting oneself in the world, a worldview, then explicit transcending—philosophizing—entails an explicit cultivation of a worldview" (GA27 354–355). "Philosophy is not one worldview among others, not one way of comporting among others, but the comportment that comes from the ground of transcendence, the grounding comportment pure and simple" (GM 678; cf. GA27 397). In philosophizing, as explicitly letting Dasein's transcendence happen from its ground, the most originarily possible comportment takes place (GA27 396).

Philosophy as a wake-up call and as the occasion for free decision and interpretation—this is philosophy's exhortative function, which Aristotle already designated as a protreptic. This function of philosophy is connected to two temporally determined and interwoven features of the transcendence of Dasein: its freedom and its historical particularity. Philosophizing—letting transcendence happen from its ground—means precisely the development of that transcendence of Dasein which we call freedom. Likewise, philosophy is the liberation of the historically particular Dasein (GA27 401). Philosophizing, as letting the historically particular leeway of freedom happen for the peak moment of decision and the possibilities that have temporally ripened in that moment, is itself the primal action of letting-be (cf. GA27 205), of *Gelassenheit*—"an originary action of the freedom of Dasein—indeed, the happening of the space of freedom of Dasein itself" (GA27 214), "a 'deed' of the highest and original kind, which is possible only on the basis of the innermost essence of our existence—freedom" (GA27 103). "Letting transcendence happen as philosophizing involves the originary letting of Dasein, the human's trust in the Da-sein within itself and in its possibilities" (GA27 401). "This entity [called] Da-sein .. in and through its being, lets such a thing as a 'there' [a historical space of openness and disclosure] first be" (GA27 136).

And this "there" is always temporally particular, in each instantiation mine, yours, ours, and this means in each instance historical. As Dasein never exists in general, so "philosophy does not occur in general, in some undetermined somewhere or indefinite Dasein, or in itself" (SM 682 = GA27 399). "Dasein never exists in general. As concrete, it exists in a particular circumstance and, depending on these circumstances, in each instantiation secures for itself the essential and inessential situations [of action]" (GA27 227; cf. SM 407). The explicit and decisive leap into worldview as a comportment is necessarily the leap into one's own historicity, into concrete historical circumstances, into the specific historicity of one's own questioning from the whole of one's own historical situation (cf. GA27 400). In a radical sense, philosophy leaps into the historicity of its own factic Dasein in order to attain originality and strength and to be what is essential (cf. SM 682–683). The fact that the essential and originary is revealed only in historical concretion is a difficulty that is considered along the third path to the full essence of philosophy, the path through history. This difficulty is nothing other than the problem of the essence of philosophical truth as opposed to scientific truth, and thus the problem of the essence of truth as such. This problem of truth belongs together with the problem of being (in the first path) and the problem of the world (in the second path) within the architectonic of philosophy. More precisely, each of these problems constitutes the whole of philosophy (cf. SM 683).

Excursus on formal indication. The above paragraph highlights a theme that arose in tandem with the thematic of phenomenological philosophy as a primal science and, like the latter theme, is about to come to its climax at the end of Heidegger's phenomenological decade (1919–29), namely, the theme of formal indication. From the start, it is closely tied to the search for a nonmetaphysical, pretheoretical language for philosophy that would precede and underlie the duality of subject and object. Heidegger's quest for a nonobjectifying language of being in the framework of a phenomenological logic of philosophical concept formation becomes particularly clear in the dramatic closing hours of the 1919 war emergency semester (GA56–57 107–117/TDP 90–99). Here he tries to free the main methodological concept of phenomenology, the concept of intentionality, in its application to the "original something" (life in and for itself, lived experience), from all traces of a formal logical misinterpretation as a rigid dualism of subject and object. Objectifying life and treating it theoretically serve to strip life of its very vitality (devivification), tear it out of its historical context (dehistoricizing), un-world (*entweltet*) and designify (*entdeutet*) it. In its pure phenomenological formality, intentionality is purely and simply a direct ing-itself-toward. As comportment as such, it is indicated in its pure moment of the formal "toward," which Heidegger considers the heart, the center, the middle, the origin, the concealed source, of life—the intimate happening of its being. The toward-which (*das Worauf*) of this comportment is initially described as a unitary intentional relation from motivation to tendency and back, in an intentional "circular" motion of "motivated tendency or tending motivation" (GA56–57 117/TDP 99). It then becomes passionate action before it is described more fundamentally as thrown projection in *Being and Time*. There, "the toward-which [*das Woraufhin*] of the primary projection" constitutes the meaning of Dasein *qua* temporality, whose circular motion is redescribed as a thrown projecting of a prestructured context (the world) "according to which something becomes comprehensible as something" (SZ 151, 324). Meaning is thereby constituted by the circular interplay between the toward-which, the telic purposive) direction of Dasein, and the precedented context of the world in which "things fall into place and make sense" in the present.

Formal indication becomes the "methodological secret weapon" in Heidegger's logic of philosophical concept formation.[5] In the published First Half of *Being and Time* it is mentioned about a half-dozen times without explanation (SZ 53, 114, 116–117, 179, 231, 313–315; but also "provisional indication," 14, 16, 41). The undiscussed theme of "formal indication," as hermeneutic phenomenology's guiding "logic of philosophical concept formation," thus would have to become a central topic of discussion in the third division. This is confirmed by a footnote (deleted after the 6th edition of SZ) that dispatches the following themes for discussion in a specific chapter (2) of Division III: "Only in terms of the temporality of speech— that is, of Da-sein as such—can the 'origin' of 'meaning' be clarified and the possibility of concept formation be made ontologically understandable" (SZ 349).

On the way to *Being and Time*, Heidegger passes through a whole series of increasingly more profound formal indications. But each should be seen not only as a struggle to bring out different nuances of the motivated tendency of human life but also as a formal deepening of the dynamic prestructuring (*Praestruktion*) of intentionality, which is first understood as pure directing-itself-toward: as an intentionality with the three dimensions of relational sense, containment sense, and actualization sense (1920–22), supplemented by a unifying temporalization sense and a truthful safekeeping in 1922; as Da-sein (1923), being-in-the-world (1924), to-be (*Zu-sein*, 1925), ex-sistence (1926), and transcendence (1927–30). Thus the pure formula for the structure of care in *Being and Time*, "ahead-of-itself-being-already-in-(the-world) as being-amidst-(entities encountered within-the-world)" (SZ 192), is clearly intentional in the broader pretheoretical sense. The "new start" of Division III "on a more historical path," in SS 1927, thus reaches the following conclusion by way of a series of formal indications: "Intentionality is the *ratio cognoscendi* of transcendence. Transcendence is the *ratio essendi* of intentionality in its diverse modes" (GA24 91/BP 65). In Kantian terms, transcendence becomes the "condition of the possibility" of intentionality.

Finally, the entire series of formal indications will prove to have "the condition of its possibility in temporality and temporality's ecstatic-horizonal character" (GA24 379/BP 268). Intentionality, transcendence, existence: at their root they each formalize their temporal structuration and indicate the temporal telos that together constitute the very sense (*Sinn*) of existence. What in factic life could be more formal than time? And with regard to its indicative indexical function, what in factic life could be more concrete and immediate and nearer to us than time, my time, your time, our time? Time is at once the ultimate formality and the most intimate and immediate proximity of being, the original thrust of its facticity. In a note that belongs among the new attempts to elaborate Division III, Heidegger remarks: "Temporality: it is not just a fact, but itself the essence of the fact: facticity. The fact of facticity (here the root of the 'turn-around of ontology.' Can one ask, 'How does time originate?' ... Only with time is there a possibility of origination. ... But then, what is the meaning of the impossibility of the problem of the origination of time?"[6]

There are accordingly two interrelated aspects of time that must be thought together in formal indication, its dynamic prestructuring and its concretion, factic life in the uniqueness of its facticity, "the fact of facticity." Heidegger formally indicates this uniquely singular aspect of Dasein in the following pronominal terms: "The be-ing that concerns this being in its very be-ing is in each instantiation mine [yours, ours]" (SZ 42). In other contexts, the ontological indexicals of the personal pronouns, "I am, you are, we are," are expressed in the more overtly temporal particularities of "my time, your time, our time" to indicate the unique one-time-only lifetime that each of us is allotted as our very own (GA31 129–130/EF 89–90). Underlying the *Je-meinigkeit* (in-each-instance-mine-ness) of Dasein is thus the *Je-weiligkeit* (to each its while) of being. Time has long been regarded as a principle of individuation, but it is important here to identify this as the time proper to each of us in order to distinguish it from the common time that we all share in the public domain. It is therefore time proper that is the principle of individualization. My (your, our) history is also very much a factor in proper time, for we are clearly individualized by the particular historical context into which we find ourselves thrown. Precursors to Dasein in Heidegger's early development include the "historical I" and the "situation I" or, together, the historically situated I. Coming to terms with our proper temporal selves as Da-sein involves the hermeneutic task of explicating our unique selves in our proper historical context. And on the ontological and preontological levels, the hermeneutics of facticity is a formally indicative hermeneutics where, fundamentally, be-ing as time is properly singular, historical, and finite.

Winter semester 1929–30. Philosophy is not a science but a directive exhortative protreptic. The course of WS 1929–30 emphasizes this point from the unique perspective of Heidegger's very last, and most definitive, treatment of formal indication. Finding ourselves situated in existence, thrown into a historical world that is in fact very much our own, we, each of us, are called upon to overtly own up to this situation as a whole and properly make it our very own. This call (exhortation, solicitation, challenge, demand) elicited by the existential situation into which we find ourselves thrown is the function of the formally indicative concepts of philosophy. "The meaning-content of these concepts does not directly intend or express what they refer to, but only gives an indication, a pointer to the fact that anyone seeking to understand is called upon by this conceptual context to actualize a transformation of themselves into their Dasein" (GA29–30 430/ FCM 297). Because such concepts—Heidegger's terse examples are "death, resolute openness, history, existence"—can only convey the call for such a transformation to us without being able to bring about this transformation themselves, they are but indicative concepts. They in each instance point to Dasein itself, which in each instantiation is my (your, our) Da-sein, as the locus and potential agent of this transformation. "Because in this indication they in each instance point to a concretion of the individual Dasein in the human being, yet never bring the content of this concretion with them, such concepts are *formally* indicative" (GA29–30 429/FCM 296). In contrast to scientific concepts, all philosophical concepts are formally indicative. For when concepts are generic and abstract rather than proper to the concrete occasion in terms of which they are to be interpreted, "the interpretation is deprived of all of its autochthonous power, since whoever seeks to understand would not then be heeding the directive that resides in every philosophical concept" (GA29–30 431/FCM 298). Yet the kind of interpreting that seeks out its very own facticity in each instance is not "some additional, so-called ethical application of what is conceptualized, but .. a prior opening up of the dimension of what is to be comprehended" (GA29–30 428–429/FCM 296). The concepts and questions of philosophizing are in a class of their own, in contrast to science. These conceptual questions serve the task of philosophy: not to describe or explain man and his world, "but to evoke the Dasein in the human being" (GA29–30 258/FCM 174 .

These formally indicative, properly philosophical concepts thus only evoke the Dasein in human being, but do not actually bring it about. There is something penultimate about philosophizing. Its questioning brings us to the very brink of the possibility of Dasein, just short of "restoring to Dasein its actuality, that is, its existence" (GA29–30 257/FCM 173). There is a very fine line between philosophizing and actualizing across which the human being cannot merely slip, but rather must overleap in order to dislodge its Dasein. "Only individual action itself can dislodge us from this brink of possibility into actuality, and this is the moment of holistic insight [into the concrete situation of action, and be-ing]" (GA29–30 257/FCM 173). It is the originary action (*Urhandlung*) of resolute openness, letting be, or freedom toward ground, in each instantiation concretely reenacted in accord with one's own unique situation and particular while of history which authenticates our existence and properizes our philosophizing. It is in such originary action, repeatedly reenacted from one generation to the next, that ontology finds its ontic founding. Just as Aristotle (and so the metaphysical tradition) founded his *prote philosophia* in *theologia*, so Heidegger now founds his fundamental ontology on "something ontic—the Dasein" (GA24 26/BP 19).

Beyond *Being and Time* toward a New Direction for "Time and Being"

The path through *Being and Time* was finally abandoned by the end of 1930, adjudged to be an overgrown path littered with unsuccessful drafts of "Time and Being" that could no longer be trodden, as Heidegger confides to several of his intimate correspondents. The larger reading public was not informed of the abandonment of this path until the seventh edition of *Being and Time* published in 1953, which deletes the phrase "First Half" from the title with the following prefatory explanation: "After a quarter century, the second half can no longer be added unless the first half were to be presented in a new way. Yet the path it has taken remains a necessary path even today, if our Dasein is to be aroused and moved by the question of being" (SZ v). The necessity is derived from the Da-sein experience in its radical interrogative power, secure in the revolutionary direction of its questioning and the interrogative domain of being that it projects and into which it finds itself thrown. "SZ (1927) ... originated ... as an initial path of making the question-of-being evident as fundamentally as possible and at once in an actual performance [of this question] in a gestalt that points beyond all former ways of posing that question" (GA66 413/M 366). Accordingly, "what was unsatisfactory in the division that was withheld was not an insecurity in the direction of questioning and its domain, but only an uncertainty in its proper elaboration" (GA66 414/M 367). Secure in its direction of questioning, but inadequate in its proper elaboration—to the point of being incomprehensible to sharp minds like Rilke and Jaspers: where exactly is the fatal flaw in the Third Division, which after repeated attempts to elaborate it, was never to appear? The improper elaboration would gradually be attributed to the language of metaphysics. Heidegger's explanation in the "Letter on Humanism" (1947) strikes us as a good summary and final overview of the detailed accounts of these various failures of elaboration. In this context, Heidegger is trying to deflect the misinterpretation of the "projection" of the understanding-of-being as an achievement of subjectivity. It can be thought only as the ecstatic relation to the clearing of being:

> The adequate actualization and completion of this other thinking that abandons subjectivity is surely made more difficult by the fact that in the publication of *Being and Time* the third division of the First Part, "Time and Being," was withheld [cf. *Sein und Zeit*, 39]. Here everything is reversed. The division in question was held back because thinking failed in the adequate saying of this turning [*Kehre*] and did not succeed by means of the language of metaphysics. The lecture "On the Essence of Truth," thought out and delivered in 1930 but not published until 1943, provides a measure of insight into the thinking of the turning from "Being and Time" to "Time and Being." This turning is not a change of standpoint from *Being and Time*, but in it the thinking that was sought first arrives at the locality of that dimension out of which *Being and Time* is experienced, that is to say, experienced in the fundamental experience of the oblivion of being. (GA9 327–328/PM 249–250)

The key to what follows regards the nature of the new "insight" into the thinking of the turning from "Being and Time" to "Time and Being" that is provided by the lecture "On the Essence on Truth." The lecture famously concludes with the distinction between two extremes of truth as concealment, insistence in the everyday concealment of errancy and ex-sistence in the lifetime concealment of mystery, which proves to be insuperably concealed. Terminologically, we shall follow Thomas Sheehan, who has situated the very last draft of "Time and Being" at the very heart of Heidegger's hermeneutic phenomenology. Beginning with the tacit field of meaning exposed by way of the hermeneutic-phenomenological reduction, he asks about the meaning-giving source that enables that field of meaning. Whence sense? What makes meaning at all possible? What lets meaningfulness come about at all? In his briefest account, Sheehan provides a two-concept answer to this question, one from the very core of *Being and Time* and the other from the core of the later Heidegger. What makes meaning possible at all? The answer: *die Lichtung*, the lighted clearing that opens a realm of intelligibility for the human being and demarcates its essentially hermeneutic situation. But what then makes the clearing possible? The answer *das Ereignis*, the properizing event of appropriation that throws us into the unique clearing of intelligibility into which we happen to find ourselves thrown.

A longer and more detailed account[7] follows the development of Heidegger's thought from his repeated failure to complete the published fragment of *Being and Time*, which prompts a radical change in direction of his thought that is gradually made known through his talks, lecture courses, and writings from the thirties on, most of which were not published until well after the war. Our story begins with the repeated attempts to draft the third division of the First Part of *Being and Time*, entitled "Time and Being," without success. The fulcrum of the story is a reconstituted version of "Time and Being" that Heidegger jotted down in his "cabin copy" of *Sein und Zeit* no earlier than the late 1930s, in my estimation, that sketches out the stages of the reversal into the new direction that the later Heidegger was pursuing (GA2 53 n.):

[1]. The transcendental difference.
[2]. Overcoming the horizon as such.
[3]. The turnaround into the source [*Herkunft*].
[4]. Meaningful presence out of this source.

[1]. This title recalls the overall title of Part One of *Being and Time*, which was to conclude with the never-published Third Division entitled "Time and Being": "The interpretation of Dasein in terms of temporality and the explication of time as the *transcendental* horizon for the question of Being."

[2]. As we have seen above, the lecture courses of 1927–30 seek to further elaborate the ecstatical-horizonal unity of temporality, which was begun in §69c of *Being and Time* in a section entitled "The Temporal Problem of the Transcendence of the World." Toward the end of this period, the single yet threefold horizon of time is subjected to increasing critique in view of its blatant objectifying tendencies, in particular, the objectification of being itself. As it was hinted above, horizonal temporality will eventually be displaced and replaced by grounding Dasein in the temporal playing field (*Zeit-Spiel-Raum*), usually simply time-space (*Zeit-Raum*) (GA65 18/CP16, GA65 234–235/CP184–186), which is located in the integral moment (*Augenblick*) of holistic insight and decision.

[3] and [4]. The talk that Heidegger first delivered in 1962 entitled "Time and Being" most clearly makes the turn into the source and derives meaning and meaningful presence (*Anwesen*) from out of this meaning-giving source. The source, at first identified neutrally as an It, is initially said to let or allow meaningful presence, *Anwesenlassen*. The letting is more originally understood as a giving, such that It gives being, It gives time. The giving is then specified further as It sends being, It extends time, or more precisely, time-space. And the It itself? The t that gives is *das Ereignis*, which "appropriates being and time into their own out of their relationship" (GA14 24/TB 19). Moreover, in giving, "the sending source keeps itself back and, thus, withdraws from unconcealment" (GA14 27/TB 22). The meaning-giving source itself is self-concealing and remains insuperably concealed, the ultimate facticity beyond which we can go no further.

Notes

1. This file is to be found in a larger folder at the Deutsches Literaturarchiv in Marbach entitled *"Sein und Zeit" Vorarbeiten und Nachträge* under Zugangsnummer 75.7315 in Gattung/Gruppe B 36.

2. Martin Heidegger and Elisabeth Blochmann, *Briefwechsel 1918–1969*, edited by Joachim W. Storck (Marbach am Neckar: Deutsches Literaturarchiv, 1989), p. 54.

3. Rudolf Bultmann and Martin Heidegger, *Briefwechsel 1925–1975*, edited by Andreas Grossmann and Christof Landmesser (Frankfurt/Tübingen: Klostermann/Mohr Siebeck, 2009), p. 172.

4. The two sentences on a "transcendental horizon" before the paragraph in question were likewise not read aloud. I have compared the edition of GA27 with a much more comprehensive transcript of the course by Simon Moser and have supplemented and improved my citations from the edited version with clarifying turns-of-phrase drawn from the Moser transcript (hereafter referred to as SM). A copy of this Moser transcript is to be found in the Simon Silverman Phenomenology Center at the Duquesne University Library.

5. Theodore Kisiel, "Die formale Anzeige: Die methodische Geheimwaffe des frühen Heideggers," in *Heidegger—neu gelesen*, ed. Markus Happel (Würzburg: Königshausen & Neumann, 1997), pp. 22–40.

6. Martin Heidegger, "Unbenutzte Vorarbeiten zur Vorlesung vom Wintersemester 1929/30: 'Die Grundbegriffe der Metaphysik. Welt—Endlichkeit—Einsamkeit.'" *Heidegger Studies* 7 (1991), pp. 5–12, at p. 9.

7. Cf. Thomas Sheehan, "The Turn," in *Martin Heidegger: Key Concepts* (Durham, NC: Acumen, 2010), ed. Brett W. Davis, pp. 82–101. The "briefest account" above is distilled from one of his unpublished papers.

9   On Being as a Whole and Being-a-Whole

Denis McManus

Many—probably most—interpreters react to the fact that *Being and Time* is merely a "torso"[1] by setting aside "the Question of Being." Instead they set about stripping the body for what might yet prove to be assets in the context of some project or other of their own. In contrast, John Haugeland boldly insisted that

> *Everything in Being and Time* has to do with the question of being. ... [For example, the] existential concepts are introduced for this reason and this reason only. Our task as readers is to understand how. (Haugeland 2000, 66)

I confess that this strikes me as a pure act of faith on Haugeland's part. I have argued elsewhere that we have plenty of reason to wonder whether the best reference point by which to understand Heidegger's early thought is "the Question of Being" and, with it, "the Being and Time project"—as I will call it—the broader project to which the published book was declared to be contributing.[2] That project is only one of a number of "frames" that Heidegger sets around his work in the 1920s and one that he abandons within a couple of years of the book's publication.[3]

He does so seemingly because of continuing dissatisfaction with his own efforts to bring it to fruition. A case could be made for thinking that we have much of the material that might have made up Part Two of the completed book. But there are fewer reasons for such optimism with respect to Division III of Part One. Retrospectively Heidegger talks of that division being "held back" (BW 231) and—as early as 1929 (EG 105, n. b)—he identified the 1927 *Basic Problems of Phenomenology* lectures as a "new elaboration of the Third Division of the First Part of *Being and Time*" (BP 1). These comments suggest that, in essence, the work was done but never reached quite the publishable form Heidegger sought; and that may seem to be confirmed by Heidegger's report in 1941 that—through conversations with Jaspers in December 1926 and January 1927—"it became clear to me that the elaboration of this all important Division (I, 3) drafted up to that point had to be incomprehensible."[4] But in the same letter, he continues:

Of course, at the time I thought that in the course of the year everything could be said more clearly. That was a delusion.

So Heidegger's opinion in 1941 suggests that nothing he had written since *Being and Time*—*Basic Problems* included—quite added up to that missing division.[5]

Having said all of the above, I have also argued elsewhere that interesting possibilities may still open up if we do take seriously the "Question of Being" and the particular framing of Heidegger's early thought that we find in *Being and Time*. In particular, I have offered an account of the project to which that book was devoted, the work left to Division III, and the importance of that work, along with—however—reasons to think there may be problems of principle that prevent such a completion.[6] According to that account, Heidegger envisaged the Being and Time project as solving a problem that Aristotle revealed and that Heidegger's own insights—into the diverse forms that the Being of entities takes—exacerbated. The problem is that there is reason to think that the very possibility of the discipline of ontology presupposes that there is sense to the idea of "Being in general" and reason to think that there is no such sense. What I want to do here is suggest one way that the account I have offered might be filled out, in particular, by sketching a way in which the discussion of authenticity in *Being and Time* might have been structurally significant for the above project.

Phenomenology, Ontology, and Diversity

In *Being and Time*, Heidegger bemoans the baleful influence of the "priority of the present-at-hand [*Vorhanden*] in traditional ontology" (SZ 147), "the domination of the ontology of the 'substantial'" (SZ 320, n. xix).[7] He argues that we must instead recognize diverse forms of Being, distinguishing, for example, *Vorhandenheit* from *Zuhandenheit* (readiness-to-hand), from the mode of Being of the world within which entities of those sorts are found, and from that of the entity that encounters them in that world, *Dasein*.[8]

Heidegger maintains that the "priority" of the *Vorhanden* exists in a symbiotic relationship with a corresponding and similarly baleful "priority" of "pure beholding [*puren Anschauen*]" (SZ 147); for this reason, a recognition of the diverse forms that our understanding of entities takes may also help to break up prejudices about the "objects" of that understanding, a kind of phenomenological reflection on the ways in which those objects are grasped, revealing the diverse ontological forms that they take.[9] So, for example, though we may grasp the *Vorhanden* through "pure beholding,"[10] we grasp the *Zuhanden* by being "occupied with it in using it" (HCT 191) and other *Dasein* through "Being-with" (SZ 113); and recognizing this diversity—in what Heidegger at one stage calls "subject-correlates [*Subjektkorrelate*]"[11]—helps us "broaden the idea of objectivity," the latter "exhibited in its content in the investigation of the corresponding intuition" (HCT 72). We tend to overlook the diversity such "intuitions"—such "subject-correlates"—take too but, by remedying this *Verstehensvergessenheit*, we can expose the symbiotically related *Seinsvergessenheit*.[12]

There may seem to be a circularity in this approach: one would seem to need a grasp of *Zuhandenheit*, for example, if one is to identify which mode of understanding of ours *is* our understanding of the *Zuhanden*. But Heidegger believes we have such a grasp anyway: "Being is never alien but always familiar, 'ours'" (MFL 147). The problem is that—in a sense—we "forget" it. As *Dasein*, our mode of existence is one of "understanding Being" (SZ 12). But that understanding—which is manifest in our adept everyday dealings with the variety of entities we encounter—fails to inform our reflections on such entities and such understanding. Instead we fixate on entities possessed of a particular mode of Being—"the substantial"—and its "subject-correlate"—"pure beholding." The phenomenological response described above is a technique to aid "recollection" of other modes of understanding and, through that, of other modes of Being.[13]

An early example of this recollecting reflection in action can be found in Heidegger's lectures on St. Paul and St. Augustine. There Heidegger approaches "the task ... to determine the sense of the objecthood of God" (PRL 67)—"the sense of the Being of God" (PRL 84)—by starting "from the modes of access," from a proper appreciation of the "original region of life and performance of consciousness (or feeling), in which religion alone realizes itself as a certain form of experience" (PRL 222, 243). By placing such a subject-correlate first in our thinking, we may shake off the temptation to fall into thinking of God "by analogy with the theoretical and the constitution of the object of cognition," a temptation that distorts our "experiential comportment to God" into a "holding-as-true" and God into "simply a special object" (PRL 232, 149). By reflecting instead on God as the "correlate of the act-character of 'faith'" (PRL 252)—as the recipient of prayer, love, and service[14]—we resist the corresponding ontological assimilation and open up the possibility of recognizing God's "originary objecty [*Objectität*]" (PRL 252).[15]

But while his early work stresses such diversity, Heidegger also insists that "the *question* that determined the way of [his] thought' is 'what is the simple, unitary determination of Being that permeates all its manifold meanings?' (LR x). The "quest" for an answer to this question became— as Heidegger retrospectively put it—"*the* relentless impetus for the treatise *Being and Time*" (CV 9); "the question of the possible *multiplicity of Being* and therewith at the same time that of the *unity of the concept of Being in general*" was for him "urgent," "demand[ing] to be raised" (BF 120, 282). So why?

Diversity and Fragmentation

In the 1924–25 lecture series on Plato's *Sophist*, Heidegger celebrates Parmenides' formulation of "the seemingly trivial principle," "beings are" (PS 303). This, Heidegger proposes, represented "the very first decisive inception of ontology" (PS 307):

> The ancients tried to clarify and make intelligible beings ...—what is already there— by deducing them from particular beings. [But] Parmenides ... considers beings as such, i.e., he sets apart the whole of beings in an ontic sense and says that "they are." (PS 302)

Parmenides' breakthrough was to attempt to "enter into the dimension of the *Being* of beings" (PS 305), to reach—so to speak—for a concept of "Being," for a "feat" or feature that all entities share in simply by virtue of the fact that "they are."

But his successors recognized the true difficulty of that venture, Plato insisting that "there must be *manifold Being*" (PS 307) and Aristotle that "Being is said in many ways" (Aristotle, *Metaphysics* Γ, 2, 1003a33). The difficulty is not merely that such ontological diversity would seem to call for a general ontological theory of greater complexity; it may also seem to cast doubt on the very possibility of such a theory, by casting doubt on whether there is a singular subject matter for any such theory to address.

Heidegger reports that he found the "urgent" question of "the *unity of the concept of Being in general*" "concealed" in Aristotle (LR x);[16] and there are several ways in which the latter's thought can raise the above doubt. G. E. L. Owen spells out one:[17]

> In [Aristotle's] view, to be was to be something or other: for a threshold, he says, "to be" means "to have such and such a position," for ice it means "to have solidified in such and such a way." And at the level of greatest generality, to be is to be either a substance of some sort or a relation or a quality or a member of some other category.

There is no general sense to the claim that something exists over and above one of the particular senses. (Owen 1986, 181)

If there is no such general sense that subsumes the particulars—and hence "no class of *existing things* which will embrace men and miles and modesty" (Owen 1986, 216)—then "a single synoptic science of all existing things" (Owen 1986, 278) would seem to lack a topic.

Heidegger's own stress on ontological diversity makes such a worry over the "the disintegration [*Zerfall*]" of Being (AM 23) more vivid still. When one says that a *zuhanden* item exists, a *vorhanden* item exists, and another *Dasein* exists, one says—roughly speaking—that something is useable for some purpose, that something occupies a certain space, and that we share an understanding of the world with someone.[18] But what entitles us to think that these are variations on a single "achievement" or "feat"—"existence," "Being"? Even if the most pressing "task" for ontology is "classifying the whole of Being into regions" (PRL 41)—"partition[ing] the totality of beings" (PRL 39)—there must still be such a "totality"—such a "whole"[19]—if such a partitioning is to be a contribution to something that merits the name "ontology"—"a science … [that] stud[ies] all things that are, *qua* being" (Aristotle, *Metaphysics* Γ, 2, 1003b, 15–16). If there isn't "any single unifying concept of Being in general that would justify calling these different ways of Being ways of *Being*" (BP 176), then whatever distinctions we may be marking, they will not be entitled to the label "ontological distinctions."

This worry can show up in other ways: for instance, as a worry about the perspective from which the ontologist might draw her distinctions. If we grasp the *Vorhanden* through "pure beholding" and the *Zuhanden* by being "occupied with it in using it," through which "subject-correlate" might we have the difference between such entities in view? We may come to worry that there is no single unifying concept of "understanding" or "grasping" entities that would justify calling "pure beholding" and "being occupied with something" "ways of understanding or grasping," or any perspective from which the difference between these entities—that such "ways of understanding or grasping" understand or grasp—might be understood or grasped.

Polt has suggested that "Heidegger assumes" that, although "Being takes various forms," "all the varieties of Being cohere … so that we can ask what it means to be in general" (Polt 2005, 2). It would be fairer to say not that Heidegger makes this assumption, but rather that he believes both that we all make this assumption—"if we conceive of philosophical cognition as something possible and necessary" (SZ 16)—and that this is an assumption to which we must show we are entitled.[20]

The Being and Time Project

Aristotle offers one way of meeting the latter need, proposing that though "there are many senses in which a thing is said to be, ... all refer to one starting-point":

> Some things are said to be because they are substances, others because they are affections of substance, others because they are a process towards substance, or destructions or privations or qualities of substance, or productive or generative of substance, or of things which are relative to substance, or negations of one of these things or of substance itself. (*Metaphysics* Γ, 2, 1003b, 5–18)

As Owen glosses this view, "the primary sense" of "Being" "is that in which substances ... exist" and the "others ... are variously derivative," in that the notion of substance "reappear[s] as a common element in our analyses of the existence of non-substances such as colours or times or sizes" (Owen 1986, 217).[21] But for Heidegger, this view precisely exhibits "the domination of the ontology of the 'substantial.'"

The project to which *Being and Time* was to have contributed offered an alternative response: something *else* is to play the kind of role that substance plays for Aristotle, namely, time. Heidegger's "provisional aim" in *Being and Time* is "the interpretation of *time* as the possible horizon for any understanding of Being" (SZ 1): "within the horizon of time the projection of a meaning of *Being in general* can be accomplished" (SZ 235, italics added). If so, time *"enabl[es] ... the thematic interpretation of Being* and *of its articulation* and *manifold ways,"* and "thus makes ontology possible" (BP 228).

But we cannot leap straight to this conclusion—not least because we cannot claim to know what it means once Heidegger has warned us that the "time" in question is not time as it has been "ordinarily understood" (SZ 17). Indeed Heidegger sees the latter as yet another expression of "the domination of the ontology of the 'substantial'": through a process of "levelling off," time is itself rendered a sequence of "nows" that are "somehow *vorhanden*" (SZ 422, 423). Considerations of what Being in general is face similar prejudices to those that blind us to the nature of the *Zuhanden*, *Dasein*, world, and so on. So even if we have the sophistication to think that Being in general has something to do with time—perhaps in recognition of time's having acted throughout philosophy's history as an "'index' for the differentiation and delimitation of domains of Being as such" (HCT 5)—here too "the domination of the 'substantial'" is waiting in the wings in the form of the "ordinary conception of time."

So how, then, are we to proceed? I will tentatively suggest that Heidegger employs here too the approach that I sketched in the first section above. We saw there how Heidegger seeks to break our ontological prejudices through a phenomenological re-duction—literally, a leading back to the ways in which entities show themselves to us. This approach frees up our ontology of *x* by asking what understanding *x* "looks like"—what the subject who intends *x* has to be like. We see this in *Being and Time*'s reflections on how we grasp the *Zuhanden*, the *Vorhanden* and other *Dasein*; and my suggestion here is that the overarching Being and Time project might perhaps be seen as extending this treatment to the particular and metaphilosophically crucial case of Being in general: it would free up our vision of Being in general by asking what understanding Being in general "looks like," what the subject who intends Being in general has to be like. Though, in one sense, all *Dasein* grasp Being in general constantly, I will suggest that—for Heidegger—we see what this actually amounts to only when we consider the demands of authenticity: there is a further sense in which a condition of *Dasein*'s acknowledging Being as a whole is *Dasein*'s having achieved a kind of wholeness itself, a wholeness that only the authentic achieve.

Division I and the Question of *Dasein*'s Wholeness

Heidegger opens Division II of *Being and Time* with a discussion of the question of what it is for *Dasein* to be a whole. But this discussion can seem odd and undermotivated. He claims that we cannot speak of *Dasein* as being "whole" in the ways that, for example, we may speak of a *zuhanden* object being whole;[22] we may imagine striving to grasp *Dasein* when it is "complete," for example, but that would be to "grasp" it when it is dead and gone. Seemingly on the basis of such failures, he then drives us into a consideration of death and Being-toward-death.

But it is easy to feel uncomfortable with this. Fleischer, for example, sees no real need as being met when Heidegger presents the investigations embodied in Division II as necessary by virtue of our not having yet grasped *Dasein* as a whole, since Heidegger has already offered the notion of "care" as encapsulating what it is for *Dasein* to be in its entirety (Fleischer 1991, 39, 196). Why isn't this an adequate form of wholeness for our analysis to have achieved? Heidegger may very well have reasons to move us on to discuss Being-toward-death; but is this lack of wholeness—"the question of arriving at the wholeness of *Dasein*" if we are to "mak[e] *Dasein* available as an object for consideration" (HCT 310)—a good one?

Heidegger as much as accepts this worry later in the book. In the light of his analysis of death, conscience, guilt, and so on,

the question of *Dasein's* potentiality-for-being-a-whole … slough[s] off the character indicated at the beginning [of Division II], when we treated it as if it were just a theoretical or methodological question of the analytic of *Dasein*, arising from the endeavour to have the whole of *Dasein* completely "given." (SZ 309)

As he puts it in HCT, that question "is the secondary difficulty":

The primary one is whether *Dasein* is the entity which one oneself is and which of *its essence* entails that it *be in each case mine*, and whether this entity has the possibility *to be* its wholeness. It is only on the basis of this possibility of being that we could have the further possibility of experiencing this self-being of *Dasein* in its wholeness now also in an explicit fashion. (HCT 310–311)

The "primary difficulty" then is establishing the sense in which *Dasein* can *be* whole, the "secondary difficulty" being the "methodological" question of whether we can get such a whole in view. But why then bring the "secondary difficulty" up in the first place? Why give the question of *Dasein's* wholeness such importance in introducing Division II's deepening analysis of authenticity into the work of the Being and Time project?

In an effort to elucidate one possible way of understanding why authenticity matters to that project,[23] and of seeing a genuine methodological necessity in turning to reflections on *Dasein's* wholeness, I propose that those who "flee" from the above "possibility of [*Dasein's*] being" a whole also "flee" from a disclosure of "Being in general." There is a sense, which I will explain, in which only those who realize that possibility "condense" into unified perspectives on things; and by grasping the formal structure of their mode of existence—the structure it has by virtue of being a unified perspective on things, whatever "content" that perspective might have—we uncover what could be called the "horizon" within which "the projection of a meaning of *Being in general* can be accomplished."[24]

Authenticity as the "Subject-Correlate" of Being as a Whole

In the *Sophist* lectures, Heidegger considers Socrates' description of the true philosopher as one who "looks down upon life from above"; "that implies," Heidegger tells us, that the philosopher himself, in order to be able to carry out such a possibility in earnest, must have attained a mode of existence guaranteeing him the possibility of such a look and thereby making accessible to him life and existence in general. (PS 168)

Dasein's mode of being is, of course, one of *Sein-bei* entities—being amid them (SZ 54)—and hence it does not "look down upon life" even when it grasps Being in general. But that is not to deny that it does indeed— "somehow"—grasp it:

As surely as we can never comprehend [*erfassen*] absolutely the whole of beings in themselves we certainly do find ourselves stationed [*gestellt*] in the midst of [*inmitten*] beings that are revealed somehow as a whole. (WM 87)

Our efforts to comprehend particular kinds of entities bring with them, however, a kind of concealing of this whole. "The originary disclosure of beings as a whole" is an "open[ing] up [of] the open region [*das Offene*] for every measure" (OET 143)—for each particular way in which we may classify or evaluate what we find around us. But when such a "measure" "lets beings be in a particular comportment that relates to them and thus discloses them, it conceals beings as a whole" (OET 148). Any such measure embodies "only *one* kind and possibility of making manifest of entities" (EP 203), and, therefore, in adopting it, one forfeits the possibility of addressing other aspects of the world. "So much for the 'revelation of beings somehow as a whole'!" one might say. But Heidegger's discussion of authenticity can be seen as pointing to a mode of existence in which we do acknowledge this whole and do so precisely by being a whole ourselves.

Reminding ourselves of the terms in which Heidegger describes inauthenticity may make this proposal—which I can no more than sketch here— seem at least a little less odd. The life of the inauthentic, let us recall, is one of "dispersal," "distraction," and "disconnectedness" (SZ 390, 347, 371). It is a life of "inconstancy [*Unständigkeit*]," in which one is "absorbed in the everyday multiplicity and the rapid succession of that with which one is concerned," "the endless multiplicity of possibilities which offer themselves as closest to one" (SZ 337, 321, 384). In the midst of this "jumble of hovering possibilities," the inauthentic person "drift[s] back and forth between 'worldly' possibilities which it has not seized upon" (SZ 342, 344).

At the same time, though, it is a life of fixation or "falling," one in which we "cling" to "what is proximally at [our] everyday disposal": the inauthentic person "busily los[es] *himself* in the object of his concern" (SZ 195, 410). All "other possibilities" are "crowded out" or "closed off" and what remains—those objects so understood—"becomes the 'real world'"

(SZ 195). Similarly—to introduce a temporal theme to which we will return—there is a sense in which inauthentic *Dasein* "always live[s] in the present" (WDR 169): it "orients its concerns to the now" WDR 170), "leap[ing] away from its authentic future and from its authentic having been" (SZ 349).

We may "drift," then, from one mode of "losing ourselves" to the next in this "rapid succession of that with which one is concerned" but we do so in a mode of "tranquilization" (SZ 189). It can be 'tranquil' because, in this "inconstancy"—this *Unständigkeit*—we do not achieve the authentic person's "steadfastness [*Standfestigkeit*]"—her "having achieved some sort of a position [*Standgewonnenhaben*]" (SZ 322)—a position from which such inconstancy might manifest itself to us. The authentic person achieves a single overarching perspective—or "position"—on life, a general view of things that might be called her own, and which expresses—though typically only implicitly—an assessment of which of the "multiplicity of possibilities which offer themselves" to her are most worthwhile. The possibilities on which the inauthentic person acts, on the other hand, change as he moves from role to role and context to context. As a result, he is recognizably "dispersed" and does not live life *as* a whole. Instead his actions express a shifting and fluctuating conglomeration of perspectives, with none of which he can be identified. "The inauthentic Being of *Dasein*" is *Dasein* "*als unganzes*"—as "*less* than a *whole*," or as Stambaugh puts it, "fragmentary" (SZ 233).

Heidegger describes the inauthentic person's "losing *himself* in the object of his concern" as a "levelling off of *Dasein*'s possibilities to what is proxi-mally at its everyday disposal," and as "a dimming down of the possible as such" (SZ 195). The authentic person's "having achieved some sort of a position" may evoke a closing down of possibilities—a narrowing of view; but, in fact, as we will see below, it is in their acceptance of the *need* for "some sort of a position" that we see a take on things in general emerge, an experience that one might tentatively identify with one of "Being in general" or "as a whole." One might articulate this proposal in a number of ways, and the next two sections will explore how Heidegger's discussions of "guilt" and "Being-toward-death" might be seen to do so.

Guilt

To return to the terms used in OET (quoted above), the adoption of one "measure" at the exclusion of others expresses—one might say—an evalua-tion of "beings as a whole," in this adoption's taking one particular aspect of beings as worthy of comprehension. Indeed, one faces the problem of unifying one's understanding of the world in this way whenever one acts: there may be many principled demands arising out of a situation, and, when we act, we select among those demands, thereby expressing an assessment of what *overall* is most important. To be *an* actor we must condense the multidimensional world that we confront into *a* world. In doing so, we—as finite creatures—cannot avoid the possibility that the act we perform will not address all the demands that we may recognize. As a result, our existence is marked by an "ontological" or "absolute" guilt.

Heidegger explains his notion of guilt by reference to two "nullities," according to the second of which

in having a potentiality-for-Being [*Dasein*] always stands in one possibility or another: it constantly is *not* other possibilities, and it has waived these in its existentiell projection. ... Freedom ... *is* only in the choice of *one* possibility—that is, in tolerating one's not having chosen the others and one's not being able to choose them. (SZ 285)

In WDR, we read:

Every action is at the same time something marked by guilt. For the possibilities of action are limited in comparison with the demands of conscience, so that every action that is successfully carried out produces conflicts. To choose self-responsibility, then, is to become guilty in an absolute sense. Insofar as I am at all, I become guilty whenever I act in any sense. (WDR 169)

There is nothing one can do to alleviate such "guilt," as it is inherent in our nature as finite creatures—creatures who cannot be in two places at once. But—in a way that the next section will make clearer—inauthenticity is a way of "fleeing" this guilt—of pretending it is not a fact of life—and authenticity a way of acknowledging it. When authentic, I achieve a unifying perspective on things, to which corresponds a "horizon" against which I project what one might provisionally call an understanding of "Being in general": an appreciation of the aspect of things revealed by the measure upon which I act, the indefinitely many other aspects of things revealed by the measures upon which I do *not* act, and the fact that when I act—indeed "insofar as I am at all"—I express an evaluating unification of that multiplicity. But any such unification rests on a further unifying understanding in light of which the authentic live and which—by virtue of that further depth—has a better claim to be the "horizon" we are seeking to "recall."

Death and Ecstatic Temporality

In taking passages like WM 87 as presenting a picture of grasping "Being as a whole," I overlooked, of course, its explicitly concerning beings as a whole; this might seem to be a prime example of *Seinsvergessenheit*, and my talk of the possibility of a unified "take on things" might be seen as augmenting this confusion. But following the clue of OET 143 and 148, I used the latter expression to refer to a unifying ranking of "measures" and—thereby—of those aspects of things upon which one might act, the ways in which they may be. For that reason, I have so far taken such a ranking as a not-unreasonable approximation for a "grasp of Being in general." But can this first approximation be trusted, or might it itself rest on a deeper disclosure more deserving of such a label? "All ontological interpretations are more like a groping about than an inquiry clear in its method" (BP 322), and might we have not yet got to the bottom of the influence on our reflections of "the domination of the substantial"?[25]

Recognition of ontological guilt yields a unification that gives one sense to authentic *Dasein*'s "Being-a-whole"—yielding a kind of synchronic wholeness in the many "ways of being" upon which one might act. But this presupposes a kind of diachronic wholeness, and hence temporality—and a particular kind of temporality—now comes to the fore.[26] One way of looking at the dream of somehow disowning "ontological guilt" is as an unwillingness to be someone who acts on particular measures at the cost of not acting on others. Since such a cost is an inescapable part of what it is for a finite creature to act at all, this would be a refusal to perform determinate acts, a refusal to be a particular person; it would be a denial of one's having a particular identity in favor of a dream of being "everywhere and nowhere" (SZ 177, 347). Now this clearly is a dream, and a "tranquilizing" one, at that; but to see how one might come to dream it, let us note how a certain denial of death plays its part.

The thought is simple. "Freedom" is not "the choice of *one* possibility" and "tolerating one's not having chosen the others" *if* one can make up for that choice by acting on those others later; "the possibilities of action" are not "limited in comparison with the demands of conscience" *if* one can meet later the demands one does not meet now. But clearly this assuages our (ontological) guilt only on one condition, namely, that "there is still plenty of time" (CT 69). "Death certainly comes, but not right away" (SZ 258) is the inauthentic person's characteristic "pushing away and suppressing [of] 'the thought of death'" (PIRA 163): he "pushes away the indefiniteness of death"—"the possibility that it can come at any moment"—"into the realm of postponement" (WDR 167, HCT 317).[27] Such a "pushing away" denies the need for a singular (unifying) response to the situation in which we find ourselves obliged to act, and the attendant "ontological guilt" it brings with it. For such a pseudo-agent, "all doors are open"; "everything is within its reach" as it "float[s] unattached" and "uprooted," "*never dwelling anywhere*" (SZ 177, 170, 173).

In this way, inauthenticity brings with it a certain denial of one's past— of one's thrown, determinate situatedness through which one can live in only a single way—and one's future—in particular, the certain "possibility of impossibility," the possibility that one may not be able to make up for some of the choices one does not make, and the necessity that one cannot make up for all. Acknowledgment of this "*finite* temporality" (SZ 348) of ours is then, in contrast, the living of life against the horizon of what Heidegger calls an "ecstatic temporality," our being "held out" into our past and finite future; when authentic,

the Present is not only brought back from distraction with the objects of one's closest concern, but it gets held in the future and in having been. (SZ 338)

This is the (diachronic) "horizon" that one must deny if one is to spare oneself the "guilt"-laden task of achieving a (synchronic) take on one's life as a whole and its "possibilities of action." Correspondingly, this is the horizon that the authentic acknowledge—live in the light of—by being-a-whole, by resisting the temptation to be the "dispersed" everyone and no one that is the They-self. Whatever content one's take on things in general may be—whatever "position one achieves"—this is the "horizon" against which such a take will be "projected."

There is, I think, a certain architectonic aptness to the idea that *Dasein* does not acknowledge Being as a whole unless it itself is-a-whole, an aptness that Heidegger's picture of the inauthentic person as being "*less* than a *whole*" makes vivid.[28] Such a person "clings" to particular possibilities while all others are "dimmed down"—a "fragmentary" *Dasein* encountering only a fragment of the world. The authentic person, in contrast, embodies an appreciation of that full range of possibilities and a recognition of the need to unify them not only if she is to act but "insofar as [she is] at all." But we then dug deeper and saw how the inauthentic must "liv[e] always in the present " By thinking through what is implicit in the authentic person's synchronic grasp of "Being in general"—as we might be tempted to describe such a unifying grasp of "possibilities of action"—we uncovered a further diachronic horizon in acknowledgment of which it is distinctive of such a person to live, that of an "ecstatic" time in which one is "held in the future and in having been." Elucidating that horizon—and at least part of the work that Division III was to do was surely that—is elucidating what it is that those who live in the light of such a synchronic grasp of Being in general live in the light of, the further diachronic "horizon" against which their distinctive form of understanding is "projected."

Concluding Thoughts

The devil, of course, is in the details. The above discussion is without doubt speculative, has passed at great speed over a lot of very difficult terrain, assuming a host of interpretive decisions without justification, raising as many questions as it is answers, and no doubt inviting many objections. In this last section, I will consider one such objection. Responding to it will help clarify the proposal that my discussion offers but also point to limitations we must surely encounter in attempting to confirm any proposal of this kind.

For example, one might wonder how an acknowledgment of our "guilt" can possibly set us on the road to a horizon for an understanding of Being in general. That acknowledgment may require an appreciation of the many "measures" on which we might—but do not—act. But what does this "many" denote? And "we" meaning who? If it means "we thrown, factical individuals"—presented with a finite set of measures as "live options," to use James's expression (James 1956, 3)—then it is not clear that acknowledging *that* range of possibilities can be any analogue of the Socratic "look down upon life and existence in general."

Or might it? I suggested above that it is the form rather than the content of the authentic "look" that matters. My proposal makes key one's escape from an inauthentic lostness in "the object of one's concern." One might understand this as the failure to recognize that this aspect of reality upon which one is acting is but *one* possible basis for action. But this underdescribes inauthentic lostness. In such a condition, one fails to recognize the aspect of reality upon which one acts as a *possibility*, one instance of a generality that is "ways things can be"; when all other ways that things can be are "crowded out" or "closed off," one is left confronting no even— so to speak—*one* possibility, because the horizon against which it would show itself *as a possibility* is obscured. Instead, as Heidegger put it, one confronts what one simply takes as the "real world." From this perspective, the inauthentic person's failure does not contrast with—say—the authentic persons' (somehow) acknowledging all possibilities of every possible

Dasein, but instead with their acknowledging the factical possibilities that they do have *as possibilities*. The latter recognition is of a multiplicity of ways things can be, and, as such, it presupposes an appreciation of a broader concept under which (what we now see as) those instances are subsumed; this appreciation is a grasp of what it is for something to *count* as a "way of being," rather than some more concrete but facticity-denying familiarity with each and every instance of that broader concept. To offer (what may be more than merely) an analogy, this would be akin to knowing what counts as a reason, rather than knowing all the reasons on which it is possible for a person to act.

This might seem to leave us with a rather thin notion of "Being in general." But does it? Let us recall that the horizon onto which our understanding is projected when we display a mastery of the above unity in "ways of being" turns out to be that of a presupposed and, hence, deeper unity—that of ecstatic temporality. Is that a thin notion? Heidegger insists that "the idea of Being in general is just as far from being 'simple' as is the Being of *Dasein*" (SZ 196); and ecstatic temporality playing a key role in both would seem to confirm that.

More importantly, is the resultant idea of "Being in general" likely to be *too thin* to do the work the Being and Time project requires it to do? We have a flavor of the kind of work that project was to have done in the discussion in Chapter Four of Division II of the temporality of understanding, *Befindlickeit*, falling and discourse. Heidegger offers this discussion as showing that these phenomena "*in principle* can*not* be clarified in terms of the 'now'" (SZ 338). Rather,

The ecstatical unity of temporality—that is, the unity of the "outside-of-itself" in the raptures of the future, of what has been, and of the Present—is the condition for the possibility that there can be an entity which exists as its "there." (SZ 350)

He makes parallel cases concerning our "circumspective concern" with the *Zuhanden* and the "theoretical discovery of the *Vorhanden*" (SZ 352, 356). In grasping them, we "make use of time": we grasp these kinds of Being too "in their temporal constitution" (BP 291); and hence, one might see here an attempt to show that not only *Dasein* but these phenomena too only show themselves against the horizon of ecstatic temporality, a common horizon that provides a basis for our "calling these different ways of Being ways of *Being*" (BP 176, quoted above).

But any candidate concept of "Being in general" needs to do significantly more than that. In criticizing Aristotle's proposal that the question, "what is Being?" "is just the question, what is substance?" (Aristotle, *Metaphysics*

Z, 1028b4), Heidegger stresses that the "many ways" in which "Being" is "said" can be understood in narrower and wider senses. In addition to the unity that renders being *Dasein, Zuhandenheit,* and *Vorhandenheit* "ways of Being," we must also establish a unity that subsumes these *plus* Being's further "regions" of "accidental and non-accidental Being," "true and untrue Being," and "potential and actual Being" (AM 9).[29]

Can, then, the horizon that is ecstatic temporality—on a thin or yet-to-be-articulated thicker construal—deliver an account of "Being in general" that can meet these needs?[30] I do not know how far one can go in resolving these matters.[31] Heidegger himself explicitly mentions in *Being and Time* the need to "clarify the ontological meaning of the kind of talk in which we say that 'there is truth'" (SZ 214),[32] but then kicks the question of how we are to handle this need into the long grass of Division III. "Being and truth 'are' equiprimordially" and "Being … is something which 'there is' only in so far as truth is"; but even the "concrete asking" of the question, "What does it signify that Being 'is'?"—let alone answering it—is possible for us "only if the meaning of Being and the full scope of the understanding of Being have in general been clarified" (SZ 230). And there the matter is left.

Heidegger himself suggests he had succumbed to a "delusion" in thinking he had in mind a project for Division III that could be rendered clear;[33] I have also offered reasons elsewhere for thinking there may be a problem of principle inherent in the attempt to articulate the horizon upon which "Being in general" is "projected."[34] If that problem is insurmountable, attempts to make sense of the Being and Time project must fail in the end; and a difficulty that we face in trying to understand the texts that we do have is knowing when the principle of charity—and the expectation that a good reading of those texts will make sense of them—should be set aside.

Acknowledgments

For helpful comments on material on which this essay is based, I would like to thank Anthony Beavers, Jim Conant, Barry Dainton, Katalin Farkas, Rafe McGregor, Ed Minar, Adrian Moore, Stephen Mulhall, Aaron Ridley, Joel Smith, Tom Sorell, Joshua Tepley, Andreas Vrahimis, Daniel Whiting, Dan Zahavi, and, in particular, Lee Braver. I would also like to thank the University of Southampton and the Arts and Humanities Research Council for periods of research leave during which work on which this essay is based was done.

Notes

1. This is Spiegelberg's well-known description, quoted in, e.g., Kisiel 2005, 189.

2. Cf. McManus 2012, ch. 9.

3. As the two available translations of *Sein und Zeit* also give the pagination of the German original, I will give references to the latter, though generally I will follow the translation of Macquarrie and Robinson (Oxford: Blackwell, 1962). I use the established translations of Heidegger's works in most cases, but diverge from them on occasion.

4. Translation quoted from Kisiel 1993, 486.

5. There are also clear indications in BP itself that he feels the task he set himself there remains unfinished. See, e.g., BP 308.

6. See McManus 2013b.

7. This equation of the *Vorhanden* with substances is often made—see, e.g., Guignon 1983, 101, 144, and Dreyfus 1991, 71—but is problematic. In McManus 2012, ch. 3, I discuss these worries, but I set them aside here.

8. Other forms of Being that Heidegger seems to entertain but which he does not discuss at any length in *Being and Time* include those instantiated by animals, God, and truth. I discuss the second of these briefly in a moment and the third in my concluding remarks.

9. Or so I argue in McManus 2012.

10. For complications I will not discuss here that concern Heidegger's understanding of how we grasp the *Vorhanden*, see McManus 2012, chs. 3, 8.

11. Cf., e.g., TDP 37, PRL 240, 241.

12. The connection between phenomenology and ontology that I sketch here is looser than that which Heidegger seems to defend in SZ. (Cf., e.g., SZ 35 and 38, and for one interpretation, see Braver, introduction to this volume.) But I will set that worry aside here.

13. For further discussion, see McManus 2012, sec. 1.1, and of this notion of "recollection" in particular, McManus 2013c.

14. Cf. PRL 79, 107, 234, 254.

15. For further discussion of this example, see McManus 2012, sec. 1.2, and, for greater detail, 2013a.

16. Cf. LR x, CV 9, and TB 74 on this and the important role that Brentano's study of Aristotle (Brentano 1975) played in revealing that question's presence to Heidegger.

17. McManus 2013b, sec. 3, spells out another.

18. See BP on how a *Zuhanden* item is individuated not by "space- and time-position" but by "its equipmental character and equipmental contexture": "functionality" is "exactly what makes [such a] thing what it is" (BP 292, 164). "To exist," which is *Dasein*'s distinctive mode of Being, on the other hand, "is essentially ... to understand" (BP 276).

19. I will treat the expressions "Being in general" and "Being as a whole" as interchangeable. Though there may be issues here, Heidegger's own note to SZ 37 (published in the Stambaugh translation of SZ) would seem to sanction this.

20. Another way of thinking of the importance of identifying such a unifying sense arises out of Heidegger's description of philosophical confusion as our using words whose meaning has descended into "indeterminate emptiness" (HCT 269). Just as Heidegger worries—for example—over whether (and, if so, how) "*the possibility of being itself*" is "attested" in *Dasein*'s lived experience, so too one might wonder whether "Being in general" has a "demonstrable meaning" (SZ 23, 59). "The fundamental concepts of metaphysics" might then "amount to nothing more than the possession of words," having "a neutral, faded content" by virtue of not "originally aris[ing] from" any determinate "sphere of experience" (PRL 246, IPR 7). (For discussion, see McManus 2013c.) In response, the account below would identify— "attested" in the life of *Dasein*—an "experience" from which an idea of "Being in general" might "arise."

21. Heidegger discusses this view at BCAP 126–127, 133–136, 222, and AM 27–39.

22. Cf. SZ secs. 46–48 and HCT 311.

23. The basis of others can be found in McManus 2012, sec. 9.2, and 2013c.

24. What follows draws on a broader understanding of authenticity that I cannot defend here. I present aspects of this in McManus 2015, (forthcoming) and as-yet-unpublished works.

25. Another kind of worry one might raise concerning my "first approximation" is whether *Dasein*'s unified grasp of the array of possibilities of action open to it can be identified even provisionally with a grasp of various modes of being—a worry one might raise in at least two ways. (1) One might propose that, when one acts, one understands the entities upon which one acts as—and *only* as—*zuhanden*. A case can be made for such a view (see, e.g., Rouse 1985 and Blattner 1995 for some relevant thoughts) but I have argued elsewhere (McManus 2012, sec. 3.4) that it remains problematic: in particular, it is hard to establish an interpretation of such a view that gives it both substance and the necessary breadth. (2) One might think that the

unity of Being concerns the unity of very broad ontological kinds rather than that of many different and particular "measures" on which one might act. But if—*contra* (1)—we can indeed act on the basis of entities being so where this is not simply a matter of their *Zuhandenheit*, then the unified grasp of entities being so that is necessary for act on must be capable of encompassing all the different ways that such entities can be so; the "horizon" against which entities—as understood through many different "measures"—are projected must also be one against which the many—though presumably fewer—ontological kinds that they instantiate are projected.

26. Though I concentrate here on one particular notion of diachronic wholeness, I do not discount the relevance of others, such as that explored in various ways in the work of Charles Guignon. See, e.g., Guignon 2000.

27. See also SZ 253, 255, HCT 315.

28. Heidegger identifies authentic Being-a-whole with "individualization" (see, e.g., SZ 266) and the importance that my reading assigns to our understanding the unity of the subject that intends Being in general for our understanding of Being in general and its unity makes unsurprising connections such as that proposed in the following: "Being, as the basic theme of philosophy, is no class or genus of entities, yet it pertains to every entity. ... *Being is the transcendens pure and simple.* And the transcendence of *Dasein's* Being is distinctive in that it implies the possibility and the necessity of the most radical *individuation*" (SZ 38). There are also clear Kantian echoes here, and my reading suggests connections with themes in the discussion of transcendental apperception, to which a number of Heidegger's comments on SZ's unwritten sections allude (see, e.g., SZ 319, n. xvi). (McManus 2013b, sec. 6, identifies other Kantian aspects of the Being and Time project.)

29. This echoes Brentano's identification of the problematic diversity to be unified as that of "Being according to the figures of the categories" plus "accidental Being," "Being in the sense of being true" and "potential and actual Being" (Brentano 1975). Recognition of the need to accommodate these further "regions" gives further substance to the tentativeness of what I call above my "first approximation" of what "Being in general" must subsume. But perhaps the trickiest case—of all such candidate further "regions of Being"—is that of the Being of the "horizon" that is ecstatic temporality. See n. 34 below.

30. Heidegger sees Aristotle's discussion of substance as leaving this broader unity "obscure" (AM 38).

31. There also remains the task of convincing us that ontology as we know it has indeed played itself out—however unwittingly or confusedly—against the background that the above account tries to identify, the task perhaps of the "torso's" other missing parts, the three divisions that would have been Part Two. In making his claims about the horizon against which an understanding of Being in general is

possible, Heidegger is also making a claim about "the basic theme of philosophy" (SZ 38)—indeed about "the inner and hidden life of the basic movement of Western philosophy" (MFL 154)—a claim that needs to demonstrate its histori al plausibility.

32. Cf. LQT 23: "There are automobiles, Negroes, Abelian functions, B ch's fugues. 'Are there' truths too? Or how could it be otherwise?"

33. See the letter to Jaspers quoted above.

34. See McManus 2013b, sec. 7. The problem concerns how we are to understand the Being of that horizon itself, indeed whether it can coherently be said to possess a mode of Being—and be said to be or to be thus-and-so—while still per orming the "function" Heidegger assigns it.

References

Aristotle. 1928. *Metaphysics*. Trans. W. D. Ross. Oxford: Oxford Universit Press.

Blattner, W. D. 1995. Decontextualisation, standardisation, and Dewey science. *Man and World* 28:321–339.

Brentano, Franz. 1975. *On the Several Senses of Being in Aristotle*. Trans. R. George. Berkeley: University of California Press.

Dreyfus, Hubert. L. 1991. *Being-in-the-World*. Cambridge, MA: MIT Press.

Fleischer, M. 1991. *Die Zeit Analysen in Heideggers Sein und Zeit: Aporien, Probleme and ein Ausblick*. Würzburg: Königshausen and Neumann.

Guignon, Charles. 1983. *Heidegger and the Problem of Knowledge*. Incianapolis: Hackett.

Guignon, Charles. 2000. Philosophy and authenticity: Heidegger's search for a ground for philosophizing. In *Heidegger, Authenticity, and Modernity*, ed. M. A. Wrathall and J. Malpas, 79–101. Cambridge, MA: MIT Press.

Haugeland, John. 2000. Truth and finitude: Heidegger's transcendental existentialism. In *Heidegger, Authenticity, and Modernity*, ed. M. A. Wrathall and J. Malpas, 43–77. Cambridge, MA: MIT Press.

James, William. 1956. The will to believe. In his *The Will to Believe and Other Essays in Popular Philosophy*, 1–31. New York: Dover.

Kisiel, Theodore. 1993. *The Genesis of Heidegger's Being and Time*. Berkeley: University of California Press.

Kisiel, Theodore. 2005. The Demise of *Being and Time*: 1927–30. In *Heidegger's* Being and Time, ed. R. Polt, 189–214. Lanham, MD: Rowman & Littlefield.

McManus, Denis. 2012. *Heidegger and the Measure of Truth*. Oxford: Oxford University Press.

McManus, Denis. 2013a. Heidegger, Wittgenstein, and St. Paul on the Last Judgment: On the roots and significance of the "theoretical attitude." *British Journal for the History of Philosophy* 21:143–164.

McManus, Denis. 2013b. Ontological pluralism and the Being and Time project. *Journal of the History of Philosophy* 51:651–674.

McManus, Denis. 2013c. The provocation to look and see: Appropriation, recollection and formal indication. In *Wittgenstein and Heidegger*, ed. D. Egan, S. Reynolds, and A. Wendland, 50–65. London: Routledge.

McManus, Denis. 2015. Anxiety, choice, and responsibility in Heidegger's account of authenticity. In *Heidegger, Authenticity, and the Self*, ed. D. McManus, 163-185. London: Routledge.

McManus Denis. Forthcoming. Being-towards-death and owning one's judgment. *Philosophy and Phenomenological Research*.

Owen, G. E. L. 1986. *Logic, Science, and Dialectic*. Ithaca, NY: Cornell University Press.

Polt, Richard. 1999. *Heidegger: An Introduction*. London: UCL Press.

Polt, Richard. 2005. Introduction. In *Heidegger's* Being and Time: *Critical Essays*, ed. R. Polt. Lanham: Rowman & Littlefield.

Rouse, J. 1985. Science and the theoretical "discovery" of the present-at-hand. In *Descriptions*, ed. D. Ihde and H. J. Silverman. Albany: SUNY Press.

10   What Is Missing? The Incompleteness and Failure of Heidegger's *Being and Time*

Eric S. Nelson

Introduction

Martin Heidegger's early magnum opus *Being and Time* (*Sein und Zeit*) provides a unique challenge to readers: the published work remains a fragment, and it is difficult to interpret the course of its argumentation without a sense of the projected whole. The double hermeneutical movement of interpreting the part through the whole while interpreting the whole through the part that usually bootstraps the text's meaning is here short-circuited. The reader is forced to project and reconstruct missing arguments, textual details, and a sense of the whole based on brief indications from the published fragment of *Being and Time* and other documents—such as lecture courses, letters, and the statements of contemporaries—as well as its intellectual milieu.

Hurried into print in 1927 because of career demands, the published version of *Being and Time* includes only the first two divisions of the first part: (1) the existential analytic of Dasein (conventionally translated as "being-there") and (2) the explication of Dasein through its temporality.

The unpublished Division III was to have analyzed temporality as the transcendental horizon of posing and responding to the question concerning the sense and meaning of being (*Sein*). This division, which Heidegger called "Time and Being," was reportedly worked out in some form but was left unfinished and unpublished after conversations between Heidegger and Jaspers in December 1926.[1] The planned three divisions of the second part were to offer a "destruction" (*Destruktion*), or a destructuring reading, revealing in reverse chronological order the constitutive role of temporality and its concealment in the metaphysics of time at three key moments of the history of Western ontology: the schematism in Kant's *Critique of Pure Reason*, the cogito in Descartes's *Meditations*, and the analysis of time in Book IV of Aristotle's *Physics*. The full articulation of time through which being is to be interpreted remains incomplete and leaves the project and philosophical success of *Being and Time* as a whole in doubt.

In this essay, I first consider several prevalent interpretations of the fragmentariness and "failure" of *Being and Time*, including three of Heidegger's divergent and at times conflicting self-interpretations. I then turn to questions of hermeneutics that are provoked by this incompleteness and its reception in relation to Heidegger's approach to hermeneutics as the art of interpretation. Heidegger's practice and elucidation of destructuring, creative, and violent interpretations that intend to liberate the "unthought" in the text appear to clarify his own subsequent depictions of *Being and Time*. But there remains a discrepancy and distance between the contingent incompleteness of *Being and Time* owing to the circumstances of its publication and the role this incompleteness is later given as part of the history of being. I accordingly examine the "gap" between the thought (or unthought) and the contingent empirically or ontically existing "author." I conclude that Heidegger's best interpretations of the significance of *Being and Time* in his philosophical journey entail a different understanding of the relationship between "life and work" than the one Heidegger himself maintained—one that is closer to the hermeneutical perspective and interpretive strategies, which embrace critical autobiographical and biographical reflection, encouraged by Wilhelm Dilthey and Georg Misch.

The Incomplete Failure of *Being and Time*

Heidegger's *Being and Time* appears to be a brilliant and provocative work at the same time as its fragmentary character leaves readers dissatisfied. This has led some commentators, such as William D. Blattner, to conclude not only that Heidegger "never completed the ontological task of *Being and Time*" but that "we do not possess any indications of how he would have completed it."[2] Such an extreme interpretation of incompleteness, the lack of "any indications" emphasized by Blattner, cannot be entirely true given the many indications provided by Heidegger, particularly in the lecture courses and in *Kant and the Problem of Metaphysics* (1929), that can be mapped in part onto the missing sections of *Being and Time*.

Researching sources in the archives and as they appear in print has allowed for ambitious reconstructions of the formation, scope, and "failure" of the project of *Being and Time*, most notably by Theodore Kisiel.[3] Heidegger's lecture course *The Basic Problems of Phenomenology*, held at the University of Marburg during the summer semester of 1927, is a compelling—if in the end only partial, as Blattner rightly stresses—indication of the themes and issues Heidegger planned to discuss in Division III and Part Two of *Being and Time*, making it less than an ineffable mystery.[4] We can thus neither skeptically deny or naively affirm the sense of the project of *Being and Time* as a whole.

There is a more troublesome suspicion than incompleteness lingering over the project of *Being and Time*: "failure." The incompleteness of *Being and Time*—in addition to Heidegger's varying and inconsistent explanations—has been construed as the result of a more serious underlying failure. That this incompleteness constitutes a philosophical failure of Heidegger's overall project, instead of an accidental feature of the publication history of the work, is maintained by a number of authors, in addition to Blattner and Kisiel. This interpretation can also be buttressed by a number of Heidegger's own later self-interpretations. Charles Guignon accordingly remarked: "The overall project of *Being and Time* is, as Heidegger suggests in his later writings, an illuminating—and perhaps inevitable—failure."[5]

Heidegger's philosophical failure has also been connected to his ensuing political failure. Herman Philipse has contended, for instance, that the failure of the turn within *Being and Time*—that is, the anticipated but undelivered turn toward "time and being," which Philipse described as a "metaphysical turn" and " an attempt to find God in some metaphysical sense"—led to the greater moral-political failure of Heidegger's "voluntaristic enthusiasm" for National Socialism.[6]

Three Attempts to Contextualize *Being and Time*

Turning Away from *Being and Time*

Heidegger proposed a variety of ways of understanding and reinterpreting *Being and Time*, from the time of its publication through his later writings. I will examine three of them here.

First, Heidegger often connects the issue of the meaning of *Being and Time* with the so-called reversal or turn (*Kehre*) in his thought. He speaks at times of the "false paths" and "detours and retreats" in *Being and Time*,[7] contending for instance in the "Letter on Humanism" that "the division in question was held back because thinking failed in the adequate saying of the turning and did not succeed with the help of the language of metaphysics."[8] Heidegger describes in *Zum Ereignis-Denken* ("Toward Thinking Enowning") the predicament of philosophical language to appropriately address the matter to be thought (*die Sache des Denkens*) in the wake of *Being and Time* that led to a new mindful-poetic language of the enowning or appropriating event (*Ereignis*). *Being and Time* remained captured by the language of metaphysics and it is Heidegger's encounter with poetic language, particularly that of the poet Hölderlin, which redirected his thinking of being.[9] Heidegger does not identify this failure as his own personal failure. It is always a failure in the context of its hermeneutical situation or its location in the history of being (*Seinsgeschichte*). His statements concerning the inability of thinking (*denken*) to follow through on the turning to "time and being," and overcome the limitations of traditional metaphysical language, are the sources for the "failure" mentioned by Guignon and the "failure of language to express the insight contained in the very title" described by Kisiel.[10]

Heidegger himself noted in *Contributions to Philosophy: From Enowning (Beiträge zur Philosophie: Vom Ereignis)*, composed between 1936 and 1938, how the failure of his early project resulted from inadequately emphasizing the radicalness of the ontological difference (*Differenz*) between beings (*Seiende*) and being (*Seyn*), since being cannot be comprehended from the perspective of beings at all, including that being that I am (*Dasein*). In the *Black Notebooks (Schwarze Hefte)* and other writings from the mid- and late 1930s, he asserted the overwhelming predominance (*Übermacht*; literally "superior power") of being over all beings.[11] The shift in Heidegger's use of *Überantwortung* is revealing: whereas Dasein is delivered over and responsible (*überantwortet*) to others and itself in care (*Sorge*) according to *Being and Time*, here humans have no capacity to constitute the sense of being to which they are delivered over and entrusted (*überantwortet*).[12] In Heidegger's interpretation of the preeminence of being in this period, *Being and Time* fails to think being because it treats it as a "mixture" (*Vermischung*) of being and beings rather than thinking this difference out of the nothing, as in the 1928/1929 essays "What Is Metaphysics?" ("Was ist Metaphysik?") and "On the Essence of Ground" ("Vom Wesen des Grundes"), or by way of the appropriating or enowning event (*Ereignis*) of being, as he does in the *Contributions*.[13]

Reiner Schürmann remarked that "the *Contributions* succeeds where *Being and Time* failed," as it relies on a heuristic rather than transcendental temporality and proceeds from a fractured and discordant condition that allows it to depart from the lingering "transcendental subjectivism" of *Being and Time*.[14] This claim reflects Heidegger's own assessment at that point that a new beginning would make a continuation or return to *Being and Time* unnecessary. Schürmann and Heidegger identify the step away from subjectivity and its temporality with a thinking of difference. It is in the *Contributions* that Heidegger concluded that the question of being can be approached only through its difference from beings, including Dasein, rather than through the intangible or illusive reflection (*Wiederschein*) of the unity of being that eluded his earlier thought.[15] The project of *Being and Time* collapses because it inappropriately objectifies or reifies being by elucidating being from the position of a being, Dasein, instead of from its difference.[16]

The "ontological difference" itself proved to be overly restraining according to Heidegger in the *Contributions*. It restrains thinking of being without reference to beings whatsoever, even in their difference. In the seminar in Le Thor in 1969, Heidegger reprises the idea that it was the reliance on the ontological difference from 1927 to 1935 that necessarily led off track to an impasse (*Holzweg*).[17] Prioritizing being (*Sein*) in to the context of the ontological difference is here identified as the limitation of his early thinking. The appropriating or enowning event cannot be thought from the concept of being, and the ontological difference disappears (*verschwindet*) with the disappearance of being.[18] It would be a mistake to consider Heidegger as a philosopher of being, since the question and history of being proceeds from the impending coming into unconcealment and of enowning.

Heidegger states in the *Contributions* that he held back the unpublished remainder of *Being and Time* to avoid the objectification (*Gegenständlichung*) of being and allow the "truth of being" (*Wahrheit des Seyns*) to be visible independently of the "temporal explication of being."[19] The analytic of *Dasein*, in which Dasein vis-à-vis its temporal way of being transcendentally constituted the "sense of being," proved to be an impediment to the truth of being as a disclosive event constituted by being in which humans comport themselves.[20]

Heidegger quickly experimented with and abandoned new philosophical projects in the immediate years after the appearance of *Being and Time* such as an "absolute science of being," "metontology," and a "metaphysics of freedom."[21] In the decade after its publication, Heidegger repeatedly spoke of its failure and the need to overcome it. But this narrative of failure is not the only one offered by Heidegger, including during this period. Heidegger became less willing to dismiss *Being and Time* as the limitations of the *Contributions* and the difficulty of an utterly new and other beginning—initially identified with the aspirations of the "new Germany" and its national revolution—became clearer to him.[22]

Failure as the Way: Errancy as Freedom or Rhetoric?

Second, failure does not signify an abrupt end if it can be interpreted as a methodology or way. The way of failure as the genuine way of thinking is indicated in a later text through the image of woodpaths (*Holzwege*): the woodpaths that twist, turn, and abruptly come to "dead ends" and clearings in the forest.[23] Heidegger advocated recurrently risking and experiencing failure in pursuing the matter to be thought in contrast with the academic establishment's obsession with a narrow instrumental conception of reputation and success. With reference to Plato and Aristotle Heidegger agued in the winter semester 1928–29 lecture course *Introduction to Philosophy* (*Einleitung in die Philosophie*) that thinking, one instance of which is visible in *Being and Time*, relentlessly fails in posing the question of being and thus must inevitably pose this question anew.[24] Failure in the path of thinking also takes place in his writings from the 1930s. Failure rather than calculable instrumental success is the mark of genuine thinking.

Less than ten years later in *Mindfulness* (*Besinnung*), Heidegger upholds the inescapability of failure of the kind of thinking he is endeavoring to undertake. Posing the question of being necessarily and repeatedly faces failure that in turn intensifies and radicalizes its questioning. The project of *Being and Time* must fail and be shattered ("muß scheitern") to the degree that the destructuring and overcoming of metaphysics is inexorably understood in a metaphysical sense.[25] That is to say, the most decisive posing of the question cannot avoid its own reification and fallenness.

What then is the question that *Being and Time* cannot overcome? Heidegger's thinking after the turn offered a new consideration of the "failure" of *Being and Time*. Frank Schalow has argued that the perceived "impasse" consisted in Heidegger's growing recognition of the problematic character of transcendental philosophy. Schalow notes how Heidegger's attempted "destructive-retrieval of transcendental philosophy" in his work on Kant sets the stage for the turn.[26] Heidegger stressed in his later notes to *Kant and the Problem of Metaphysics* how Part IV of this work adjusts his previous transcendentalism, the priority of the subject, and the "misinterpretation" of the incompleteness *Being and Time*, remarking: "*Beiträge*: beginning to a new beginning" (*Anfang zu neuem Anfang*).[27] The aspiration for a radical new beginning, and the subsequent failure of such a new beginning to transpire, clarifies both Heidegger's earlier move away from and later step back toward *Being and Time*.

Another clue in support of Schalow's reading is visible in Heidegger's focus on reinterpreting the notions of transcendental philosophy and metaphysics in works following the publication of *Being and Time*. Heidegger's book on Kant and the lecture courses *The Metaphysical Foundations of Logic* and *Introduction to Philosophy* indicate his renewed concern for the question of transcendental philosophy. According to this interpretation, the paradigm of transcendental philosophy and his struggles to overcome it continue to inform the categories and deep structures of Heidegger's thinking, notwithstanding the existential, hermeneutical, and life-philosophical embellishments visible in his thought in the 1920s, as he increasingly articulates in the 1930s the need for a more mindful unconcealment of an "other beginning" (*der andere Anfang*) that is only implicit in the questioning of *Being and Time*. Its incompleteness is less a failure than an incomplete step away from transcendental philosophy that opens the way for the more fundamental and radical transformation of thinking that Heidegger embarked on in the *Contributions to Philosophy*.

The Step Back toward *Being and Time*

A third approach becomes paradigmatic for the mature Heidegger after the Second World War. No "other beginning" had been achieved in Germany and Heidegger is compelled to assert the continuity of his thought in contrast with the discontinuities emphasized in the 1930s. The question of being led to the disclosure of the truth of being, its enowning event (*Ereignis*), even as *Ereignis* must be thought beyond the limitations of the question of being. The turn is in a sense already implicit in the questioning pursued in *Being and Time*, albeit limited by it, when it is appropriately understood as a moment in the history of being. *Being and Time* becomes a limited and yet still promising step that can be returned to and renewed in another direction rather than a mere failed and misleading impasse.

Heidegger at times spoke of "failure" (*scheitern*), as we have seen; at other times he contested the assessment of *Being and Time* as a mere failure or a fruitless "dead-end" (*Sackgasse*) that has been overcome by his critics or by himself. The etymology of "scheitern" might provide a clue to Heidegger's meaning: it means shattering to pieces, as when a ship shatters to pieces on the rocks (*zerscheitern*).[28] The word has come to signify in the modern German language an unexpected breakdown or falling through. Heidegger often uses "scheitern" in an ordinary sense of failure. But in the "Letter on Humanism," Heidegger stated that philosophizing about failing *("Philosophieren" über das Scheitern)* cannot be identified with a shattered failed thinking (*scheiternden Denken*) on condition that it immanently and responsively remains with the matter itself (*Sachen selbst*) that is to be thought and welcomes falling through as a fortunate gift of being.[29] There are innumerable unexpected twists, turns, and reversals on the way, but no failure—or success—as such. Such unexpected reversals and setbacks are necessary to allowing the truth of being to come to words.[30]

Heidegger argued in his later works, against his own occasional remarks about failure, for the underlying continuity and deepening of the standpoint of *Being and Time* through the turn into his later thinking of being:

The thinking of the reversal *is* a change in my thought. But this change is not a consequence of altering the standpoint, much less of abandoning the fundamental issue, of *Being and Time*. The thinking of the reversal results from the fact that I stayed with the matter that was to be thought in *Being and Time*, i.e., that I inquired into that perspective which already in *Being and Time* (p. 39) was designated as "Time and Being."[31]

In this letter to William J. Richardson from 1962, Heidegger describes the "reversal" in his thinking as inherent within the movement of *Being and Time* itself toward "time and being."[32] This reinterprets the incompleteness of *Being and Time* as a specific moment in the overall wayfaring of his philosophical sojourn rather than its incompletion constituting an outright failure.

Being and Time should not be construed to be a broken fragment that signifies an intrinsically flawed and "failed" project if it is interpreted from the standpoint out of which it is thought. Heidegger's own work should be read as he himself reads the philosophical canon, from out of its implicit unthought and the forgetting of being. Heidegger accordingly remarked, continuing the passage quoted above, in the "Letter on Humanism":

The lecture "On the Essence of Truth," thought out and delivered in 1930 but not printed until 1943, provides a certain insight into the thinking of the turning from "Being and Time" to "Time and Being." This turning is not a change of standpoint from *Being and Time*, but in it the thinking that was sought first arrives at the location of that dimension out of which *Being and Time* is experienced, that is to say, experienced from the fundamental experience of the oblivion of Being.[33]

We can see that Heidegger formulated multiple narratives concerning the incompleteness and failures of *Being and Time*. I have argued that these self-presentations diverge over time and are on occasion inconsistent, especially what I described as the turn away from *Being and Time*. Heidegger's varying assessments reflect the contexts in which they are formulated such that their "coherence" is not that of an intended thought or an implicit unthought but rather of "a life." This life can be traced through a critical reflective interpretation of Heidegger's path and its contexts. Such a "philosophical profile" encompasses and relies on the kind of biographical elements and critical autobiographical and biographical reflection that Heidegger himself excluded from the proper task of philosophy.

Hermeneutics and the Unthought

The Hermeneutics of Understanding Better

One hermeneutical maxim calls for taking agents' first-person perspectives and authors' self-interpretations seriously in order to understand the person from her or his own perspective ("aus ihm selbst"), interpreting authors as they "understood themselves." Such strategies of interpretive trust have their limits in the face of suspicions about self-ignorance, self-deception, and ideological and other forms of systematically distorted belief.

In the case of Heidegger, we have well-established reasons to limit our hermeneutical trust in his assertions. Heidegger has proven himself to be an inconsistent and unreliable interpreter of his own life and thought, whether it concerns his own intellectual development or his problematic political involvement in promoting National Socialism for the sake of an ostensibly nonvulgar and spiritual National Socialism.[34] His critics take an additional step: Walter Kaufmann once remarked that Heidegger's self-interpretations reveal a lack of capacity for any genuine self-understanding.[35] If Heidegger is not a dependable guide to interpreting his own words, then a different hermeneutical maxim may be appropriate: interpreting the author better or more insightfully than the author's own expressed self-interpretation.[36] This reconstructive hermeneutical strategy conforms to Heidegger's own interpretive practice of not taking an author's stated self-interpretation as authoritative about her meaning.

Heidegger adopted and transformed this notion of "understanding better" in opposition to his understanding of Dilthey's hermeneutics: the thinker *qua* thinker is not interested in the biography, individuality, or psychology of the author whose contingent individual life (*zufällig-indi-viduellen Lebens*) does not constitute the center of the intellectual work.[37] Dilthey sought to contextualize and individualize the thinker, making the implicit explicit and indeterminate determinate through the hermeneutical movement between individual and context in order to articulate an individuated life-nexus (*Lebenszusammenhang*). Heidegger, on the other hand, separated the thinker from her life-conditions even when he was closest to Dilthey's hermeneutical life-philosophy in the early 1920s. This feature of Heidegger's thought was developed more than a decade earlier than his questionable political engagement, so it is not simply a revisionist attempt to disentangle his thought from his own life.

Despite the early Heidegger's protests against abstract conceptual thought dissociated from the existential conditions of human life, he never adopted existentialism and life-philosophy's thesis of the unity of life and thinking in an author. Heidegger remarked in his 1924 lecture course the *Basic Concepts of Aristotelian Philosophy* that it is sufficient for the thinker to know that "Aristotle was born, worked, and died."[38] The primary philosophical task is to focus on the immanent structure of the thought as independent of the contingent ontic aspects of the life of the thinker. Words are not simply expressions that can be traced back to the life of the mind or the subject. Heidegger sided, in fact, with Frege and Husserl in the early 1920s against the "historicism" and "naturalism" that threaten to reduce thought to its historical or natural conditions; the thought (*der Gedanke*) aims at the object that is "intended" (*das Gemeinte*).[39]

Formal Indication, Emptiness, Politics

Heidegger takes this separation a step further: he divides the thought from the ontic contingencies of life while connecting thinking to the formally indicated structures of existence.[40] Heidegger described "formal indication" as the basic character of philosophical concepts as late as the *Fundamental Concepts of Metaphysics* in winter semester 1929–30.[41] Heidegger depicted his early methodology of formal indication as not having the function of binding (*Bindung*); it releases (*Freigabe*) or opens up the concrete variety of the phenomena without being absorbed and lost in them.[42]

Formalization is a process of emptying (*entleeren*) particular contents, including the long-standing and commonly accepted understandings and interpretations that are dominant in everyday life and philosophical thought, until one reaches the "formal-ontological."[43] This is an emptying out of contents that ought to lead back to the concrete phenomena in their self-showing. Formal indication is as a consequence in the first instance a negative prohibitive step, according to Heidegger.[44] That is to say, for example, the formal indication "Dasein" destructures traditional interpretations of what it is to be human and releases a variety of concrete forms of existence without being identical or reducible to one form or understanding of human life. The idea that Dasein is a formal indication—as opposed to a given concrete reality—points toward why Heidegger considered it to be "neutral" prior to its factical brokenness, dispersal, and concretion instead of being defined by its biology, anthropology, or gender.[45] Heidegger himself abandoned this terminological expression, though it continues to resonate in his conception of way, and noted after the turn the danger of a "detached formal indication of Da-seyn."[46]

The strategy of formal indication or hermeneutical anticipation is the dimension of Heidegger's early project that gave rise to the allegation of pseudo- or phony concreteness. This charge has been made in various ways by critics such as Misch, Herbert Marcuse, and Günther Anders.[47] Marcuse, for instance, retrospectively describes this problem in an interview with Frederick Olafson.[48] Marcuse expresses unease that Heidegger's formalized and reutralized concreteness entails a lack of practical and political determinacy that cannot be compensated for and is only worsened by his ambiguous ethos of a contentless resoluteness (*Entschlossenheit*), which Jürgen Habermas described as "the decisionism of empty resoluteness."[49] *Being and Time* is necessarily incomplete and incompletable owing to the arbitrariness, emptiness, and rhetorical aura of its basic concepts. It is part of its charm and danger that this work stages a philosophy that seemingly can be taken and individuated in multiple ways, including the Heideggerian–Marxist direction that fascinated the early Marcuse, while structurally tending toward radical nationalistic conservativism and National Socialism.

Given Heidegger's deployment of his philosophical concepts in support of the new National Socialist regime, his implementation of its university policies during his year-long service as rector of the University of Freiburg, and legitimate questions concerning whether the turn has a deep connection with his political thinking, as is evident in the *Black Notebooks*, Heidegger's critics are correct that questions of incompleteness and failure are not only bound up with the turn as a purely intellectual transformation. Heidegger's turn is intertwined with his political involvement in the 1930s. Its philosophical vocabulary is all the more—rather than less—entangled in German nationalism than the language of *Being and Time*. Better accounts of Heidegger's philosophy *qua* philosophy do not resolve these suspicions; they intensify the doubt that something elemental is lacking insofar as they disconnect the thought from the empirical philosopher and his ethnocentric and rationalist (*völkisch*) political thinking.[50] The variations in the philosophical thought cannot be formalized and detached without distortion from the ontic biographical life of the philosopher "Heidegger."

The Thought and the Unthought

Heidegger contended in the 1920s that thought is not solely a matter of logic, cognitive thinking, and discursive argumentation.[51] At the same time as the early Heidegger rejected the priority of a narrowly defined logic and rationality, he resisted the reduction of thinking to the empirical state of affairs of individual thinkers, particularly the ideal content of the thought to the psychological states of individuals, as in the variety of naturalism called "psychologism."[52] Heidegger's rejection of the distinction between the real and the ideal does not entail that he overcame the "Platonism" of his academic formation.[53] Heidegger noted in his early and late remarks concerning Husserl how it was the critique of psychologism in the *Logical Investigations*, the work that he described as Husserl's most decisive, which constituted a radical philosophical "breakthrough"; it is only the first negative step but a necessary one for pursuing phenomenology.[54]

Heidegger did not rest with the intended "thought" liberated from ontic and empirical affairs. He repositions the thought in relation to formally indicated dispositional affective moods and that which is hidden, silent, and prereflectively "unthought" by the biographical thinker that structures her or his thinking. In his Marburg lecture course on Plato's *Sophist* in the winter semester of 1924–25, Heidegger commented that the interpreter cannot rely on the author's statements concerning what is essential in the work. Nor can one appeal to the "intended" predicative proposition. One ought to turn instead toward that which is concealed in silence in order to interpret more decisively what the author assumes to be the essential.[55]

Heidegger regarded "understanding appropriately" or "correctly" in this context as "understanding better." He maintained in the winter semester of 1927–1928 that the interpretive process cannot be considered as correctness or as a correct reproduction of the given. Interpretation has to engage and confront what is to be understood in what is to be thought. This confrontation "is no mere rejection of what is understood, but rather is giving it 'validity.'"[56] To allow the author to speak and the thought to come to its "validity" calls for engaging in a differentiating confrontation (*Auseinandersetzung*) and "the philosophical struggle [*Kampf*] that goes on within every real interpretation."[57]

Heidegger presses the case for the necessity of interpretive violence in his book on Kant: "Certainly, in order to wring from what the words say, what it is they want to say, every interpretation must necessarily use violence. Such violence, however, cannot be roving arbitrariness."[58] It is not erratic capriciousness if textual violence liberates the latent unspoken in the saying: "The authentic interpretation must show what does not stand there in the words and which is nevertheless said. For this the interpretation must necessarily use violence."[59] Heidegger's unconventional hermeneutics requires a kind of violence against the author in the name of the matter to be thought. It interprets authors according to the hidden unthought (*das Ungedachte*) of their thinking (*denken*) and, as he deepens his destructuring art of interpretation, the history of the thinking of being itself.

Heidegger repeatedly denied, then, the possibility of the "failure" of a philosophy, including the project of *Being and Time*, through an argumentative refutation. Genuine thinking is never a matter of logic and proof. Heidegger remained consistently unconcerned with objections to his thought—such as those made by Rudolf Carnap and Oskar Kraus in 1931 to his conception of nothingness—based on its lack of logical consistency.[60] Heidegger remarked in an interpretation of Nietzsche that a philosophy cannot be "overcome" through argumentation and refutation. As an alternative to formal systematic reasoning, Heidegger calls for a way of thinking in which the explicit and thematic thought (*das Gedachte*) is to be overcome and the implicit unthought in its being thought ("das Ungedachte in seinem Gedachten") returned into its original truth.[61] This original truth is the same (*das Selbe*), I am suggesting, as the originary dimension from which we ought to interpret *Being and Time*: the unthought as an indication or trace of being in the play of its historical concealment and unconcealment.

Heidegger stresses that readers should turn away from a subjective identification with the thinking of authors toward the thinking that is implicit in the matter to be thought: the concealment and unconcealment of being. Such a confrontation does not concern itself with what the author knowingly intended or meant. Heidegger's readings of canonical occidental philosophers tenaciously and violently seek to liberate the concealed unthought of the text, in confrontation with the author's "intentions," and disclose the roles of the text's "said" within the fateful trajectory of the history of Western ontology or the history of being. Heidegger consequently maintained from his early to later philosophy that there is either an ideal intentional (early phase) or a concealed ontological (later being-historical phase) thought within philosophical texts independent of the thinker to which it occurs. This thought is more fundamental than the contingent empirical thinking of individual authors—which encompasses contexts and conditions as well as the intentions and first-person perspective of individuals—emphasized by Dilthey.

As I argued above, Heidegger's articulated anticipative concepts such as life, finitude, facticity, existence, Dasein, care, and so on, not as concrete empirical-ontic realities; in opposition to such "reification" and the false objectivity of regional ontic domains, formally indicative and destructuring-releasing concepts are accordingly ontological.[62] It is in the context of Heidegger's formalism that the transformation from the thought to the unthought needs to be interpreted. While Heidegger—under the influence of Husserl's phenomenology—identified the target of interpretation with the "intended thought" in the early 1920s, the target shifted to the proto-intentional unthought in increasingly radicalized forms thereafter.

Husserl could no longer recognize the transcendental-phenomenological moment in *Being and Time* and *Kant and the Problem of Metaphysics*.[63] Husserl accordingly held the reverse of the usual assessment of the "failure" of *Being and Time*—that it is due to its lingering commitments to transcendental subjectivity. Attributing it to its betrayal of transcendental philosophy, Husserl criticized Heidegger for transforming phenomenology into an existential anthropology akin to Dilthey's life-philosophy construed as a "new form of anthropology."[64] I have contended that Heidegger's "liberating" destructuring of the unthought has little to do with the ontic or empirical features of biographical authors, or their anthropological and psychological conditions. Heidegger rejected not only psychologism but the specter of it that he, like Husserl and Rickert before him, perceived in the descriptive and analytic contextualizing approach to the "life of the mind," relying on a variety of critical reflectiveness—as Dilthey conceptualized *Besinnung*—informed by and yet irreducible to the sciences, which proved to be so significant for Dilthey and Misch. As Charles Bambach argued, Heidegger remained committed to a transcendental analysis in *Being and Time* in order to ward off the historical relativism he considered to be a consequence of Dilthey's variety of historically oriented thinking.[65]

Despite Heidegger's reluctance to use merely biographical information about a thinker, his own shifting narratives about failure make better interpretive sense when they are related to the conditions, contexts, and elements of "a life"—with all of its epochal and generational complexities and complicities—instead of impersonally linked to the history of being and its fatefulness.[66] The missed chance to connect philosophical thinking to the "authentic historical event [*eigentlichen geschichtlichen Ereignisse*]" of the embodied worldly self, including the formation (*Bildung*) of moral personality, is one of the limitations of *Being and Time* according to Misch's early critique in *Life-philosophy and Phenomenology*.[67]

Conclusion: Retrieving Heidegger's Unthought?

"To think with Heidegger against Heidegger," to reiterate Habermas's catch-phrase, has come to signify the critical uncovering of the limitations and/or the recovery of the promise of the thinking associated with his philosophical project(s).[68] Such an endeavor to think with and against is one that Heidegger himself repeatedly undertook—with respect to his own thinking if not to his political involvement—as he reposed and reformulated questions and responses anew.

I have noted above that which Heidegger considered to be the "unthought" of *Being and Time* that becomes explicit only through the turn into his later thinking: it is "the fundamental experience of the oblivion of being."[69] *Being and Time* is accordingly a moment that marks a turning point in the history of being. It discloses—while performatively enacting and being entangled in—the forgetting of being and the plight of human beings within this forgetting. Suspicions concerning Heidegger's reconstruction of his journey can be raised again here: is this retrospective "unthought" the same as its "original" incompleteness? Did Heidegger halt the composition of *Being and Time* as a result of an inkling of his future thinking? Or was there something else in his immediate present—a doubt or interruptive consideration raised by Jaspers in that decisive conversation? We must conclude with these questions, since they ask about unknown characteristics belonging to the empirical biography of the thinker that may or might not be discovered through further historical research.

There have been frequent deconstructive and reconstructive readings of the unthought of *Being and Time*, which is not merely a question of the person "Heidegger": what did this work not think, or not think adequately enough? And is this the same as an unthought? One interpretation that has shaped the English-language reception of Heidegger is found in Richard Rorty's reconstruction. Rorty has argued that the failure of *Being and Time* is due to the limitations of Heidegger the person rather than its groundbreaking antifoundational therapeutic project.

Heidegger failed in Rorty's estimation to effectively think through the art of "groundless" existential philosophical therapy promoted in *Being and Time* in a thorough and consequent manner.[70] The project of *Being and Time* is not necessarily a failure if its essential argumentation was made in the published work and if it can be interpreted as either a coherent form of open-ended pragmatism or incarnation of transcendental philosophy concerned with how the "subjectivity of the subject" arises from Dasein. Both accounts appear to miss elements of Heidegger's project as well as the twisting journey of his thinking. Heidegger's thinking before the turn interprets the a priori of the subject in its concrete enactment bringing it closer to Dilthey's immanent "categories of life"; Heidegger, after the turn, relentlessly criticizes the transcendental notion of the subjectivity of the subject and the modern notion of the subject that Heidegger condemned as ahistorical and worldless.[71]

Comparable difficulties pursue the pragmatic account. Rorty's interpretation, for instance, problematically minimizes its transcendental-ontological moment that encompasses a further range of philosophical commitments than needed by a work of pragmatic therapy. Regardless of the limitations of Rorty's reading, it suggests a way of looking at *Being and Time* critically and immanently as an incomplete and flawed yet open and promising source of structured philosophical argumentation and analysis as well as existential and therapeutic insight. Rorty argues that Heidegger's incompletion and turn away from the project of *Being and Time* constituted a betrayal and a "failure of nerve."[72] The reputed failure of *Being and Time* is a failure of our own—and, according to Rorty, Heidegger's—imagination.

As a factical nexus of contingent conditions, passions, and actions, as entangled with and mediated in the empirical and ontic existence of "a life," work and person are not as easily separable as Rorty suggests.[73] The failures of the person and the work call for critical biographical reflection as well as social and ideology critique. If the claims of hermeneutics are taken seriously, then questions about Heidegger's biography and its contexts are not external to those concerning Heidegger's thought even if the validity of a thought or proposition cannot be reduced to the factical social-political states of affairs and psychological states of mind of the thinker. Likewise, the incompleteness and limitations of *Being and Time* are immanent to the work itself. They have become integral to its interpretation, reception, and any reimagining of it.

Acknowledgments

I want to thank Lee Braver, François Raffoul, and Frank Schalow for their suggestions. I also would like to express my gratitude to Jin Y. Park for questions that helped change this essay for the better. All references and citations are to the pagination of Heidegger's works in the *Gesamtausgabe* (GA) (Frankfurt am Main: Vittorio Klostermann, 1975–) unless otherwise noted.

Notes

1. Heidegger reported this crucial conversation with Jaspers in GA49 39–40.

2. William D. Blattner, *Heidegger's Temporal Idealism* (Cambridge: Cambridge University Press, 1999), 259.

3. Theodore J. Kisiel, *The Genesis of Heidegger's* Being and Time (Berkeley: University of California Press, 1993), 445. Kisiel's pioneering work still remains the most ambitious and comprehensive reconstruction of the context and emergence of *Being and Time*. See also Theodore Kisiel, "Das Versagen von *Sein und Zeit*: 1927–1930," in

Martin Heidegger: Sein und Zeit, ed. Thomas Rentsch (Berlin: Akademie, 2001), 253–279.

4. Blattner, *Heidegger's Temporal Idealism*, 259.

5. Charles E. Guignon, *Heidegger and the Problem of Knowledge* (Indianapolis: Hackett, 1983), 20.

6. Herman Philipse, *Heidegger's Philosophy of Being: A Critical Interpretation* (Princeton: Princeton University Press, 1998), 244.

7. See Dieter Thomä, "*Being and Time* in Retrospect: Heidegger's Self-Critique," in *Heidegger's Being and Time: Critical Essays*, ed. Richard Polt (Lanham: Rowman & Littlefield, 2005), 215.

8. GA9 327–328.

9. GA73 1.

10. Guignon, *Heidegger and the Problem of Knowledge*, 20; Kisiel, *The Genesis of Heidegger's Being and Time*, 445. See also Theodore Kisiel, "The Demise of *Being and Time*: 1927–1930," in *Heidegger's Being and Time*, 189–214.

11. GA94 362; see also GA36–37 100; GA39 31.

12. On being delivered over in the sense of being responsible to oneself, see GA2 41–42, 135; GA26 17; GA27 324; on being delivered over into and accepting being, see GA38 162–163; GA65 488.

13. GA65 250, 450–451.

14. Reiner Schürmann, "Ultimate Double Binds," in *Heidegger toward the Turn: Essays on the Work of the 1930s*, ed. James Risser (Albany: SUNY Press, 1999), 243, 245.

15. GA65 250.

16. GA65 451.

17. Heidegger, "Vorausgreifend müßte man nämlich auch die fortgesetzte Bezugnahme auf die ontologische Differenz von 1927 bis 1936 als notwendigen Holzweg sehen," GA15 104.

18. GA15 104.

19. GA65 451.

20. Cf. Philipse, *Heidegger's Philosophy of Being*, 479.

21. See Peter Trawny, *Heidegger und der Mythos der jüdischen Weltverschwörung*, 2nd exp. ed. (Frankfurt am Main: Klostermann, 2014), 17.

22. Cf. Trawny, *Heidegger und der Mythos der jüdischen Weltverschwörung*, 25–28.

23. See Iain D. Thomson, *Heidegger, Art, and Postmodernity* (New York: Cambridge University Press, 2011), 83.

24. GA27 216.

25. GA66: *Besinnung*, 413–414/*Mindfulness*, trans. Emad and Kalary, 356–367. Heidegger interpreted failure as "epochal errancy" in relation to the history of being. The "freedom to fail" is interpreted as an anarchistic emancipatory impulse in Heidegger's thinking in Peter Trawny, *Freedom to Fail: Heidegger's Anarchy* (Oxford: Polity Press, 2015).

26. Frank Schalow, "Heidegger and Kant: Three Guiding Questions," in *Bloomsbury Companion to Heidegger*, ed. François Raffoul and Eric S. Nelson (London: Bloomsbury, 2013), 109–110.

27. GA3 xiii/KPM xvii. Schalow, "Heidegger and Kant," 109–110.

28. See Joachim Heinrich Campe, *Wörterbuch der deutschen Sprache: U bis Z*, vol. 5 (Braunschweig: In der Schulbuchhandlung, 1811), 848; Christian Friedrich Meyer, *Handwörterbuch deutscher sinnverwandter Ausdrücke* (Leipzig: Brockhaus, 1849), 372.

29. GA9 343.

30. Cf. GA9 343–344.

31. Heidegger, "Letter to Father Richardson," in Heidegger, Günter Figal, and Jerome Veith, *The Heidegger Reader* (Bloomington: Indiana University Press, 2009), 302.

32. Ibid.

33. GA9 327–328.

34. See, e.g., the now classic discussion of divergent visions of National Socialism and spirit (*Geist*) in Jacques Derrida, *Of Spirit: Heidegger and the Question*, trans. Geoffrey Bennington and Rachel Bowlby (Chicago: University of Chicago Press, 1989). The currently available volumes of the *Black Notebooks* (GA94–97) confirm Heidegger's continued commitment to an ethnocentric "Germanism" (*Deutschtum*) superior to "vulgar" National Socialism into the postwar period.

35. Kaufmann claimed: "Heidegger's failure to understand himself far exceeded even Hegel's." Walter Kaufmann, *Nietzsche, Heidegger, and Buber* (New York: McGraw-Hill, 1980), 218.

36. "Jede Auslegung einer Dichtung geht über das, was auszulegen ist, hinaus; sie muß den Autor besser verstehen als er sich selber verstanden hat, damit wir uns dadurch ein Positives schaffen" (GA36–37 167).

37. See, e.g., Holger Zaborowski and Anton Bösl, eds., *Martin Heidegger: Briefe an Max Müller und andere Dokumente* (Freiburg: Alber, 2003), 49.

38. GA18 5.

39. Cf. GA59 65; GA63 11; GA24 297. On the intended in Heidegger and Husserl, see Leslie MacAvoy, "Heidegger and Husserl," in *Bloomsbury Companion to Heidegger*, ed. François Raffoul and Eric S. Nelson (London: Bloomsbury, 2013), 135–142.

40. On the formation and signification of formal indication, see Theodore Kisiel, "On the Genesis of Heidegger's Formally Indicative Hermeneutics of Facticity," in *Rethinking Facticity*, ed. François Raffoul and Eric S. Nelson (Albany: SUNY Press, 2008), 41–6⁷. See also Leslie MacAvoy, "Formal Indication and the Hermeneutics of Facticity," *Philosophy Today* 54 (SPEP Supp. 2010): 84–90; Eric S. Nelson, "Die formale Anzeige der Faktizität als Frage der Logik," in *Heidegger und die Logik*, ed. Alfred Denker and Holger Zaborowski (Amsterdam: Editions Rodopi BV, 2006), 31–48.

41. GA29–30 421. Compare the discussion of formal indication as method in John Haugeland, *Dasein Disclosed: John Haugeland's Heidegger*, ed. Joseph Rouse (Cambridge, MA: Harvard University Press, 2013), 73–75.

42. GA9 65.

43. GA17 250.

44. GA61 41.

45. GA26 136–138; GA27 146. On Dasein's neutrality and the body, see Kevin A. Aho, *Heidegger's Neglect of the Body* (Albany: SUNY Press, 2009), 55–61. This line of thinking is often interpreted as preventing Heidegger from simply adopting biological forms of racism and as motivating his numerous criticisms of biological-racial thinking in the 1930s. But this rejection does not entail the exclusion of nonbiologically based varieties of racism, such as legitimations based in "being-historical thinking," as Trawny discusses in *Heidegger und der Mythos der jüdischen Weltverschwörung*, 39–45.

46. GA88 243.

47. Georg Misch, *Lebensphilosophie und Phänomenologie: Eine Auseinandersetzung der Diltheyschen Richtung mit Heidegger und Husserl* (Bonn: F. Cohen 1930), 228; Guenther Stern (Anders), "On the Pseudo-Concreteness of Heidegger's Philosophy," *Philosophy and Phenomenological Research* 8, no. 3 (Mar. 1948): 337–371. Marcuse adopted this phrase retrospectively in describing his departure from Heidegger's influence. See Herbert Marcuse, *Heideggerian Marxism*, ed. Richard Wolin and John Abromeit (Lincoln: University of Nebraska Press, 2005), 166.

48. Marcuse, *Heideggerian Marxism*, 2005, 165–175.

49. Jürgen Habermas, *The Philosophical Discourse of Modernity* (Cambridge, MA: MIT Press, 1987), 141.

50. Cf. Trawny, *Heidegger und der Mythos der jüdischen Weltverschwörung*, 26–27.

51. See GA61 21; Martin Heidegger and Heinrich Rickert, *Briefe und Dokumente 1912–1933*, ed. Alfred Denker (Frankfurt am Main: Klostermann, 2001), 58.

52. GA20 160.

53. GA2 217. Cf. Taylor Carman, *Heidegger's Analytic: Interpretation, Discourse, and Authenticity in "Being and Time"* (Cambridge: Cambridge University Press, 2003), 91–92.

54. See GA58 16; GA20 160; and also the later remark in *Zur Sache des Denkens*, translated as *On Time and Being*, GA14 83. Heidegger took time in the *Black Notebooks 1939–1941* to praise Husserl's critique of psychologism and historicism in the midst of claiming that his phenomenology could not reach the realm of essential decisions because of the empty calculative rationality of Judaism (*Judentum*) in GA96 46–47.

55. "Gerade das, was ein Autor verschweigt, ist das, wobei man ansetzen muß, um das zu verstehen, was der Autor selbst als das Eigentliche bezeichnet" (GA19 46).

56. GA25 4.

57. Ibid.

58. *Kant and the Problem of Metaphysics*, trans. Richard Taft (Bloomington, Indiana University Press, 1997), 202; GA3 141.

59. *Introduction to Metaphysics*, trans. Gregory Fried and Richard Polt (New Haven: Yale University Press, 2000), 173; GA40 124.

60. Rudolf Carnap, "Überwindung der Metaphysik durch logische Analyse der Sprache," in *Scheinprobleme in der Philosophie und andere metaphysikkritische Schriften* (Hamburg: Meiner, 2004), 87–103; Oskar Kraus, *Wege und Abwege der Philosophie: Vorträge und Abhandlungen* (Prague: I. G. Calve, 1934), 123–124. On Carnap's logical and life-philosophical critique of Heidegger, see Eric S. Nelson, "Heidegger and Carnap: Disagreeing about Nothing?" in *Bloomsbury Companion to Heidegger*, ed. François Raffoul and Eric S. Nelson (London: Bloomsbury, 2013), 151–155.

61. "Das Gedachte eines Denkers läßt sich nur so verwinden, daß das Ungedachte in seinem Gedachten auf seine anfängliche Wahrheit zurückverlegt wird" (GA8 23–24).

62. On formal indication, see GA58 198; GA61 145; GA29–30 429.

63. Husserl's notes and comments on Heidegger are collected in Edmund Husserl, *Psychological and Transcendental Phenomenology and the Confrontation with Heidegger* (1927–1931), Collected Works 6 (The Hague: Nijhoff, 1997).

64. Husserl, *Psychological and Transcendental Phenomenology*, 505; see also Edmund Husserl, "Phänomenologie und Anthropologie," in Edmund Husserl, *Aufsätze und Vorträge (1922–1937), Gesammelte Werke XXVII*, ed. Thomas Nenon and Hans Rainer

Sepp (Dordrecht: Kluwer, 1989), 164–181. Cf. Kaufmann, *Nietzsche, Heidegger, and Buber*, 188.

65. Charles R. Bambach, *Heidegger, Dilthey, and the Crisis of Historicism* (Ithaca: Cornell University Press, 1995), 228.

66. Misch, *Lebensphilosophie und Phänomenologie*, 244. For further discussion of Dilthey and Heidegger, see Eric S. Nelson, "Heidegger and Dilthey: A Difference in Interpretation," in *Bloomsbury Companion to Heidegger*, 129–134; and Eric S. Nelson, "Heidegger and Dilthey: Language, History, and Hermeneutics" in *The Horizons of Authenticity: Essays in Honor of Charles Guignon's Work on Phenomenology, Existentialism, and Moral Psychology*, ed. Megan Altman and Hans Pedersen (Dordrecht: Springer, 2014).

67. Misch, *Lebensphilosophie und Phänomenologie*, 18.

68. Jürgen Habermas, "Mit Heidegger gegen Heidegger denken: Zur Veröffentlichung von Vorlesungen aus dem Jahre 1935," *Frankfurter Allgemeine Zeitung*, July 25, 1953, 67–75.

69. GA9 327–328.

70. Richard Rorty, "Overcoming the Tradition: Heidegger and Dewey," in *Heidegger and Modern Philosophy*, ed. Michael Murray (New Haven: Yale University Press, 1978), 250–258. On Rorty's reading of Heidegger, see Leslie MacAvoy, "Heidegger's Anglo-American Reception," in *Bloomsbury Companion to Heidegger*, 429–430.

71. For the transcendental sense of subjectivity, and posing the question of it more radically, see GA2 24, 106, 229, 382; GA26 129, 160, 190, 205, 211; GA27 11. For Heidegger's later critique of the subject, see GA5 243: GA69 44; GA79 101, 139.

72. Richard Rorty, *Essays on Heidegger and Others: Philosophical Papers*, vol. 2 (Cambridge: Cambridge University Press, 1991), 63.

73. Richard Rorty, "Diary," *London Review of Books* 12, nos. 3–8 (February 1990), 21.

11   From the Understanding of Being to the Happening of Being

Richard Polt

To see your lovely faces
as they once were is deadly, I'm afraid,
and it is hardly meet to wake the dead.
—Hölderlin, "Germania"

Our enterprise is a morbid one: to resurrect a text murdered by its own author, a manuscript he chose to "annihilate" by fire (GA66 413–414; GA2 582)—even though he preserved nearly every other draft, sketch, and note that he penned over the decades. What good can come of sifting through the ashes?

Waking the dead can be deadly if it seduces us into a fantasy of retrograde time travel, into an imaginary alternate history that denies a crucial aspect of our finitude: our thrownness, our inability to undo what has been handed down to us. Grave robbery is also unsalutary if it merely serves an antiquarian reconstruction of past ideas, and fails to stimulate our own active thought. But if we draw creatively on the hints that Heidegger left behind, the traces of his annihilated text may help us project new ways to think, and even to be.

This recovery effort requires particular attention to the role of time in Heidegger's thought, for it was the connection between time and being that he saw as his "sole lightning bolt" of insight,[1] and the vicissitudes of that insight are central to understanding his evolution through and past *Being and Time*. Part One, Division III of *Being and Time* would have treated Dasein's temporality as providing "horizonal schemata" that delimit and unify the possible senses of being (BT 365, BP 302). Time would serve as the ultimate condition of the possibility of experience. Heidegger would thus have provided a transcendental account that would shed new light not only on Dasein's own being, but on the being of all beings. Heidegger's shift away from this transcendental approach has sometimes been taken as a rejection of an overly subjectivist conception of Dasein, a view that takes our understanding of being as an achievement of subjectivity. But *Being and Time* explicitly forswears subjectivism—and even before this text, Heidegger's interpretations of Kant had emphasized the *receptivity* that is involved in the temporal understanding of being. Why, then, did he destroy Division III? I propose that Heidegger was uneasy with this text because he began to feel the need for a new line of thought. As we will see, he came to believe that he had to address the origin of the "primal fact" of temporality itself, and sought such an origin in a mysterious event that founds Dasein's time. This theme could not be encompassed in a transcendental inquiry, even a nonsubjectivist one. This is at least part of the meaning of Heidegger's move "from the understanding of being to the *happening of being.*"[2]

In what follows, I review what it means to inquire into "being" and how Heidegger intended to clarify the meaning of being by way of Dasein's temporality. I then sketch a temporal ontology along the lines that he suggests, and show how his own thoughts brought him to questions about the origin of time that could not be raised within the transcendental framework of that temporal ontology. These new questions do not simply cancel out the project of *Being and Time*, because that project cannot be reduced to its transcendental interpretation. *Being and Time* keeps provoking us to explore the connection between time and being, as do Heidegger's later inquiries into the "event" that originates time.

The Question of Being

The goal of *Being and Time*, announced on its opening page and in its very title, was to reveal time as the horizon for the understanding of being. In other words, Heidegger wished to show that our threefold temporality—our projective reach into possibilities, our thrown dependence on what we have been given, and our engagement in a current world—makes it possible for anything to make sense to us as what is, rather than what is not. Time gives us access to being.

But what does Heidegger mean by "being"? The question is difficult and controversial.[3] To get a clear and complete concept of being, we would need to have completed the project of *Being and Time* itself. However, as Heidegger emphasizes from the outset, we already have an implicit, vague understanding of being that we can work with—as he does in his book. The following remarks, then, are inexact elucidations of Heidegger's usage of the word *Sein*, not strict definitions.

First, Heidegger often uses "being" as one might use "essence" or "nature": for instance, to examine "the kind of Being which belongs to the living as such" is to establish what defines something as alive (BT 10). Heidegger calls this "what-being" (BP 77–121).

"Being" also has what is often called an existential sense, or "that-being." An entity, something that *is* (or, in common parlance, exists), is something instead of nothing. "Being lies in the fact that something is [as well as] its Being as it is" (BT 7).

Furthermore, Heidegger emphasizes that being is not an entity. It "is" not, but it is given to Dasein as the entity who understands being (BT 183). Being is essentially related to Dasein's understanding; it is that in terms of which Dasein understands entities as entities (BT 6).[4]

These various usages cohere, as long as we are willing to challenge some standard distinctions such as the split between what-being and that-being. What it means for something to "exist" (that-being) may depend on what sort of entity it is (what-being), and vice versa.[5] If we keep what-being and that-being utterly separate, we easily end up assuming that "existence" has one and the same sense for all kinds of entities. That is precisely the unquestioned, reductive understanding of being that Heidegger found pernicious.

To suggest the multiple yet related senses of "being" and being's essential connection to Dasein, we can gloss being as "the difference it makes that there is something instead of nothing."[6] There is no such difference without someone (Dasein) to whom the difference can be made. The difference has an "existential" sense but also an "essential" one, for various kinds of entities display their various essences precisely in the particular sorts of difference it makes for them to be something instead of nothing. As we tease apart the senses of being, we discover the differences it makes that there are, for instance, artworks rather than nothing, or atoms rather than nothing. An artwork does not "exist" in the same way an atom "exists"; the difference between their ways of existing is precisely the essential difference between the two kinds of entity.

Another way to express the notion of "making a difference" is to observe that to *be*, for us, is to be potentially worthy of note—to be something that can be acknowledged, that can be taken into account. This acknowledgment includes even the most trivial and passing notice we take of something. Even an indifferent glance has meaning: it recognizes some entity as having some minimal import. By drawing the line between being and nonbeing, as we constantly do in both thought and practice, we establish what can count as memorable and valid.

The boundary between being and nonbeing permits us to comprehend, use, and recognize things. Without such a boundary, we could not deal with beings as beings. Thus, "We always conduct our activities in an understanding of being" (BT 5). The boundary between being and nonbeing may go unrecognized, and usually does. When we attempt to grasp it explicitly, we inevitably draw on a historically formed tradition (BT 20–22, BP 22). This tradition may be warped and inappropriate, for it may prevent some distinctive aspects of entities from being properly acknowledged and articulated.[7]

Thus, beyond its intrinsic philosophical interest, the question of being has far-reaching implications for our thought and action, and we may need to deconstruct and reconstruct our understanding of being by testing it critically against the phenomena. If the meaning of being amounts to a boundary between what we can accept as valid or real and what we disregard as invalid or illusory, then it behooves us to become aware of the prejudices and limits in our current understanding.

Dasein, Time, and Being

In particular, Heidegger had long chafed at a metaphysical prejudice that he found in traditional philosophy, science, and common sense. All these ways of thinking often assume that to *be* is to be *present-at-hand*—to subsist as an actual thing or object with given properties, which in principle can be specified and defined. That assumption is stifling. Presence-at-hand cannot do justice to the wealth of what is: tools, space, and history, for example, are all more than merely present-at-hand beings. Above all, traditional metaphysics fails to reveal our *own* being: every well-meaning attempt to distinguish soul from body, or subject from object, ends up merely positing a different kind of present-at-hand thing, because such theories fail to rethink what it means to *be* in the first place.

The clue to that rethinking, Heidegger saw, lay hidden in the problematic concept of presence-at-hand itself. What if presence in general, as a sense of being, depends on the temporal present and thus on time? This idea was "the sole lightning bolt that struck my thinking Da-sein."[8] What if time, then, is not just another entity, but an enabling, enveloping matrix for all interpretations of entities? What if the breadth and diversity of time point us toward richer, unexplored senses of being?

The temporal revival of the question of being was Heidegger's own form of grave robbery. This project required a deconstruction of the philosophical tradition, which had been piling dirt on the question's grave for millennia (BT 20–22, BP 22–23). Bringing the question back to life might free us from being represented as a present object with properties. Instead, in Heidegger's vision, we are "Dasein."

Dasein is not an object: it is the "there" (BT 135, 220–221). It is not a thing, but an opening. To be the "there" is to encounter what *is*, to engage with beings as a whole, to exist as the field in which things can make a difference. Such an opening can never be understood as if it were simply one item among those available *within* the opening.

Dasein has no properties: it has possibilities that engage with its situation. Our being is an issue for us: we have always adopted a position on who we are, and we are perpetually challenged to renew our position. Our existence remains a problem, and our selfhood never crystallizes into a rigid identity. To own up to this condition is to exist in a self-owned or authentic way. To evade or forget this condition is to fall, to exist inauthentically.

Dasein is not simply present: it is temporal. This does not just mean that it changes: it is a truism that things change, and philosophies of becoming are among the most hackneyed metaphysical standpoints. Dasein's time is better understood in terms of three "ecstases" (BT 329). (1) Deliberately or not, we are engaged in possible ways to be. Heidegger calls this our understanding, our projection of possibilities. (2) In turn, we are claimed by our circumstances, which are thrust upon us as given. This is our thrownness, our having-been. (3) Through projecting possibilities while being claimed by the past, we arrive at the present: we dwell at home in the midst of things in our current world. These three ecstases allow us to "stand out" from any determinate spatiotemporal point, so that we can be an open "there" that extends into future, past, and present.

The detailed description of the way of being of Dasein, as the entity who understands being, is the "fundamental ontology" that is supposed to prepare the way for a well-developed "concept" (BT 6) of being as such.[9] That concept—the answer to the question of the meaning of being—was supposed to be laid out in Part One, Division III of *Being and Time*.

We should not misunderstand the term "fundamental ontology" in a Cartesian way. Heidegger is not trying to lay down a set of certainties about Dasein that will serve as the indubitable foundation for an ontological system. If one views his project in this light, it can only seem like a vicious circle: to found a theory of being as such on some "clear and distinct" truths about the being of Dasein would beg the question, because one would already have to know what it is to be before one established truths about a particular entity's being.[10]

Heidegger is well aware of the circularity in his project, but he denies that it is vicious. It is a virtuous circle, a hermeneutic circle that starts with the implicit, inarticulate sense of being that we already have; we keep returning to the phenomena as we articulate and refine this sense of being (BT 152–153, 315). This approach embodies a non-Cartesian conception of knowledge, where static, propositional assertions and the ideal of clarity and distinctness are replaced with a process of progressively deeper interpretation.

We see some cycles of the hermeneutic circle in the text as it stands: Heidegger redescribes his early accounts of Dasein in terms of care (BT §41) and temporality (BT §§66–71). Likewise, Division III would have had to review and deepen the description of Dasein after elucidating being as such (BT 333). As a whole, Part One of *Being and Time* would move from the fundamental ontology of Dasein to a concept of being as such, and then back to Dasein in the light of this concept.

More specifically, we have a list of particular questions that Division III was supposed to address.[11] How is being given, if it is not an entity (BT 230)? How can we properly conceive of it (BT 39)? What are all the "variations" of being (BT 11, 241, 333)? How are they all connected (BT 45)? (As a good reader of Aristotle, Heidegger would never expect a univocal sense of being, but rather an organically linked family of senses.) Why, among these variations, does presence-at-hand tend to emerge as the primary meaning of being (BT 437)? How does being relate to truth (BT 230, 357)? How does it relate to beings (BT 230)? How does it relate to nonbeing (BT 286)? Does time have its own way of being (BT 406)? How does time relate to space (BT 368)? How does Dasein's temporality make intentionality possible (BT 363n23)?

We will learn more about the contents of the lost text when certain manuscripts are published. In particular, some 200 handwritten pages of notes on Division III exist among Heidegger's papers in Marbach. These notes indicate the structure and themes of the division; their topics include the ontological difference, the varieties of temporal modes (such as expectative, presentative, and perfective), and time as a "self-projection upon itself."[12]

In order to grasp Dasein's temporality (*Zeitlichkeit*) as the horizon for being, Heidegger proposes to construe it as Temporality (*Temporalität*) (BT 19). Above all, this means describing how the three temporal ecstases bring us out toward three "horizonal schemata" that make the varieties of being available (BT 365, BP 302). The essential idea is presented in *Being and Time*, §69c, and is developed a little farther in *The Basic Problems of Phenomenology*, the lecture course immediately following *Being and Time*.

Thus, the ecstasis of the present directs us to a horizonal schema that Heidegger designates as *praesens* (*Praesenz*, BP 305). This schema enables us to understand not only what is present, but also what is absent: for instance, a ready-to-hand thing that is unavailable is understood in its unavailability thanks to *praesens* (BP 306, 311).

The past and future temporal schemata can be called *what has been* and the *for-the-sake-of-itself* (BT 365). The for-the-sake-of-itself provides "futurity as such, i.e., possibility pure and simple. Of itself the ecstasis does not produce a definite possible, but it does produce the horizon of possibility in general, within which a definite possible can be expected" (MFL 208). Heidegger does not elaborate on the schema of what has been.

This is all, literally, schematic: it sketches a new "language game,"[13] but it gives us little indication of how the particular questions Heidegger reserved for Division III would have been worked out. How might his account of being as such have emerged?

A Venture in Temporal Ontology

While we cannot fully answer this question, we can indicate some ways in which the various modes of being might be interpreted and unified temporally. The point of this exercise is not only to reconstruct some of Division III, but to think for ourselves about the being of all that is, insofar as it is intelligible by virtue of time.

Any reconstruction of the missing text has to be largely imaginative: it is speculation, an exploration of a possibility. Appropriately enough, then, it has to begin with the future, the dimension of the possible.

Futurity

Futurity yields possibility. In futurity, we are challenged to find a possible way to exist—to come to grips with our own being as a problem and a task, to address the question of who we are.

The future allures us, beckons us, invites us. It introduces us to the imagined, envisioned, and anticipated.

The future also threatens, oppresses, and burdens us, since the question of who we are can never be settled, and possibility can always be blocked and extinguished. Futurity introduces us to failure, claustrophobia, despair, and mortality—the constant possibility of running out of possibilities.

These are nothing but platitudes as long as we remain within an understanding of being that pictures the future as the not-yet-present. We represent it as a section of the timeline that lies ahead of the section we inhabit.

The statements above would then mean nothing except that we know little about what has not yet happened, that we try to affect what will happen, and that at some point our own presence will cease.

But this picture of the future would fail to grasp futurity altogether. A possible way to exist as Dasein can never be reduced to a set of present-at-hand qualities—features that are given either now or in some coming moment. One's self-understanding, one's projection of who one is, is not a list of facts; it is a guiding interpretation in terms of which one approaches life. If I interpret myself, for instance, as a parent, that possible way of being is irreducible to the fact that I have offspring, or to the sum total of my interactions with them; it is part of the difference it makes that I am who I am, instead of no one. And since the question of who one is cannot be settled as if it were a question about present-at-hand characteristics, it is always possible for my self-interpretation as parent to be shaken, super-seded, or transformed, regardless of what the facts about my relation to my children may be.

But futurity does not only disclose our own being. It intersects, as we will see, with the other ecstases; and as it joins with what has been to illu-minate our present situation, we can attend to how other beings involve possibility (cf. BT 144–145). In many cases, this possibility takes the form of *potentiality*—the capacity to become a certain kind of thing or take on cer-tain characteristics. The tree in my garden has the potential to bear oranges; I understand this because I understand myself, for instance, as a parent who takes care to feed himself and his children. By the same token, I understand manmade entities, such as a paring knife I use to peel an orange. The poten-tial of these things is disclosed with reference to the goals and practices that are involved in my own self-understanding. By understanding myself, I understand the purposes of things—along with the concomitant phenom-ena of the purposeless and purpose-free (BP 295). (In general, the temporal ecstases disclose both the positive and the negative—the various meanings of both being and nonbeing.)

We need not reduce all potentiality to utility for our own interests. We can notice that other trees bear fruit that we will never eat. Plants are dis-closed not just as edible, but also as knowable. With Aristotle, we can even view the whole cosmos as consisting of potentials in the process of being actualized. Note, however, that this vision cannot comprise Dasein itself, whose actuality is always exceeded by its potential and whose identity can never come to full fruition.[14]

In addition to Dasein's possibilities and the potentials of natural and arti-ficial things, there are derivative types of possible being. There is *epistemic possibility:* that is, a situation in which we do not know whether something is the case but we suspect it or cannot rule it out. We may even be able to estimate its likelihood, as when we say there is a 70 percent chance of rain. And there is *logical possibility*, the fact that some state of affairs involves no contradiction. Both of these types of possibility are defined in relation to assertion (we assert certain things about the weather and draw inferences, or we find that we cannot coherently assert both that a figure is circular and that it is rectangular). Assertion is an important and legitimate way of grasping certain features of beings, but it is made possible by a more basic, broader, and temporal way of encountering beings in the first place. For instance, I interpret myself as a weatherman, an informed citizen, or a commuter; thanks to such possibilities of my Dasein, I can comprehend the epistemic possibility of the 70 percent chance of rain.

The derivative types of possibility cannot explain the futurity that makes them accessible. My ability to understand myself as a parent is quite different from (though not unrelated to) a statistical likelihood that I have reproduced or will reproduce. My inability to understand myself as a samurai is not due to a logical contradiction, but to my thrownness, as we are about to see.

Pastness

Pastness is the domain of the *factum*—of what has been done and cannot be undone. What is completely past has been finished; it admits of no appeal. Our own former acts, the acts of others, the totality of the circumstances into which we have been thrown: all this presents itself as inalterable, to the extent that it has already happened. The "it was" stares us down as mercilessly as death itself, to which pastness is akin, insofar as it lacks possibility.

As the realm of what cannot be undone, pastness gives us access to *facticity* and *factuality* (BT 56). Facticity is the givenness of our own situation, which cannot be gotten around or replaced. Factuality is the givenness not just of ourselves, but of all the things we encounter as ingredients of our facticity. *Thinghood* involves this factual, settled element. Factuality is the basis of the law of noncontradiction: things have turned out one way rather than its opposite; they cannot have happened in both ways. To *know* is to grasp this factuality, to have factically seen the character that beings already have.

But the inalterable, the no longer possible, is simultaneously the basis of new possibilities: it is the ground on which we can build. In this way, pastness serves as source and resource for futurity. For although the past cannot be *un*done, it demands to be *re*done. To redo the past is not to erase or rewrite it, but to retrieve it creatively, to appropriate it as a model of what can be achieved or should be avoided. Redoing the past means extending it, so that the meaning and purpose of the "it was" has not yet been exhausted. Pastness serves as a provocation, an irritation, a challenge. This challenge can be ignored; we can fail to redo the past by denying, repressing, or procrastinating. But all of these failures are themselves indirect acknowledgments of the challenge.

As the realm of what can be redone, pastness discloses heritage, tradition, and models of virtue and vice. Pastness is the basis of law, of loyalty, and of normative conventions and habits. Pastness reveals justice and injustice, since it allows us to experience what has been done as calling for redress, reward, or repeal. Pastness also discloses the *ought* in the form of a promise—a freely adopted and reiterated commitment. The fact that I have freely chosen to undertake some project cannot be undone; if I am to carry my choice forward, to extend my freedom, I now ought to continue this undertaking.[15]

In pastness, we also encounter the memorable and forgettable. In redoing the past, we distinguish between the notable and irrelevant as we pursue monumental, antiquarian, or critical ways of interpreting what has been (cf. GA46). Again, these are not simply anthropological facts, but parameters for interpreting all facts—approaches to the domain of the factual as such.

Presence

Presence opens at the intersection of futurity and pastness. As we pursue possible ways of existing, we redo the past, thus disclosing the present. I interpret myself as a builder by appropriating factual things and factical models of builders. As we have seen, futurity in conjunction with pastness reveals potentials: I can build, and things can be handled as tools and building materials. A practical situation unfolds, and the being of the things in it emerges as *readiness-to-hand.* Or I may interpret myself as an astronomer by appropriating factual scientific equipment and factical models of scientists, disclosing the present situation as one in which I can study stars; the being of stars emerges for me as *presence-at-hand.*

Both readiness-to-hand and presence-at-hand thus involve a certain pastness or settled givenness, in combination with possibilities that are disclosed thanks to futurity. At this juncture, entities emerge as what can be *dealt with* or *handled* in the broadest sense—either theoretically or practically.[16] They emerge as knowable or usable—or as currently unknowable or unusable, which are deficient modes of the same phenomena.

Through their knowability and usability, entities disclose their *spatial* relations. They appear as already situated in certain locations and as susceptible to various interactions and motions. These locations, interactions, and motions cohere in a space, either as a practical environment or as measurable extension. Although space may seem to be a timeless set of relations, it is made intelligible by temporality.[17]

Presence, then, is the third dimension of temporality. It cannot stand on its own, it cannot define the other ecstases, and it cannot, by itself, make being meaningful. Without futurity or pastness, no situation would disclose itself to us, and things would be unavailable and unintelligible to us. They would interact with us causally, but could not emerge as present. Thus, temporality makes possible all intentional relations to what is present.

Nevertheless, presence tends to push to the fore as if it were the primary horizon for being. We "fall" into presence, since that is the dimension in which beings come forth as directly appealing or repellent, enticing or alarming. It is the dimension in which we engage with things. When we attempt to disengage in order to grasp how things are, we theorize—thus revealing things as present-at-hand. Yet theorizing is itself only a particular form of engagement in the present; its effect is to narrow down the sense of being and to obscure the importance of past and future.

Presence can be understood in a rich Greek sense as the emergence and enduring of beings, or *physis*. It can also be narrowed down to quantifiable objectivity, or other restricted forms of presence-at-hand. But no matter how rich presence is, in a temporal ontology it must be subordinated to the other dimensions of time.[18]

This sketch may be enough to suggest the temporal coherence of the various modes of being—our own being and that of all entities.

As we noted, the interpretation of being gained in Division III would have to be applied back to Dasein. One notable implication is that we could no longer understand ourselves solely within one of the multiple senses of being. For example, we must not take ourselves simply as collections of facts, simply as potentials in the process of actualization, or simply as systems of norms. All of these senses of being illuminate aspects of human beings, but none can stand on its own. And even the sum total of ontological interpretations of humanity will fail to grasp us if we do not see that we are, first and foremost, those whose own temporality enables them to engage in such interpretations. This insight remains crucial at a time when the continuing success of natural science and technology can easily tempt us into reductive assumptions.

Being and Time as Transcendental Philosophy

But why did Heidegger retreat before this temporal ontology? What went wrong in his draft of Division III? The answer must have something to do with the transcendental tenor of his investigation. The term "transcendental" appears only rarely and ambiguously in *Being and Time* (e.g., BT 38–39). But time, as the horizon for being, seems to have what is generally understood in post-Kantian philosophy as a transcendental status: temporality makes it possible for us to understand all beings in their being, and hence to make ontic judgments about them. Heidegger is thus working back from ordinary experience to its conditions of possibility.[19] The similarity to Kant here is emphasized by Heidegger's term "horizonal schema," which echoes the Schematism of the Pure Concepts of the Understanding in the *Critique of Pure Reason*. The Schematism, which interprets the categories in temporal terms, was precisely the focus of Heidegger's studies of Kant in the 1920s. In some sense, then, *Being and Time* can be seen as a transcendental work, and even as a broadly Kantian one.

It is precisely this aspect of his thought that Heidegger appears to criticize a decade later, in texts such as the *Contributions to Philosophy*. He now says that the transcendental approach was merely "provisional" (GA65 305). It is overly indebted to a conception of being as a universal that serves as the condition of possibility for beings (GA65 250, 468). This line of thought is merely a preparation for "the turnaround and the leap" (GA65 305) into the "grounding of the essence of truth" (GA65 455).

A standard interpretation of Kant's "Copernican revolution in philosophy" is that for Kant, a priori synthetic principles are no longer objective facts, but achievements of subjectivity—not, of course, voluntary acts, but ways in which the subject's consciousness must constitute itself. This version of transcendentalism, which we can call subjectivism, comes in for heavy criticism in the *Contributions*. Heidegger claims to have left subjectivism behind for good (GA65 259), so that there is no possibility of understanding being as a product of the subject, the mind, or even Dasein. Instead, Dasein is thrown into belonging to being; it is indebted to the event of appropriation (*Ereignis*) that first brings Dasein into its own (GA65 250–251). Heidegger's later texts go further in emphasizing our dependency and our receptivity to being, our need to wait and listen rather than actively impose our will.

But what exactly is Heidegger criticizing? Is it a certain misreading of his earlier thought,[20] an erroneous aspect of that thought itself,[21] or the misleading language in which his thought was couched?[22] His thinking obviously evolves after *Being and Time*, but does he see that text as hopelessly infected with a subjectivist point of view? Did Heidegger destroy the manuscript of Division III because he decided at the eleventh hour—during the very typesetting (GA49 40)—that he had fallen prey to subjectivism?

For all his criticisms of the particular approaches and vocabulary that he used in *Being and Time*, Heidegger is unwilling to say that the project was essentially subjectivist. In 1938 or 1939 he claims that in *Being and Time*, "not just the subjectivity of man but the role of man is shaken, as one will recognize someday" (GA67 90). When preparing *Introduction to Metaphysics* for publication in 1953, he writes: "The 'transcendental' [in the phrase "time as the transcendental horizon for the question of Being," BT 39] does not pertain to subjective consciousness; instead, it is determined by the existential-ecstatic temporality of Being-here [Da-sein]" (IM 20).

In order to decide whether *Being and Time*'s transcendental project is subjectivist, it makes sense to return to Heidegger's interpretations of Kant in the 1920s to see whether Heidegger's Kant develops transcendental philosophy by exalting the activity of the subject. In fact, in his 1925–26 lectures on Kant (LQT), Heidegger already takes the approach that he will develop in his post–*Being and Time* interpretations of the first *Critique* (GA25, KPM): Against the neo-Kantians, Heidegger argues that time, which is shown in the Schematism to be essential to any comprehension of experience, is available to us through our *receptivity* and is in no way the product of subjectivity (LQT 225, 230–231). Experience proves to depend on our *openness* to time.

Given this evidence, it is implausible to charge *Being and Time* with a one-sidedly subjectivist point of view. In fact, the text avoids ascribing the fundamental features of Dasein to some primal activity, even when it comes to the projection of possibilities. Projection is not a plan or vision that we construct (BT 145), but an inevitable forwardness that underlies any human action, and Heidegger does not attribute this forwardness to a necessary subjective activity of synthesis; instead, it is a movement in which we are always already involved. Similarly, "the significance-relationships which determine the structure of the world are not a network of forms which a worldless subject has laid over some kind of material" (BT 366). The subject does not generate significance, either voluntarily or involuntarily, but finds itself drawn into a world.

Thus, Dasein's temporality is not an active achievement of Dasein, but the way in which Dasein is essentially drawn out and drawn in. We are drawn *out* to the reaches of time: to the possible, the preestablished, and the present. We are thereby drawn *in* to a field in which all that s can be for us. It would be inappropriate to construe the horizonal schemata as products of Dasein, as the effects of a spontaneous self-positing of he subject. Willful and constructive forms of consciousness are certainly possible, but what makes them possible is a prevoluntary, preactive transcendence—a happening that primordially engages and opens us. This transcendence is the deeper basis of the Kantian transcendental problematic (PM 109).

Heidegger's position becomes clearer if we distinguish two types of transcendental philosophy. The subjectivist type, developed in different ways by thinkers such as Fichte, the neo-Kantians, and Husserl, holds that the (necessary) activity of the subject generates the conditions of possibility of experience. My claim is that Heidegger never subscribed to such subjectivism, but instead developed a nonsubjectivist type of tran-cendental thought in *Being and Time*. The horizonal schemata of time serve as conditions of possibility of experience, but they are not products of Dasein's activity; instead, time *happens to* Dasein, so to speak. We find ourselves constituted by temporal ecstases that operate on a level more basic than any subjective activity. To discover the temporality that enables all experience is not to set ourselves up as the creators of being, but to understand how we are temporally drawn into transcendence—into our condition as those who understand being and beings.

Toward the Happening of Being

If it is fair to describe transcendence in *Being and Time* as a happening rather than as an achievement of subjectivity, so that the text's transcendentalism is not of the subjectivist type, then what did go awry in Division III? And what does Heidegger mean when he writes in the mid-1930s of a transition "from the understanding of being to the *happening of being*" (IM 233)? What is it about the project of *Being and Time* that was insufficiently oriented toward "happening"?

The answers are murky and complex, but I would like to highlight one strand: in the years following *Being and Time*, Heidegger becomes increasingly concerned with the *initial entry* of Dasein into temporality. The moment of this entry would be, as it were, the time when time begins. The threefold temporal ecstases described in *Being and Time* are already an ongoing "happening," but the event that first plunges us into this ecstatic condition is a happening in a different sense—a unique, founding eruption of time itself. This is "the event of grounding the there," or for short, "the event" (*das Ereignis*) (CP 144, 195).

The project of thinking of such an event does not make sense within a transcendental point of view, whether subjectivist or nonsubjectivist. Transcendentalism identifies the conditions of possibility for all experience—that is, for all interpretations and judgments. To attempt to reach a further judgment about the origin of the conditions themselves would seem to be a misunderstanding. The a priori conditions of experience and thought cannot themselves be traced back to some further ground, because grounding—like all thinking—it itself governed by these conditions.[23] According to *Being and Time*, the fundamental condition of possibility of experience is the ecstatic transcendence of Dasein; thus Heidegger tries to show (in MFL and "On the Essence of Ground") that all grounding is based on such transcendence. What sense could it make to seek a further ground for transcendence itself?

But Heidegger, as we will see, attempts to develop a way to think about the event that generates the very condition of transcendence, the event that originates time itself. Such an event cannot be comprehended as if it were an entity within normal experience; it will always elude such understanding Yet Heidegger, for better or worse, comes to believe that he can develop a way of thinking and speaking that does justice to this intrinsically obscure origin, without violating its obscurity.

My hypothesis, then, is that Heidegger became uneasy with Division III because he began to suspect that it could not address the question of how Dasein enters temporality. The problem was not that *Being and Time* was too subjectivist, but that the origination of Dasein's temporality was threatening to be covered up by a transcendental framework that seemed to rule out any inquiry into the topic. If I am right, then in abandoning Division III, Heidegger did not simply discard its ideas, but he laid aside their systematic exposition and their transcendental trappings to follow the stirrings of what he considered deeper and more urgent questions. He did not abandon his account of temporality,[24] but he felt the need to inquire in a nontranscendental manner into the origin of time. Heidegger felt this need only obscurely at first, until it culminated in the *Contributions to Philosophy* a decade after *Being and Time*. This is not the place to tell the whole story of this development, but only to point out a few milestones.[25]

In *The Basic Problems of Phenomenology*, Heidegger wonders: if we understand being thanks to the horizon of time, then does not time also need to be understood in terms of some further horizon? Are we not faced with an infinite regress (BP 280)? He provides only a few hints for an answer: time does not need a further horizon because primordial time is finite (BP 308), and because time is "the origin of possibility itself" (BP 325).

What might Heidegger have meant? First, it is clear that time is "the origin of possibility" because of futurity: we understand possibility and potential because we project possible ways to be. But futurity is finite because it is shadowed by mortality—our possibilities are always faced with the threat of complete negation.

What would it mean, then, to understand time? Time allows us to grasp things, but it itself cannot be grasped. It allows us to seize possibilities, but cannot itself be taken up into some higher possibility. We can do nothing with time, and we can do nothing about it; we find ourselves caught up in it far beyond the power of our action and thought. Just as we did not bring ourselves into the temporal condition of having possibilities, and just as we cannot overcome the mortality of that condition, we cannot project some further possibility that embraces temporality itself.

In one sense, time is understood along with whatever else we may understand; it is implicitly understood because it fundamentally enables all understanding (BP 307–308). Yet in another sense, time cannot be understood. To grasp time explicitly, to stand over it, as it were, is impossible. To "understand" our own temporality is to run up against it as a primordial *given*, as that which we find ourselves unable to transcend. To appreciate time is to collide with its ultimate facticity and opacity. In this sense, time is "*earlier than any possible earlier* of whatever sort, because it is the basic condition for an earlier as such" (BP 325). "The primal fact ... is that there is anything like temporality at all" (MFL 209).

End of story, one might conclude. But the more Heidegger runs up against the sheer givenness of time, the more he is inclined to wonder about it. By 1929–30, he is asking, "What does it mean to say that time is a horizon? ... We do not have the slightest intimation of the abysses of the essence of time" (FCM 146).

If time is the ultimate given, "Can one ask, 'How does time arise?'"[26] Can we inquire into the giving of time? Certainly this giving cannot itself be understood in a positive way, as one develops understandings of this or that entity; all understanding is itself temporal and presupposes time. But perhaps the giving of time can be understood in a negative way—that is, in its very opacity, in its concealment.

Heidegger thus begins to think in terms of a mysterious founding event in which we are thrust into temporality. "This originary time transports our Dasein into the future and past, or better, brings it about that our being as such is a transported being. ... In such time, time 'comes to be'" (GA39, 109). "Ever since time arose and was brought to stand, since then we *are* historical."[27] The origin of time is an "inception" (*Anfang*) (GA70). In an inception, a clearing opens against concealment; the boundary between being and nonbeing is first drawn. Our mission as Dasein is to participate creatively in this event that is the source of truth, worldhood, history, and Dasein itself.

While the transcendental aspect of *Being and Time* suggests that temporality is a fixed structure that we occasionally recognize, Heidegger now presents it as gushing forth at great historical moments that establish a way of existing for a people or an age. He has made the transition "from the understanding of being to the *happening of being*." This happening is not just an ongoing movement in which we are engaged, but the original founding of such a movement, an abyssal ground that must remain a mystery, yet can still be thought in its very mysteriousness. By the early '30s, Heidegger's philosophical diary is focused on this "happening of being" (e.g., GA94, 6, 32, 59) and emphasizes the way in which being falls contingently to Dasein (*Zu-fälligkeit*: GA94, 60). Thus, time in *Being and Time* turns out to be the first indication of what the *Contributions* call "that which takes place in the uniqueness of the ap-propriation as the truth of the essential occurrence of beyng [*Seyn*]" (GA65, 74).

This is not the end of Heidegger's path, as in his late thought he seems to draw back from the sharp singularity of the appropriating event; *Ereignis* comes to look more like an ongoing condition than an extraordinary outburst.[28] But we have at least glimpsed some ways in which his thought turns to questions beyond the temporal ontology of *Being and Time*, without simply renouncing the central insights of that text.

What is left of those insights once their transcendental framework falls away? Consider the distinctive phrases *immer schon* (always already) and *je schon* (in each case already) that appear throughout *Being and Time*. The word *schon* emphasizes that we do not begin from nothing, that we are not in a position to lay the foundation for our own being; it has already been laid for us. The subject's activity presupposes a thrownness that subjectivity cannot master. As for the words *immer* and *je*, they suggest universality and necessity: in *no* case can we *ever* lay our own foundation. This is the aspect of *Being and Time* that smacks most strongly of traditional transcendental philosophy, with its quest for a priori knowledge of necessary limits. But ironically, that very quest sets us up, in effect, as knowers who *can* establish a firm and certain ground: a clear conception of our essence and its inevitable finitude. At the same time, as we have seen, the transcendental approach blocks any attempt to inquire into the origin of ecstatic temporality in an event that may be profoundly contingent, and may thus resist all attempts to ascertain some necessary ground for it. Ultimately,

then, transcendentalism must be considered a residual attachment to presence and a vestige of modern metaphysics. The *immer* and *je* should be
dropped.[29] We are left with the *schon*—a description of how we, n fact, find
ourselves existing. We can notice the thrown, temporal character of experience without taking any stand on whether experience is possiɔle only by
virtue of that temporality. Thus, even when we let the overtones of necessity fade away, *Being and Time* retains much of its thought-provoking power
simply as a description of our current ways of encountering beings in their
being—an attempt to tell it like it is, whether or not it has tɔ be. *Being
and Time* can then be read in tandem with Heidegger's later work, which
attempts to say how we find ourselves thrown into a particular historical
truth of being, while eschewing all claims of necessity.

The questions that *Being and Time* explores remain vital today. Our being
remains in question and, for this very reason, being as such remains in
question. It can never become a settled doctrine or self-evident concept, but
must be renewed and reinterrogated. In this way, a resurrection o˙ the problem of being and time is far more than an antiquarian or escapist enterprise.
It is not deadly, but brings new life.

Notes

1. Heidegger, "Der Weg: Der Gang durch *Sein und Zeit*" (unpublished typescript
dated 1940–41), p. 12.

2. Heidegger, *Introduction to Metaphysics*, 2nd rev. ed. (New Haven: Yale University
Press, 2014), Appendix I, 233. "IM" will refer to this edition.

3. See, e.g., Jean Grondin, "Why Reawaken the Question of Being?" in *Heidegger's
"Being and Time": Critical Essays*, ed. Richard Polt (Lanham, MD: Rowman & Little-
field, 2005); Thomas Sheehan, *Making Sense of Heidegger: A Paradigm Shift* (London:
Rowman & Littlefield International, 2014), prologue.

4. Hence, Thomas Sheehan identifies being with meaning. I have argued that while
meaning is central to Heidegger's project, the broader question of being also includes
meaning's relation to what exceeds meaning, and—in later Heidegger—the event in
which meaningfulness is given. See Richard Polt, "Meaning, Excess, and Event,"
Gatherings: The Heidegger Circle Annual 1 (2011): 26–53.

5. Cf. John Haugeland, *Dasein Disclosed: John Haugeland's Heidegger*, ec. Joseph
Rouse (Cambridge, MA: Harvard University Press, 2013), pp. 21–22, 52, 62, 105, 191,
226.

6. Compare the question, "Why are there beings at all instead of nothing?" that
ends "What Is Metaphysics?" and begins IM. In Heidegger's hands, the question is

not asking for a first cause or supreme entity; instead, it draws our attention to the question of what it means to be, and how being means anything to us at all.

7. Exactly how an understanding of being can be untrue is a question for another occasion, but Heidegger clearly thinks that this is possible; in particular, he holds that the being of Dasein has been understood in an impoverished and confused way.

8. Heidegger, "Der Weg," p. 12.

9. The phrase *das Sein überhaupt*, which first appears on BT 11, is rendered in the English translations as "Being in general" or "being in general." In order to avoid the suggestion that being is a genus, I prefer the expression "being as such." "Fundamental ontology" usually refers to the analysis of Dasein's existence (e.g., BT 14), but sometimes it appears to refer to the account of being as such in Division III (e.g., BT 183). The two topics are, of course, intimately connected.

10. Compare Descartes's claim that being is a concept so simple and self-evident that it is not even necessary to discuss it before proceeding to know that one's own mind *is*: *Principles of Philosophy*, in *Selected Philosophical Writings*, trans. J. Cottingham et al. Cambridge: Cambridge University Press, 1988), p. 163.

11. On the projected contents of Division III, see Theodore Kisiel, "The Demise of *Being and Time*: 1927–1930," in *Heidegger's "Being and Time,"* and Sheehan, *Making Sense of Heidegger*, chapter 6.

12. Kisiel, "Demise," 211. About 15 percent of the text has been published as "Aufzeichnungen zur Temporalität (Aus den Jahren 1925 bis 1927)," *Heidegger Studies* 14 (1998): 11–23. Heidegger's running commentary on *Being and Time*, to be published in GA82, will also be valuable; this text dates from 1936.

13. Kisiel, "Demise," p. 197.

14. See Richard Polt, "Potentiality, Energy and Sway: From Aristotelian to Modern to Postmodern Physics?" *Existentia* 11 (2001): 27–41.

15. An example is the commitment of love: "That once we told ourselves this tale / says what we ourselves long failed / to hear—but finally hear it asking, / calling us to bear it, tasking ...": "*Amo: Volo ut sis*," GA81, 109.

16. This point explains Heidegger's somewhat counterintuitive claim that "the horizonal schema for the *Present* is defined by the '*in-order-to*'" (BT 365). One might expect the in-order-to to be futural, but the future is primarily the dimension in which we understand our *own* possibilities for existing (the "for-the-sake-of-which," BT 84), whereas the present is where entities are uncovered in more concrete purposive relations.

17. Heidegger's full views on the relation between time and space are considerably more complex and obscure. *Being and Time* claims that a spatial "region" opens only

on the basis of making-present, which is one dimension of temporality (BT §70). Yet the text also asserts, with little explanation, that because spatiality involves *ecstatic* temporality, "space is independent of time" (BT 369). In 1962, Heidegger declares that "the attempt in *Being and Time*, section 70, to derive human spatiality from temporality is untenable" (TB 23). However, the same lecture claims that "true time itself ... is the prespatial region which first gives any possible 'where'" (TB 16).

18. For a clear statement that Heidegger's ultimate aim is not to revive being as *physis*, see GA94, 241.

19. "Der Weg" even describes the project of *Being and Time* as a "transcendental question squared" (*potenzierte transzendentale Frage*, 9): the book inquires not just into being as the condition of possibility of the experience of beings, but into time as the condition of possibility of being.

20. *Being and Time* was "misinterpreted as transcendental philosophy" (GA67 25).

21. *Being and Time*'s doubly transcendental way of thinking blocks us off from "the truth of being" ("Der Weg," p. 13).

22. "The division in question was held back because thinking failed in the adequate saying of this turning and did not succeed with the help of the language of metaphysics" ("Letter on Humanism," BW 231).

23. For similar reasons, Steven Crowell rejects Heidegger's post–*Being and Time* turn away from transcendental philosophy as incoherent: "Metaphysics, Metontology, and the End of *Being and Time*," *Philosophy and Phenomenological Research* 60 (2) (March 2000): 307–331.

24. A sign that Heidegger retains many of the positions of *Being and Time* is his exposition of temporality in the Zollikon seminars of the mid-1960s, which is remarkably faithful to his insights of forty years earlier (Zo 33–67).

25. For another overview of this development see Richard Polt, "Being and Time," in *Martin Heidegger: Key Concepts*, ed. Bret W. Davis (Chesham: Acumen, 2010). For an extended interpretation of *Ereignis* as the origination of time and being, see Richard Polt, *The Emergency of Being: On Heidegger's "Contributions to Philosophy"* (Ithaca: Cornell University Press, 2006).

26. "Unbenutzte Vorarbeiten zur Vorlesung vom Wintersemester 1929/1930: *Die Grundbegriffe der Metaphysik: Welt, Endlichkeit, Einsamkeit*," *Heidegger Studies* 7 (1991): 9.

27. Heidegger, "Hölderlin and the Essence of Poetry," in *Elucidations of Hölderlin's Poetry*, p. 57.

28. For a survey of Hedegger's uses of *Ereignis*, see Richard Polt, "*Ereignis*," in *A Companion to Heidegger*, ed. Hubert L. Dreyfus and Mark Wrathall (Oxford: Blackwell, 2005).

29. By the time of the *Contributions*, phrases such as "always already" have almost completely vanished: see Polt, *Emergency of Being*, p. 107.

12   The Incompletion of *Being and Time* and the Question of Subjectivity

François Raffoul

The Incompletion of *Being and Time*

The incompletion of *Being and Time*, and in particular the nonpublication of the announced Third Division of Part One, "Time and Being," is often portrayed or characterized as a "failure." In fact, it might well be the case that this interruption testifies to a secret movement in Heidegger's thought the preparation of a new beginning in thought, a turn or crossing that could not be pursued within the structure, language, and orientation of the 1927 treatise. It may also express the singular fate and itinerary of a thought always seeking to bring into language the event and truth of being as such in a language that at first must always fall short, and which thus needs to be repeated and deepened each time. If there is failure, then, it would be in the sense in which one speaks of words "failing us" in our attempt to say or think what is to be said. This is indeed what Heidegger stated in the "Letter on Humanism," explaining that "The division in question [the third division of Part One of *Being and Time*] was held back [*zurückgehalten*] because thinking *failed* in the adequate saying of this turning [*Kehre*] [*weil das Denken im zureichenden Sagen dieser Kehre versagte*] and did not succeed with the help of the language of metaphysics."[1] Indeed, in a 1941 course (*Die Metaphysik des deutschen Idealismus—Schelling*, volume 49 of the *Gesamtausgabe*), Heidegger describes the language of *Being and Time* as "a language that is in a quest, an exposition in search of the word it does not find."[2] As we know, Heidegger was "on the way" toward a genuine thinking of being, its meaning and its truth—an improper expression, if it is the case, as he explained in the *Beiträge*, that far from a linear progression, the process is more tantamount to a peculiar stumbling or interrupting, a deepening and a repeating of the *same* question differently: "On this 'way'—if stumbling and getting up again can be called that—the same question of the 'meaning of be-ing' is always asked, and *only* this question. And therefore the locations of questioning are constantly different. Each time that it asks more originarily, every essential questioning must transform itself from the ground up. Here there is no gradual 'development.'"[3] The incompletion of *Being and Time*, then, far from being a mere failure, harbors crucial stakes in Heidegger's thinking in its attempt to name the truth of being.

As is well known, Heidegger presents the outline of *Being and Time* in paragraph 8 of the treatise. The work was to have been composed of two parts. The first one was to treat of "The Interpretation of Dasein on the Basis of temporality [*Zeitlichkeit*] and the Explication of Time as the Transcendental Horizon of the Question of Being," and the second would have been devoted to the "Basic Features of a Phenomenological Destruction of the History of Ontology along the Guideline of the Problem of Temporality [*Temporalität*]." In turn, the first part was to have been divided into three divisions, as was the case for Part Two. However, only the first two divisions of Part One were published. The Third Division of Part One, titled "Time and Being," was written, but Heidegger, apparently following intense discussions with Jaspers in late 1926 or early 1927 in Heidelberg (*Being and Time* would appear in April 1927), decided not to include it in the final manuscript. In the 1941 course, he explains that

the understanding of the concept of existence used in *Sein und Zeit* was rendered all the more difficult due to the fact that the "existential concept" of existence according to *Sein und Zeit* was only fully developed in the division that, because of the interruption of the publication, was not communicated. *The decision for this interruption was made in the last days of December 1926 with Jaspers, during a sojourn in Heidelberg, when in the course of friendly and intense discussions, and with the galley proofs in hand, it appeared clearly that the elaboration that had been reached in that third division, the most important one* (I, 3), *was necessarily bound to remain unintelligible.* The decision to interrupt the publication was made the day we learned of the death of R. M. Rilke [Rilke died on December 29 and was buried on January 2]. (GA49 39–40; my emphasis)

One can also find several letters from Heidegger to Jaspers in 1926, and in particular the letters from April 24 and October 4, in which he addressed the forthcoming publication of *Sein und Zeit*, referring to the length of the manuscript and the academic context for this enterprise—the need to publish in order to secure a position as a Professor Ordinarius. He writes on April 24: "On April 1st, I began the proofs of my treatise, *Being and Time*. It comprises about thirty-four sheets [*Druckbogen*]. I am really in full swing, and I am only irritated about the coming semester and the narrow-minded atmosphere that will again surround me. The faculty wants to nominate me again and to attach the already printed sheets. The whole thing has been botched, and it is a matter of indifference to me."[4] Then in his letter from October 4, 1926, he realized that the manuscript would in fact exceed the thirty-four sheets originally projected (which would have been about 544 pages in print, as was estimated): "I suspended the printing in the middle of the semester and, after a very short rest, went back to work with revisions. The work has become more extensive than I thought so I must now divide it about every twenty-five sheets. I must deliver the remainder [*der Rest*] of the first volume [*Band*] by November 1st, so everyday is precious."[5] In the end, the work came out without the Third Division of Part One and without Part Two, although several sections of which appeared in the 1927 summer semester course, *The Basic Problems of Phenomenology*.[6]

Being and Time is thus only known as the juxtaposition of the first two divisions of Part One. Division I develops the "preparatory fundamental analysis of Dasein," and Division Two analyses "Dasein and temporality [*Zeitlichkeit*]." In a sense, it is the existential analytic as a whole, and not only Division I, that is "preparatory" or "provisional" (*vorbereitenden*). Indeed, the analysis of the being of Dasein (the very task of the existential analytic of *Being and Time*) must, in the final analysis, allow for the interpretation of that which is *sought after* in the questioning, namely the *meaning of being*, and in fact presupposes it.[7] Heidegger insists that the analytic of Dasein "is wholly oriented towards the guiding task of working out the question of Being" (GA2 17). This subordination of the existential analytic to the question of the meaning of being in a sense already announces a "beyond" of the existential analytic toward the thinking of being as such and thus already gestures toward "the turn," a turn that is indicated by the interruption of *Being and Time*. For Heidegger states that the existential analytic will need to be repeated "on a higher, genuinely ontological basis" (GA2 17). The meaning of being as such, and not simply the being of Dasein (object of the first two divisions), would have been addressed in Division III of Part One of *Being and Time*. Division III would have approached time in terms of the question of the meaning of being as such (and not only as the ecstatic-transcendental horizon of Dasein). At issue was the temporal meaning of being, or, as Heidegger put it in his letter to Father Richardson, how being "is determined by the scope of time."[8] An indication from such letter to Richardson is worth citing in this respect: "The disquieting, ever watchful question concerning Being as presence (present) developed into the question concerning Being in terms of its temporal character. Through this process it became clear that the traditional concept of time was in no way adequate for even correctly posing the question concerning the temporal character of presence, let alone for answering it. Time became questionable in the same way as Being. *The ecstatic-horizontal temporality delineated in* Being and Time *is not by any means already the most proper element of time that is sought as a correlate of the question of Being"* (HR 300, my emphasis). It was thus already in Division III of Part One, "Time and Being," a matter of *turning* from time as transcendental horizon of Dasein's being to a meditation on what is most proper to time, a meditation that would only be accomplished in the lecture from 1962 bearing the same title, "Zeit und Sein."

In considering the turn, operative in the interruption of *Being and Time*, one is led to recognize that it is not simply a movement within Heidegger's thought, but already plays within the question of being itself. Indeed, as Heidegger insisted in his letter to Father Richardson, "The reversal [*Kehre*] is in play within the matter itself [significantly Heidegger clarifies this expression by referring to the headings of *Being and Time*: "the very matter designated by the headings ['Being and Time,' 'Time and Being']. Neither did I invent it nor does it affect merely my thought. Up to now I know of no attempt to reflect on this matter and analyse it critically. Instead of the groundless, endless prattle about the 'reversal,' it would be more advisable and fruitful if people would simply engage themselves in the matter mentioned" (HR 302).[9] Before returning to the issue of the turn, and how it affects the question of the incompletion of *Being and Time*, let us begin by recalling that in the *Beiträge*, Heidegger explains that his entire effort consists in giving thought to the truth of being itself, and no longer to beings or even beingness (*Seiendheit*), as the metaphysical tradition had done. In paragraph 4 of the *Beiträge*, Heidegger makes the following statement: "The question concerning the 'meaning' [of being], i.e., in accordance with the elucidation in *Being and Time*, the question concerning grounding the domain of projecting-open—and then, the question of the *truth of being*—is and remains *my* question, and is my *one and only* question for this question concerns what is *most sole and unique*. In the age of *total lack of questioning anything,* it is sufficient as a start to inquire into the question of all questions" (GA65 10/11; CP 8). Heidegger's thinking, a "thinking in the crossing," as he calls it (*Das übergängliche Denken, Das Denken im Übergang*) thus does not start from beings, that is, this or that being, but is already engaged in a "leap [*sprung*]" beyond beings and into the truth of being as such. This corresponds to a passage or a transition—a crossing if not already a "turning"—from the "guiding-question [*Leitfrage*]" of metaphysics which questions about beingness, to the "grounding-question [*Grundfrage*]" of being, which inquires about the truth of being.[10] Now what is particularly revealing for our problem is how Heidegger explains that this crossing—turning—toward the "other beginning" of thought was already at stake in *Being and Time*. "Going from the guiding-question to the grounding-question, there is never an immediate, equi-directional and continual process that once again applies the guiding-question (to be-ing); rather, there is only a leap, i.e., the necessity of an *other* beginning. Indeed and on the contrary, a *crossing* can and should be created in the unfolding overcoming of the posing of the guiding-question and its answers as such, a crossing that prepares the other beginning and makes it generally visible and intimitable. *Being and Time is in service to this preparation*" (GA65 76; CP 53; my emphasis). To this extent, it is not possible to speak of a failure of *Being and Time*, as the 1927 work was underway to prepare the turn and crossing toward another beginning, although, as Heidegger would explain in the "Letter on Humanism," it was unable to accomplish this turn through the "language of metaphysics" that was still weighing on *Being and Time* (for instance: the reliance on the notions of the "transcendental" or transcendence, which presuppose beings as that which is transcended, or the ambiguous reference to subjectivity, among other motifs). As we saw, Heidegger explained that the nonpublication of the Third Division of Part One of *Being and Time* was due to the necessity of overcoming the language of metaphysics. The task became one of an overcoming of metaphysics, which was already the implicit horizon of the project of fundamental ontology, as is visible in *Being and Time* in the definition of the very method of ontology as *Destruktion* of our tradition. The significance of the incompletion of *Being and Time*, of its interruption, is to be sought in the turn toward the overcoming of metaphysics, an overcoming that was to occupy Heidegger in the years following *Being and Time*. As Heidegger explained in the 1949 introduction to "What Is Metaphysics?": "The thinking attempted in *Being and Time* (1927) sets out on the way to prepare an overcoming of metaphysics [*Überwindung der Metaphysics*]" (PM 279).

The Question of Subjectivity

Now, it appears that in such turning, the question of "subjectivity," of the human Dasein, and ultimately of the proper being of humans, is central. This is no doubt due to the very fashion in which *Being and Time* developed, that is, as an analytic of Dasein: an ontological analysis of the being that we each time are. The question regarding the meaning of being *turned* into an analysis of human Dasein, which came to the fore in the analysis for essential reasons. What are those reasons? What is the necessity for the human

Dasein, for the "subject" (recalling here Heidegger's comments according to which the subject, ontologically understood, *is* Dasein[11]), to come to the fore in an ontological analysis that seeks to clarify the meaning of being? As we know, Heidegger presents Dasein in the early paragraphs of *Being and Time* as that entity that is *interrogated* (*das Befragte*) by the question of being, as the very locus where the question of the meaning of being comes into play. Dasein is accessed in *Being and Time* in terms of the questionableness (*Fraglichkeit*) of being. The fact that Dasein emerges in a question already reveals that ultimately we must essentially remain a question. As Heidegger writes in *Introduction to Metaphysics*, "The determination of the essence of the human being is *never* an answer, but is essentially a question."[12] Hence the uncanniness of the human being: "The human being is *to deinotaton*, the uncanniest of the uncanny" (GA40 114; IM 159). In opening the question of being, human beings themselves become questionable, situated, as Heidegger writes in the *Beiträge*, in a domain in which they can become questionable (GA65 53; CP 38). The issue is to raise the *question* of the Being of beings in such a way as to also put our own being in question, to make it questionable (*fragwürdig*). Heidegger presents this implication in "What Is Metaphysics?" in the following way: "First, every metaphysical question always encompasses the whole range of metaphysical problems. Each question is itself always the whole [*das Ganze*]. Therefore, second, every metaphysical question can be asked only in such a way that the questioner as such is also there within the question, that is, is placed in question" (PM 82). The human being thus comes to the fore in the question of being, Heidegger going so far as to claim that "*the properly posed question of Being, thus the question concerning being and time, concerning the essence of time, necessarily leads to the question of the human being*"[13] or that, "The grounding question of philosophy, the question of being, is, in itself, correctly understood, the question of the human being."[14] Ultimately, the thinking of Being, either as fundamental ontology or as a reflection on *Ereignis*, in principle includes a reflection on human beings in their selfhood, Heidegger stating in the *Beiträge* that "as mindfulness of be-ing [*Besinnung auf das Seyn*], philosophy is necessarily self-mindfulness [*Selbstbesinnung*]" (GA65 48; CP 34). Heidegger returned to this place of the human being in the thinking of being in a letter he wrote to Jean Beaufret in 1946, explaining that it was for essential reasons that, on the way to an elaboration of the question of the meaning of being, the question of the "human Dasein [*menschlichen Daseins*]" emerged as *fundamental*: "And because human beings have a privileged relation to being, because they stand in the clearing of being—which in a hidden way is time itself—we must enquire into the original relation of time to the essence of human being (*Wesen des Menschen*). That is why the beginning of *Being and Time* refers to the temporality of human *Dasein*."[15]

In *Being and Time*, Dasein's implication in the general question of the meaning of being is analyzed as Dasein's privilege or priority (*Vorrang*), a privilege that ultimately is to be situated in the *Seinsverständnis*, which Heidegger presents, quite simply, as a "fact" (*Faktum*) (GA2 5). Heidegger stresses that Dasein is distinctive because it has—*is*—an understanding of being, and to that extent "has proven itself to be that which, before all other beings, is ontologically the primary being to be interrogated" (GA2 13). Dasein emerges as what is "interrogated" in the question on the meaning of being because it has an understanding of being, that is, because it is that being who can *understand* the question of what it means to be. Therefore, "The explicit and lucid formulation of the question of the meaning of being requires a prior suitable explication of a being (Dasein) with regard to its being" (GA 2, 7), which implies that "to work out the question of being means to make a being—one who questions—transparent in its being" (GA2 7). The question of being thus turns toward Dasein as that being who has an understanding of being, Heidegger writing in *The Basic Problems of Phenomenology* that, "Being is given only if the understanding of being, hence Dasein, exists. This being accordingly lays claim to a distinctive privilege in ontological inquiry. It makes itself manifest in all discussions of the basic problems of ontology and above all in the fundamental question of the meaning of being in general" (GA24 26/19). This is why, in the 1930 course on *The Essence of Human Freedom*, Heidegger went so far as to state that "we have access to the problem of being only through the understanding of being" (GA31 125; EHF 86–87). The understanding of being—that is, Dasein, for only Dasein has an understanding of being—is taken as the sole possible access to the problem of being.

One should not be surprised, then, if in *The Basic Problems of Phenomenology* Heidegger stresses that the central role of Dasein is a permanent feature of every philosophy, and of every ontology: "Furthermore, we stressed repeatedly that *all* ontology, even the most primitive, *necessarily* looks back [*zurückblickt*] to the Dasein. Wherever philosophy awakens, Dasein already stands in the sphere of vision" (GA24 172/122). The necessity and permanence of this look back is rooted in the "distinctive function" (GA24 172/122) of human Dasein, its "fundamental ontological function" (GA24 173/122), which as we saw lies in the *understanding of Being*. In this sense, the "return to the subject" as performed in the modern epoch manifests nothing but a *permanent* and *constitutive* tendency of philosophy, Heidegger going so far as to assert that "the path he [Kant] follows, *by returning to the subject* [Rückgang auf das Subjekt] *in its broadest sense, is the only one that is possible and correct"* (GA24 103/73, my emphasis). The human Dasein proves to be the very locus of the question of being, the "privileged field" of that battlefield [*Kampfplatz*] where, since the Greeks, the "battle between giants" over the question of the meaning of being has taken place; and this, necessarily:

> The struggle over beings shifts to the field of thinking, of making statements, of the soul, of subjectivity. Human Dasein moves to the center! Why is this? Is it an accident that the battle gets shifted onto this field? Is it up to the whims of philosophers, according to each of their would-be world-views or ethics, according to just how important they, in each case, take the "I" to be? Is it a peculiar, irrational enthusiasm for the inwardness of the soul, or an especially high esteem for free personhood, or a blind subjectivism, which here in this basic problem selects human Dasein, as such, for the battlefield? *None of these! Rather, the content pertinent to the basic problem itself, and this alone, requires this battlefield, makes human Dasein itself into this privileged field.* (GA26 19; MFL 15; my emphasis)

Now, due to this orientation in the analysis, as Heidegger admitted in the second volume of his Nietzsche volumes (among other texts), there was a risk of misunderstanding *Being and Time* as subjectivism. The way in which *Being and Time* unfolded, namely as an analytic of Dasein, len itself to the subjectivist misunderstanding, as shown in the Sartrean existentialist reception of Heidegger.[16] It was in order to conjure such a risk, Heidegger explained, that *Being and Time* was interrupted: "The reason for the disruption is that the attempt and the path it chose confront the danger of *unwillingly becoming merely another entrenchment of subjectivity."*[F] In this passage, Heidegger insists on two other points: first, on the overwhelming tendency of modern thought to reduce every reflection on the human being to an anthropology, and second, on the hermeneutic situation of a way of thinking that is "developed historically," and which for that reason must *necessarily* and *constantly* rely upon the very thing it is trying to overcome, that is, in this case, the modern subjectivist tradition. For instance, when Heidegger defined Dasein as transcendence, being-outside-of-itself, ek-staticity, it was still in direct opposition to the classical determination of the subject as self-consciousness, to the immanentist conception of subjectivity, as is betrayed in this passage from *The Basic Problems of Phenomenology*: "The Dasein itself is what oversteps in its being and thus is exactly *not the immanent"* (GA24 425/299). Now Heidegger is not simply content to reverse subjectivity, but rather intends to give thought to the truth of being as such. This is why he clarified: "The ecstatic essence of existence is therefore still understood inadequately as long as one thinks of it as merely a 'standing out,' while interpreting the 'out' as meaning 'away from' the interior of an immanence of consciousness or spirit" (PM 284). At issue is a genuine overcoming of the *metaphysics* and *tradition* of subjectivity, veritable obstacles to the thinking of the truth of being. "In the entirety of modern thought, stemming from Descartes, subjectivity thus constitutes the barrier to the unfolding of the question of being."[18] In short, the thinking of being does not fall within the problematic of subjectivity. This is what Heidegger explained in his letter to Father Richardson: "Whoever is ready to accept the simple fact that, in *Being and Time*, the starting point of subjectivity is deconstructed [*abgebaut*], that every anthropological enquiry is kept at a distance, and moreover that the sole decisive experience is that of Da-sein with a constant look ahead to the Being-question, will agree that the 'Being' which *Being and Time* inquires into cannot remain something that the human subject posits" (HR 302). This is why the coming to the fore (to the "center") of Dasein in the analysis should not be taken as a sign of anthropocentrism, as Heidegger clarified in a footnote from *On the Essence of Ground* (*Vom Wesen des Grundes*):

All concrete interpretations [in *Sein und Zeit*], above all that of time, are to be evaluated *solely* in the perspective of *enabling* the *question* of being. ... As regards the reproach . . of an "anthropocentric standpoint" in *Being and Time*, this objection ... says nothing so long as one omits to think through the approach, the *entire thrust*, and the goal of the development of the problems in *Being and Time* and to comprehend how precisely through the elaboration of the transcendence of Dasein, "the human being" comes into the "center" in such a way that his nothingness amid being as a whole can and must become a *problem* in the first place. What dangers are entailed, then, by an "anthropocentric standpoint" that precisely puts its *entire* effort *solely* into showing that the *essence* of Dasein that there stands "at the center" is ecstatic, i.e., "*excentric.*" (PM 371, n. 66)

Being and Time thus already enacts a break with anthropocentrism and subjectivism and is already engaged in the turn toward the thinking of being as such.

The turn first consists in abandoning subjectivism. Let us nonetheless clarify straight away that an ontological analysis of the being of the subject, as Heidegger called for around the time of *Being and Time* in no way amounts to subjectivism. Indeed, what is subjectivism? For Heidegger, subjectivism consists in the conjunction peculiar to modern philosophy of an epistemological primacy given to the subject with an absence of ontological inquiry regarding its being. The modern tradition, even while taking the subject as a center norm or ground, neglects to question the meaning of its being by applying inadequate categories to it. To affirm the primacy of the subject, as the modern ontological tradition has done with Descartes, in no way ensures that its specific mode of being would be elucidated, which is the very task of the existential analytic. In this connection, the following passage from *The Basic Problems of Phenomenology* is particularly illuminating:

We are thus repeating afresh that in the active stress put upon the subject in philosophy since Descartes there is no doubt a genuine impulse toward philosophical inquiry which only sharpens what the ancients already sought; on the other hand, it is equally necessary not to start simply from the subject alone but to ask whether and how the *being* of the subject must be determined as an entrance into the problems of philosophy, and in fact in such a way that orientation toward it is *not one-sidedly subjectivistic*. Philosophy must perhaps start from the "subject" and return to the "subject" in its ultimate questions, and yet for all that it may not pose its questions in a one-sidedly subjectivistic manner. (GA24 220/155)

It is a matter of clarifying the "ontological foundation" of the *ego cogito* (GA2 22), of the subject, of the I. "Working out the tacit ontological foundations of the '*cogito sum*' will constitute the second stage of the destruction of, and the path back into, the history of ontology" (GA2 24). This passage merely reiterates *Being and Time*'s stated project. Indeed, according to the plan of the work (§8), a second part was to have been devoted to a "phenomenological destruction [*Destruktion*] of the history of ontology" (GA2 39) and proposed to inquire into the ontological foundations of the *cogito sum*, as well as how medieval ontology has been taken over into the problematic of the *res cogitans*. This second part was never completed, but the manner in which Heidegger formulated its object left little doubt concerning the direction that it would have taken. It would have been committed to clarifying the very presuppositions of an ontological tradition that had not been interrogated. What Heidegger deplores in the new Cartesian "beginning" is thus to have neglected to clarify ontologically its main "object": "Modern philosophy made a total turnabout of philosophical inquiry and started out from the subject, the ego. *It will be surmised and expected* that, in conformity with this fundamental diversion of inquiry to the ego, the being now standing at the center would become decisive in its specific mode of Being. *It will be expected* that ontology now takes the subject as exemplary entity and interprets the concept of being by looking to the mode of being of the subject—that henceforth the subject's *way of being* becomes an ontological problem" (GA24 174/123; my emphasis). Now this is precisely what did not happen. One must therefore distinguish between the return to the "I" as it testifies to Dasein's fundamental ontological function, and the modern return to the subject. For how is the *modern* return to the subject defined? Not in the sense in which Dasein would appear as that which is *interrogated* by the question of Being, as the very locus where the question of the meaning of being comes into play, but on the basis of philosophical presuppositions regarding the *ontical* and *epistemological* primacy of the subject. The priority accorded to the subject in modern philosophy is accompanied by an *indetermination* of its being.[19] As for the privilege of Dasein, it "obviously has nothing in common with a vapid subjectivizing of the totality of beings" (GA2 14). It is in this very hiatus between subjectivism and an ontological analysis of the being of subjectivity that the turn begins in Heidegger's thinking.

The Turn

The interruption of *Being and Time* thus was motivated by the attempt to overcome *subjectivism*, or what lent itself to the subjectivistic misunderstanding. Nonetheless, Heidegger admitted that his earlier work was still too attached—reactively or "defensively"—to the metaphysical subjectivistic way of thinking, and attempted to think, beyond transcendence and beyond the very ontological difference, the truth of be-ing out of itself. Dasein is now approached from the key word in his thought, *Ereignis*, that is, from the happening of the truth of be-ing. Heidegger explains in the *Beiträge* (GA65 295; CP 208) that "in *Being and Time* Da-sein still stands in the shadow of the 'anthropological,' the 'subjectivistic,' and the individualistic,'" and he explains as well, in paragraph 138 (GA65 259; CP 182–183), that the initial position of the question of being in *Being and Time* in terms of "meaning of being" and "understanding of being" suffered from an excessive dependence upon the language of subjectivity. To that extent, it exposed itself to a series of misunderstandings, all sharing the same subjectivism: "Understanding" is taken in terms of the "inner lived-experiences" of a subject; the one who understands is taken in turn as "an I-subject"; the accessibility of being in an understanding is taken as an indication of the "dependency" of being upon a subject and therefore as a sign of idealism. In the "Letter on Humanism," we find a similar analysis: "If we understand what *Being and Time* calls 'projection' as a representational positing, we take it to be an achievement of subjectivity" (PM 249), and consequently we do not grasp the notion of "understanding of being" *in the way it was intended in a work of fundamental ontology*, "namely as the ecstatic relation to the clearing of Being [*als der ekstatische Bezug zur Lichtung des Seins*]," or as "ekstatic in-standing [*ekstatisches Inne-stehen*] within the clearing" (PM 249). It is in this context that Heidegger then explicitly mentions the interruption of *Being and Time*: the "adequate execution and completion of this other thinking that *abandons subjectivity* is surely made more difficult by the fact that in the publication of *Being and Time* the third division of the first part, 'Time and Being,' was held back (cf. *Being and Time*, ┌. 39)" (PM 249–250). And why was the publication held back? Because it could not be undertaken with the help of the language of metaphysics, and required another beginning. As I mentioned above, the turn from "Being and Time" to "Time and Being" could not be accomplished within the confines of that one book, as if that interruption of the 1927 work was due to an impasse having to do with an excessive reliance on the language of metaphysics and in particular the *language of subjectivity*. "Here everything is reversed [*Hier kehrt sich das Ganze um*]. The division in question was held back because thinking failed in the adequate saying of this turning [*Kehre*] and did not succeed with the help of the language of metaphysics" (PM 250). Citing that passage in his letter to Richardson, Heidegger clarifies: '"Here the whole is reversed.' 'The whole': this means the matter of 'Being and Time,' 'Time and Being'" (HR 302), thus explicitly referring the turn in his thinking to the question of the incompletion of *Being and Time*.

To go beyond such language of subjectivity, Heidegger turned from the expression "meaning of being" to that of "truth of be-ing." In 1969, in the Thor seminar, Heidegger clarified that in contrast with the metaphysical question concerning the beingness of being, he attempted in *Being and Time* to pose the question concerning the "is-ness" of the "is" in terms of the *meaning* of being. For, precisely, metaphysics does *not* ask about the meaning of being, but only about the beingness of beings. The expression "meaning of being" is thus to be taken as a first attempt to step out of the metaphysical conflation of being with beingness or beinghood. "According to the tradition, the 'question of being' means the question concerning the being of beings, in other words: the question concerning the beinghood of beings, in which a being is determined in regard to its being-a-being [*Seiendsein*]. This question is *the* question of metaphysics. ... With *Being and Time*, however, the 'question of being' receives an entirely other meaning. Here it concerns the question of being as being. It becomes thematic in *Being and Time* under the name of the 'question of the meaning [*Sinn*] of being'" (FS 46). Now, "meaning of being" is further clarified in *Being and Time* in terms of the project or projecting unfolded by the understanding of being. "Here 'meaning' is to be understood from 'project' which is explained by 'understanding'" (FS 40). At this point, Heidegger notes that this formulation is inadequate *because it runs the risk of reinforcing the establishment of subjectivity*: "What is inappropriate in this formulation of the question is that it makes it all too possible to understand the 'project' as a human performance. Accordingly, project is then only taken to be a structure of subjectivity—which is how Sartre takes it, by basing himself upon Descartes" (FS 41). It was in order to avoid the subjectivizing of the question of being that the expression "truth of being" was adopted. "In order to counter this mistaken conception and to retain the meaning of 'project' as it is to be taken (that of the opening disclosure), the thinking after *Being and Time* replaced the expression 'meaning of being' with 'truth of being'" (FS 41), a shift that is at the core of the turn. Indeed, how does Heidegger explain the shift from "meaning of being" to "truth of be-ing"? In terms of a *turning* of the question of being, a turning that would have the question part from a certain subjectivism and anthropocentrism still dangerously threatening to affect the analyses of *Being and Time*. Heidegger gives examples of such a "turning in thinking," when, for instance in paragraph 41 of the *Beiträge*, he explains that the word "decision" can be taken first as an anthropological human act, "until it suddenly means the essencing of be-ing [*das Wesen des Seyns*]" (GA65 84; CP 58; trans. modified). This indeed raises the issue of the turn or of the *reversal*, the reversal of the understanding of Dasein on the basis of being itself: "This does not mean that be-ing is interpreted 'anthropologically' but the reverse [*umgekehrt*]: that man is put back into the essential sway of be-ing and cut off from the fetters of 'anthropology'" (GA65 84; CP 58). As such, the expression "truth of be-ing" leads away from all subjectivism, for it points to a dimension beyond the opposition between subject and object. Truth "of" be-ing does not mean: truth about being (objectification), nor is it to be taken simply as a subjective genitive. In fact, Heidegger clarifies that the "of" "can never be grasped by the heretofore 'grammatical' genitive." The "of" instead names the event of the happening of the truth "of" be-ing (which is the happening of the be-ing "of" truth), a dimension that is more originary than the subject–object opposition. This is why Heidegger renames the genitive "of" an "original own" (*ein ur-eigener*) (GA65 428; CP 302).

In a sense, *Being and Time* was already engaged in this turn toward the overcoming of subjectivity. For far from establishing the primacy of subjectivity, the existential analytic as we saw was defined on the basis of the project of fundamental ontology (GA2 13). In the 1928 course, *The Metaphysical Foundations of Logic*, Heidegger would make explicit the fundamental-ontological import of the analytic of Dasein. The whole of the analytic is governed by a single objective, that of the elaboration of a fundamental ontology, as existential analytic: "The analysis [of existence] proceeds solely with the purpose of a fundamental ontology; the point of departure, execution, limit, and mode of concretizing certain phenomena are governed by

this purpose" (GA26 171; MFL 136). Heidegger carefully distinguished the
existential analytic from a project of philosophical anthropology by projecting, for example, *Zeitlichkeit* onto *Temporalität*, that is to say, "the meaning
of the entity that we call Dasein" onto the meaning of being as such, object
of the held back Third Division of Part One, "Time and Being." The thought
of Dasein thus constitutes a radical break with the traditions of anthropology and subjectivity, a break that Sartre and the early existentialists missed
in their misunderstanding and translation of Dasein as *"réalité humaine,"*
or human reality. In fact, the very terminological choice inherent in the
notion of Dasein was motivated by the project "to liberate the determination of the human essence from subjectivity, but also from the definition
of *animal rationale"* (PM 282–283). Rather, with the term Dasein, Heidegger
undertook an ontological questioning on the human being, interrogated
solely in terms of its *being*, that is to say, in terms of being itself. This is what
Heidegger clarified in 1940 in *Der europäische Nihilismus*, explaining that in
Being and Time, on the basis of the question concerning no longer the truth
of beings but the truth of being itself, "an attempt is made to determine the
essence of the human being solely in terms of his relationship to Being [*aus
seinem Bezug zum Sein*]. That essence was described in a firmly delineated
sense as *Da-sein"* (GA6.2 194; *Nietzsche III*, 141; trans. modified). The term
Da-sein—oftentimes hyphenated in order to stress this sheer relatedness
to being—designates in the *same* stroke man's relation (opening) to being
and being's relation to man: "To characterize with a *single* term both the
relation of Being to the essence of man and the essential relation of man
to the openness ('there' ['*Da*']) of Being [*Sein*] as such, the name of Dasein'
[there-being] was chosen for the essential realm in which man stands as
man" (PM 283). And to decisively overcome any subjectivism, Heidegger
insists that "any attempt at thoughtfulness" would be "thwarted as long
as one is satisfied with the observation that in *Being and Time* the term
'Dasein' is used in place of 'consciousness.' As if this were simply a matter
of using different words!" (PM 283). Dasein is not another word for either
consciousness or subjectivity. With the choice of the term Dasein, it is a
question of a topological revolution of the essence of the human being.
"The term 'Dasein' neither takes the place of the term 'consciousness,' nor
does the 'matter' designated as 'Dasein' take the place of what we represent
to ourselves when we speak of 'consciousness.' Rather, 'Dasein' names that
which is first of all to be experienced, and subsequently thought of accordingly, as a place [*Stelle*]—namely, as the locality of the truth of Being [*die
Ortschaft der Wahreit des Seins*]" (PM 283).

Therein lies the break with the tradition of the subject: what matters first "is not at all and no longer to begin with man as a subject [*Subjektum*], before he is beforehand grasped in terms of the question of being, and only in this way" (GA65 489; CP 345). Indeed, Dasein's being consists not in subjectivity but in the dimension of being itself, especially since "in the determination of the humanity of the human being as ek-sistence what is essential is not the human being but being—as the dimension of the *ecstasis* of ek-sistence" (PM 254). Now we recall how Heidegger explained in his 1941 course that the understanding of existence in terms of being alone was "only fully developed" in the held back Division III of Part One of *Being and Time*. It then appears that the interruption of *Being and Time* involved this rethinking of existence and the being of Dasein outside of the tradition of subjectivity. Da-sein, as "overcoming (*überwindung*) of all subjectivity arises from the essential occurrence of being [*Wesung des Seyns*]" (GA65 303; CP 214; trans. modified).

This is what overcoming subjectivity means: reopening the thinking of being. "Descartes can be overcome only through the overcoming [*Überwindung*] of that which he himself founded, only through the overcoming of modern, and that means at the same time Western, metaphysics. *Overcoming means here, however, the primal asking of the question concerning the meaning ... of Being.*"[20] Therein lies the turn in thinking, from a thinking centered on Dasein's openness to being to a thinking that meditates the openness of being to Dasein: "The thinking that proceeds from *Being and Time*, in that it gives up the word 'meaning of being' in favor of 'truth of being,' henceforth emphasizes the openness of being itself, rather than the openness of Dasein in regard to this openness of being. This signifies 'the turn,' in which thinking always more decisively turns to being as being" (FS 47). The turning in the question leads not to an abandonment of the reference to the human being, but rather to its relating to the truth and event of being. This is what Heidegger stated in his letter to Richardson, when he explained that the "thinking of the reversal" or of the turn "brings about the adequate determination of Dasein, i.e., of the essence of the human as thought in terms of the truth of being as such" (HR 303).

Conclusion

The turn thus pursued what the existential analytic was attempting to develop, and in this respect was already present in *Being and Time*, insofar as the thinking of Dasein exceeded the problematic of subjectivity. In his letter to William Richardson (1962), Heidegger stressed that *Being and*

Time was already engaged in such turning: "Being is something that matters to Da-sein as the presence determined by its time-character. Accordingly thought is also already called upon, in the initial steps of the being-question of *Being and Time*, to undergo a change whose movement corresponds with the reversal [*Kehre*]" (HR 302). In that same letter, Heidegger insisted on the deep continuity of his thought: "The thinking of the reversal *is* a change in my thought. But this change is not a consequence of altering the standpoint, much less of abandoning the fundamental issue, of *Being and Time*. The thinking of the reversal results from the fact that I stayed with the matter that was to be thought in *Being and Time*, i.e., that I inquired into that perspective which already in *Being and Time* (p. 39) was designated as 'Time and Being'" (HR 302). Heidegger had also insisted on this point in the "Letter on Humanism," explaining that "This turning is not a change of standpoint from *Being and Time*, but in it the thinking that was sought first arrives at the locality of that dimension out of which *Being and Time* is experienced, that is to say, experienced in the fundamental experience of the oblivion of Being" (PM 250). Let us clarify, then, that the turning in the question of being does not mean that there would be two distinct questions, as if Heidegger had abandoned any reference to the human being after the turn, insofar as his thinking increasingly turned toward the truth of be-ing as such. For the turning in the question leads not to an abandonment of the reference to the human being, but rather to its *transformation* (a "becoming other in what is ownmost to him" [GA65 83; CP 58]). In fact, as we alluded at the outset, there is only one and single question. However, because that same question is asked ever more originarily, the "locations" of questioning are each time different, and the question itself must "transform itself from the ground up."[21] Therein lies the *"transformation of human beings themselves"* (GA65 84; CP 67), from the subjectivistic horizon to the belongingness to the truth of be-ing (Da-sein). This reveals that the turn, the "reversal" from "Being and Time" to "Time and Being," as Heidegger himself characterized it (in the "Letter on Humanism," we read: "The lecture 'On the Essence of Truth,' thought out and delivered in 1930 but not printed until 1943, provides a certain insight into the thinking of the turning [*Kehre*] from 'Being and Time' to 'Time and Being,'" PM 250), comes out of the matter itself, the question of being. Heidegger explains in his letter to Richardson that "the reversal between Being and Time, between time and Being, is determined by the way Being is granted, time is granted [*wie Es Sein, wie Es Zeit gibt*]," then referring to the lecture from 1962, "On Time and Being," where time and being are thought out of the gift of *Ereignis*; he adds: "I tried to say a word about this 'is granted' [*Es gibt*] in the lecture

'Time and Being' which you heard yourself here [in Freiburg], on January 30 1962" (HR 303). What is the turn? The turn, which arises out of the matter itself, ultimately names the "relation" of Dasein to being.[22] Da-sein is *itself* by standing in the opening of be-ing. The turn lies in that being only "essences" where and when there is Dasein, and that *in turn* Da-sein "is" only where and when there is be-ing. Dasein now designates the *belonging-together of the human being and Being*. "En-ownment in its turning [*Kehre*] is made up neither solely of the call nor solely of the belongingness, is in neither of the two and yet resonates deeply in both" (GA65 342; CP 240). The thinking of the truth of being unfolds as a thinking of the most proper being of humans. "The human being can belong to *be-ing* (not only among beings), insofar as he draws out of this belongingness—and precisely out of it—what is most originarily his ownmost" (GA65 499–500; CP 351, trans. modified). It was that thought of the most proper being of humans that was at stake in the turn. For Heidegger, it was a question of thinking from the perspective of a primordial event and appropriation through which humans are given over to themselves,[23] an event that the motif of "subjectivity" could not appropriately capture, thus leading to the interruption of *Being and Time*, and the opening of the turn.

Notes

1. Martin Heidegger, "Letter on Humanism," in *Pathmarks*, ed. William McNeill (Cambridge: Cambridge University Press, 1998), 250, my emphasis. Hereafter cited as PM, followed by the page number.

2. Martin Heidegger, *Die Metaphysik des deutschen Idealismus: Zur erneuten Auslegung von Schelling: "Philosophische Untersuchungen über das Wesen der menschlichen Freiheit und die damit zusammenhängenden Gegenstände"* (1809/1941), ed. Günter Seubold (Frankfurt am Main: Vittorio Klostermann, 1991, 2006, 2nd rev. ed.), GA49 41.

3. Martin Heidegger, *Beiträge zur Philosophie (vom Ereignis)*, ed. Friedrich-Wilhelm von Herrmann (Frankfurt am Main: Vittorio Klostermann, 1989), 84. *Contributions to Philosophy (From Enowning)*, trans. Parvis Emad and Kenneth Maly (Bloomington and Indianapolis: Indiana University Press, 1999), 58–59. Hereafter cited as GA65 for the German edition and CP for the English translation.

4. *The Heidegger–Jaspers Correspondence* (1920–1963), ed. Walter Biemel and Hans Saner, trans. Gary E. Aylesworth (Amherst, NY: Humanity Books, Prometheus Books, 2003) 65.

5. *The Heidegger-Jaspers Correspondence*, 69. On these letters, see the indications from Jean-Francois Courtine in his essay, "Heidegger, l'échec de *Sein und Zeit*," in *Lectures d'Être et Temps de Martin Heidegger*, ed. Philippe Cabestan and Françoise Dastur (Paris: Le Cercle herméneutique, 2008), as well as Claude Romano's recent book, *L'inachèvement d'Être et Temps et autres études d'histoire de la phénoménologie* (Paris: Le Cercle herméneutique, 2013), 197–244.

6. Indeed, Heidegger begins *The Basic Problems of Phenomenology* by presenting the course in the following way: "A new elaboration of division 3 of part 1 of *Being and Time*." *Die Grundprobleme der Phänomenologie*, ed. Friedrich-Wilhelm von Hermann (Frankfurt am Main: Vittorio Klostermann, 3rd ed., 1997), 1. *The Basic Problems of Phenomenology*, trans. A. Hofstadter (Bloomington: Indiana University Press, 1982), 1. Hereafter cited as GA24 for the German edition, followed by the English translation pagination.

7. See Martin Heidegger, *Sein und Zeit* (1927), ed. Friedrich Wilhelm von Herrmann (Frankfurt am Main: Vittorio Klostermann, 1977), GA2, 7–8. English translations used: *Being and Time*, trans. John Macquarrie and Edward Robinson (New York: Harper, 1962). *Being and Time*, trans. Joan Stambaugh, revised and with a foreword by Dennis J. Schmidt (Albany: SUNY Press, 2010). Hereafter cited as GA2, followed by original pagination.

8. Martin Heidegger. "Letter to Father Richardson," in *The Heidegger Reader*, ed. Günter Figal, trans. Jerome Veith (Bloomington: Indiana University Press, 2009), 303. Hereafter cited as HR.

9. On the different senses of the turn in Heidegger's work, distinguished as the turn of (1) reciprocity (*Gegenschwung*), (2) reversal (*die Kehre*), and (3) resoluteness (*Entschlossenheit*), see Thomas Sheehan, "The Turn: All Three of Them," in *The Bloomsbury Companion to Heidegger*, ed. François Raffoul and Eric Sean Nelson (London: Bloomsbury, 2013), 31–38.

10. "The question of being is the question of the truth of be-ing [*Seyns*]. When accomplished and grasped as it historically unfolds, it becomes the *grounding-question*—over against the hitherto "guiding-question" of philosophy, which has been the question about beings" (GA65 6; CP 5).

11. For instance: GA2 111.

12. Martin Heidegger, *Einführung in die Metaphysik*, ed. Petra Jaeger (Frankfurt am Main: Vittorio Klostermann, 1983), GA40 107. *Introduction to Metaphysics*, trans. Gregory Fried and Richard Polt (New Haven, CT: Yale University Press, 2000), 149. Hereafter cited as GA40 and IM.

13. Martin Heidegger, *Vom Wesen der menschlichen Freiheit: Einleitung in die Philosophie*, ed. H. Tietjen (Frankfurt am Main: Vittorio Klostermann, 2nd ed., 1994), GA31,

123. *The Essence of Human Freedom*, trans. Ted Sadler (London: Continuum, 2002), 85, modified. Hereafter cited as GA31 and EHF.

14. Martin Heidegger, *Logik: Metaphysische Anfangsgründe der Logik im Ausgang von Leibniz*, ed. Friedrich-Wilhelm von Herrmann (Frankfurt am Main: Vittorio Klostermann, 1990), GA26 20. *The Metaphysical Foundations of Logic*, trans. Michael Heim (Bloomington: Indiana University Press, 1984), 16. Hereafter cited as GA26 and MFL.

15. Martin Heidegger, "The Basic Question of Being as such," in *Heidegger Studies*, vol. 2 (Berlin: Duncker & Humblot, 1986), 5. Translation slightly modified.

16. On this reception (or nonreception), see Françoise Dastur, "The Reception and Nonreception of Heidegger in France," in *French Interpretations of Heidegger*, ed. David Pettigrew and François Raffoul (Albany: SUNY Press, 2008).

17. Martin Heidegger, *Nietzsche* II (1939–46), ed. Brigitte Schillbach (Frankfurt am Main: Vittorio Klostermann, 1997), GA6.2 194, my emphasis. *Nietzsche III: The Will to Power as Knowledge and Metaphysics*, ed. David F. Krell, trans. Joan Stambaugh (New York: Harper & Row, 1987), 141. Hereafter cited as GA6.2 and Nietzsche III.

18. Martin Heidegger, *Four Seminars*, trans. Andrew Mitchell and François Raffoul (Bloomington: Indiana University Press, 2004), 70. Hereafter cited as FS.

19. As early as 1921–1922, Heidegger had linked the epistemological primacy of the I to its ontological neglect: "The fact that Descartes could deviate into epistemological questioning have moved towards the position of an epistemological question … merely expresses the more basic fact that to him the *sum*, its Being and its categorial structure, were in no way problematic. On the contrary, he intends the word *sum* in an indifferent, formally objective, uncritical, and unclarified sense." Martin Heidegger, *Phänomenologische Interpretationen zu Aristoteles. Einführung in die phänomenologische Forschung*, ed. Walter Bröcker and Käte Bröcker-Oltmanns (Frankfurt am Main: Vittorio Klostermann, 2nd ed., 1994), GA61 173. *Phenomenological Interpretations of Aristotle: Initiation into Phenomenological Research*, trans. Richard Rojcewicz (Bloomington: Indiana University Press, 2001), 130.

20. Martin Heidegger, *Holzwege*, ed. Friedrich-Wilhelm von Hermann (Frankfurt am Main: Vittorio Klostermann, 1977), GA5 100. *The Question Concerning Technology and Other Essays*, trans. William Lovitt (New York: Harper & Row, 1977), 140–141. My emphasis.

21. Let us note that in the Thor seminar in 1969 (FS 40–41, 47), Heidegger announced that his thinking of being has taken three essential formulations: as meaning of being, as truth of being, and as topology of being.

22. In fact, the term "relation" is inadequate because it presupposes two distinct spheres entering *a posteriori* into a relation. In paragraphs 134 and 135 of the *Beiträge*,

Heidegger notes that "strictly speaking, talk of a relation of Da-sein to be-ing is misleading, insofar as this suggests that be-ing holds sway 'for itself' and that Da-sein takes up the relating to be-ing" (GA65 254; CP 179).

23. As Heidegger wrote in "On Time and Being": "Appropriation has the peculiar property of bringing the human being into his own. ... Thus appropriated, the human being belongs to Appropriation" (GA14 28, 12; TB 23; trans. modified).

13 Did Heidegger Ever Finish *Being and Time*?

Thomas Sheehan

Actually, Heidegger *did* finish "being and time"—not the book by that name but the project that he set for himself in 1926. And yet Heidegger scholarship has been notoriously uncertain about at least four issues: (1) what Heidegger's project was ultimately about, (2) whether the project changed or remained the same throughout the half-century of his career, (3) what Heidegger's basic question was, and (4) whether he ever answered it. A few comments on each of these issues:[1]

(1) *As regards the ultimate goal of Heidegger's project*: Since the 1960s the mainstream consensus in Heidegger studies, which I will call "the classical paradigm," has argued that "the thing itself"—the final aim of all Heidegger's work—was "being" (= *Sein*, sometimes spelled as *Seyn* and sometimes written under erasure as S̶e̶i̶n̶ or S̶e̶y̶n̶), even though Heidegger himself declared that when it comes to the very core of his project, "there is no more room even for the word 'being.'"[2] If not "being," then what?

(2) *As regards the continuity of the project*: According to the classical paradigm the early Heidegger held that *Dasein* (which I will translate as "ex-sistence": see n. 1) "projects being"—that is, existentielly (= personally) opens up the clearing—whereas in the 1930s his project took a "turn," a "reversal of direction," such that thereafter "being projects ex-sistence"— this despite Heidegger's insistence in 1962 that his later work entailed no "*change in the standpoint*, much less an abandoning of the fundamental issue, of *Being and Time*."[3]

(3) *As regards the basic question*: The classical paradigm holds that Heidegger was focused on "the question of being" (*die Frage nach dem Sein*), even though he clearly said that metaphysics had already answered that question many times over. He himself insisted his question was not about *Sein* but about the *source* of being (*die Herkunft des Seins, das Wesen des Seins*),[4] or in other terms, whatever it is that "allows for 'being'" (*das Lassen des Seins*). Moreover, Heidegger understands *Sein* phenomenologically. "Being"

is not the objective existence (*existentia, Vorhandenheit*) of things apart from and prior to man (e.g., the existence of flora and fauna in the Triassic period). Rather, the "being" of things is exclusively their *meaningful presence* (*Anwesen*) to human beings in correlation with the understanding of that meaningfulness: no *Dasein* = no *Sein*.[5] The guiding question of metaphysics ("How come there are things at all?") found its answer in one or another articulation of being (as εἶδος, ἐνέργεια, *esse*, etc.), whereas Heidegger's meta-metaphysical question ("How come there is *being* at all?") aims at whatever it is that makes *Sein* possible and necessary in human experience.[6] That is: If we are able to relate to things only mediately and discursively, only by understanding their whatness and howness (= their "being"), why is such discursive knowledge necessary for us, and how is it possible?

(4) *As regards the fulfillment of Heidegger's project*: Some scholars hold that he never answered his basic question about the source of "being" but left it aporetic, and necessarily so, because there can be no answer to the "mystery" (*das Geheimnis*) of "being." But on the contrary, Heidegger not only named the source of *Sein* in all its forms but also discussed it at length. He called this origin-of-being "appropriation" (*Ereignis*) or more fully "the appropriated clearing" (*die ereignete Lichtung*),[7] about which he had quite a lot to say between 1936 and 1976.

Moreover, Heidegger identified both appropriation and the clearing with the very structure of ex-sistence. As regards "appropriation," Heidegger insisted that *Ereignis* should never be translated as "event" (hence not even as "the event of appropriation").[8] Rather, *Ereignis* is simply the later Heidegger's reinscription of what he had earlier called *Geworfenheit* or *das geworfene Entwurf*: the thrown-openness of ex-sistence.[9] "Ap-*propri*-ation" names the existential-structural fact that ex-sistence has always already been "brought into its proper state" (*ad proprium*). That proper state is its thrown-openness, its being always already drawn out (*angezogen*) or stretched open (*erstreckt*).[10] As appropriated, ex-sistence is always already opened up *as* the clearing, the space within which things can be taken as what-and-how-they-are, that is, in terms of their current "being" (*das jeweilige Sein*) or, phenom-enologically, their current form of meaningful presence. As appropriated, ex-sistence is the clearing, the *Da*, which Heidegger understands not as the "here" or "there" or "t/here" ("Da ≠ ibi et ubi")[11] but as the "open space" within which the meaningful presence (their "being") can occur.

For me, "*Da-sein*" does not mean the same as *me voilà*, "Here I am!" but rather—if I might express it in a perhaps impossible French—*être le-là*. And the *le-là* is Ἀλήθεια: disclosedness—openness.[12]

This *Da* or openness is the very essence of human being.

The clearing: the *Da—is* itself *ex-sistence.*[13]

[Ex-sistence *is* itself the clearing.[14]

Ex-sistence s the way in which the open, the clearing, occurs, within which "being" as cleared is opened up to human understanding.[15]

Thus once one sees what Heidegger's basic question was and was not, it becomes clear that he *did* complete the task he set for himself in 1926 (albeit in an often needlessly obscure language). I have presented the evidence for this thesis thematically in *Making Sense of Heidegger: A Paradigm Shift*, and here I will merely sketch out diachronically the fulfillment of the "being and time" project from 1926 to 1976.

There are three presuppositions that underlie this chapter: (1) Heidegger's work was phenomenological from beginning to end; (2) what Heidegger means by *das Sein* is the significance of things, their meaningful presence (*Anwesen*) to discursive intelligence (λόγος), whether practical or theoretical; and (3) Heidegger's final goal, the so-called "thing itself," was not the meaningful presence of things (traditionally, their "being") but rather what makes such presence possible. At this point I will comment only on the first presupposition.

As regards phenomenology: Heidegger began his public career in 1927 with the phenomenological ontology of *Being and Time*, and as late as the 1960s he insisted that his work was still phenomenological. In September of 1962, commenting on his approach in the lecture "Time and Being," he was emphatic that "this procedure can be designated as phenomenological"; and in 1968 he maintained that his question about the essence of "being" was a "phenomenological question."[16] By "phenomenology" Heidegger was referring not to the watered down version of "letting things show themselves as they are in themselves" (something that analytic philosophers also do, not to mention scientists, artists, and carpenters). Rather, he meant phenomenology in its strict and proper sense, based on what in 1927 he called the phenomenological reduction of things *from* their natural-attitude status as simply "out there," independent of human constitution, *to* their presence within meaning-constituting worlds of human concerns and interests.

For *us* the phenomenological reduction means leading the phenomenological vision *back from* the apprehension of a thing, whatever may be the character of that apprehension, *to* the understanding of the "being" of the thing (i.e., understanding the thing in terms of the way it is disclosed).[17]

For Heidegger the "being" of a thing does not stand on its own, independent of any relation to ex-sistence, as it does in traditional metaphysics.

Rather, it is the *significance* of things to human beings. Prior to the reduction, we already understand the significance of the things in our everyday lives, at least tacitly, but we mostly overlook it.[18] The phenomenological reduction wakes us up to what is always already the case. It is the methodological procedure that focuses our attention *explicitly* on the ever-operative correlation between the thing in question and our interests in the thing and our concerns about it. The reduction restrains or "brackets out" (ἐπέχειν) our natural tendency to overlook our own constitution of the meaningfulness of things as we look *through* the meaning of things to those very same things as they allegedly are "in themselves." The reduction takes us back reflectively and thematically to where we always already stand without noticing it: in relation to the thing as *concerning* us in such and such a way, as *meaningful* in this way or that. For Heidegger a thing is still out there (*vorhanden*) and unchanged after the reduction, but as such it is not the focus of his philosophy. The subject matter of a phenomenological inquiry is things only insofar as one is meaningfully engaged with them. After the phenomenological reduction, the only philosophical problems one may properly pursue are those of sense and meaning. And in Heidegger's phenomenology, the "being" of something is the significance it has for us, the sense it makes to us.

Finally, we must note the notorious sloppiness with which Heidegger employed the word "being." In the partly fictitious "Dialogue on Language," based on a 1953–54 conversation, Heidegger's interlocutor, Professor Tomio Tezuka of the Imperial University of Tokyo, lays most of the blame for the muddle about "being" at Heidegger's own doorstep:

Tezuka: [The problem is due] mainly to the confusion that was created by your ambiguous use of the word "*Sein*."

Heidegger: You are right. [Nonetheless, my thinking] knows clearly the distinction between "*Sein*" as the "the being of things" and "*Sein* as *Sein*" with regard to its own proper sense, which is dis-closedness (clearing).

Tezuka: Then why didn't you immediately and decisively hand back the word "*Sein*" exclusively to the language of metaphysics? Why didn't you immediately give your own name to what you were seeking as the "*Sinn des Seins*" on your path through the essence of time?

Heidegger: How can I give a name to what I'm still searching for? Finding it would depend on assigning to it the word that would name it.

Tezuka: Then we have to endure the confusion that has arisen.[19]

The confusion Tezuka refers to is Heidegger's scandalous practice of using the same word, *Sein*, to refer to two very different phenomena:

1. *the "being" of things*, whether that be understood metaphysically (as their "substance," their essence or their existence) or phenomenologically (as their meaningful presence to us); and
2. *the thrown-open clearing* that makes possible the "being"/meaningful presence of things.

This confusion has thrown Heidegger scholarship off track for over eighty years, and Heidegger's efforts to distinguish between the two ("the being of things" vs. "being as being," as above) has had little success. In what follows I will distinguish the two (1) by reserving the word "being" exclusively for the "being"-of-things, but only in a *phenomenological* sense, that is, as their significance within contexts of human interests and concerns; and (2) by never using the word "being" to refer to the thrown-open clearing (i.e., ex-sistence as appropriated to its thrown-open status), which is the source of all forms of meaningful presence.

We now turn from these preliminaries to three major moments in the unfolding and the completion of Heidegger's "being and time" project.

1   The Project in 1926–1927

When it was published, *Being and Time* was to have unfolded in two parts, each with three divisions. I abbreviate the parts and divisions of the book, both as published and as promised, as follows: SZ I.1; I.2; I.3; and II.1; II.2; and II.3. The shaded areas indicate which divisions were actually published.

SZ I: Fundamental ontology

SZ I.1	SZ I.2	SZ I.3
What ex-sistence is (chs. 1–2) How it makes sense of things (ch. 3) How it is the clearing (chs. 5–6)	Mortality (ch. 1) Resolve and authenticity (ch. 2–3) Temporality and historicity (ch. 3 and 5)	How time (i.e., the temporal "horizon") determines all formations and regions of being as the meaningful presence of things.

SZ II: Destruction of the history of ontology

SZ II.1	SZ II.2	SZ II.3
Kant (= GA 3)	Descartes	Aristotle

Heidegger's basic question, like all questions, is made up of three moments:

* *das Befragte*: the subject matter under investigation
* *das Gefragte*: the focus on, and thus the question about, the subject matter
* *das Erfragte*: the heuristic outcome ("X") that the question is seeking

The *Befragtes* or subject matter of Heidegger's question is significance or meaningful presence (*das Anwesen*), which is always the significance or meaningful presence *of things*. The *Gefragtes* or focus is meaningful presence *taken in and for itself* and *in terms of its source*. The *Erfragtes* or sought-for "X" is whatever makes meaningful presence possible and necessary. But since significance or meaningful presence occurs only with human beings, Heidegger's question about what makes it possible turns the tables and begins by questioning the questioner, the human being who is asking about meaningful presence. Why are we obliged—even "condemned"—to making sense of things? Why are we structurally required to mediate discursively between things and their meanings instead of knowing things directly through an intellectual intuition?

By understanding "being" phenomenologically as the meaningfulness of things in correlation with human intelligence, *Being and Time* stands in the centuries-long tradition of the transcendental turn to the subject (*die Wende zum Subjekt*), which reaches back at least as far as Descartes and, for Heidegger, arguably as far back as Parmenides.[20] In that transcendental tradition, the way to solve a philosophical problem is to turn the inquiring subject into the subject of the inquiry.[21] Heidegger's unique place within the transcendental tradition is defined by the debate he initiated over what is meant by the subject. He radically reinterpreted the essence of human being not as "sub-ject" but as "e-ject," as "thrown out and ahead" in such a way that its essence is ex-sistence, its having been made to stand "out" (*sistere* is a causative verb: "to *make* something stand"). As such, ex-sistence, by its very essence, is ineluctably made to stand out beyond its actuality into itself *as possibility* ("Possibility stands higher than actuality")[22] and also beyond things into *their* possibilities.

But ex-sistence is also fundamentally λόγος, the need and ability to make sense of things, that is, to interpret them discursively in terms of their possible meanings. Correspondingly, therefore, that *into which* ex-sistence is thrown-out-and-ahead is always *possible meaningfulness*, both of itself and of the things it encounters. I "have" myself always and only as an interpreted self, understood in terms of this or that possibility of myself. Likewise I meet up with things only in terms of *their* possible meaningfulness. I do not merely bump up against them with my bodily senses and then add significance to them. Rather, I have an a priori relation *not* to the specific meaning of the thing but to its general intelligibility: (1) its *ability* to have a specific meaning within a specific context, and (2) the *necessity* that it have some meaning or other in terms of which it can be encountered. Heidegger defines ex-sistence as *In-der-Welt-sein*, that is, as being-in-the-world-of-meaning, where "being in" means "engaged with."[23]

Located within the transcendental tradition that makes the inquiring subject into the subject of the inquiry, *Being and Time* as fundamental ontology had three distinct tasks, each of which corresponds to one of the three divisions of SZ I:

- first (SZ I.1): to establish what the existential "e-ject" is and how it makes sense of things, and then to ground such sense-making capabilities in man's radical thrown-openness.
- second (SZ I.2): to show that thrown-openness is mortal, to argue that it can be "taken over" in an act of resolve, and to interpret it in terms of "temporality," which is the basis of human historicity.
- third (SZ I.3): to show how "temporality" unfolds as the "temporal" horizon for all forms of "being"—this under the rubric of "time and being," or as he later put it, "clearing and meaningful presence" (*Lichtung und Anwesenheit*).[24]

The progression of SZ I.1 and I.2 is well known, and we need not repeat all the details. But a brief overview is necessary if we are to see how Heidegger completed his project, even without writing SZ I.3.

In my everyday ex-sistence I usually meet things not as stand-alone entities but rather in ensembles of interrelations: knife with fork with plate with food. Things come in meaningful contexts that Heidegger calls "worlds" of significance, which are structured by my concerns and purposes. Within those worlds the changeable meanings of things are derived from their possible relation to those concern and purposes.[25] Say I am camping and need to set up a tent, but have forgotten to bring a mallet to hammer in the tent pegs. From my purpose, which lies "ahead" of me ("Gotta set up this tent before it rains"), I pick up a rock to do the job. The lived context of camping, focused on my need for shelter, gives the rock its current meaning as a mallet. After using it, I toss it aside, and it returns to being "only a rock." In other words, things get their current meaning when we "return" to them from our "aheadness" in the concerns that shape the worlds of meaning we inhabit (in this case, the world of camping). As Heidegger puts it,

In taking up a tool [here, a rock], we return to the tool [from our aheadness in our purpose] and understand it in terms of the work-world that has already been opened up.[26]

Viewing the world of our concerns as a meaning-giving "horizon," he continues:

[We] come back from those horizons to the things we encounter within them. Returning to these things and understanding them [e.g., as useful] is the existential meaning of letting-them-be-encountered by rendering them meaningfully present.[27]

But how must we be structured *in order* to perform this "movement" of living ahead in our concerns and returning from them to render things meaningfully present? As in medieval scholasticism, Heidegger argues from actuality to possibility, from a specific activity to the state-of-being that makes it possible, in accordance with the axiom *operari sequitur esse*: activities are consonant with and derive from a thing's nature or being[28]—or as Heidegger himself puts it: "Each thing ... achieves only what it is."[29] What, then, allows us to take a rock as a mallet? Or for that matter, to take anything *as* this-or-that (e.g., to understand Socrates as an Athenian)? As Aristotle might put it: What makes it possible for us "to interpret something *as* this-or-that" (τὶ κατὰ τινὸς λέγειν)?[30]

Heidegger argues that to "take something *as* ..." is to think or act *discursively*, that is, to have to "run back and forth" (*dis-currere*) between "this" and "that" (between the tool and the task, or between the thing and its possible meaning) as we check out whether there is a fit between the two. This means, metaphorically speaking, that we have to "traverse an open space"[31] (the clearing) that makes possible an "as," that is, a relation between the relata. This space is opened up by—and in fact *is*—the thrown-aheadness, the thrown-openness, of ex-sistence. That is what allows us to take something in terms of *what and how we think it is*—which in a traditional lexicon is its "being" and in phenomenological terms is its meaning, its current significance to us. In that sense, ex-sistence, as thrown-open, opens up the clearing and thus is the focal issue ("the thing itself") of all Heidegger's work.[32]

Three further and important points: (1) Insofar as ex-sistence as the clearing is never an over-and-done-with actuality but always a matter of open-ended possibility, it is *intrinsically finite*. (2) The finitude of ex-sistence entails the possibility of its impossibility at any moment.[33] Ex-sistence is always *at-the-edge-of-death* (not "being-*towards*-death"): it is inevitably mortal. (3) Ex-sistence (= each of us) can personally acknowledge and embrace

Table 13.1

HOW EX-SISTENCE MAKES FINITE SENSE OF THINGS

Existentially			
I *can* understand	an actual thing	in terms of	its possibilities
	1. Socrates	as	an Athenian
	2. This rock	as suitable for	hammering in tent pegs

only because

Existentially I *always already am* the clearing, i.e.:	$\longrightarrow$	thrown-ahead as possibility among possibilities ... ,
	. . . whence I return so that I and everything I meet get their meanings.	$\longleftarrow$

its essential mortality and thus "become what it already is."[34] Such a resolve to live mortally (*vivere moriendo*) is what Heidegger calls "authenticity."[35]

In the final analysis, this ever-finite aheadness-and-return (ex-sistence's way of being present to itself *as* thrown-ahead possibility) is what Heidegger means by "temporality" (*Zeitlichkeit*).

This being-ahead-of-oneself as a returning [*Sich-vorweg-sein als Zurückkommen*] is, if I may put it this way, a peculiar kind of movement that ex-sistence *qua* "temporal" constantly makes.[36]

Heidegger is at pains to make it clear that the "temporality" and "time" he has in mind is not a matter of a chronological past-present-future but rather is this aheadness-and-return as the *Lichten der Lichtung*, the ever-operative opening up of the space-for-meaning.[37] (I put these time-words in scare quotes to indicate that they do not refer to time in the usual sense.) There is a correlation operative here. On the one hand, "temporality" (*Zeitlichkeit*) names thrown-open *ex-sistence* as ahead-and-returning; and on the other hand, "time" and "time-character" (*Zeit* and *Temporalität*) are equivalent names for the *clearing* that thrown-open ex-sistence itself is and sustains. In his clearer moments, Heidegger either dropped "time" and "temporality" from his lexicon or explicitly reinterpreted them in terms of the thrown-open clearing.

"Temporality" [*Zeitlichkeit*] constitutes the clearedness of the open [the *Da*] in a thrown-open, horizon-forming way.[38]

The unfolding of *Temporalität* [= the "time-character" of the clearing] is a preliminary name for the openness of the clearing.[39]

"Time" ["*Zeit*"] is … the clearing of being itself.[40]

"Time" is a preliminary name for the openness of the clearing.[41]

"Time" as a preliminary name for the thrown-open domain [*Entwurfbereich*].[42]

"Temporality" and its [correlative term, the] "*time-character*" [of the clearing]: a way
of announcing the open-ness of the open."[43]

Thus the trajectory of Heidegger's project in 1926, the year in which he
wrote *Being and Time*, begins to come clear. Structurally-existentially (and
not by a will-act of its own), ex-sistence as "temporality" (*Zeitlichkeit*) a
priori unfolds as, holds open, and *is* a "temporal" space (*Zeit* or *Temporalität*) within which all forms of taking-as—and, therefore, all forms of meaningful presence—occur. As intrinsically "temporal"—that is, as finite—this
thrown-open space determines that the meaningful presence of things will
always be "temporal"/finite. Hence, the project that was to be worked out
in the unpublished SZ I.3 was to show that "time" or finitude determines
all forms of "being," that the mortal thrown-openness of ex-sistence as the
clearing is what makes discursive meaningfulness possible and necessary.

A final note on ex-sistence as the clearing in 1926: Some invoke Heidegger's statement that man stands "in relation to" the clearing as "that
which man is not"[44] and then go on to allege that ex-sistence is not the
clearing. However, Heidegger immediately explains what he means by that
phrase when he continues: "… insofar as human being *receives its determination from the clearing*."[45] That is, the clearing is not different from ex-sistence
but is the structural determination of human being, the very essence of ex-
sistence, the reason why ex-sistence ex-sists at all. There are not two separate things, ex-sistence over here, and the clearing over there, the "two"
somehow glued together. The "two" are actually the same phenomenon
considered from distinct points of view: either *ex-sistence* as the clearing
or the same *clearing* as making possible all forms of "being." This oscillat-
ing sameness (*Gegenschwung*)[46] was first designated as *In-der-Welt-sein*. On
the one hand, the being of ex-sistence is to-be-the-world, the possibility-
of-meaning ("As ex-sisting, ex-sistence *is* its world" and "The clearing, and
it alone, is the world").[47] And on the other hand, the ever-open world is
the very being of ex-sistence.[48] Heidegger never loses sight of the structural
unity of ex-sistence-as-the-clearing, a "*unitary* phenomenon [that] must be
seen as a whole."[49] As the later Heidegger puts it:

The relation is not a bond stretched between the clearing and man. … The relation
is the clearing itself, and man's essence *is* that same relation.[50]

The task of SZ I.3 was to show how this thrown-open ("ex-static") clearing determines all forms and regions of the meaningful presence of things.

2 Summer 1927: The Failure of the Transcendental Project

Being and Time, as Heidegger frequently said, was a transitional work.[51] In 1926 his fundamental ontology was based on a phenomenological-*transcendental* correlation: (1) thrown-open ex-sistence (2) forms the "horizon" (his provisional term for the clearing) that determines all forms of the meaningful presence of things. The never-published SZ I.3 was to show how the schema-forming moments of thrown-openness affect the whole range of intelligibility (the "being" of things), including its possible variations and different regions. But that transcendental approach fell by the wayside almost immediately.

Just ten weeks after *Being and Time* was published, Heidegger began his Marburg course "Basic Problems of Phenomenology" (April 30–July 17, 1927), which he envisioned as "a new elaboration of *Being and Time*, Part One, Division 3."[52] However, Heidegger spent most of the course providing background about being (in Kant, Aristotle, Descartes, and logic: May 7–July 2) and about time (Aristotle's *Physics* IV: July 6)—neither of which corresponded to what *he* meant by "being" and "time"—as well as briefly reviewing the core of *Being and Time* (July 13 and 16). It was only in the last half of the last day of the course (July 16, 1927) that he left the material of SZ I.1–2 behind and made a brief sortie into the "new" material of what was to be SZ I.3. The results were meager: Heidegger made an inconclusive and not very informative effort to elaborate only the "temporal" horizon of "the present."

In *Being and Time*, the closest Heidegger had come to discussing the clearing as the horizon for all forms of "being" was §69c, "The Temporal Problem of the Transcendence of the World." Heidegger had already established that the structure of ex-sistence as aheadness-and-return is what allows things to be meaningfully present.[53] At §69c he reiterated that same point, but in specifically transcendental-horizonal language:

[Ex-sistence] already maintains itself in the *horizons of its ex-stases*, and, as it unfolds in that way [*sich zeitigend*], it returns to the things it encounters in the open.[54]

By the "ex-stases" (my misspelling to stress the etymology) Heidegger is referring to the three moments that make up aheadness-and-return ("temporality"). Ex-sistence "stands outside" insofar as it is (1) *always-already thrown* (2) *ahead* into meaning-giving possibilities (3) in terms of which it renders things meaningfully *present*. These three "temporal" ex-stases correspond to the three moments of *Sorge* or care: (1) always already (2) ahead as possibility in possibilities, thereby (3) rendering things meaningfully present.[55] In SZ §69c Heidegger went on to assert—briefly, dogmatically, and without elaboration—that these three unified modes of self-transcendence shape a correlative threefold horizon. He left the matter at that, and concluded:

> By tracing being-in-the-world back to the ex-static horizonal unity of "temporality," we have made intelligible the existential and ontological [horizon-forming] possibility of this fundamental constitution of ex-sistence.[56]

That is: precisely as "temporal," ex-sistence is thrown-open *as* empty horizonal formations (the schemata) that provide a "temporal" shape to the meaningful presence of whatever we encounter. However, that is as far as Heidegger had gotten by February 1927, that is, in *Being and Time*.

Now, in the course "Basic Problems of Phenomenology," he made a further stab at explaining how the transcendental-horizonal clearing determines two things: (1) the "directionality" of thrown-openness, and, in turn, (2) the "temporal" meaningfulness of whatever we encounter.[57] He picks up the argument in §21a of "Basic Problems."[58] Correlative to the three ways that ex-sistence is thrown open as possibility there are three specific and distinct "schemata," possible ways of "having" (shaping the meaning of) ourselves and possible objects.[59] He declares: "each ex-stasis as such has a horizon that is determined by it and that first of all completes that ex-stasis's own structure."[60] Thus, at one pole, the three unified moments of thrown-openness; at the other pole, the three unified moments of the open horizon—the whole of this as constituting a "temporal" transcendental correlation that is the articulated shape of ex-sistence as the clearing.

However, section §21a of "Basic Problems" ("Temporalität und Sein") adds little to what Heidegger had already said in SZ §69; and in fact, the few steps he takes into the supposedly new material are quite hesitant. "In order not to complicate too much our view of the phenomenon of 'temporality,'" he says, "which in any case is difficult to grasp,"[61] he imposes a double limit on his treatment. (1) He restricts himself to only *one* of the three horizonal schemata, the one corresponding to the ex-stasis of *Gegenwärtigen,* having something meaningfully present. (2) Within that one horizonal schema, he further restricts himself to dealing only with tools, to the exclusion of whatever else one could render meaningfully present. Briefly:

Having-a-tool-present, as an ex-static moment of ex-sistence, has a schematic pre-indication (*Vorzeichnung*)[62] of that out-toward-which transcendence reaches, namely, the horizon of *Praesenz* (also called *Anwesenheit*). *Praesenz* thus constitutes "the condition of the possibility of understanding usefulness as such."[63] The exstasis of having-present, in fact, understands whatever it has-present in terms of this field of *Praesenz* and so understands those things as having a "presential sense" (*ein praesentialer Sinn*) and thus as "meaningfully present things" (*als Anwesendes*).[64] Moreover, as he had done earlier in SZ §69c, so again in "Basic Problems" Heidegger analyzes the breakdown of a tool and finds therein a privative modification of the ex-stasis, namely, from having-it-present to having-it-un-present. In the corresponding horizonal schema there is a modification of the tool's "being" from usefulness to unsuitability (from *Zuhandenheit* to *Abhandenheit*), that is, from presentness to un-presentness (*Anwesenheit, Abwesenheit*).[65] He uses the "un-" to indicate that the no-longer-useful tool is still *there* in the carpenter shop but no longer meaningfully present as it was before.

At that point (GA 24: 443.24 = 312.4), Heidegger's advance into SZ I.3 stops, and it is a very meager advance at that. "Basic Problems" §21a has merely established that, correlative to the ex-stasis of *Gegenwärtigen*, there is the horizonal schema of *Praesenz*, with *Absenz* (un-presentness) as its privative modification corresponding to the un-usefulness of a tool. End of story. Heidegger has sketched out, almost formulaically, only one horizonal schema corresponding to the one ex-stasis of having-present in the one area of tool-use. Left undiscussed are: (1) the other two schemata in which tools are experienced, along with their privative modifications; (2) *all* the schemata of nontools; and above all, (3) the unified "temporal" meaning of the horizon-for-being as such. The course "Basic Problems of Phenomenology" hardly represents a notable advance into SZ I.3—a sign, perhaps, that the project of SZ as planned was in trouble as soon as it was published.

Despite Heidegger's failure to make progress in working out SZ I.3 in the spring and summer of 1927, he still maintained, for one more year, the fourfold outline of SZ I.3 that he had provided in "Basic Problems of Phenomenology." In that 1927 course Heidegger's outline was:

1. the ontological difference
2. being as *essentia* and *existentia*
3. the possible modifications and unity of being
4. the disclosed-character of being.[66]

In his last semester at Marburg he repeated that outline at the end of his course "The Metaphysical Foundations of Logic" (July 10, 1928), along with an unremarkable change. (The third and fourth sections were rearranged.)

1. the ontological difference
2. the articulation of being into whatness and thatness
3. the disclosed-character of being
4. the regionality of being and the unity of the idea of being.[67]

That fall (October 24, 1928), during his first semester in Freiburg as Husserl's successor, Heidegger told the Australian philosopher (and translator of Husserl's *Ideen I*), W. R. Boyce Gibson, that it would be "some little time"—not likely by the next issue of Husserl's *Jahrbuch*—before the rest of *Being and Time* appeared.[68] After that we hear nothing more about the completion of Heidegger's *magnum opus*. The project of SZ, which basically remains enclosed within the Marburg period, had apparently ground to a halt. Finally, in the 1953 foreword to the seventh edition of *Being and Time*, we read:

> While the previous editions have borne the designation "First Half" [= SZ I.1–2], this has now been deleted. After a quarter of a century, the second half [especially SZ I.3 but perhaps also II.1–3] could no longer be added unless the first were presented anew. Nonetheless, the road it has taken remains even today a necessary one, if our ex-sistence is to be stirred by the question of being.[69]

3   1930–1976: The Project Completed

As William J. Richardson pointed out fifty years ago, Heidegger's lecture "On the Essence of Truth," delivered in December 1930 but not published until 1943, is the "decisive point" in Heidegger's development and constitutes the "breakthrough" in which "Heidegger I becomes Heidegger II."[70] That breakthrough consisted in Heidegger's momentous insight into the intrinsic hiddenness of the appropriated clearing. In 1926–27 *Being and Time* had spoken of the hiddenness of thrown-openness, but not of the clearing itself.[71] In 1929 Heidegger's inaugural lecture at Freiburg "What Is Metaphysics?" took a small step forward when it spoke, somewhat hesitantly, of "the essential impossibility of determining" the clearing, here understood as the no-thing encountered in dread.[72] However, it was not until a year later, in "On the Essence of Truth," that Heidegger began to articulate his dawning insight that the clearing is hidden *in and of itself* and not because of the limitations of our knowing powers.

"On the Essence of Truth" reaches its climax in section 6, where Heidegger declares for the first time in his career that, in contrast to the disclosedness of things, the clearing-as-appropriated remains ever *un*-disclosed and that this un-disclosedness is the very essence of the clearing. Unfortunately, in that crucial passage Heidegger made two mistakes. First, contrary to his own principles,[73] he used the misleading language of "truth" to refer to the disclosedness of both *things* and the *clearing*.[74] ("Truth" should be reserved only for the correctness of judgments.) And second, he did not adequately distinguish between the disclosedness of things and the disclosedness of the clearing.

A close paraphrase of the crucial but difficult German sentence may clarify the matter. (The bracketed numbers are mine.)

[1] Die Verborgenheit ist dann,
[2] von der Wahrheit als Entborgenheit her gedacht,
[3] die Un-entborgenheit und somit die dem Wahrheitswesen eigenste und eigentliche Un wahrheit.[75]

[1] The intrinsic hiddenness of the appropriated clearing,
[2] when compared with the dis-closedness of things,
[3] is *un*-disclosedness: hiddenness as the most proper and essential characteristic of the clearing as such.

That is: While enabling the meaningful presence of things, the clearing itself—ἀλήθεια in its most fundamental sense—remains intrinsically "lethic," undisclosed or "hidden," that is, unknowable as regards its why and wherefore. There is nothing mystical about this, and one is not talking about the clearing "hiding *itself*" as if it possessed some weird kind of agency. When applied to the clearing, verb forms like *sich entziehen* and *sich verbergen* are to be read as "The clearing *is* withdrawn, *is* hidden" instead of "The clearing *ups and hides itself.*" (Compare *etwas zeigt sich*: something *shows up* vs. shows *itself*.)[76] In any case, this text from the 1930 lecture records Heidegger's breakthrough into his later work. We may mark it with the formula ἀλήθεια-prime = λήθη-prime—that is, the appropriated clearing, as the ultimate (groundless) ground for the disclosure of everything meaningful, is itself intrinsically hidden. This is the ur-insight, the founding vision that drove all Heidegger's work, early and late. To adapt the words of William J. Richardson, it is "the living center of Ur-Heidegger."[77]

This insight opened the door to Heidegger's "history of being." The intrinsic hiddenness of the appropriated clearing is the reason that the clearing has been overlooked and forgotten throughout Western metaphysics. Heidegger confusingly speaks of *Seinsvergessenheit* (the forgottenness of *"being"*) when he actually means *Lichtungsvergessenheit* or *Ereignissesvergessenheit* (the forgottenness of the appropriated clearing). We must distinguish two "levels" of hiddenness:

1. the intrinsic and un-overcomeable hiddenness of the clearing (hiddenness *in se*);
2. the overcomeable forgottenness of the clearing in metaphysics and in our daily lives (hiddenness *quoad nos*).

In both cases there is a "bracketing out" (ἐποχή) of the clearing. I will call the intrinsic hiddenness of the clearing "ἐποχή-1" and the resultant forgottenness of the clearing "ἐποχή-2." Heidegger's "history of being" is about various instances of ἐποχή-2 in metaphysics, that is: (1) an individual philosopher's awareness of the "being" of things, whether as εἶδος, ἐνέργεια, esse, etc., while (2) always overlooking ἐποχή-1 as the ever-hidden source of such formations of "being." In the later Heidegger, overcoming or getting free of metaphysics/ἐποχή-2 entails recollecting ἐποχή-1 but always actively leaving it in its intrinsic hiddenness. Such an effective acknowledgment of the hiddenness of the appropriated clearing breaks the stranglehold of ἐποχή-2/metaphysics, just as in the early Heidegger resolve (taking over one's mortal thrownness) awakens one from one's fallen absorption in meaningful things.

Heidegger's 1930 insight into the intrinsic hiddenness of the clearing also marked the end of his earlier transcendental approach to the question of the clearing. In the 1930s, even as the original project held, Heidegger began transitioning away from transcendentalism to a seinsgeschichtlich articulation of what was to have been the content of SZ I.3. The verb schicken, which lies at the heart of the adjective seinsgeschichtlich, bespeaks the fact that the appropriation of ex-sistence opens up the clearing and thus allows for ("sends" or "gives") various possibilities of taking-things-as, and thus various possibilities of the "being"/significance of things. Thus we might interpret Heidegger's new orientation as one based on "appropriation-making-meaningful-presence-possible." The phrase hardly rolls off the tongue, and I do not propose it as a translation, only as a periphrastic interpretation. But it is more accurate than speaking of the later Heidegger's "being-historical approach."

How had the transcendentalism of Being and Time thrown up obstacles to Heidegger's progress? Why did he find that approach inadequate to unfolding his project? In his 1945 "dialogue on a country path" entitled "Ἀγχιβασίη" ("Approaching"), Heidegger provides one of his more discursive (if largely metaphorical) comments on overcoming the transcendental-horizonal approach of Being and Time. A horizon, he says, is the field of vision (Gesichtskreis) that "encircles" us and our objects, making possible both our presentational intentionality and the meaningful appearance of our objects.[78] In that sense, the horizon lies "beyond" the objects, "just as transcendence passes beyond the mere perception of the object to the apprehension of the significance/"being" of the object.[79] Heidegger emphasizes that in a transcendental approach, transcendence and its correlative horizon are defined and determined only relative to intentional objects and the presentation (*Vorstellung*) of them as meaningful—this, as a way of saying that the transcendental approach is inadequate for getting at what *opens up the horizon itself* in the first place. The horizonal field of vision is certainly open, but it "does not have its openness from the fact that we look into it."[80] It's the other way around. We *can* look into the horizon only because it is *already* opened up.

What has the character of a horizon is thus only the side turned toward us of a surrounding openness, an openness that is filled up with [intentional-presentational] viewings of the meaningful appearances of what shows up as objects to our presenting [*Vorstellen*] of them as objects.[81]

Even if Heidegger had remained within the early transcendental-horizonal approach of *Being and Time*, even then the openness of the horizon would still not be due to either presentational intentionality or Promethean projectivity. The openness of the open field that allows for transcendental, object-presentational thinking is prior to all that and cannot be accounted for by it.

The question then becomes: What opens up the open itself, if we disregard the fact that it can *also* appear as the horizon of our intentional-presentational thinking? Heidegger's metaphorical answer to that question plays on the German preposition *gegen*, less in the sense of "over against" and more in the sense of the Latin *contra*, "in front of."[82] The open clearing is like the expansive *country*side (*die Gegend*) that en-*counters* us (*entgegen-kommt*) as always already open.[83] The usual translation of *die Gegend* by the opaque "region-that-regions" (which says absolutely nothing, even in Heidegger-speak) misses Heidegger's nuanced metaphorical sense of the clearing as the *country*side that already lies open before us (*contra*) before we do anything within it (strolling through the fields, for example, or picnicking on the grass). This countryside *lies open before us* without ever being an object *standing over against* us (*Gegen-stand*). Heidegger's *Gegend*-metaphor evokes "the open countryside" (= the clearing) in which we already find ourselves and within which particular things are meaningfully present to us. And its openness is due not to any *existentiel* intentionality or act of personal-Promethean transcendence on our part. The clearing is always already opened up thanks to our existential structure as thrown-openness.

Through all its shifts and transitions, its clarifications and improvements (and its not infrequent obfuscations), Heidegger's work from 1926 to 1976 remained directed to one and the same end: to show that finite, mortal ex-sistence as the appropriated clearing is what allows for all forms of the significance or meaningful presence (the "being") of things. Heidegger was clear about this point:

Das Dasein ist das je vereinzelte "es," das gibt; das ermöglicht und ist das "es gibt."[84]

Ex-sistence is the ever individualized *es* that gives. It makes possible and is the "*es gibt.*"

Heidegger even went so far as to say:

[Das Da] gehört zum Sein selbst, "*ist*" Sein selbst und heißt darum das Da-sein.[85]

[The *Da*, i.e., the open] belongs to being itself, "*is*" being itself and thus is called *Da-sein*, ex-sistence.

Given that, we may say that the core of Heidegger's project was mostly achieved by 1927. In 1936, Heidegger noted:

Being and Time has not become something past for me, I have still not "gotten any further" today because I know with every increasing clarity that I must not get any "further." But perhaps I have gotten closer in some things to what was attempted in *Being and Time*.[86]

The content of Heidegger's project entailed the long-planned change of focus (*Blickwendung*) from (1) *ex-sistence* as the clearing to (2) *the clearing* as making possible all meaningful presence. This change of focus was necessary to articulate Heidegger's fundamental conviction that the clearing is the *Worumwillen* of ex-sistence—its *raison d'être*, its very essence—and, as such, that which makes possible all forms of "being." But this does not mean that the clearing is some super-human phenomenon that is other than ex-sistence and endowed with a higher ontological status. That is, the clearing is not the hypostasized Super-*Sein* of recent Heideggerian fiction, which somehow "gives itself to" and "withholds itself from" ex-sistence at will.[87] Any alleged "priority" of the clearing to ex-sistence comes down to the fact that the clearing is the essence, the very *proprium*, of ex-sistence and thus is always already operative "before"—that is, existentially prior to—any *existentiel* acts we might perform.

And yet, for all that, the project of "being and time" was not an end in itself. It was, Heidegger said, only a preparation for (*Vorbereitung*) and an exhortation to one's own personal-existentiel act of becoming what one already is by embracing one's appropriation and making it one's own. Read properly, then, his project realizes its goal only when an individual personally "enters into *Ereignis*,"[88] that is, lives mortally in terms of his or her groundless thrown-openness.

Notes

1. Regarding references, sources, and translations: I cite Heidegger's texts by page and line (the line number follows the period) in both the *Gesamtausgabe* and the current English translations. An exception: I cite *Sein und Zeit* in the more readily available eleventh, unchanged edition (Niemeyer, 1967) and in the Macquarrie-Robinson translation. A list of translations is given in my *Making Sense of Heidegger: A Paradigm Shift* (New York: Rowman & Littlefield, 2015), from which some material is adapted. I translate *Dasein*, in both its existentiel and existential usages, as "existence" in order to stress the etymology: *sistere* (a causative verb) + *ex*: to be made to stand (1) *out* as possibility and (2) *beyond things*, into their possibilities. Thus *Existenz*, Heidegger's name for the essence of human being, already implies "thrown-openness." I translate *das Seiende* as "things" or "entities." Because *Sein* in Heidegger properly refers to the meaningful presence (*Anwesen*) of things, I place "being" in scare quotes whenever it has that meaning. I often use my own translations from the German, or change and adapt the published English translations. The word "man" refers to human being, not the male of the species.

2. GA 15: 365.17–18 = 60.9–10: "ist sogar für den Namen Sein kein Raum mehr."

3. GA 11: 149.23–24 = William J. Richardson, *Heidegger: From Phenomenology to Thought*, 1st ed. (The Hague: Martinus Nijoff, 1963), xvi.27–28; my emphasis.

4. GA 10: 131.19–20 and 131.28 = 88.27 and 88.34: "Wesensherkunft des Seins." Cf. GA 6, 2: 304.11 = 201.13–15: "Herkunft von Anwesen." Also GA 2: 53, n. a = Stambaugh 37 n. †: "Das Anwesen aus dieser Herkunft"; and GA 73, 2: 984.2: "nach ihrer Wesensherkunft (Ereignis)."

5. SZ 152.11–12 = 193.31–32; 183.29–30 = 228.12–14; and 212.4–5 = 255.10. GA 45: 212.10–11 = 179.29–32. GA 65: 254.22–23 = 200.23–24. GA 73, 1: 337.5. Cf. GA 73, 2: 975.24.

6. GA 16: 66.15–16: "worin gründet die innere Möglichkeit und Notwendigkeit der Offenbarkeit des Seins."

7. GA 7 : 211.8. Regarding the origin of "being": Heidegger called this origin the Urphänomen and Ur-Sache at GA 14: 81.13–14 = 65.30–32.

8. GA 14: 25.33–26.1 = 20.29–33; GA 11: 45.19–20 = 36.18–19, where in the German note 76 Heidegger glosses "Geschehnis" and "Vorkommnis" with "eine Begeben-heit," an incident or occurrence; and GA 70: 17.19.

9. GA 65: 34.9 = 29.7: "die Ereignung, das Geworfenwerden; ibid., 239.5 = 188.25: "geworfener . . . d.h. er-eignet"; and ibid. 304.8 = 240.16: "Das Dasein ist geworfen, ereigne-"; ibid., 325.37 = 373.14–15—"die Übernahme der Geworfenheit"—compared with GA 65: 322.7–8 = 254.36–37: "die Über-nahme der Er-eignung." Cf. GA 9: 377, note d = 286, note d: "Geworfenheit und Ereignis." See also GA 65: 252.23–25 = 199.3–4; and GA 94: 337.7–8. This topic is discussed in *Making Sense of Heidegger*, chapter 8.

10. Re angezogen: see Cf. GA 8: 11.10 = 9.17 (where it is mistranslated as "attracted"). Re erstreckt: SZ 371.32 = 423.15 and 375.2–3 = 427.10: "Bewegtheit des *erstreckten Sicherstreckens.*" GA 26: 173.34 = 138.17: "Dasein als Erstreckung." GA 66: 315.18 = 280.31: "er-streckt und aus-streckt."

11. GA 71: 211.4 = 180.30. See Heidegger, "Die 'Seinsfrage' in *Sein und Zeit*," *Heidegger Studies* 27 (2011), 9.27–28: "'Da' nicht demonstrativ (wie 'dort') ontisch, sondern: ekstatisch—dimensioniert."

12. Heidegger, "Lettre à Monsieur Beaufret (23 novembre 1945)," in *Martin Heidegger, Lettre sur l'humanisme*, ed. and trans. Roger Munier, new revised edition (Paris: Aubier, Éditions Montaigne, 1964), 182.27–184.3. See also Heidegger, *Zollikoner Seminare* 156.33–35 = 120.20–21.

13. "Die 'Seinsfrage' in *Sein und Zeit*" (see n. 11), 9.23: "die Lichtung: das Da—*ist* selbst *das Dasein.*" GA 3: 229.10–11 = 160.32: "ist der Mensch das Da, mit dessen Sein der eröffnende Einbruch in das Seiende geschieht." GA 70: 125.12: "[die] Lichtung des Da-, die als Da-sein west." See also GA 14: 35.23–24 = 27.31–33.

14. SZ 133.5 = 171.22: "daß es [= Dasein] selbst die Lichtung ist." Cf. GA 56: 129.5 = 109.7–8: "das 'Da,' die Lichtung." GA 69: 101.12–13: "*Die Lichtung—sein*—in sie als Offenes sich loswerfen = das *Da*-sein."

15. GA 49: 60.25–27: "Das Da-sein ist vielmehr die Weise, wie das Offen-, die Lichtung west, in der 'das Sein' als gelichtetes dem menschlichen Verstehen sich öffnet." Also GA 15: 415.10–13 = 88.18–21: "Es gilt, das Da-sein in dem Sinne zu erfahren, daß der Mensch das 'Da,' d.h. die Offenheit des Seins für ihn, selbst *ist*, indem er es übernimmt, sie zu bewahren und bewahrend zu entfalten. (Vgl. 'Sein und Zeit,' S. 132f.)"

16. GA 14: 54.2–3 = 44.32–33: "Dieses Vorgehen [in 'Zeit und Sein'] kann als phänomenologisch bezeichnet werden." GA 14: 147.15–16 = 201.1: "die weitere Frage [re das Wesen des Seins], die ich as phänomenologische beanspruche."

17. GA 24: 29.15–18 = 21.25–30; my emphasis. GA 19: 8.25–26 = 6.8–10: "Phänomen bezeichnet das Seiende, so wie es sich zeigt, in den verschiedenen Möglichkeiten seines Erschlossenwerdens."

18. GA 8: 113.8–10 = 110.11–13: "Das Sein des Seienden ist das Scheinendste; und doch sehen wir es gewöhnlich überhaupt nicht." Heidegger references Aristotle, *Metaphysics* II, 1, 993b9–11: we are as blind as a bat to that which, by nature, is most evident of all.

19. GA 12: 104.16–105.3 = 20.14–212.

20. GA 26: 179.20–21 = 143.24–25: "insofern bei Parmenides zum erstenmal zur Sprache kommt, daß Sein subjektsbezogen ist."

21. SZ 7.24–27 = 27.7–9. Cf. Plotinus, *Enneads* V.1.1.31–32: "It is necessary for the soul to know what kind of entity is doing the searching. ..."

22. SZ 38.29–30 = 63.2: "Höher als die Wirklichkeit steht die *Möglichkeit*," inverting Aristotle, *Metaphysics* IX, 8, 1049b4.

23. For Heidegger the structure of Welt is Bedeutsamkeit. Hence, properly interpreted, *In-der-Welt-sein* means *In-der-Bedeutsamkeit-sein.*

24. "Clearing and meaningful presence": GA 14: 90.2 = 73.2 and GA 11: 151.21–28 = Richardson, *Heidegger*, xx.25–33. I put "temporality" and "temporal" in scare quotes to indicate that they do not refer to a chronological past-present-future. "Temporal ty" (*Zeitlichkeit*) refers to ex-sistence as always already (1) ahead in meaning-giving possibilities and (2) returning from there to the things that are thus rendered meaningful. The "temporal" horizon (*Zeit* or *Temporalität*) is the realm of possible meaningfulness (the "clearing") that is opened up and sustained by such aheadness-and-return. See *Making Sense of Heidegger*, 95–100 and 169–178.

25. Note the relation between these two claims: "Intelligibility is an existentiale of ex-sistence. ... Ex-sistence alone 'has' intelligibility" (SZ 151.34 and 0.36 = 193.11 and 193.13) and: "When an innerworldly thing is discovered with the being of ex-sistence—that is, when it comes to be understood—we say it has intelligibility": SZ 151.22–24 = 192.35–37; ibid. 207.12–13 = 251.3–4: "Mit dem Dasein ... erschlossen."

26. SZ 352.35–36 = 404.2–3.

27. SZ 365.15–19 = 417.16–17.

28. For example, Thomas Aquinas, *Summa theologiae*, I, 75, 3, corpus, ad finem: "Similiter unumquodque habet esse et operationem." Or to reverse the direction, "Qualis modus essendi talis modus operandi": a thing's way of being determines its way of acting.

29. GA 4 65.26–28 = 87.27–29: "Jegliches ... je nur das leistet, was es ist."

30. See, e.g., *De interpretatione* 5, 17a21 and 10, 19b5; *Metaphysics* VIII, 3, 1043b30–31.

31. GA 15: 380.6 = 68.43: "eine offene Weite durchgehen." See GA 14: 81.35 and 84.3–4 = 66.19 and 68.9 (durchmißt, duchmeßbaren) and GA 7: 19.12 = 18.32 (durchgeht).

32. See GA 73, 1: 642.27–28.

33. SZ 250.38–39 = 294.25.

34. SZ 145.40–41 = 186.4–5, implicitly referring to Pindar, *Pythian Odes* II, 72: γένοι' οἷος ἐσσ μαθών. See also GA 40: 108.26–28 = 111.12–14.

35. "Vivere moriendo," to live as dying: Augustine, *Epistula XCV*, no. 2, *Patrologia Latina*, ed. Jacques-Paul Migne (Paris: Imprimerie Catholique, 1857–1856), vol. 33: 352.38.

36. GA 21: 147.23–26 = 124.19–20. I here correct my earlier reading (ibid.) of "Zeit" in place of "Dasein."

37. GA 49: 41.25–28: "Ent-wurf besagt: Er-öffnung und Offenhalten des Offenen, Lichten der Lichtung, in der das, was wir Sein (nicht das Seiende) nennen und somit unter diesem Namen auch kennen, eben als *Sein offenkundig* ist."

38. SZ 408.7–8 = 460.20–21: "Weil die Zeitlichkeit die Gelichtetheit des Da ekstatisch-horizontal konstituiert," italicized in the original; ibid., 410.25–26 = 464.20–21: "als ekstatisch-zeitliches je schon erschlossen"; ibid., 4_0.34–35 = 463.29–30: "Zeitlichkeit ... Erschlossenheit des Da" (italicized).

39. GA 9: 159, note a = 123, note a: "Zeitigung der Temporalität als Vorname der Wahrheit des Seyns." GA 69: 95.3–5: "Zeitlichkeit zeitigt den Lichtungsbereich für das Sein (die dort [in *Sein und Zeit*] sogenannte 'Temporalität'). Zeitlichkeit ist der Vorname für die Wahrheit des Seyns." SZ 408.7 = 460.20–21: "Weil die Zeitlichkeit die Gelichtetheit des Da ekstatisch-horizontal konstituiert" (all italicized in the original).

40. Heidegger, *Schellings Abhandlung* 229.4 and 0.6 = 188.38–40. Here Heidegger himself puts "Zeit" in scare quotes.

41. GA 9: 376.11 = 285.26–27: "die 'Zeit' als der Vorname für die Wahrheit des Seins." GA 49: 57.2–3: "Der Name 'Zeit' is hier der *Vorname* für die Wahrheit des Seins." GA 65: 74.10–11 = 59.20–23: "'Zeit' ist ... Wahrheit der Wesung des Seins." GA 66: 145.25 = 124.6: "Lichtung (Zeit)." GA 73, 1: 758.2: "'Zeit' hier als Zeit-Raum im Sinne der Gegend."

42. Heidegger, *Schellings Abhandlung* 229.6 = 188.38.

43. GA 88: 46.7–8: "(Zeitlichkeit und ihre *Temporalität* als Anzeige der Da-heit des Da.)"

44. GA 15: 390.9–11 = 75.45: "zu dem ... was nicht der Mensch ist."

45. GA 15: 390.10–11 = 75.4–5: "indem er doch von dort seine Bestimmung empfängt." My emphasis in the English.

46. Heidegger's neologism "Gegenschwung" ("oscillation") appears in his notes beginning in 1936 and disappears (unfortunately, in my opinion) after 1945. See GA 65: 29:10 = 25.18 et passim; also, e.g., GA 70: 126.18; GA 75: 59.15; GA 78: 335.13. I favor dropping the overdetermined word "Kehre" and using "Gegenschwung" to name the sameness of ex-sistence and the clearing.

47. SZ 364.34–35 = 416.8: "Dieses [= das Dasein] *ist* existierend seine Welt" and GA 9: 326.15–16 = 248.37–38: "Die Lichtung, und nur sie, ist Welt."

48. GA 9: 154.18–19 = 120.24–25: "Welt ist … die Bezeichnung für das menschliche Dasein im Kern seines Wesens." See also SZ 64.19–20 = 92.32; 365.38 = 417.11; 380.28–30 = 432.17–18; GA 24: 237.8–10.

49. SZ 53.12–13 = 78.22–23: "ein *einheitliches* Phänomen. … Dieser primäre Befund muß im Ganzen gesehen werden."

50. GA 73, 1: 790.5–8, my emphasis: "Der Bezug ist jedoch nicht zwischen das Seyn und den Menschen eingespannt. … Der Bezug ist das Seyn selbst, und das Menschenwesen ist der selbe Bezug." "Einspannen" has the sense of yoking together, harnessing, as well as stretching between.

51. GA 65: 305.24 = 241.24: "Fundamentalontologie das Übergängliche." GA 65: 251.3 = 197.21: "Im übergänglichen Denken." See also GA 70: 194.28–30.

52. GA 24: 1, note 1 = 1, note 1: "Neue Ausarbeitung." Presumably an "old" version of SZ I.3 had existed before and was put aside.

53. See above, notes 24 and 25.

54. SZ 356.4–6 = 417.19–21; my emphasis. The verb "zeitigen" should never be translated as the barbaric "to temporalize." Heidegger provides its meaning at *Zollikoner Seminare,* 203.7–8 = 158.10–11: "Zeitigung als Sich-zeitigen ist Sich-entfalten, aufgehen und so erscheinen."

55. SZ 192.11–12 = 237.11–12.

56. SZ 356.32–34 = 418.7–9.

57. SZ 365.20–21 = 416.30–32: "Der Horizont der ganzen Zeitlichkeit bestimmt das, *woraufhin* das faktisch existierende Seiende wesenhaft *erschlossen* ist."

58. GA 24: 431–445 = 303–313.

59. The word "schema" (Greek: σχῆμα) is derived from the verb ἔχω, "to have," through the second aorist infinitive σχεῖν. The Latin for σχῆμα (as likewise for ἕξις) is "habitus": the way something has itself, bears itself. From that come the meanings "figure, shape, form" (as well as "looks, appearance").

60. GA 24: 435.10–12 = 306.21–22.

61. GA 24: 435.32–33 = 306.37–38.

62. GA 24: 435.20 = 306.23.

63. GA 24: 434.9–10 = 305.35–36.

64. GA 24: 433.22 = 305.17 and 436.6 = 307.2, respectively.

65. GA 24: 433.17 = 305.17 and 436.7–8 = 307.4–5, respectively.

66. GA 24: 33.5–11 = 24.12–17 (May 4, 1927).

67. GA 26: 191.29–194.2 = 151.24–153.4.

68. William Ralph Boyce Gibson, "From Husserl to Heidegger: Excerpts from a 1928 Freiburg Diary," ed. Herbert Spiegelberg, *Journal of the British Society for Phenomenology* 2 (1971), 72b.22–23.

69. SZ v.10–14 (*Vorbemerkung*) = 17.10–14.

70. Richardson, *Heidegger*, respectively 211.3, 243.17, and 254.12. The essay itself is found at GA 9: 177–202 = 136–154.

71. SZ 348.28–30 = 399.35–400.2: *Verschlossenheit, Geworfenheit, Faktizitä.*

72. GA 9: 111.29 =88.23–24: "die wesenhafte Unmöglichkeit der Bestimmbarkeit" of "das Nichts," i.e., of the clearing; however, Heidegger did not thematize that in terms of intrinsic hiddenness.

73. See Heidegger's polemic against translating ἀλήθεια as "truth": SZ 219.33–37 = 262.26–29 ("verdecken den Sinn"); GA 45: 98.8–12 = 87.20–24 ("Weder ... veritas noch ... Wahrheit"); GA 15: 262.5–10 = 161.31–34 ("nichts zu tun" and "schob sich dazwischen"); and GA 14: 86.16–20 = 70.2–5 ("nicht sachgemäß und demzufolge irreführend").

74. He complicates matters even further by speaking of "non-truth proper" and "the proper non-presence of truth": GA 9: 194.13–14 = 148.28: "die eigentliche Un-wahrheit. Das eigentliche Un-wesen der Wahrheit."

75. GA 9: 193.24–27 = 148.12–14.

76. Also GA 66: 340.13–14 = 303.18–19: "nimmt sich aus wie": "*is taken* as f."

77. Richardson, *Heidegger*, 640.28–29.

78. GA 77: 111: 19–20 = 72.14–15. See also GA 26: 269.5–6 = 208.13–14. Here and in what immediately follows, I translate *vorstellend* as "presentational."

79. GA 77: 111.22–23 = 72.17–18.

80. GA 77: 112.6–8 = 64.13–15.

81. GA 77: 112.13–16 = 64.20–23.

82. Cf. "Contra Costa County," which lies open before a San Franciscan who looks east across the Bay.

83. See GA 77: 113.17 = 73.23: *entgegenkommt.* See also GA 83: 157.5 and 157 11–20: "Das Gegnende: die zu-kommend sich öffnende umgebende Weite" understood as the χώρα: "Von wo her etwas [here: a thing in its "being"] anwest" (both phrases italicized in the original).

84. GA 73, 1: 642.27–28.

85. GA 6:2: 323.14–15 = 218.4–5.

86. Heidegger, *Schellings Abhandlung* 229.14–18 = 189.6–9.

87. See GA 66: 340.13–14 = 303.18–19, where Heidegger distances himself from the following error: "Das Sein nimmt sich aus wie 'Etwas.'" Compare Richard Capobianco, *Engaging Heidegger* (Toronto: University of Toronto Press, 2010) and *Heidegger's Way of Being* (Toronto: University of Toronto Press, 2014), as well as his lecture of May 9, 2015, "*Heidegger's Way of Being:* Reaffirming and Restating the Core Matter," *Proceedings of the Forty-Ninth Annual Meeting of the Heidegger Circle,* pp. 106–119.

88. Cf. GA 14: 51.33–34 = 42.30–31: "[die] Einkehr in das Ereignis"; see also GA 14: 50.23 = 41.24 and GA 15: 390.12 = 75.6.

14   The Failure of Philosophy: Why Didn't *Being and Time* Answer the Question of Being?

Iain Thomson

> *Being and Time* is a failed project.
> —Theodore Kisiel[1]

Introduction: Thinking Failure

Let us add another item to the long list of lessons still to be learned from *Being and Time*: We need an ontology of philosophical failure. What *is* failure in philosophy? I am not asking about failing at philosophy by failing to do it or by doing it badly. I mean the more deeply puzzling phenomenon of doing philosophy as well as it has ever been done and yet failing in that philosophy nonetheless. What does it mean to say, rightly, that *Being and Time* fails, or that it is (in Kisiel's words) "a failed project"? In what way can and should the most influential philosophical work of the twentieth century be considered a failure, judged by the most sympathetic standards of an "internal" or immanent reading (that is, by its own lights or on its own terms) rather than by some measure "external" to the text itself?[2] What did *Being and Time* set out to accomplish, and why did it fail to achieve that goal? Is this a failure Heidegger could have avoided or rectified if he had time to complete the book in the way he originally planned? Or is this a necessary failure, one that follows from some inexhaustibility inherent in the subject matter of *Being and Time* itself, and so from the impossibly ambitious nature of its attempt to answer "the question of being"? In what way must philosophy *fail itself* (to employ a polysemic locution), necessarily falling short of its own deepest, perennial ambitions? What is the lesson of such necessary philosophical failure?

Questions look easier than answers, but in fact our questions guide and circumscribe our search. As Heidegger points out near the beginning of *Being and Time*: "Every question is a kind of seeking, and every search must be guided beforehand by what is sought" (BT 24–25/SZ 5–6). If we do not ask the right questions, we stand little chance of finding the right answers. Yet, sometimes philosophers get lucky (though at first such luck appears to be anything but), and our misguided questions lead to an impasse or *aporia*, requiring us to go back and revise our earlier questions. This, we will see, is exactly what happened to "the question of being" Heidegger asked in *Being and Time*. He went looking for the wrong sort of answer and, failing to find it, eventually found something else instead, something better because more true. Or, in the terms of *Being and Time*, we could say that Heidegger's first quest to answer the question of being had to *die*, to be reborn differently only in his later work. For, to *be* "a failed project" (as Kisiel fortuitously puts it) is precisely what *Being and Time* means by existential "death." (This is ontological death—*being* dead—as opposed to the mortal phenomenon of ontic "demise," which is something we can never *be* since mortal demise takes away our being, as Epicurus observed long ago.) With such allusions to existential death and rebirth—especially that *philosophical* death and rebirth that used to be called Heidegger's "turn" (until that location too died, prematurely, before being fully understood)—we are already "running out ahead" of ourselves, "anticipating" what is to come.[3]

Such death and rebirth also form the path to what *Being and Time* famously calls "authenticity," though to begin to see this we must pass through and beyond the death of the project guiding that text, as Heidegger did. Following this path will suggest that the failure of *Being and Time* can be understood as the failure of philosophy itself, the death of the most fundamental project that has animated Western philosophy since it first began with Thales. Yet, this death of philosophy is cause for celebration, even if reaching that point requires a period of mourning for the failed philosophical ambitions Heidegger will call metaphysics or, more precisely, *ontotheology*. For, philosophy's failure—the death of philosophy in and through Heidegger—opens up the possibility of *thinking* in another way, an "authentic" thinking that learns to embrace the inescapable limits of our finitude by remaining creatively and responsibly grounded on the earth rather than escaping into philosophical metaphysics and its ontotheological castles in the sky.[4] To walk such a precarious path we first need to find our hermeneutic footing, so: "Back to the text itself!"

Fundamental Ontology as the "Onto-" of Ontotheology

According to "The Outline of the Treatise" that concludes *Being and Time*'s "Introduction" (see para. 8, BT 63–64/SZ 39–40), the text published in 1927 (and reprinted with only minor alterations ever since) includes just the first two of the book's envisioned six divisions, or *one-third* of the treatise as originally outlined.[5] This means Heidegger published only the "preparatory" part of *Being and Time* (BT 38/SZ 17). The published text—the rightly famous 'existential analysis" of the structures conditioning our "being here" or *Dasein* (in Division I) and the deeper analysis of the temporal foundations of those existential structures (in Division II)—was supposed to *prepare* Heidegger to delve into such temporality in order to disclose "a fundamental ontology [*einer Fundamentalontologie*]," that is, a *single* answer to "the question of the meaning of being in general [*die Frage nach dem Sinn von Sein überhaupt*]" (BT 61/SZ 37). As he writes: "The analytic of Dasein ... is to prepare the problematic of fundamental ontology, *the question of the meaning of being in general*" (BT 227/SZ 183). The ultimate goal of the text is to answer "the fundamental ontological question of the meaning of being in general [*die fundamentalontologische Frage nach dem Sinn von Sein überhaupt*]" (BT 241/SZ 196). *Being and Time* analyzes the meaning of our own "being here [*Dasein*]" in order to *prepare* to answer the question of the meaning of "being [*Sein*] in general." In other words, the "existential analysis" of the meaning of our being here is supposed to serve as a preliminary or propaedeutic bridge to understanding the meaning of "the *being* of entities [*das Sein des Seienden*]" (BT 59/SZ 35): What do *all* entities share in common insofar as they *are*? What is it simply to *be*? What, in the end or "after all" (*überhaupt*), does "being" *mean*? Heidegger's ultimate ambition in *Being and Time* is to answer this "question of the meaning of being in general" by uncovering a single "fundamental ontology" (BT 61/SZ 37), a bedrock ontological account of what it means for anything at all to be.

The fact that Heidegger thinks this "question of the meaning of being" is also "the fundamental question of philosophy in general" (BT 49–50/SZ 27) indicates the incredible magnitude of *Being and Time*'s ambition. Heidegger is seeking to answer what he takes to be to the most fundamental question of all philosophy (and, indeed, of human existence), a question he believes has *never* been satisfactorily answered in the entire history of Western philosophy and has now "been forgotten," requiring him to "reawaken" it (BT 19–21/SZ 1–2). (*Hubris, nemesis*, as the Greeks taught. Or, in the Christian proverb: "Pride goeth before a fall.")[6] In *Being and Time*, "the question of being [*die Seinsfrage*]" takes shape *as* a quest for a "fundamental ontology"; these are the book's "guiding question [*leitenden Frage*]" (BT 49–50/SZ 27), "thematic object" (BT 49/SZ 27), and "cardinal problem" (BT 61/SZ 37). They are also, nonetheless, a question the text never answers, an object it never reaches, and a problem it never resolves. Despite some misleading suggestions to the contrary, Heidegger *never* uncovered a "fundamental ontology" that could answer "the question of being," not in *Being and Time* nor in any of his later work, published or unpublished.

Instead, his quest for a fundamental ontology reached its apogee in 1929 and then hit a dead end (as we will see), and Heidegger began to *turn* away from it as deeply misguided, as an unwitting (or "errant") expression of the "metaphysical" tradition he now sought to transcend.[7] In his transitional middle period (from about 1929 to 1938), he began—slowly, sometimes reluctantly, and with significant backsliding—to profoundly rethink the way he had posed and pursued the "question of being" in *Being and Time*. Experiencing the failure of metaphysics firsthand, in the collapse of his own metaphysical ambitions, Heidegger began again, more thoroughly deconstructing the metaphysical tradition (which he came to understand more clearly as ontotheology) and developing another kind of thinking (with which he sought to transcend ontotheology from within). From the perspective of this later thinking, "fundamental ontology" can easily be recognized as an instance of the ontological side of ontotheology, that dual metaphysical ambition to ground the entire intelligible order from its innermost (ontological) core to its outermost (theological) expression.[8]

Our main goal here is to understand the philosophical reasons for the failure of fundamental ontology and the consequent transformation of the question of being. Doing so will help us address that misreading (long common among orthodox Heideggerians) according to which *Being and Time* did not fail in this way; instead, Heidegger delivered a fundamental ontology when he showed that our understanding of being is grounded in time (or, more specifically, in the temporal structures that fundamentally condition our "being here"). On this view, Heidegger's later thinking simply develops the consequences of *Being and Time*'s deepest insight that being is necessarily conditioned by temporality. This reading thus understands Heidegger's philosophical development as fundamentally "unified," not as *turning* radically around a breakdown in the middle of his thought-path, a philosophical failure so profound that it constituted the central existential death from which his later thinking had to be reborn (and, with it, the philosophical tradition itself), as I am suggesting.[9]

What that widespread view gets right is that Heidegger did indeed recognize in *Being and Time* (and subsequently never stopped believing) that *being is conditioned by temporality* (although Heidegger's understanding of the way temporality conditions being changes dramatically between his early and later work).[10] What the view gets wrong is the further claim that this insight either is or somehow leads to the fundamental ontology for which *Being and Time* was searching. The view is also right that Heidegger never stopped asking "the question of being" (and this lifelong quest provides an important formal continuity to his thinking). But it is wrong once more not to recognize that the answer Heidegger was looking for changed dramatically in his later thinking, so much so that he came to reject *Being and Time's* quest for a fundamental ontology as itself metaphysics. (To put it in Heidegger's own terms, *Being and Time's* search for a fundamental ontology was an attempt to understand the meaning of "the being of entities"; like all metaphysics, it thus effaced "being as such," that apparently inexhaustible Ur-phenomenon which informs and makes possible but is never completely captured by any metaphysical understanding of "the being of entities.")[11] To see all this, of course, we need to delve more deeply into the details of Heidegger's early project.

We saw that *Being and Time* hoped to uncover a "fundamental ontology" (an "understanding of the meaning of being in general") by way of an existential analysis of our "being here." (As that ontic entity who has an ontological understanding of being, we form the bridge between the ontic and ontological domains.)[12] More specifically, interpreting the meaning of our "being here [*Dasein*] in terms of temporality" was intended to establish "time as the transcendental horizon for the question of being [*die Seinsfrage*]" (BT 63/SZ 39). The climax of *Being and Time* comes in Division II, when Heidegger demonstrates that the three existential structures of our "being here" articulated in Division I (*Befindlichkeit, Rede,* and *Verstehen,* or roughly the "attunement of mood," our "conversance" with things, and our guiding self-"understanding") are themselves grounded in more fundamental temporal horizons (of having-been, making-present, and futurity, respectively). Our "being here" or *Dasein*—that is, our making-intelligible of the world in which we find ourselves—is grounded in temporality, in that (1) the mood-attunement that shapes our world-disclosure originates from our *always-already* "having been." (Simply put, the past is always present as the mood that shapes our world.) (2) The conversance with things (prelinguistic and conceptual, practical and theoretical) that constitutes the *significance* of our everyday worlds comes from our way of "making present." (What we call "the present" takes shape primarily through our skillful use of "hands-on" [*zuhanden*] equipment with which we are integrally and inconspicuously involved—the pen we write with, the shoes we walk in, and so on—and only secondarily through our express deliberations about a separate domain of objects "on-hand" [*vorhanden*].) And (3) the life projects that we "understand" (that is, the practical projects we project into or *stand-under*—teacher, father, philosopher, revolutionary, and so on—projects that shape and guide our basic sense of self) disclose "futurity" or the "to come." (So the future is here now too, in the way our life-projects organize and orient our basic sense of self.)[13] The existential structures of our *Dasein* or "being here" are thus made possible by these interlocking temporal horizons, which come together—as "a future that makes present in the process of having been" (BT 401/SZ 350)—to constitute the temporally "ecstatic" way we "exist" or "stand out" (*ek-sistere*) into a meaningful world.

Readers have often supposed that with this breathtaking demonstration—of the way our "being here" is grounded in temporality—Heidegger delivered the fundamental ontology he had been pursuing throughout *Being and Time*. Yet, the text itself is relatively clear that this is not the case:

With this interpretation of Dasein as temporality, however, the answer to our guiding question about the meaning of being in general is not already given. But the soil [*der Boden*] will have been made ready to reap such an answer. (BT 38/SZ 17)

By showing that our being here is grounded in temporality, Heidegger believes he has prepared "the soil"—namely, "temporality"—from which to "reap" an understanding of the meaning of being in general, but this reaping itself does not take place. Heidegger does not even show us *how* temporality constitutes the meaning of being in general, let alone *what* that fundamental ontology is supposed to be.[14]

In a later marginal note to the first sentence just quoted, Heidegger specifies that in trying to answer *Being and Time*'s "guiding question about the meaning of being in general," he is looking for what all entities share in common simply insofar as they *are*, the fundamental ontological "unity, the thing itself [*katholoy, kath auto*]" (GA2 24, n. a). As this use of the Greek suggests, *Being and Time* is still pursuing the question of what unifies all the different senses of being, the very same "question of being" Heidegger had been asking since 1907, when the eighteen-year-old was given Brentano's 1862 dissertation ("On the Manifold Meaning of Being in Aristotle") by the Catholic headmaster of his boarding school in Constance, Dr. Conrad Gröber.[15] *Being and Time* was finally supposed to answer that "question of being" by uncovering the "meaning of being in general," but this fundamental ontology never materialized. It is not surprising that this failure would prove to be so momentous for Heidegger (nor that he would struggle against acknowledging it throughout much of the 1930s), since it meant the collapse of the pathway he had been on ever since his first philosophical awakening in 1907. In 1946, however, Heidegger describes his early philosophy as "breaking against the hardness of the matter" he was trying to think (P 261/GA9 343), a dramatic admission made all the more telling by (what I have described as) "Heidegger's nearly constitutional incapacity to admit his own mistakes," the fact that he typically prefers to drastically reinterpret his own early works (often quite incredibly) to render them consistent with what he has come to believe, rather than admit he had been wrong.[16]

Nonetheless, Heidegger makes clear that he did abandon this early quest for a fundamental ontology in numerous places, including in another of the elliptical notes he wrote in the margins of his copy of *Being and Time* (this one next to his published outline's reference to the unpublished Division III on "Time and Being"). We saw that *Being and Time*'s analysis of Dasein's temporality was supposed to establish "time as the transcendental horizon for the question of being" (BT 63/SZ 39). This means that the "fundamental ontology" *Being and Time* seeks can be discovered only by way of an understanding of Dasein's temporality or, more specifically, the ecstatic "horizons" of intelligibility that Dasein's temporality constitutes.[17] Instead of trying to reap the ontological fruits of such temporal horizons, however, Heidegger's later note calls for "the overcoming of the horizon as such." Rather than thinking we can answer the question of being by understanding Dasein's temporal structures as conditions for the possibility of any understanding of being (including a fundamental ontological understanding of the meaning of being in general), he now suggests that we need to "turn back into the origin" and so discover "the presencing of the origin [*das Anwesen aus dieser Herkunft*]" (BT2 37/GA2 53). Here we witness *Being and Time*'s "transcendental" approach—Heidegger's search for necessary "conditions of possibility" (so heavily under the influence of Kant)—giving way to his later phenomenology.[18] For Heidegger is referring to the "presencing [*Anwesen*]" of "being as such" in its *difference* from "the being of entities" that metaphysics pursues (P 246/GA9 322), including the metaphysics of fundamental ontology. This temporally dynamic and seemingly inexhaustible phenomenological "presencing" is precisely what fundamental ontology cannot account for, a condition of possibility it must thus deny, obscure, and so contradict—or so I shall suggest in what follows. Elsewhere I have shown how Heidegger's later phenomenology undermined the quest to uncover a fundamental ontology that lured him on throughout *Being and Time* (and many of the other texts that followed over the next decade). Here I shall focus primarily on the prior question of why "time" or "temporality" *cannot* itself be the answer to the question of being that Heidegger was looking for in *Being and Time*. Why *must* such an answer fail to satisfy the deepest ambitions of *Being and Time*? We can then ask: What are the main consequences of this failure? These are complex matters, but I shall try to address them briefly.[19]

Beneath Fundamental Ontology: The Temporal Abyss of Being

Faced with the fact that he never finished *Being and Time*, Heidegger reluctantly deleted the words "First Half" from its title page in 1953, explaining (in his preface to its seventh edition) that "after a quarter century" the long-promised "second half could no longer be added unless the first were to be presented anew. Yet, the path [*Weg*] it follows remains a necessary one even today, if our being here is to be moved [*bewegen*] by the question of being" (BT 17/SZ vii). Here Heidegger exaggerates how much of the book he published.[20] But he often reiterates the sentiment that his formative passage through his unfinished book was "necessary" in order for him to develop his later thinking about being. In his preface to Father Richardson's *Heidegger* book, for example, Heidegger writes: "Only by way of what Heidegger I [that is, the 'early' Heidegger] has thought does one gain access to what is to be thought by Heidegger II [or the 'later' Heidegger]."[21]

Let me thus be clear: When I suggest that *Being and Time* failed *by its own standards*, I do not want to reinforce that widespread misreading according to which Heidegger considered the book a simple *failure* and said as much by repeatedly referring to it in later years as a *Holzweg*. For Heidegger, a *Holzweg* is not a mere "dead end" but (more fully thought) designates a forest path that leads to a "clearing" (*Lichtung*), that is, a place in the forest from which the trees have been removed. Such a "clearing" affords us an ontological epiphany (that is, an insight into being). Out of an encounter with *nothing*, initially, we come to notice the light through which we ordinarily see the forest. A clearing thus helps us "see the light" by redirecting our attention from entities to being, that usually unnoticed ontological light through which things appear.[22] This clarification provides us with an important hint as to why *Being and Time* had to remain unfinished: Heidegger himself came to see the light (to redeploy that rich and revealing locution), and what he saw—although it looked like "nothing" at first—unfolded itself in a way that prevented him from following through on *Being and Time*'s original plan. In other words, the impasse to which *Being and Time*'s question of being led is also what opened up the perspective from which all Heidegger's later works were born.[23]

To see clearly that the early Heidegger failed to answer the question of being in *Being and Time* (and subsequent texts), we need to understand how exactly that answer was supposed to allow Heidegger to fulfill the text's neo-Husserlian ambition to establish phenomenology as the queen of the sciences. As I show in *Heidegger on Ontotheology: Technology and the Politics of Education*, Heidegger sought to uncover the meaning of being in general in *Being and Time* because he believed that only such a fundamental ontology would prove capable of uniting all the different academic disciplines, reversing their "boundless and aimless dispersal" and thereby unifying the *University*.[24] Heidegger's basic idea (inherited from Husserl's critique of the natural sciences but developed differently) is that every well-formed academic discipline must presuppose an ontological understanding of what the class of entities it studies *is* (BT 29–31/SZ 9–11): Research in biology presupposes some understanding of what "life" *is*; historical research presupposes what history *is*; research in psychology presupposes what "consciousness" *is*; and so on. Practitioners in every field of research (or "positive science") need to be guided by such an ontological understanding (or "posit") simply in order to be able to pick out the relevant entities to study: Biologists must have some sense of what it means to *be* alive just to be able to distinguish living from nonliving entities; historians need some sense of what it means to *be* historical in order to sort those entities from the past destined for oblivion from those needing to be preserved in history books, museums, and so on. In Heidegger's early work, the distinctive role of philosophy is to focus on these ontological presuppositions themselves: What is the *being* of life; that is, what does it mean to *be* alive?[25] What is the *being* of history; that is, what does it mean to *be* historical? Indeed, that last question (and this is still too infrequently recognized) is precisely the one Heidegger is trying to answer when he explicates the "historicality [*Geschichtlichkeit*]" of the historical in *Being and Time* (BT 424–455/SZ 372–404).[26]

It is not surprising that history is the ontological domain in which Heidegger made the most progress, given that it is the field to which Husserl originally assigned him, and the one he had last been working on the longest (since at least 1915, when he published "The Concept of Time in the Science of History").[27] *Being and Time* does advance a fairly robust (and subsequently controversial) view of what it means to be historical, arguing (to simplify) that each generation must constitute its own guiding historical mission through a creative and critical *inheritance* of "the tradition," in which the missions that guided heroic figures and movements from the past are updated so that they speak to people's most pressing contemporary needs. We can probably imagine how such an account of historicality might guide the specific research of historians (and the dangers of *revisionism* loom large here). But how does Heidegger's account of historicality answer such questions as the one he inherits from Dilthey's central concern with the relation between the natural and the human/social sciences, namely: How should we understand the relation between the history of human beings and our social and cultural institutions, on the one hand, and the history of nonhuman entities and events, on the other? What, for example, do the history of cultures and constitutions have in common with the history of geological and even cosmological processes? What understanding of the *being* of history can account for *both* human and nonhuman history by telling us what all history *is*? *Being and Time*'s treatment of historicality ends abruptly with the remark that no further progress can be made on this question until Heidegger has succeeded in "clarifying, through fundamental ontology, the question of the meaning of being in general" (BT 455/SZ 403). Only by understanding what it means for anything to *be*, in other words, will Heidegger be able to say what anything historical *is*.

That, of course, is a proverbial leap from the frying pan into the fire. (Heidegger is saying, in effect, "Before I can tell you what 'history' is, I have to tell you what 'Isness' itself *is*.") This also turns out to be a strategy of endless deferral (since the question of what "Isness" *is* will get deconstructed rather than answered). But this helps make clear how much is riding on Heidegger's promise in *Being and Time* that his deconstruction of the philosophical tradition will allow him to uncover a fundamental ontology. Such an understanding of the meaning of being in general would tell us what *all* entities share in common, what unites the being of all things. If we could uncover such a fundamental ontology, Heidegger thinks we would then be able to understand how this general understanding of "being" divides into its three constituent "regional ontologies" of *history*, *nature*, and *language*, thereby allowing us to understand what unifies and distinguishes all historical entities, natural entities, and linguistic entities as such (and so answer Dilthey's question, among many others).[28]

As this suggests, Heidegger treats the regional ontologies of history, nature, and language as the three basic kinds of entities (the three most basic ways of slicing up the *being* pie, as it were). Fundamental ontology divides into these three regional ontologies of nature, history, and language, and then these three regional ontologies get sliced up further to yield the domains of being studied by all "mature" or well-formed academic disciplines. So, once we see how the three regional ontologies get divvied up into the particular ontological "posits" that guide each of the "positive sciences," we will have recognized the deeper unity connecting all the academic disciplines. For, we will have seen how all the academic disciplines' different ways of understanding the being of the classes of entities they study stem from regional ontologies that are themselves ultimately rooted in a single fundamental ontology or meaning of being in general. Such a comprehensive, hierarchical vision might indeed help the philosopher who articulated it to unify the university—and perhaps even, behind it, the German nation. (As that suggests, Heidegger's metaphysical quest for a fundamental ontology explains the more authoritarian dimension of the political program he attempted to initiate in his Rectorial Address of 1933.)[29]

Being and Time pursues this fundamental ontology right to the end, where the book breaks off with leading questions: "Is there a way which leads from primordial *time* to the meaning of *being*? Does *time* itself reveal itself as the horizon of *being*?" (BT 488/SZ 437). Here, however, the caution Heidegger expresses in an earlier passage from *Being and Time* proves to be far more prescient:

The question of being [*die Seinsfrage*] will achieve its true concreteness only when we have carried through our deconstruction of the ontological tradition. ... In this domain where "the thing itself is deeply veiled" [as Kant wrote in his first *Critique*], every investigation should avoid overestimating its own results. For such questioning is constantly compelled to face the possibility of disclosing an even more primordial and universal horizon from which to answer the question: What does "being" mean? (BT 49/SZ 26–27)

In fact, Heidegger's quest for a fundamental ontology reaches its apogee in 1929, in *Kant and the Problem of Metaphysics*, which Heidegger originally presented as "a first working-out of Part Two of *Being and Time*" (KPM xix/ GA3 xv). In the first ("A") edition of Kant's *Critique of Pure Reason*, Kant postulated a third faculty of the "imagination" that mediates between the faculties of sensation and understanding, explaining how mind and world are joined together through the temporal process of "schematization" (in which the categories of the understanding get subconsciously applied to the data of sensation in order to yield an intelligible world). Kant largely effaced this faculty of imagination (and with it the central role temporality plays in constituting the intelligible world) from the second ("B") edition of the *Critique*—hence Heidegger's dramatic charge in *Being and Time* that "Kant shrinks back ... in the face of something which must be brought to light as a theme and a principal if the expression 'being' is to have any demonstrable meaning" (BT 45/SZ 23).

Kant and the Problem of Metaphysics picks up this task (which, *Being and Time* emphasizes, Kant called the "duty of philosophers" [BT 45/SZ23]). Heidegger goes so far as to suggest that he can derive Kant's categories from the temporal structures of our "being here [or *Dasein*]" discovered in *Being and Time*. Heidegger even tries to derive the category of "substance" (or what "stands beneath" and persists throughout all change) from the temporal horizon of making present. Time "shows its own permanence" in the fact that it "is always now," and in such temporal permanence, "time gives the pure look of something like lasting in general," thereby constituting the "ground" of that which persists beneath all change (KPM 75–6/GA3 106–107). Yet, what Heidegger thus inadvertently shows is that only one facet of temporality (namely, our sense that all our experience happens in the now) leads us to search for a single, unchanging ontological ground beneath all things, and temporality has other facets that undermine that search for a fundamental ontology. Most important here is Heidegger's dawning recognition of that temporally dynamic "presencing" referred to earlier, a subtle coming into and passing out of being that plays an even more important role in constituting our intelligible worlds than the final ontological foundations sought out by metaphysics of substance.

As Heidegger deepens his analysis—proudly applying hermeneutic "violence" to uncover what Kant left "unsaid and force it into words" (KPM 141/GA3 202)—he works through this problem vicariously. Thus, instead of asserting that Kant "shrinks back" from the temporal foundations of being, Heidegger now writes that "Kant's falling back before the ground which he himself unveiled, before the transcendental power of imagination, is ... that movement [Bewegung] of philosophizing which makes manifest the breaking open of the foundation [Bodens] and thus makes manifest the abyss of metaphysics [den Abgrund der Metaphysik]" (KPM 150–151/GA3 215). In other words, the Western tradition of substance metaphysics (that is, the metaphysics of presence) systematically overlooks that dynamic phenomenological excessiveness (the bottomless abyss of "presencing") which is needed to explain how the metaphysical tradition can change over time (and, with it, the historical constellations of intelligibility that this tradition helps constitute and transform), and this temporally dynamic presencing (Heidegger comes to realize) can never be completely captured by any single fundamental ontological understanding of the meaning of being.[30]

Heidegger later inscribed a brief handwritten note on the title page of his first edition of *Kant and the Problem of Metaphysics* (a note he then published in the fourth edition of 1973), admitting that his attempt to use Kant to develop the project of fundamental ontology not only "over-interpreted" Kant (here Heidegger finally rejects that hermeneutic "violence" he still proudly acknowledged in the second edition of 1950) but also led to a dead end: "The *Kant* book. With *Being and Time* alone—; soon clear that we did not enter into the authentic question [die eigentliche Frage]" of being; instead, "the particular path was blocked [der eigene Weg versperrt]"

(KPM xvi /GA3 xiii). What this rightly suggests is that, during the 1930s, when Heidegger carried out the "deconstruction of the history of ontology" famously called for in *Being and Time*, he was not able to "recover" the fundamental ontology for which he had long been searching (BT 44/SZ 11). When Heidegger traces the regional ontologies of nature, history, and language back to the pre-Socratic Greek understanding of *phusis*, *alêtheia*, and *logos*, respectively, then traces this *phusis-alêtheia-logos* constellation back to a conceptually inexhaustible ontological "presencing," this is as close as he ever comes to actually "grounding" the regional ontologies in a fundamental ontology, and it is quite instructive. For it shows that the relations between the positive sciences, the regional ontologies, and fundamental ontology are too murky and indistinct to allow for a top-down, authoritarian reorganization of the University in which the philosopher who has learned to be receptive to phenomenological presencing will be able to see how the regional ontologies emerge out of this fundamental ontological presencing and then build the new academic disciplines around the ontological posits emerging from these regional ontologies.[31]

Instead, as Heidegger carries out his deconstruction of the history of ontology, he discovers that a series of metaphysical "ontotheologies" have temporarily grounded and justified a succession of ontological "epochs" or historical constellations of intelligibility. Each historical age in the West has been unified by such a basic metaphysical understanding of what and how entities *are*. This series of dual, ontotheological understandings of "the being of entities" temporarily "doubly ground" the intelligible order only by denying "being as such" (the dynamic and inexhaustible source of intelligibility that both informs and exceeds every ontotheology). Heidegger will thus conclude that the ontological posits that guide each of our positive sciences come not from some unchanging fundamental ontology beneath all of Western history but rather from our contemporary age's reigning ontotheology. The later Heidegger would suggest that present-day biology, for example, takes over its implicit ontological understanding of what life *is* from the metaphysical understanding of the being of entities that governs our own epoch of technological "enframing." And indeed, one has to admit that when contemporary philosophers of biology proclaim that life *is* a self-replicating system, it certainly appears that they have unknowingly adopted the basic ontotheological presuppositions of Nietzsche's metaphysics, according to which life *is* ultimately the eternal recurrence of will-to-power, that is, sheer will-to-will, an ongoing struggle between competing forces by which life perpetuates itself.[32] In the same way, when contemporary philosophers of psychology suggest that consciousness *is* merely an emergent property, the fortuitous (but in itself meaningless) result of an evolutionary struggle to integrate all the various sensory modalities (vision, touch, taste, etc.), does not this picture of the *being* of consciousness fit only too well with our Nietzschean ontotheology, according to which all entities are *nothing* but inherently meaningless forces endlessly competing with one another? Cannot the same be said of our historians' view that history *is* the study of the struggle between those forces that have most powerfully shaped our self-understanding (hence, paradigmatically, wars)? Or of the increasingly widespread view in literature departments that literature *is* an arena for representatives from different groups to give voice to the struggles that have most profoundly shaped their competing identities?

Because the later Heidegger comes to believe that *all* of the different disciplines' guiding ontological posits are implicitly taken over from this nihilistic Nietzschean ontotheology underlying our "atomic age" I have suggested that the first task of his mature understanding of *ontological education* involves making us reflective about the way in which our experience of what is commonly called "reality" has already been shaped by these fundamental conceptual parameters and ultimate standards of legitimacy. For when we become aware of the way our age's reigning ontotheology implicitly shapes our understanding of the being of ourselves and our worlds—and thereby come to recognize the subtle but pervasive influence of this nihilistic, "technologizing" understanding of all things as nothing but resources to be optimized—we begin to open up the possibility of understanding ourselves otherwise.[33]

Being Unfinished

Let us end by returning to one of the unanswered questions with which we began: How should we understand the unfinished nature of *Being and Time*? Heidegger had been developing the philosophical ideas he published in *Being and Time* for more than a decade, and intermittently writing the book itself since at least 1924.[34] Still, he had to finish the book under great time pressure (working furiously in a rented farm house near his famous "hut," where he could write all day long for months, away from the competing demands of his family, hoping finally to publish the major work he needed to secure a professorship). It is thus understandable that the question repeatedly arises: Could Heidegger have finished *Being and Time* in the way he originally envisioned if pressures coming from "outside" philosophy had not encouraged him to publish the text before he had time to complete it? I have tried to show that the answer to this question is *no*;

when he had time to carry out the project he ended up deconstructing and transcending it. Instead of trying to deliver a fundamental ontological understanding of "the being of entities" that would finally *answer* the question of being, Heidegger recognized that all such answers are but temporary metaphysical dams in the ontohistorical river (ontotheological dams that allow an historical *epoch* to form by "holding back" the floodwaters of historicity for a time). He came to see that these metaphysical ontotheologies are themselves made possible by something (which is not a thing but rather a "noth-ing," a dynamic phenomenological "presencing" Heidegger also calls "the earth") that they can never render fully intelligible and so permanently stabilize in the light of our historical worlds.

Still, I think the question remains interestingly problematic. It is true that the imperative to "publish or perish" led Heidegger to send off the manuscript of *Being and Time* before he could finish it in the way he had planned. Such mundane pressures to publish philosophical work in hopes of securing or advancing a professional career are increasingly ubiquitous in the world of professional philosophy, and we are often right to bemoan the ways these pressures can rush and so undermine philosophical work. Indeed, we should recognize the growth of such pressures as a symptom of the optimization imperative that quietly rules our late modern age of technological "enframing." Wittgenstein, who published very little (and yet proved almost as influential as Heidegger), might even have been right to suggest that philosophers should greet one another with an emphatic reminder: "Take Your Time!"[35] Nonetheless, it would be false to imagine that there was ever some golden age in which philosophy was free of the pressures of time, and it is naïve to think of such pressures as simply "external" to philosophy itself—nostalgic mistakes Heidegger sometimes makes.

For the later Heidegger, Socrates was "the purest thinker of the West." Socrates was drawn into the withdrawal of being "all through his life and right in to his death"—tirelessly asking, What *is* piety? What *is* justice? What *is* friendship? What *is* love?—yet never finding a satisfying answer about what any of our most important concepts *are*. This, Heidegger suggests, is why Socrates never tried to *write down* any of his thoughts; Socrates left to Plato that impossible task of capturing his thinking's restless, relentless search for being, preferring to be drawn by the winds of thought that issue from being's withdrawal instead of fleeing this "draft [*Zugwind*]" into the refuge of writing.[36] Heidegger even suggests that "all great Western thinkers after Socrates, regardless of their greatness, had to be such fugitives and refugees [*Flüchlinge*]" (WCT 17/GA8 20). The great philosophers help focus, shape and transform their ages' understanding of "the being of entities," yet their great *answers* to the question of being prove that they were unable to endure the unending onslaught of "being as such" in the manifest inexhaustibility of its "question-worthiness." (For it is, paradoxically, through the apparently inexhaustible excessiveness of its phenomenological "presencing" that being *withdraws*, eluding every attempt to capture and so still its polysemic movement in a single philosophical answer or metaphysical system.) This, Heidegger hints (twenty-five years after *Being and Time*), is "the secret of a still concealed history" (ibid.); Western philosophy is a history written by such fugitives and refugees from being, driven by their own greatness to try the impossible: To *answer* the question of being, once and for all. Heidegger seems loath simply to admit it here (preferring, out of a telling combination of modesty and pride, to keep his own secret), but the author of *Being and Time* knows (and so hints) that he too was in flight from being when he wrote his most famous book; he too knows the failure—the *necessary* failure—of such great philosophy firsthand.

Indeed, who could deny that Heidegger faced the pressures that led to the publication of *Being and Time* brilliantly when he submitted an unfinished book manuscript that nevertheless went on the become an overnight success and, eventually, the most celebrated philosophical work of the twentieth century? In thus negotiating the pressures of his own being in time, Heidegger provides a dramatic illustration of the constraints that inevitably condition *all* philosophy (and not just all metaphysics, but all thinking too). The notoriously compromised genesis of *Being and Time* reminds us that all philosophical work (from the greatest to the most humble) must negotiate with the unavoidable limitations that arise from our *finitude*, constraints we might indicate with such terms as *temporal scarcity, historical situatedness*, and *perspectival limitation*. Such ineliminable constraints condition (and always have conditioned) *all* philosophy, *all* thinking (even that of our noble Socrates), at least to some degree—a degree we can seek to minimize or negotiate in creative ways but can never completely control, let alone elimimate.[37] Such constraining conditions make philosophy both possible and impossible (as Derrida liked to say); more precisely, they make philosophy possible in the only way it can ever be possible, namely, as impossible ever to perfect, finish, complete—impossible to somehow establish safely beyond all lack, absence, or imperfection—impossible to secure beyond, in a word, all philosophical *failure*.

The lessons of such failure (as I have only begun to suggest here) are endless, or so we may hope, as we too strive toward the impossible in our own inescapably mortal and finite ways. The necessity of such failure is not simply a tragedy. For us finite beings, a text survives only so long as it continues to provoke debate, discussion, critique, development, and so on. It can survive, in short, only so long as it *fails* to attain and maintain some unquestionable state of timeless perfection. (I suspect, moreover, that even an immortal could never *finish* a text that would be perfectly complete. For, owing to the holism of meaning, one thing leads to another *ad infinitum*. As long as there is being *and* time, there will be genesis, emergence, and the new, as well as death, decay, and passing away, and thus instability, rearrangement, and transformation. Making sense of things generates more things to make sense of, so the work of philosophy is never done.) Failure is thus a necessary part of even the greatest works.[38] The unavoidable nature of such failure suggests that we need to rethink its meaning in and for philosophy. In my view, the fact that our otherwise tragic-seeming finitude makes meaning inexhaustible for us mortals is a crucial part of what allows us to embrace our mortality and finitude.[39]

What, then, is the main philosophical lesson of *Being and Time*'s failure? I have tried to suggest that the metaphysical failure at the very heart of the project is inseparable from its destiny—and, perhaps, our own, insofar as we remain inspired by Heidegger's later critique of metaphysics as onto-theology. Despite its halting and painful genesis (unavoidable for a mortal philosophy), Heidegger's deconstruction of metaphysics teaches us to recognize the creeping nihilism of our current age, helping us learn to discern the roots of this nihilism in our typically unnoticed metaphysical understanding of all things as nothing but intrinsically meaningless resources awaiting optimization. Understanding the failure of metaphysics *in* Heidegger can also help us find ways to transcend this nihilism ourselves. For it teaches us too to *think* the "noth-ing" that surrounds us not as nothing at all but as the not-yet-a-thing, the presencing of inchoate but meaningfull possibilities of that which is yet to come into being, thereby giving our impure thinking an ontologically maieutic task to which we can continue to creatively and responsibly attend—*after* Heidegger.

Renouncing the failure of metaphysics will not allow us to think from some place beyond failure. But we can seek to find other, more meaningful ways of thinking failure, of neither effacing nor denying failure but incorporating its unavoidability into our projects in more creative and meaningful ways. Beyond the failure of metaphysics, the failures of thinking beckon us on. It is in this hopeful half-light (where dusk turns into dawn) that we might see again those oft-quoted words of Beckett: "All of old. Nothing else ever. Ever tried. Ever failed. No matter. Try again. Fail again. Fail better."[40]

Acknowledgments

I would like to thank Lee Braver for inviting me to contribute this chapter to his book and for offering me extremely helpful suggestions. Thanks too to Kelly Becker, Taylor Carman, David Cerbone, Daniel Conway, Ben Crowe, Hubert Dreyfus, Megan Flocken, Rick Furtak, Beatrice Han-Pile, Claire Katz, Stephan Käufer, Sean Kelly, Jonathan Lee, Paul Livingston, Raoni Padui, James Reid, John Richardson, Robert Stolorow, Any Wendling, Dale Wilkerson, Julian Young, and Nate Zuckerman for their critique and encouragement of this chapter.

Notes

1. Theodore Kisiel, *The Genesis of Heidegger's Being and Time* (Berkeley: University of California Press, 1993), 3.

2. There are, of course, a potentially infinite number of ways in which *Being and Time* fails. It fails to float, to be a couch, to make good eating, etc., but these are silly and trivial "failures," of little philosophical interest. One could also argue, nontrivially, that *Being and Time* fails to be an important feminist text, or a major contribution to Marxist thinking, or a visionary blueprint for a liberal-democratic political order, and so on. However significant those latter kinds of failure might be, I am not interested in them here, because *Being and Time* is not explicitly and centrally trying to be a feminist text, or a contribution to Marxist thinking, or a blueprint for a liberal-democratic order, and so on. I am interested in the way *Being and Time* fails to do the very thing Heidegger most wants it to do in the book, as well as the way that failure teaches him, and so potentially us, a profound lesson about what philosophy can and cannot be henceforth. I shall thus suggest that this failure—rather than taking away from the greatness of *Being and Time*—should be recognized as a crucial part of what makes it the seminal and uncircumventable philosophical work that it is.

3. On such "anticipation" (*vorlaufen*) or "running out ahead" (into the existential death of "projectless projecting") as *ontological death* (and its relation to and difference from *ontic demise*), see Iain Thomson, "Death and Demise in *Being and Time*," in *The Cambridge Companion to Heidegger's* Being and Time, ed. Mark A. Wrathall (New York: Cambridge University Press, 2013), 260–290. On the meaning of the "turn" in and for Heidegger—and the current and old forms of misunderstanding it—see Iain Thomson, *Heidegger, Art, and Postmodernity* (Cambridge: Cambridge University Press, 2011), 179. (In order to succinctly present my view on this difficult topic, I have found it necessary to refer to my other publications more often than I would like, a fact for which I can only ask the reader's kind indulgence.)

4. On the history of these ontotheological castles in the sky, and the way their collapse opens up another kind of thinking and so a new historical age, see my *Heidegger, Art, and Postmodernity*, chap. 1.

5. Of course, the fact that these alterations have been minor does not preclude their sometimes having been highly significant—as, to mention just the most notorious example, when Heidegger removed *Being and Time*'s opening dedication to his Jewish mentor Husserl during his own Nazi years.

6. *Proverbs* 16:18: "Pride goeth before destruction, and an haughty spirit before a fall." (The Greek and Christian expressions are not equivalent but they remain interestingly similar.) See also n. 12 below.

7. See, e.g., P 250/GA9 328. On the way fundamental ontology reached its apogee in 1929, in Heidegger's claim that the category of substance derived from the temporal horizon of making present, see below and Thomson, *Heidegger on Ontotheology: Technology and the Politics of Education* (Cambridge: Cambridge University Press, 2005), 54, n. 15.

8. According to Heidegger's favorite formulation, metaphysics seeks to understand "the being of entities" by grasping "the totality of entities as such." This involves two intertwined tasks: The attempt to grasp entities "as such" (by discovering the deepest ground that unifies them all) is *ontology*, while the attempt to comprehend the "totality" (by taking up some God's-eye view on the whole) is *theology*. The fact that metaphysics does both simultaneously is what makes it *ontotheology*. Thus ontotheology does not merely mean treating God as the highest entity (as is commonly but erroneously supposed). Instead, in the simplest terms, *ontotheology* is the attempt to grasp reality from the inside out (or bottom up) and the outside in at the same time, to comprehend reality root to stem by uncovering its deepest microscopic depths as well as its ultimate telescopic expression. When successful, an ontotheology "doubly grounds" the entire intelligible order by (temporarily) grasping *both* its innermost ontological core (that fundamental ground all entities share in common) and its outermost theological expression (as if taking up some ultimate "view from nowhere," from outside the totality of entities). I shall focus on the early Heidegger's own ontological ambitions here, since that is what his quest for a *fundamental ontology* turned out to be. The fact that Heidegger himself frequently resists acknowledging his own ontotheological "errancy" (at least in any other terms) does not make it any less true (see n. 16 below). We can see this, e.g., from Heidegger's fascinating but deeply confused "Appendix" to 1928's *Metaphysical Foundations of Logic* (MFL 154–159/GA26 196–202). Reading this appendix in light of Heidegger's mature understanding of ontotheology suggests that the short-lived project of "metontology" he advocates there—"a special problematic which has as its proper theme entities as a whole" (MFL 157/GA26 199)—is best understood as Heidegger's attempt to jump from the sinking ship of "fundamental ontology" to that project's ontotheological complement, a type of "fundamental theology" or "theiology" (cf. HCE 135/H 195).

Here in 1928, Heidegger still regards metaphysics as a positive "task," indeed, as "the one basic problem of philosophy itself," a task he still believes he will be able to *accomplish.* Nevertheless, he comes very close to his later recognition of metaphysics as ontotheology when he writes: "In their unity, fundamental ontology and metontology constitute the concept of metaphysics" (MFL 158/GA26 202). In *Kant and the Problem of Metaphysics* (1929), Heidegger again defines "metaphysics" in the very terms he will soon abandon as ontotheology: "Metaphysics is the fundamental knowledge of entities as such and as a whole" (KPM 5/GA3 8). What this all suggests, I take it, is that *Heidegger had to recognize the fatal flaws in his own ontotheological endeavors—"fundamental ontology" and "metontology," respectively—before decisively rejecting metaphysics as ontotheology.* For a fuller account of ontotheology (and the historical role ontotheologies play founding and transforming historical "epochs" or constellations of intelligibility), see my *Heidegger on Ontotheology,* chap. 1 and, for a detailed explanation of the relation between "ontology" and "theology" in ontotheology (and for how Heidegger sought to transcend ontotheology from within), see my *Heidegger, Art, and Postmodernity,* chaps. 1 and 3.

9. Otto Pöggeler is the most influential advocate of the thesis that Heidegger's development must be understood as fundamentally *unified,* but more nuanced versions of this untenable claim have been defended by such major scholars as Gadamer, Kisiel, Olafson, and White. (For a critique of White, see Iain Thomson, "On the Advantages and Disadvantages of Reading Heidegger Backward: White's *Time and Death," Inquiry* 50 [1] [2007]: 103–120. On Olafson's view, see n.14 below. For a detailed critique of those other scholars' views, see Iain Thomson, "The End of Onto-theology: Understanding Heidegger's Turn, Method, and Politics" [Ph.D. dissertation, University of California, San Diego, 1999], 23–34.) When Heidegger finally published something called "Time and Being" in 1962 (giving it the weighty name of *Being and Time*'s unpublished Third Division), he argued that time cannot explain being, no more than being can explain time. Instead, he referred to a mysterious "it" that gives us the "there is" (*es gibt*) of the world, an apparently inexhaustible source that bestows both being and time. This nonsubstantial "it" is another of Heidegger's name for "being as such," that is, for being in its *difference* from the being of entities that all "metaphysics" seeks to grasp, including the metaphysics of "fundamental ontology." See Heidegger, *On Time and Being,* trans. J. Stambaugh (New York: Harper & Row, 1972), 5/GA14 9.

10. There is thus an important difference even here. As I shall show below, in *Being and Time* Heidegger thought of temporality as a *transcendental* condition on the possibility of any understanding of being, that is, a necessary condition that is not itself conditioned by what it conditions. But in his later work, he instead came to think of being and time as "reciprocally determining" or mutually conditioning one another (TB 3/GA14 7), that is, as equiprimordial or co-originary phenomena in the play of space time, neither of which can be treated as the unilateral foundation of the other.

11. See n. 8 above and, on the way metaphysics denies and contradicts its own conditions of possibility (leaving it open to the immanent critique and deconstruction), see my *Heidegger on Ontotheology*, chaps. 1 and 3.

12. For the early Heidegger, our being (i.e., the essentially distinguishing characteristic of the entity we are) *is* to understand being. Our failure to understand the meaning of being in general would be a failure not only of Heidegger's early philosophy, or even of philosophy as such (in its fundamental ontological ambitions), but of human beings to fulfill their very being (BT 35/SZ 15; BT 96/SZ 67). Or so it looked to Heidegger initially, before he realized that to try to understand the meaning of being in terms of fundamental ontology was precisely to fail to understand "being as such," and thus that to understand (and help *realize*) being as such (e.g., by showing how "it" informs and exceeds all metaphysical conceptions of "the being of entities") is what truly fulfills human beings. (For more on this topic, see *Heidegger on Ontotheology*, chap. 4; Thomson, "Heidegger's Perfectionist Philosophy of Education in *Being and Time*," *Continental Philosophy Review* 37 [4] [2004]: 439–467; and Thomson, "Heideggerian Perfectionism and the Phenomenology of the Pedagogical Truth Event," in *Phenomenology and Virtue Ethics*, ed. Kevin Hermberg and Paul Gyllenhammer [London: Bloomsbury, 2013], 180–190.) We need not get into the debate about whether Heidegger's ontological definition of Dasein is necessarily anthropocentric or whether it can and should apply in principle to all entities capable of understanding being, be they human or not. I take the latter view because it is more philosophically defensible, but there is ample textual evidence capable of supporting both readings. (For more on the issue of Heidegger and "animality," see, e.g., Thomson, "Ontology and Ethics at the Intersection of Phenomenology and Environmental Philosophy," *Inquiry* 47 [4] [2004]: 380–412; and Matthew Calarco, *Zoographies: The Question of the Animal from Heidegger to Derrida* [New York: Columbia University Press, 2008].)

13. The collapse of these projects is what Heidegger calls ontological "death" (in distinction from ontic demise). In the projectless projecting (that follows the collapse of our projects), we encounter the bare "futurity" of the future in the way the world we can no longer inhabit comes toward us nonetheless. *Being and Time* glimpses (and even names) this "nothing" of the world (e.g., BT 321/SZ 276–277), but does not yet recognize it as the active "noth-ing of the nothing," the first guise of that Ur-phenomenon of "being as such" which makes metaphysics possible (by informing it) and yet impossible (by always exceeding and so at least partly eluding its grasp). As I have shown elsewhere, it is this "noth-ing" that eventually undermines the metaphysics of "fundamental ontology" and gives birth to Heidegger's later thinking. (See "Death and Demise in *Being and Time*" and *Heidegger, Art, and Postmodernity*, chaps. 3 and 7.)

14. I think there is more room for disagreement on the former point than on the latter. Indeed, the scholar who has done the most to show *how* exactly temporality is supposed to condition fundamental ontology in *Being and Time* concludes that

the project fails. See William D. Blattner, *Heidegger's Temporal Idealism* (Cambridge: Cambridge University Press, 1999). For the clearest argument that Heidegger did deliver a fundamental ontology by showing that *the meaning of being in general is presence* (in the lecture courses he gave right after *Being and Time* on Aristotle, Descartes, and Kant, thus completing most of *Being and Time* as originally outlined), see Frederick Olafson, "The Unity of Heidegger's Thought," in *The Cambridge Companion to Heidegger*, ed. Charles Guignon (Cambridge: Cambridge University Press, 1993). Those familiar with the later Heidegger will recognize that the thesis Olafson believes *unifies* Heidegger's thought as a whole—that *being means presence*—is problematic at best, since in fact the later Heidegger famously *critiques* that equation of being with presence as the *metaphysics* of presence (see *Heidegger on Ontotheology*, chap. 1). (Olafson obscures this point by collapsing the distinction between "presence [*Anwesenheit*]" and "presencing [*Anwesen*]" that is crucial to the later Heidegger; see "The Unity of Heidegger's Thought," 101.) More importantly, even if Heidegger did believe that thesis in his early period (before turning decisively away from it in his later work), I shall go on to suggest that such an understanding of being as presence is not sufficiently detailed and robust to serve the philosophical function that "fundamental ontology" was intended to serve.

15. See Heidegger, "My Way to Phenomenology," in *On Time and Being*, 74.

16. See "On the Advantages and Disadvantages of Reading Heidegger Backwards," 109; for detailed examples of such incredible retroactive self-reinterpretation, see 109–114.

17. In his middle period, Heidegger often seems to recognize (though he rarely admits) that *Being and Time*'s guiding methodological claim that the path to being *must* pass through an analysis of our own "being here" is very close to the metaphysical "subjectivism" he critiques (see, e.g., P 125/GA9 162, and see also n. 12 above).

18. For some debate on the issue of whether Heidegger abandoned the transcendental approach entirely or just complicated it (by, as I would say, recognizing "being as such" as that which makes all the different metaphysical ways of understanding "the being of entities" possible and yet also undermines them, as a condition of possibility they systematically deny), see, e.g., the essays collected in Steven Crowell and Jeff Malpas's edited volume, *Transcendental Heidegger* (Stanford: Stanford University Press, 2006); and Lee Braver, *A Thing of This World: A History of Continental Anti-Realism* (Evanston: Northwestern University Press, 2007), esp. 273–275. For a detailed account of Heidegger's later phenomenological method, see *Heidegger, Art, and Postmodernity*, chap. 3. On why it is not enough to say that any understanding of being must be conditioned by temporality (something Heidegger never stopped believing), see below and n. 10 above.

19. I have written two books and many articles detailing and explaining the motives and consequences of the philosophical transformation in Heidegger's thinking in

great detail. Given space constraints, I have had to frequently refer to that work here. (See esp. *Heidegger on Ontotheology*, chaps. 1 and 3.)

20. He had really published only a third of his outline, since he had not published Division II of Part One on "Time and Being" nor Divisions I–III of Part Two. Still, his (then unpublished) lecture notes on the contributions made by Aristotle (GA18, GA22, GA33), Descartes (BP/GA24) and Kant (KPM/GA3) to the history of ontology can be thought of as drafts (more and less polished, as well as more and less success-ful) of the final three divisions he had planned. But treating his significantly later essay, "Time and Being" (1962), as a version of the unpublished Division III is a much more problematic move (even if Heidegger encouraged it by giving it that portentous name), since he wrote this essay long after rejecting *Being and Time*'s quest for a fundamental ontology (which most of those earlier lectures still eagerly pursue).

21. See Heidegger, "Preface," in William J. Richardson, *Heidegger: From Phenomenol-ogy to Thought*, 2nd ed. (The Hague: Martinus Nijoff, 1967), xxii–xxiii.

22. A *Holzweg* allows us see our own way of seeing, helping us glimpse and so begin to discern the ontological prescription on those unnoticed lenses through which we ordinary make sense of all that is. (See Iain Thomson, *Heidegger on Ontotheology*, p. xiii, and the development of this point in *Heidegger, Art, and Postmodernity*, 83–84.) Let me also be clear that the fact that *all* things tend to appear in the light of our current ontotheology does not mean that all things appear *completely* in its terms (as if the dominant ontotheology could exhaust the available phenomena and fully explain all things), for that would trap us in our current epoch and render epochal transitions impossible. (I critique this still common "fatalistic misreading" of Hei-degger in "Ontotheology," in *The Bloomsbury Companion to Heidegger*, ed. François Raffoul and Eric S. Nelson [London: Bloomsbury, 2013], 324–326 and 327, n. 10.)

23. This is the most obvious sense in which *Being and Time* remains a *necessary fail-ure*. As suggested earlier, however, there are other senses as well. Most importantly, the failure of fundamental ontology is also the failure of the tradition of Western metaphysics itself. It is, more precisely, the beginning of the collapse of the onto-logical component of *ontotheology*—a collapse Heidegger himself had to pass through in order to elaborate his critique of the end of philosophy as ontotheology and his postmodern thinking of the other beginning of Western history. (I explain this in *Heidegger, Art, and Postmodernity*, chaps. 1, 3, 6, 7, and 8. On this crucial "noth-ing," around which Heidegger's philosophical development itself turned, see the refer-ences in n. 13 above.)

24. See Heidegger, *Questions and Answers*, p. 9/GA16 111; and Thomson, *Heidegger on Ontotheology*, chap. 3, esp. 99–123.

25. The early Heidegger (who remains avowedly "Ur-scientific" and pro-metaphysi-cal) is still trying to redeem Husserl's ambitious goal of establishing phenomenology

as the foundation of all the other sciences in order to avert the "crisis" arising from the sciences' lack any unifying vision or guiding self-understanding.   argue that Heidegger later abandons the commitment to fundamental ontology at the heart of this proudly "Ur-scientific" vision of philosophy but that he continues to develop his response to the larger problem of disciplinary fragmentation and its connection to cultural and historical nihilism. (That Heidegger refines rather than abandons his educational view—replacing his early task of recovering a fundamental ontology with his later one of discerning and transcending our age's reigning ontotheology—is a central thesis of my *Heidegger on Ontotheology*, chaps. 3–4.).

26. "Historicity" misleadingly suggests the fact that our understanding of being changes over time (i.e., it suggests what Heidegger will later call "the history of being"). The word "historicity" is thus a bad translation of *Being and Time*s *Geschichtlichkeit*, by which Heidegger does not mean the *history of being* but rather the *being of history*. (Those are not simply equivalent locutions; for the later Heidegger, the former is the ground of the latter; see my *Heidegger on Ontotheology*, 114 n. 76.) In *Being and Time*, Heidegger is asking what history *is*—what makes something "historical" in the first place.

27. See Theodore Kisiel and Thomas Sheehan, eds., *Becoming Heidegger: On the Trail of His Early Occasional Writings, 1910–1927* (Evanston, IL: Northwestern University Press, 2007), 77–85.

28. In his Rectorial Address, Heidegger adds "language" (a category meant to map onto his understanding of the pre-Socratic *logos*) to the regional ontologies of nature and history (which he traces back to *phusis* and *alêtheia*, respectively), suggesting that the university should be reorganized into twelve academic disciplines, which would be unified as four different ways of approaching and elucidating these three regional ontologies (Q&A 9/GA16 111). (See my *Heidegger on Ontotheology*, chap. 3.)

29. For, "if a philosophical vision which recognized that and how all the different ontological posits fit together into a fundamental ontology could reunify the university (and, behind it, the nation), then Heidegger, as the unique possessor of just such a vision, would be the natural ('fated') spiritual leader of the university, and thus … the nation. In this sense, Heidegger's neo-Husserlian ambition to restore philosophy to her throne as the queen of the sciences clearly helped fuel his political vision for the revitalization of the German University" (*Heidegger on Ontotheology*, 116–117). If phenomenology can be the queen of the sciences, then the phenomenologist can be "the philosopher king." (On the dangers and lessons of this vision, see *Heidegger on Ontotheology*, 114–139.)

30. By the late 1930s, Heidegger comes to realize that this history of being—that is, the history of different metaphysical ways of understanding the being of entities—should be recognized as neither a tragic *regress* away from an original fullness of being (achieved in the Greeks' understanding of being as presence), nor as a story of *progress* toward a single correct answer about what and how being is (as we tend to

presume in our unreflective scientific optimism). Instead, being is best recognized as a temporally dynamic, ontological *excess* (which Heidegger designates with such names as "presencing," "being as such," the "truth of being") that partly informs and yet also exceeds (overflowing and so escaping) every metaphysical way of seeking to understand and so capture "the being of entities" in a single, unchanging conceptual account. (See, e.g., Heidegger, *Contributions to Philosophy*, secs. 52–54, 87, and 116.)

31. Thomson, *Heidegger on Ontotheology*, 117–118.

32. Ibid., 118. For an explanation and defense of Heidegger's reductive yet revealing reading of Nietzsche as the unwitting metaphysician of technological enframing who consummates the tradition of Western metaphysics and so also helps us move beyond it (into a more meaningful postmodern understanding of being), see my *Heidegger, Art, and Postmodernity*, chaps. 1 and 7.

33. Thomson, *Heidegger, Art, and Postmodernity*, chaps. 1, 3, and 7. (See also my "Heideggerian Perfectionism and the Phenomenology of the Pedagogical Truth Event," 180–190.)

34. See, e.g., Kisiel and Sheehan, *Becoming Heidegger*, 77–85; and Heidegger's 1924 review essay, *The Concept of Time*, trans. Ingo Farin (London: Continuum, 2011), which (as Farin emphasizes) Kisiel calls "the very first draft of *Being and Time*" (Kisiel, *The Genesis of Heidegger's* Being and Time, 323).

35. See Ludwig Wittgenstein, *Culture and Value*, trans. Peter Winch (Chicago: University of Chicago Press, 1980), 80: "*Laß Dir Zeit!*" For a fascinating comparison of Wittgenstein with the early Heidegger, see Lee Braver, *Groundless Grounds: A Study of Wittgenstein and Heidegger* (Cambridge, MA: MIT Press, 2012).

36. How can Heidegger suppose that *writing* is somehow separate from all such drafts? If speech can do some justice to polysemy—rather than seeking to still its movement in one single correct answer (in endless pursuit of that desolate impossibility Heidegger calls monosemic exactitude)—then why cannot writing? Rather than follow Heidegger's outdated prejudice here, let us instead acknowledge, after Derrida and, ironically, after the example of Heidegger's own polysemic writing, as well as that of Derrida, Cavell, Cixious, and so many others), that Heidegger's opposition here between the purity and immediacy of speech ("only when man speaks does he think; not the other way around" [WCT 16/GA8 19]), on the one hand, and the derivative artificiality of writing, on the other hand, remains naïve and simplistic, at best the beginning rather than the end of the conversation—conversations to be written as well as spoken. (See esp. Jacques Derrida, *Of Grammatology*, trans. Gayatri Spivak [Baltimore, MD: The Johns Hopkins University Press, 1976].)

37. On such unavoidable limits and one of Heidegger's most ingenious strategies for handling them, see chaps. 6 and 8 of my *Heidegger, Art, and Postmodernity*.

38. I want to say that failure marks the best thinking in an endless vari- ty of ways: In (and through) the impossibility of metaphysics; in the way the deathly collapse of that metaphysical possibility discloses the noth-ing (first to Heidegger and then, through him, to us); in the way that noth-ing permeates intelligibility, holding open its future possibilities (as the "to-come" of the not-yet-a-thing); in the way death permeates life, reminding us of its fragility, transience, pain, and occasionally sweet rebirths (including that rebirth of philosophy as "thinking"); in the way the greatest artworks preserve an overabundance of meaning that we can sometimes discern and yet can never render fully intelligible; perhaps even in the way the most tantalizing beauty remains marked by ugliness, as in the so-called beauty-mark. (I find it lovely, at any rate, to imagine failure as the beauty-mark of philosophy.)

39. For an argument to this effect, see my *Heidegger, Art, and Postmodernity*, chaps. 3 and 8, esp. 75–77, 217–220; and Iain Thomson and James Bodington, "Against Immortality: Why Death Is Better Than the Alternative," in *Intelligent Machines/ Uploaded Minds*, ed. Russell Blackford and Damian Broderick (Oxford: Wiley-Blackwell, 2014), 248–262.

40. See Samuel Beckett, "Worstward Ho," in *Samuel Beckett: The Grove Centennial Edition*, vol. IV, ed. Paul Auster (New York: Grove Press, 2006), 471. To these famous words I would also add, given our context, a few others from the same piece: "When ever what else? Where all always to be seen. Of the nothing to be seen. Dimly seen. Nothing ever unseen. ... No saying what it all is they somehow say. ... Never by naught be nulled" (ibid., 477, 479). On "seeing (the nothing) differently" as the transformative gestalt switch from the midnight of technological nihilism to the morning of a more meaningful postmodernity, see my *Heidegger, Art, and Postmodernity*, chaps. 3 and 7.

15 Being and the Sea: Being as *Phusis*, and Time

Katherine Withy

Division III of *Being and Time* (BT) was supposed to address the question of the sense of being.[1] Being and its sense are in question because while we do understand being, it is also strangely withheld from us. That we understand being is evidenced by the fact that we have access to *what* and *that* things *are* (rather than not); that being is withheld from us is evidenced by the fact that we do not seem to be able to articulate what it is that we grasp in this. Being is both given to us and withheld from us. To be given yet withheld is to be question-worthy—and it is also to be the proper object of phenomenology (BT 35). Being is the phenomenon: that which shows itself (*phainomenon*) (BT 31) but also needs to be "let be seen" (*legein*) (BT 32). To make sense of being is to make sense of both how it shows itself and how it hides itself.

Division I explains how being shows itself by, first, explaining how we discover entities in their being and, second, explicating the structure of our openness to being (i.e., disclosedness). The next step should be to explain how being hides itself—the phenomenon that Heidegger sometimes calls "falling." But Heidegger does not do this. He is distracted by a different (albeit related) phenomenon: inauthenticity. By pursuing authenticity and inauthenticity throughout §40 and the so-called existentialist chapters in Division II, Heidegger *does* give us important insight into the riskiness and fragility of our relationship to being. But he does *not* capture the finitude that he should be aiming at: the withholding of being.[2] Lacking this, Heidegger does not have our finite openness to being fully in view. As a result, the structure of the temporality that he draws out accounts for our openness to being but not for the finitude of this openness. This finitude is not a mere limitation on our part—it is not just that we don't fully "get" being. It belongs to how being works that it withholds itself from us and so makes itself question-worthy. So, if Heidegger's goal in Division III is to show how being makes sense, then he will need to make sense of this fundamental feature of being. It is, if nothing else, the feature that sparked his investigation. But because he lost sight of the withholding of being at the end of Division I, Heidegger is not in a position to make sense of being in Division III.

By the time he starts working seriously with the notion of *phusis* in the 1930s, Heidegger has reoriented himself to the phenomenon of being's withholding. By approaching BT from the perspective of Heidegger's work in this period, then, we can see more clearly what BT accomplished and where it veered off course. I will do this by interpreting Heidegger's reading (in *Introduction to Metaphysics* [IM]) of the opening strophes of the choral ode from Sophocles' *Antigone*.[3] On Heidegger's ontological reading, these strophes show us the various features of being by speaking of the natural world: being is understood as the sea, the earth, and the living thing. I will argue that BT illuminates being as the living thing and being as the earth, and in this explains how being is given to us. But BT falters when it tries to reach being as the sea. The sea is an image of being's simultaneous granting and withholding. Because Heidegger has not thought being's withholding in Divisions I and II, he cannot go on to make sense of this withholding as simultaneous with being's granting in Division III. In short, Heidegger should have thought being as the sea in Division III, but he cannot.

Being (*Sein*) is that by virtue of which entities are, and are as they are, rather than not; it is "that which determines entities as entities" (BT 6). So, what is being? Being is presence; to be is to be present. Given traditional metaphysics, we are tempted to understand this presence as physical presence in the temporal present, or at least as being *there* rather than not in the sense of belonging to the furniture of the universe. But Heidegger is a phenomenologist. For him, the presence of entities is always the *meaningful* presence of entities.[4] An entity is a meaningful thing, and so being an entity is being meaningful or intelligible in some particular way: making sense. Heidegger wants to make sense of this sense-making; he wants to understand how being or meaning works and what makes it possible.

The first step is to understand how entities come to be meaningful—how meaning comes to "infuse" things, as it were. Things could be meaningful all by themselves; meaning could simply be given. But it turns out that this is not the case. Entities "come to be" meaningful only if the human being "makes" them meaningful. How are we to understand this? Sophocles' choral ode offers an image to work with: the hunting and—even better—the domestication of animals. Meaning is presented here as a wild animal that is caught and tamed so as to become the meaning of a meaningful thing:

Even the lightly gliding flock of birds
he snares, and he hunts
the beast folk of the wilderness
and the brood whose home is the sea,
the man who studies wherever he goes.
With ruses he overwhelms the beast
that spends its nights on mountains and roams,
and clasping with wood
the rough-maned neck of the steed
and the unvanquished bull
he forces them into the yoke.

(IM 156–157)

In hunting and domesticating, the human being "tear[s] [*reißen*] this life away from its own order" (IM 165). Similarly, in making sense of things, the human being "draws [*reißt*] being into entities" (IM 171). Being is thus domesticated. What can we say about how this happens?

First, the story of domestication is not supposed to be a story of violation, even if it is a story of violence. It is a story about bringing being into its own. To hear this, we need to think the domesticating and training of animals not as an imposition but as a process that first allows the animals fully to be what they are.[5] It is when it is trained that the horse is most able to be a horse. Similarly, meaning only "is" when it is the meaning of some entity: "being is always the being of an entity" (BT 9). Being or meaning only "is" insofar as it is trained and wrangled, "captured," and "subjugated" (IM 167, *in* entities *by* the human being. It follows that we cannot treat meaning as something independent of entities.

Further, we must treat the human being as the domesticator—I am tempted to say "wrangler" or "cowboy"—of meaning. This is an important part of the image, for it stops us from thinking the human being as the artisan. Our language (and the history of Western thought) leads us into this error. To say that the human being *makes* sense of things or *makes* entities meaningful is not to say that she *produces* either meaningful entities or meaning. In particular, she does not (in Aristotelian fashion) create or construct a meaning *qua* intelligible form that she imposes on mute matter. Rather, we should think of her capturing and subjugating as *poietic letting meaning manifest itself*, where this is *letting entities show up meaningfully as what they are*. Like domesticating, such letting be is enabling, not violating.

Nonetheless, it is violent. Meaning is "torn from its own order." Meaning's "order" is the logic of how it works, and (according to Heidegger) it works by both unconcealing and concealing itself. It is this intrinsic self-concealing that the human being must grapple with in order to bring meaning to entities. I will say more about this self-concealing later. For now, the point is that, as far as meaning is concerned, the "call of the wild" is the drive to conceal itself. In drawing meaning into entities, the human being must in some sense counter this tendency in meaning—hence Heidegger's violent imagery and language. But, as I said, drawing meaning into entities is not a violation, for meaning is also unconcealing: it is driven to manifest itself in meaningful entities. Meaning is inherently ambivalent, and this permits its being "torn from its own order" to amount to its coming into its own.

Heidegger explains exactly *how* the human being draws meaning into entities in BT: we grasp (either practically or theoretically) what is possible and impossible for an entity and grasp the entity in terms of this. For example, for an entity to be meaningful as a teacup is for me to grasp it in terms of what a teacup can be used for and what it should be used for. This "can" does not pick out what is logically or physically possible and impossible; it picks out the content of public norms about how to use teacups. The possibilities and impossibilities in terms of which a tool such as a teacup is intelligible are thus special sorts of possibilities: those appropriate to tools. Other sorts of entities will in turn be intelligible in terms of other sorts of (im)possibilities.

In grasping the entity in terms of a certain sort of possibility, I am making it meaningful as a certain sort of *what* (*essentia*). A particular kind of *that* (*existentia*) will correspond to this.[6] In other words: for different kinds of entities there are different kinds of standards for counting as *that* and *what* they are. *What* the teacup *is* is what it is *for* (in order to), since tools are meaningful in terms of what they are correctly used for. The fact *that* the teacup *is* consists in its being *available* for use: it is the case *that* there is a teacup when there is an entity that it is possible to use in the way that teacups are used. A piece of quartz, by contrast, will have its *that* being in manifesting a certain chemical composition. Its being *what* it is consists in that chemical composition falling within a range of possible patterns of oxygen, silicon, and other atoms. These examples show that there is a variety of kinds of *that*- and *what*-beings—what we might call different "ways" or "modes" of being. There is thus a variety of ways in which entities can make sense, and correspondingly different "categories of intelligibility." Since not everything is meaningful in the same way, we (like Aristotle) must conclude that being is said in many ways. Heidegger is thus an ontological pluralist.

Negotiating these various modes of being and the particular (im)possibilities that they involve is not usually a theoretical exercise. Most of our comportments toward entities are thoroughly practical. "Knowing" what and that the teacup *is* is "knowing" what sorts of things are teacups and what to do with them. Such knowing is a knowing *how* rather than a knowing *that*—it is being *able* to use teacups. Further, according to Heidegger, we do not have to posit any elaborate conceptual or cognitive apparatus in order to explain this knowing how. I grasp the entity as a teacup when I pick it up and drink from it—and my grasp is not anything different from this picking up and drinking. Domesticating being or making entities meaningful consists in comporting toward entities, and most of our comportments are practical and mundane. It is by competently navigating and engaging entities in terms of what they can and cannot do that I "discover" entities in terms of their (im)possibilities, and so allow them to encounter me meaningfully. In this, I domesticate meaning—I bring it into its own as the meaning of entities.

The possibilities and impossibilities that give meaning to entities in turn are what they are by virtue of their place within a larger system of meaning. Meaning must be understood holistically, as a system or structured network. Heidegger makes this point in terms of equipment. What a teacup *can* and *should* be used for is not a property of the teacup but belongs to a complex set of relationships between different items of equipment (tea bags, tea pots, milk, biscuits, etc.) and particular human practices (tea parties, tea time, consumption etiquette, hosting etiquette, etc.). This is true not just of tools. All entities are meaningful as what they are only in light of a totality of related meanings.

Recall the domestication of animals in the choral ode. Sophocles invokes the natural habitat of each animal—the wilderness, the air, the sea—and in doing so indicates that each animal has a position within an ecosystem, and ultimately within the system of nature as a whole. Any particular living thing is what it is only as part of a larger natural order. The human being must understand and accommodate this order if she is to domesticate the animal. Sophocles flags it by speaking of the earth:

The noblest of gods as well, the earth,
the indestructibly untiring, he wearies,
overturning her from year to year,
driving the plows this way and that
with his steeds.

(IM 156)

Unlike the earth in some of Heidegger's other texts, this earth is not what is hidden or resists. It is Mother Earth or capital-"N" Nature: what we negotiate and utilize in agriculture, what is manifest in the regular cycles of the seasons and of birth and death and in the internal order of ecosystems. Earth is a massive, complex system to which all natural entities belong and by which they are determined.

This earth is what Heidegger in BT called *world*. Of course, "world" in BT is not a name for being but is a particular meaningful entity (BT 65): it is that entity that we might ordinarily (and misleadingly) address as a worldview, conceptual scheme, or network of beliefs. But "world" in BT also names the structure or logic of any world (BT 64)—not the world as an entity, but what it takes for something to be intelligible as a world rather than not. Strictly, this is called *worldhood* (BT 65). Heidegger argues that the structure and so the worldhood of any world is significance (BT 87): a system of meaningful relations, including in-order-to, toward-this, in-which, with-which, and for-the-sake-of-which relations. These relations are ways of organizing and categorizing different sorts of possibilities, and so are constitutive for different ways of being.

For-the-sake-of-which relationships are the most important for the nature of significance, since they ultimately organize all the other relationships. A for-the-sake-of-which is a possible way of being human—a human project or identity. The most fundamental for-the-sake-of-which must be that project that makes us what we are: being a sense-maker (being Dasein). But we have all sorts of mid-level projects or identities, such as being a friend, being a juggler, or being a physicist. These projects organize the system of meanings, such that entities are ultimately meaningful in terms of their place within the context of human purposes and concerns.[7] Thus teacups are meaningful in relation to the human project of tea drinking, and instances of SiO_4 are meaningful as such in relation to the human project of understanding the world chemically.

We might think that the human being's role in making-meaningful at this level of explanation is to take on such projects. But taking up a possible way of being human is just a case of grasping an entity (namely, oneself) in terms of its (im)possibilities and so belongs to the previous stage of the story (the living thing). What is the human being's special implication in meaning when meaning is understood specifically as earth, the system of meanings? Sophocles has the human being plowing the earth. Heidegger understands this as a disturbance of the natural system—an interruption of the natural cycles of nourishment and growth (IM 164). Expressed non-metaphorically, such interruption must be a creative intervention into the system of meaning. Human beings can reformulate and reconfigure the shape of meaning, and they do so through great works of art, state craft, and philosophy.

But here Heidegger seems to miss the less disruptive intervention that his reading presupposes. Plowing—like forest fires—need not simply disturb the natural system but can also enable it. By turning over the soil and releasing the powers of growth and nutrition that were previously hidden, the farmer *allows* the natural system to fully express itself. In the same way, the system of meaning needs to be *allowed* to operate in the sense that its significance relations need to be released or freed—they need to be "lit up." This is a needlessly tortured way of saying that the relationships that structure the system of meanings need to be accessible to the human being. That is, the human being must be open to them and able to traverse them. In short: the system of meaning can govern entities only if the human being has access to that system and can move within it. Heidegger fills out the human being's openness to significance (and so tells the story of "plowing") in his account of disclosedness in BT IV. Findingness (*Befindlichkeit*) is our openness to what is already given, and understanding is our openness to (im)possibilities. It is by being open in these ways that we light up or reveal significance and so allow the system of meaning to work.

To say that we are open to significance or that the system of meanings is lit up for us is to say that being is accessible to us. We are entities who have an understanding of being or who are *in* the world. Thus Division I has shown how being, as the being of entities, is given to us. Heidegger understands his argument up to this point as working against a tradition of neglect in philosophy—a tradition that has overlooked the world and its workdhood (BT 65, 66), as well as the human being's full implication in the meaning-giving process. In particular, traditional philosophy has overlooked the variety of ways of being. Since it does not see that entities are what they are by virtue of the particular significant relations they are grasped in terms of, philosophy to date has not seen the different kinds of significant relations that make for the differences between present things, available tools, and existing human beings. When this ontological plurality is ignored, being comes to look like an empty concept—one that applies univocally to all entities, and which is plainly self-evident yet so universal as to be indefinable (BT 3–4).

But if philosophy to date has been ontologically blind and unsophisticated this is not entirely the fault of previous philosophers. There are deeper reasons that being has been forgotten and misunderstood—starting with the fact that we sense-makers tend to misunderstand ourselves. In addition to overlooking our essential implication in the meaning-giving process, we overlook being itself, as both the structure of the system of meanings (the earth) and the plurality of meanings corresponding to and constituting different kinds of entities (the domesticated and trained animal). While Heidegger does sometimes imply that such misunderstanding is individual and culpable, he also attributes it at least in part to being or meaning itself. Being is the phenomenon in the sense that it shows itself and yet hides itself, and so is the "'phenomenon' in a distinctive sense" (BT 35): "it is something that proximally and for the most part does *not* show itself at all: it is something that lies *hidden*, in contrast to that which proximally and for the most part does show itself; but at the same time it is something that belongs to what thus shows itself, and it belongs to it so essentially as to constitute its meaning and its ground" (BT 35). It is because being hides itself in this way that it can be misunderstood and forgotten. And it is because being hides itself in this way that it must be allowed to show itself, making it the proper object of phenomenology.

Heidegger mentions a number of ways in which a phenomenon may be covered up: it can be undiscovered, buried over after having been discovered, or disguised, such that it shows itself only in the mode of semblance (BT 36). These ways of being covered up apply properly to innerworldly entities like teacups and pieces of quartz, but it is hard to see how they apply to being. Of course, the system of meanings is in some sense an entity (albeit not an innerworldly one [BT 72]) and to this extent can be undiscovered, forgotten, or misunderstood by philosophy in the same way that (pieces of) quartz can be undiscovered, forgotten, or misunderstood by mineralogists. But what makes the world different from quartz is that it belongs to what we are. We are being-in-the-world. This means that the system of meanings is always "lit up" for us and we are always making sense of things in terms of it. The world is thus a phenomenon that always shows up to everyone. For philosophy to simply miss what is always thus illuminated, it must be the case that the world as a system of meanings is hidden from all of us even in its very illumination. The hiding at issue cannot be a merely ontic lack of discovery, burying over, or disguising. There must be a deeper and different kind of hiding that makes being *the* phenomenon, and this is why being "must be exhibited in a way of its own, essentially different from the way in which entities are discovered" (BT 6).

Being hides itself in a way that makes possible, but is more fundamental than, its neglect in philosophy. Its self-withdrawal is a positive phenomenon—an "*a priori* [...] enigma" (BT 4) that is perhaps "inevitable" (BT 6)— that belongs to the logic of meaning.[8] As I mentioned when I discussed the domestication of the wild animal, the drive to conceal itself is part of how meaning operates. This fundamental feature of meaning is expressed at the very outset of the choral ode as the primordial chaos of the sea:

He [i.e., the human being] fares forth upon the foaming tide
amid winter's southerly tempest
and cruises through the summits
of the raging, clefted swells.

(IM 156)

The sea is not a placid and stable body of water but a turbulent "foaming tide" of stormy waves. As Heidegger puts it, the sea "constantly drags up its own depths and drags itself down into them" (IM 164). This surfacing and submerging is the ambivalence I mentioned earlier of meaning as simultaneously unconcealing and concealing. Heidegger will later express this ambivalence as a *polemos*, a war.

If being is the sea, then the logic of meaning exceeds the structure of significance. An account of meaning must go beyond the (im)possibilities of entities (the domesticated animal) and it must go beyond how these are structured into a system of significant relationships (the earth). It must explain how and why this system works by concealing itself (the sea). How and why does the world *world* (*die Welt weltet*) through self-effacement? How and why (as Heraclitus puts it and Heidegger will later become fond of saying) does nature love to hide (*phusis kruptesthai philei*) (e.g., IM 121)? Explaining this amounts to accounting for the very necessity of the investigation into meaning in the first place. Being is question-worthy precisely because it hides itself. So what Heidegger needs to do to complete his account is to indicate that, show how, and explain why being is not only given to us but also withheld from us. There are several places in BT where we might think that he does this: in the analysis of untruth, in the account of thrownness, in the "pre-ontological" and so embedded status of our understanding of being, and in the story of falling. I will argue that the story of falling should have been the story of being's withholding but that *Being and Time* does not tell this story.

First, Heidegger explicitly discusses concealing in his analysis of truth in §44 "Truth" names the showing up of entities and—at a deeper level—Dasein's disclosedness, which is the world's showing up to it. Just as the phenomenon, as that which shows itself, has its counterconcept in "covered-up-ness" (BT 36), so too truth or uncoveredness is paired with untruth or being covered up (BT 222). However, this untruth is not the self-withdrawing we are seeking, for two reasons. First, Heidegger discusses only the

closing off or covering over of entities, not that of being, so the concealing is at the wrong ontological level. (It is at the level of the domesticable
animal rather than that of the sea.) Second, it is a concealing of he wrong
sort. Entities are concealed *prior* to (or instead of) being discovered, but the
self-concealing of being is *simultaneous* with its unconcealing. Being hides
itself precisely when it shows up—precisely when we are operating within
the system of meanings. Its illumination must in some sense be the same
movement as its withdrawing, in the same way that the sea dragging itself
up is at the same time its dragging itself down. Thus, the concealing discussed in §44 is at the wrong level and of the wrong sort.[9]

Second, we might think that the withholding of being belongs to
thrownness. For sense-making to be thrown is for it to find itself stuck
with the project of sense-making, without being able to explain how and
why it is thus.[10] We are also stuck with a particular system of meanings: a
world is something that we inherit, and in fact something that we have, at
every point, *already* inherited. We might think that it is because we are thus
thrown into a world that it withdraws from us. If we always operate within
a given system of meanings, then whenever we attempt to explain how
that system hangs together or why it hangs together in the way that it does,
we operate *within* the very system that we are explaining. We constantly
presuppose it, and we cannot step outside of it to give an independent
explanation of it. In this way, the world withdraws from our attempts at
explanation. While this is certainly true, it is a different phenomenon: the
inaccessibility of the "whence" and "whither" of the world (BT 134), not
the withdrawal of the world per se. (Consider that identifying the whence
and whither of a given world or understanding of being is the Foucauld-
ian genealogical [whence] and archaeological [whither] project, not Heidegger's ontological project.)[11]

Third, Heidegger claims that being is both self-evident and unintelligible because our understanding of being is "pre-ontological" (BT 12). By
an *understanding of being* Heidegger usually means a stand on what it is to
be meaningful at all rather than not (e.g., to be is to be present). But any
particular understanding of what it is to be rather than not is always also
an understanding of what it is to be this or that. So, to say that our understanding of being is "pre-ontological" is to say that the world—the system
of meanings—is "pre-ontological."[12] To say that this is "pre-ontological" is
to say that it is unthematic (BT 12). Human beings do not have developed,
explicit ontologies. This means that our understanding of being or the
world is concealed from theoretical understanding. But it is *not* concealed

from human beings as sense-makers. It is perfectly accessible to us in all comportments that are not theoretical.

The suggestion is that the understanding of being or the world is given to us *qua* practically comporting and withheld from us *qua* theorizing.[13] Thus it is not illuminated when we philosophize, but it is illuminated in our everyday going about. In our everyday practical comportment, being or meaning is "implicit"—where this means both that it is *embedded* in our comportment and can be *inferred* from our comportment. Meaning is the system of (im)possibilities that we work with when we engage with entities, and it is *embedded* in this engagement since it *is* only in our engaging with entities. When we come to philosophize, we cease our everyday practical comportment (to some extent) and so lose our access to the system of meanings embedded within it. This is why philosophy has tended to overlook the world or our understanding of being. To see it, we would need a specifically hermeneutic philosophy, which could interpret our everyday going about so as to *infer* from various comportments the meanings that things have in them. Such a hermeneutics would be the distinctive *logos* of phenomenology—the way phenomenology allows what shows and hides itself to be seen (BT 37). Only as phenomenological and so hermeneutic, then, could ontology be possible (BT 37).

But why think that meaning is hidden from theoretical understanding? Why and how does the philosophical move (if it is not appropriately hermeneutic) tend to distort and occlude what is given in practical comportment? The key to answering these questions seems to be that although meaning is illuminated for us in comportment, it is so in a specific way—one that is not possible in theoretical comportment. We might say that meaning is the sort of thing that we do not pay attention to or that we take for granted. This is necessary to its operation, such that when we *do* pay attention to it, we miss what is most distinctive about it and in effect fail to see it. One way that readers of Heidegger have formulated this idea is by saying that the world as a system of meanings is *backgrounded*.[14] This language is borrowed from Gestalt psychology: a figure or foreground appears in contrast to or set off against a background. This is thus a perceptual analogy for the withdrawal of meaning. Entities are like the foreground, while meaning—that "in terms of which" entities are understood—is like the background. Insofar as it is a background, being conceals itself. So why think that this logic of background and foreground applies to meaning, and that it does so necessarily rather than as a matter of psychological contingency?

Heidegger attributes something like this backgrounding to our being when he asserts that we are falling. Heidegger often uses the term *falling* to name inauthenticity, but he also uses it "to signify that Dasein is proximally and for the most part *alongside* the 'world' of its concern" (BT 175). "World" here means the entities encountered in the world (BT 54). To be alongside or amid (*bei*) these is to be absorbed in them. Such absorption is characteristic of all of our comportments, including our most distracted ones. To be absorbed in entities is to pay heed to entities rather than to their meaning or their meaningfulness. Thus the point is that we are not "alongside" the world *qua* the system of meaning (whatever that would mean).[15] There is a certain closedness or hiddenness of the world that goes along with its very illumination. We thus need to add a third element to the picture of disclosedness: not only are we open to the world in finding and understanding, we are also falling. To be falling is for being to withdraw even as entities show up in their being. It is because being or the world is always hidden from us in this way—because we are falling—that philosophy can overlook or distort it.

The closest that Heidegger comes to articulating the logic of falling as a concealing or backgrounding is in his frequently invoked "law of proximity": "We see first, strictly speaking, never the closest but always what is next closest" (P 135).[16] But what does this law govern and why does it hold? Heidegger's examples of such proximate invisibility are tools (such as eyeglasses and the street [BT 107]), which possess "the inconspicuousness of the proximally ready-to-hand" (BT 107). This suggests that the self-concealing of meaning is or is like the self-concealing of the tool or the instrument, which shows itself *by* effacing or concealing itself. Tools work most effectively when they "withdraw" (BT 69).[17] The fewer demands that a tool makes on our attention, energy, and skill—the more it "gets out of the way"—the more effective it is in allowing us to achieve our goal. The withdrawing of tools is thus their way of showing up as what they are. The hammer is most itself when it has disappeared into the hammering Meaning, perhaps, works in the same way.[18]

However, we cannot simply say that meaning *is* a tool, for it is not an innerworldly entity. As significance (the structure of the system of meanings), meaning is not an entity at all. As world (the system of meanings) meaning is an entity but not an innerworldly one (BT 72). The self-concealing of meaning is at best analogous to the self-effacing of tools. There are good textual reasons to think that this analogy does not hold—or at least, does not hold beyond the fact that both tools and meaning involve some kind of constitutive self-concealing.[19] But even if the analogy does hold, it is not enough. We have not yet identified—much less understood—the

self-concealing of meaning. We have merely drawn attention to an allegedly similar phenomenon.

Heidegger needs to say more about falling, but unfortunately he does
not. The reason is that he persistently confuses this aspect of the logic of
meaning with inauthenticity, which is made possible by falling but is not
the same as it. Inauthenticity is—in short—a misunderstanding of the sort
of thing that we are. The sort of thing that we are is a sense-maker. Being
a sense-maker is the most basic project or for-the-sake-of-which organizing the system of meanings, and it is hidden from us to the extent that
and in the same way that the system of meanings is hidden from us. It
is because this is hidden from us—because we are falling—that it is possible for us to misunderstand ourselves and so be inauthentic. So while
the two phenomena are connected, they are distinct. Heidegger, however,
repeatedly conflates them. The confusion reaches its pitch in the analysis
of *Angst*, the mood that disrupts our absorption in entities and opens us to
the system of meanings (the world in its worldhood), including our own
meaning as sense-makers.[20] Although he starts by speaking of falling, Heidegger becomes increasingly concerned with inauthenticity over the course
of this analysis. By the time we get to Division II, the phenomenon of falling *qua* being amid and the correlate withholding of meaning has all but
disappeared.

As a consequence, the temporal interpretation of sense-making that
Heidegger gives in Division II either does not or cannot accommodate the
withdrawal of meaning—and so the very possibility and necessity of Heidegger's own investigation. Heidegger offers his picture of temporality as
a way of making sense-making intelligible: temporality is supposed to be
the framework within which sense-making (and perhaps even meaning or
being itself) makes sense. Temporality has an ecstatico-horizonal structure.
To say that temporality is ek-static is to say that it is a standing out (*ek*:
out, *stasis*: standing). This captures Dasein's openness or disclosedness and
so showing up of meaning. To say that temporality is horizonal is to
say that it is bounded (as if by a horizon) and so finite. Each ek-stasis of
temporality has its boundary and these boundaries together are supposed
to constitute the finitude of sense-making. First, sense-making depends on
the entities that it makes sense of—and in some way is beholden to these
(in the sense that it must be possible to get entities right or wrong). Second,
sense-making also depends on a pregiven system of meanings; it is thrown
into a world—and the "whence" and "whither" of both the world and the
"throw" into it are obscure (BT 134). Third, the future is opaque: we do not
know what will happen (BT 330)—but we do know that our understanding

of being will always be subject to revision and so is always at risk, and that our projects will never be completed but will always be underway in some sense. These three sets of finitudes are plausibly the horizonal finitudes of the present, past, and futural ek-stases of temporality, respectively.[21] The finitude that Heidegger does *not* appear to have on the table is the withdrawal of meaning from us in falling. When he gives his temporal interpretation of falling, Heidegger discusses only inauthenticity.

Unfortunately, this is probably not a mere omission. It does not seem to me that the withdrawal of being can be a horizonal finitude at all—and, if so, then it cannot be accommodated in ecstatico-horizonal temporality. As I understand it, horizonal finitude is the limit of an ek-static reaching out. It is, as it were, as far as openness can reach, just as a visual horizon is as far as the eye can see. But the withdrawal of meaning is not any sort of limit. It is a "holding-oneself-in-even-while-reaching-out." A temporality that worked like this could not be "the *ekstatikon* pure and simple," "the primordial 'outside-of-itself' in and for itself" (BT 329). It would have to be a surging, rising, or reaching out that also draws itself back in and hides itself. It would have to be the sea—being as *phusis*, which loves to hide—rather than the *ekstatikon*, which only reveals.[22]

Let me sum up by considering Heidegger's opening expression of his thesis in BT: "[W]henever Dasein tacitly understands and interprets something like being, it does so with *time* as its standpoint. Time must be brought to light—and genuinely conceived—as the horizon for all understanding of being and for any way of interpreting it" (BT 17). Heidegger appears to accomplish this: he appears to show how time makes sense of sense-making. But he does not explain why time must be brought to light. Why and how is our temporally intelligible understanding of being "tacit" (*unausdrücklich*)? Is *this* temporally intelligible? At stake is not just the completeness of the investigation or its ability to account for itself. At stake may be the very difference between being and entities—*if* this distinction rests on the fact that being shows up in a special way: by concealing itself. If we cannot make good sense of this concealing, then we cannot make good sense of the ontological difference. (Perhaps this is why Heidegger goes on to problematize and to attempt to ground the ontological difference immediately after BT [see BP].) In any case, there is work yet to be done. BT succeeds in working out the story of meaning at the levels of both the living thing and the earth, but it does not get to the most fundamental, sealike feature of meaning: that it works by effacing itself. Instead of explaining falling *qua* the hiddenness of meaning, Heidegger gets sidetracked by the issue of inauthenticity and authenticity. Instead of exploring the phenomenon that made his investigation necessary in the first place, Heidegger diagnoses and critiques the motivated misunderstanding that would make his investigation difficult to do well. As a result, his interpretation of temporality neglects the crucial finitude in sense-making.

Heidegger will later express the self-concealing of being using the Greek concept of *phusis* and—when he reads Sophocles' ode—the image of the sea. Sophocles tells us that the human being "fares forth" into the play of meaning's concealing and unconcealing. She "cruises through the summits" but never ventures into the depths of the sea. This says that the human being is exposed to being's concealing and unconcealing but never goes deep enough to understand it. She remains at the surface, never seeing what is concealed or how or why it is concealed. Similarly, in his later work Heidegger does not attempt to make being's self-concealing intelligible. He insists that we respect it as the Enigma or Mystery. The reason, I take it, is that while being is the phenomenon that shows itself while hiding itself, its self-hiding is *not* a phenomenon. It is not something that we can experience, understand, or let show itself. It demands of us an ontological piety, which consists in experiencing the question-worthiness of being that drove BT without attempting to understand it. *If* this is right, then Heidegger's failure to analyze falling in BT is not a failure that he should have remedied—even if he did not see this at the time. And yet, do *we* really have good reason to think that there is nothing more to be said about being's self-concealing? It seems to me that in order to know even this, we would have to—and should—risk the impiety of diving deep into the sea.

Acknowledgments

I thank the audience at the University of Oxford's Post-Kantian Seminar for their comments and questions on a draft of this essay, and Lee Braver for comments on the final version. I also thank the graduate students in my Later Heidegger seminar at Georgetown University in spring 2014 for many thought-provoking discussions about the self-concealing of being.

Notes

1. Page references to BT are to the marginal (Niemeyer) pagination. I have substituted a lower case "b" for the translators' capital "B" in translating *Sein*, and I have transliterated Greek terms.

2. Daniel Dahlstrom mentions this as one of three problems Heidegger had with his BT account: it "does not stress the fundamental feature of being, namely, that it conceals itself more than it reveals and, indeed, withdraws precisely in disclosing beings" (Daniel O. Dahlstrom, *The Heidegger Dictionary* [London: Bloomsbury, 2013], 34).

3. References are to the English pagination of IM. I have substituted "entities" for "beings" (*das Seiendes*) and a lower case "b" for the translators' capital "B" in translating *Sein*. My interpretation is (to my knowledge) the first ontological interpretation of Heidegger's reading of the opening of the ode. (I interpret the rest of the ode in my *Heidegger on Being Uncanny* [Cambridge, MA: Harvard University Press, 2015]). Other readers tend to take the natural entities named in the opening of the ode to refer straightforwardly to particular natural entities, despite Heidegger's insistence that they name the overwhelming and so being (IM 163, 166).

4. For compelling arguments for this claim, see the work of Thomas Sheehan—most recently, *Making Sense of Heidegger: A Paradigm Shift* (London: Rowman & Littlefield, 2015).

5. I do not wish to take a stand on whether this is true of domesticable animals, but we must assume that it is true in order to interpret the ode properly.

6. John Haugeland takes the extra step of deriving the distinction between essence, accident, and actuality from the nature of (im)possibilities: "[A]ny comportment toward entities as entities presupposes a grasp of the distinction between what is and is not possible for them. Possibilities, however, always have to do with concomitant, concrete determinations (properties and relations, e.g.). But to say that some combination is (or is not) possible is nothing other than to say that it could (or could not) be manifested in something dasein 'lets be' (acknowledges and acquiesces in). And this trio amounts to a précis of an account of the articulation of being: essence, accidents, actuality" (John Haugeland, *Dasein Disclosed: John Haugeland's Heidegger*, ed. Joseph Rouse [Cambridge, MA: Harvard University Press, 2013], 46). (Note that Haugeland has adopted "dasein" as an English noun, which does not require capitalization.)

7. This is why saying that entities are meaningful is consistent with the BT claim that only Dasein is meaningful (BT 151). Entities "get" their meaning from their relationship to human practices, and so their meaningfulness is derived or borrowed from Dasein's meaningfulness.

8. Cf.: "However much this understanding of being (an understanding which is already available to us) may fluctuate and grow dim, and border on mere acquaintance with a word, its very indefiniteness is itself a positive phenomenon which needs to be clarified" (BT 5–6).

9. For a clear account of the different levels and kinds of (un)concealing, see Mark Wrathall, "Unconcealment," in *A Companion to Heidegger*, ed. Hubert L. Dreyfus and Mark A. Wrathall (Malden, MA: Blackwell, 2005), 337–357.

10. I develop and defend this interpretation of thrownness in Katherine Withy, "Situation and Limitation: Making Sense of Heidegger on Thrownness," *European Journal of Philosophy*, 22 (1) (March 2014): 61–81.

11. We might also think that there is something about the world as traditional and inherited that explains its self-withdrawal. Thus Heidegger accuses tradition of concealing by handing "what it 'transmits'" "over to self-evidence" (BT 21). If it is the world that is transmitted in tradition, then the world as a system of meanings could be concealed in its very obviousness. I will address such proximate invisibility when I discuss being's self-concealing as falling.

12. Note that the world is not here the *object* of the understanding of being but that understanding itself. The reason is that the system of meanings *is* only in being understood.

13. This reading complicates the explanation of how meaning works at the initial level (the domesticable animal), which held that all comportment involves grappling with concealing (which I called "the call of the wild"). This problem points to one of the key differences between so-called early and later Heidegger: BT does not include what Heidegger later calls *lēthē*, a specifically *ontological* untruth. But pointing out this lack is a way of saying that the explanation of falling that Heidegger does give is inadequate, which is of course my claim.

14. Notably, Hubert L. Dreyfus in *Being-in-the-World: A Commentary on Heidegger's Being and Time, Division I* (Cambridge, MA: MIT Press, 1990).

15. Alternatively, we could see absorption as the condition of not being "alongside" the human being's own being as a sense-maker. That is, instead of talking about the concealing of the world we could talk about the concealing of Dasein from itself. Thus one of the early expressions of falling in BT is Heidegger's claim that Dasein has a tendency to understand itself in terms of innerworldly entities (as a tool, an object, or a natural thing) and for this reason is "ontologically farthest" from itself (BT 16). This ontological distance is the concealing of the world.

16. Heidegger actually says that this *follows from* the "law of proximity," but he does not identify this law and it is not clear what else it could be. Heidegger appeals to this "law" repeatedly in BT, even if he does not name it as such there.

17. Similarly, the person who operates the tool is most effective when *she* withdraws from herself. As Heidegger puts it: "The Self must forget itself if, lost in the world of equipment, it is to be able 'actually' to go to work and manipulate something" (BT 354). (I thank Lee Braver for directing me to this passage.)

18. Wrathall articulates this interpretation clearly: "[T]he style of being that allows things to show up as having an essence is most invisible when it is most effective. That is, when everything is showing up to us in terms of flexibility and efficiency, for example, we are captivated by things—we are wholly absorbed in our dealings with them. That renders us unable to make ourselves aware of the understanding of being that is shaping our experience of the world. Looked at another way, the ready availability of beings to us depends on our losing sight of the fact that their availability is grounded in a particular understanding of the essence of beings as a whole" (Wrathall, "Unconcealment," 355).

19. I refer here to the analysis of *Angst*. *Angst* is the reversal of the world's self-concealing, and it is often held to be analogous to the reversal of the self-effacing character of tools in tool breakdown. Heidegger himself encourages the analogy by saying that in *Angst* the world becomes *obtrusive* (BT 187)—just as when a tool is missing, the remaining tools and the current project become obtrusive (BT 73). But a quick glance at the alleged analogues shows that they do not line up. The *world* is revealed in *Angst*, yet it is not the *tool* that is revealed when it is missing but instead the surrounding context. The tool in fact is missing—yet in *Angst* it is not the world that is missing but instead the specific meanings of innerworldly entities.

20. *Angst* opens us to the system of meanings both (i) in the course of our lives, as something that is withheld from us, and (ii) initially, thus inaugurating our openness. This amounts to saying that *Angst* is both an event in a life and the ground of our openness to the world. For an argument for and interpretation of this dual role, see the second chapter of my *Heidegger on Being Uncanny*.

21. For interpretations of time and its finitude(s), see William D. Blattner, *Heidegger's Temporal Idealism* (Cambridge: Cambridge University Press, 1999) and Haugeland, *Dasein Disclosed*.

22. Heidegger returns to ecstatico-horizonal temporality in the 1962 lecture "Time and Being," where he attempts to argue that there is a withholding in time of just the sort that there is in being. However, his argument fails. Heidegger identifies a "distancing" in each ek-stasis of temporality, which keeps what it opens back from the other ek-stases (such that, for example, what has been [past] does not become present [now]) (TB 15). But such an ek-static limit does not entitle Heidegger to the conclusion that the reaching out of the ek-stases themselves is somehow withheld—that "the giving of a giving is concealed" (TB 16).

16   Was There a "Turn" in Heidegger's Philosophy?

Julian Young

It has long been accepted that, for better or worse, the character of Heidegger's later thought is radically different from that of the earlier philosophy of *Being and Time* (1927),[1] that his "path of thinking" made a sharp *Kehre*—a "turning" or "reversal"—sometime during the 1930s. Father William Richardson, in his monumental 1963 study of Heidegger,[2] found the turning sharp enough to justify talk of a "Heidegger I" and "Heidegger II." (One might be inclined to speak, in a similar vein, of a "Wittgenstein I" and "Wittgenstein II.") The focus of the turning, as Richardson sees it, is "being." In *Being and Time*, being is the foundational "horizon" of intelligibility that is projected in "Dasein's"—our—practical activity. A carpenter, for instance, in hammering a nail into a piece of wood, "sees" the nail and the hammer *as* entities of a certain sort. He does so in virtue of grasping their role in the network made up of other items of equipment and other human beings that Heidegger refers to as "world." In Heidegger's later thought, however, claims Richardson, being has ceased to be a human "projection" and has become instead "an active force, a process that assumes an initiative of its own by revealing itself to [Dasein]—but concealing itself as well."[3] For Richardson, then, the *Kehre* has to do with dependence. Whereas in earlier Heidegger being is entirely dependent on the human subject and its practices, in his later thought, the human subject, as a being essentially in possession of a disclosure of "world," is dependent on being for that disclosure. It is not difficult to see that, as viewed by Richardson, there is an at least quasi-theological dimension to Heidegger's turn.

Though something like Richardson's account has long been accepted, the appearance, finally, of the 1938 *Contributions to Philosophy* in English translation[4] prompted Thomas Sheehan to argue the need for a "new paradigm" in Heidegger interpretation, a paradigm that emphasizes continuity.[5] According to Sheehan, we should no longer distinguish between "Heidegger I" and "Heidegger II," between "earlier" and "later" Heidegger, since the *Contributions* shows us that "the *Kehre* never took place" (S 195). My purpose in this essay is to defend the idea of a *Kehre*. I shall attempt, first, to show why a turning was needed and, second, to demonstrate that a turning was indeed executed. Finally, however, I shall suggest some important modifications to Richardson's account of the post-turning Heidegger, modifications which, I believe, will lay to rest some of Sheehan's legitimate worries about the idea of a turning.

Sheehan's Worries

Taken at face value, Sheehan's critique of the Richardson "paradigm" purports to show that to take Heidegger's talk of a *Kehre* as referring to something that happened in his thinking is to misunderstand it. For in the *Contributions* we discover Heidegger using the idea of a *Kehre* to refer not to an event in his intellectual biography, but rather to the fact that while our "sense"-giving projection of being, of "openness" or "world," is something we cannot exist without, conversely, openness is something that cannot exist without us. This two-way dependence, Sheehan writes, is described in the *Contributions* as

the *kehriger Bezug* (a "reciprocal relatedness" (GA65 7)[6] or simply *die Kehre*, the reciprocity of openness' ineluctable sense-making and sense-making's grounding in openedness. ... ...The *Kehre*, therefore, is not something that happened in the 1930s. In fact it never happened at all. It is simply the structure of openness. (S 195)

Appealing to this and other textual details, Sheehan wants to move us to the view that there is no fundamental shift in thinking, that in later as well as earlier Heidegger the only agent in view is human being, that there is no second something revealing itself to us (while simultaneously concealing itself from us).

On the surface, Sheehan's claim seems far from compelling. The use of "or simply" to move from *one* use Heidegger makes of *Kehre* (and then only in adjectival form) to *the* use belongs to rhetoric rather than to logic. Matters of textual detail are, however, I think, not of decisive importance since, though he is not entirely explicit about it, Sheehan's real intention seems to me not so much Heidegger-*interpretation* as Heidegger-*reconstruction*. What motivates his project of reconstruction is the thought that once one admits "being" into the Heideggerian view of things as anything more than a human projection, once one moves to the idea of being as self-revealing-but-simultaneously-self-concealing, it invariably becomes "hypostatized," "inflated" into

"Big Being," a metaphysical "Something" (however ethereal) that lies somewhere beyond entities and that we can allegedly "pursue" and "relate to." In this aggrandized and reified form, Big Being ends up performing a host of extraordinary activities (all in the middle voice, we are told): it conceals itself and reveals itself, withdraws itself yet dispenses epochs of being, calls out to us while abandoning us to technology, wraps itself in mystery and yet occasionally pulls aside the veil to show Itself. (S 189) This, Sheehan observes, is "metaphysics in its most banal and vulgar form, the destruction of everything Heidegger stood for" (S 199). He concludes his article by suggesting that though some will fear that in preferring his to Richardson's paradigm we will "lose all the important stuff in Heidegger— the cosmic drama, the mystical metaphors, the Teutonic bombast—everything that makes us Heideggerians and not analysts or pragmatists," such fears are actually groundless (S 201).

What is supposed to be wrong with "Big Being"? (Sheehan derives the phrase from the disposition of some of Heidegger's translators and interpreters to mimic the fact that Heidegger's *Sein* begins—like all German nouns—with a capital letter, by talking about "Being" rather than "being.") His use of the words "banal," "vulgar," and "bombast" gives the initial appearance that the objection is a matter of aesthetic taste. But it must, surely, be grounded in something more substantial. It may be that, as a Catholic philosopher, he objects to the (from a Catholic point of view) heretical God that Big Being looks to be.[7] More likely, however—this seems to be what "Teutonic" and "vulgar" suggest—Sheehan is tuning into the claim made by Derrida and others that Nazism was really the product of post-Kantian German metaphysics, the "ontotheological" metaphysics of, in particular, *Geist*. According to Derrida, middle-to-late Heidegger used the quasi-Hegelian idea of being's—Big Being's—"dispensing epochs of being" in a way we are powerless to resist in order to "confer the most reassuring and elevated spiritual legitimacy" on Nazism and on his own decision to join the Nazi party in 1933.[8] Sheehan's fundamental worry, I suspect, is that if Heidegger's philosophy from the 1930s onward really is committed to Big Being then it is, in a word, Nazi philosophy. For now, I shall say no more about Sheehan's worries, though I shall return to them at the close of this essay. I turn now to arguing that there really was a turning in Heidegger's intellectual biography.

Heidegger's Retrospective Remarks on *Die Kehre*

Talk of a *Kehre* in Heidegger's thinking did not emerge out of thin air. Heidegger scholars claim that there was a turning because, *pace* Sheehan, Heidegger himself did. Here is the crucial passage from the 1946 "Letter on Humanism" in which the idea is first introduced. Heidegger explains that, while *Being and Time* attempts to think away from "subjectivity,"

the adequate execution and completion of this other thinking that abandons subjectivity is surely made more difficult by the fact that in the publication of *Being and Time* the third division of the first part, "Time and Being," was held back. ... Here everything [In terms of the "what" and "how" of that which is thought-worthy and of thinking] is reversed [*kehrt sich*]. The division in question was held back because thinking failed in the adequate saying of this turning [*Kehre*] [letting it show] and did not succeed with the help of the language of metaphysics. The lecture "On the Essence of Truth" thought out and delivered in 1930 ... provided a certain insight into the thinking of the turning. ... This turning is not a change of standpoint [i.e., of the question of being] from *Being and Time* but in it the thinking that was sought first arrives at the locality of that dimension out of which *Being and Time* is experienced, that is to say, experienced in the fundamental experience of the forgetfulness of being.[9]

Three basic ideas are expressed in this passage. The first is that there *is* a turn in Heidegger's thinking, one that would have found expression in the initially planned Division III of Part One of *Being and Time* had he been able satisfactorily to complete it. Writing in 1941, Heidegger recalls that, going through the page proofs of *Being and Time* with Karl Jaspers at the end of 1926, he became convinced in the course of "friendly arguments" that Division III as it stood was "unintelligible," so that the decision was made to abandon its publication (GA49 39–40). The underlying source of unintelligibility, here, is surely clear: Heidegger's dawning recognition of the fact that the proposed Division III would need to square the circle. If Division III was to be a genuine part of *Being and Time* then its content would need to be *consistent* with what had preceded it. Yet if, in it, "everything is reversed," such consistency could not possibly be achieved. The result of adding it to Divisions I and II would be as self-contradictory as adding Wittgenstein's *Investigations* to his *Tractatus* and calling it "*Tractatus Logico-Philosophicus Division II*." And so, as Heidegger explicitly acknowledged in 1938, the new thinking required a "new approach [*neuer Anlauf*] (GA66 413) in a new and separate work (in the event, a series of works). That, certainly, was Heidegger's final view of the matter since in 1969 he described *Being and Time* as a "dead end [*Holzweg*]" (GA15 366).[10] Having seen the need for a "reversal," Heidegger's thinking had to back out of the "dead end" of *Being and Time* and find a new beginning for his "path of thinking."

The second idea expressed in the passage is that the turn is not a "change of standpoint." What animates the earlier as much as the later Heidegger is the *aperçu*, the "fundamental experience," that the real "question of being" has been lost sight of in the history of Western metaphysics. The manner, that is, in which the question has been posed and answered has resulted in the "forgetting" of its real topic, being. The history of Western metaphysics is, as it were, a production of *Hamlet* in which the Prince of Denmark is at no point allowed to appear. It is this two-millennia-long missing the point which, the introduction to *Being and Time* tells us, necessitates the "destruction of the history of ontology" (BT 19). To have any chance of posing the real question we have to clear our minds of everything that has been said about being since Plato and go back to the beginning.

The third idea, however, is that, for all its good intentions, the extant part of *Being and Time* ends up tarred with the same brush as its predecessors. It, too, ends up "forgetting being." This is because it not only deploys the "language of metaphysics" but actually *is* a form of metaphysics. As the "Letter" puts it a few pages later, in the thinking of *Being and Time* there is "a metaphysics that is still dominant" (PM 256). I shall make some remarks shortly as to what Heidegger means by "metaphysics," but for now it is sufficient to note that "metaphysics" and "forgetfulness of being" are, if not synonyms, certainly equivalent expressions. To be a "metaphysician" in Heidegger's sense is to have "forgotten being." This, then, is what necessitated the turn: the fact that *Being and Time* ends up betraying its own fundamental impulse. The turn is thus a *return*, a return to the point at which *Being and Time* started but then lost sight of.

The Importance of Frege

Although Heidegger knew that, as it turned out, *Being and Time* represented a "false path" (GA66 411) which came to a "dead end," I do not believe he ever fully understood what it was that had led him down that path. The reason is a fundamental unclarity in what, both early and late, he took to be his fundamental question: "the question of the meaning of being" (BT 1–2).

When the question is raised in the introduction to *Being and Time* the word he uses for "meaning" is *Sinn*. To anyone with Frege in his toolkit, *Sinn* ("sense") immediately calls to mind *Bedeutung* ("reference"), so that the question "What is the meaning of being?" immediately presents itself as ambiguous between "What is the *reference* of "being'?" and "What is the sense of 'being'?"[11] As Daniel Dahlstrom points out, however, though Heidegger knew of Frege's work in philosophical logic, and of Russell's too, his logic lectures of 1925 failed to recommend a single work of these cutting-edge thinkers, "giving notice," as Dahlstrom tactfully puts it, "of certain limitations in his grasp of the state of logic and the philosophy of logic at the time."[12] That Heidegger was unaware of the ambiguity in his fundamental question is manifested in the habit that persisted through his entire career of speaking of "*the* question of being [*die Seinsfrage*]" as if there were a unique *Seinsfrage*, when in reality there are (at least) two.

Even as late as 1962, in the "Letter to Father Richardson," Heidegger remains seemingly insensitive to the ambiguity at the heart of his project. The fundamental question, he writes Richardson, that has determined all his thinking is "Was heisst denn Sein?" (R xi), a formulation that appears already in *Being and Time* (BT 27). Since "Was heisst X" can mean both "What does "X" mean?" and "What is X?"—*Was heisst Verantwortung* would be most naturally translated as "What is responsibility?"—the question preserves the same ambiguity between sense and reference that infects "What is the meaning of being?" Polysemy—Heidegger's word is *Vieldeutigkeit* (GA52 15)—plays, to be sure, an important role in his account of poetry, and his persistent use of polysemous words and constructions (the ambiguous genitive, as in "the house of being," is one of his favorites) is typically intentional. Usually it produces a rich, poetic effect as well as revealing illuminating connections and productive lines of thought. Yet it also carries with it the tremendous risk of rushing down false alleys and ending up in "dead ends" such as the one he eventually pronounced *Being and Time* to be.

As conceived in the introduction, *Being and Time* is a grandly ambitious work. It aims, the introduction tells us, at the "deconstruction of the history of ontology" (BT 19) in order to return to the real "question of being," namely, that question which "provided a stimulus for the researches of Plato and Aristotle albeit falling silent [*verstummen*] from then on *as a thematic question for genuine investigation*" (BT 2). We must ask, then, what it was that "animated" the researches of Plato and Aristotle. The answer, of course, is that, as it were, the quarry of their hunt was *being*. Their question was the question of "fundamental ontology," the question, that is, *of what, fundamentally there is* as opposed to merely seems to be. (It is noteworthy that later Heidegger often prefers to talk about "that which is [*das was ist*]" [QT 22, 25] and sometimes even "the real [*das Wirkliche*]" [QT 18 23] to talking about "being.") Plato, at least, would have strongly rejected the idea that he was a conceptual analyst interested in the "sense" that we ordinarily attach to "being" since he would certainly have regarded our ordinary use of the word as ensnared in "semblance." What this means is that the question the introduction to *Being and Time* wants to rediscover *pertains to the reference of "being" rather than to its sense.*[13] *Being and Time*'s aim is to answer the ancient question fundamental to all theoretical philosophy, namely, "What (really) is being?"

What one actually finds in the body of the work, however, is an investigation not of being but rather of what it is to be *a being like us*. Fertile, fascinating, and important though that 600-page investigation is, it still does not represent what the book was supposed to be talking about. *Being and Time* thus resembles the voyage of Columbus—it sets out, as it were, to get to India but ends up discovering America.

The crucial step that produces this change of direction is the premise that, albeit "nonthematically," the human being, "Dasein," in its "average everydayness," has an "understanding of being" (BT 18, 86), so that all we need to do is to keep "interrogating" it (BT 5). If we do so for long enough, then the answer to "the" question of being will emerge—in the same kind of way, presumably, as Socrates' interrogation of the slave boy eventually reveals the answer to the question of geometry. "If," Heidegger writes, "we are enquiring about the meaning of being, our investigation does not need to become a 'deep' one [but] ... asks about being insofar as it enters the intelligibility of Dasein" (BT 152). Hence, courtesy of "meaning" doing duty for both sense and reference, the question of the reference of "being" has been transformed into the question of what "being" means *for us*. And this, from the point of view of the fundamental project of "remembering being," is a disaster.

What makes it a disaster is that it reduces being to what Heidegger calls the "being of beings" (i.e., "openness," "the clearing")—the "main trait" (ITP 38) beings must exhibit to count as possessing "presence" (R xi), to count as being in being. In *Being and Time*, for instance, that trait is represented in terms of the disjunction between Daseinhood and "equipmentality," in the later Heidegger's account of modernity it is "resource [*Bestand*]," and in the account of the being of beings Heidegger attributes to Nietzsche it is "will to power." In his "Letter to Father Richardson," Heidegger says that the way in which metaphysics "forgets being" consists in mistaking "the being of beings" for "being as such" (R xiv). Metaphysics, in other words consists in answering the question of the being of beings *and thinking that in doing so the question of being has been comprehensively answered*. What metaphysics "forgets," however, is that being *transcends* the being of beings. The introduction to *Being and Time* states, to be sure, that "*Being is the transcendens pure and simple,*" so that knowledge of being is (the phrase comes, of course, from Kant) "transcendental knowledge." (BT: 38). But all it means, thereby, is that the being of beings ("world," "the truth of being") is the precondition of anything which shows up as a being so doing. What *Being and Time*'s conception of transcendence misses is being's *double* transcendence, the fact that it transcends *both* beings *and* the being of being. This is the burden of a self-criticism contained in a marginal comment later Heidegger attaches to the "*transcendens pure and simple*" assertion: transcendence is indeed, he writes, a matter of the "horizon" which (literally translated) "provides the roof over [*überdachen*]" beings. But—and this is what *Being and Time* misses—there is there is a second transcendence, "transcendence of the truth of being [*Seyns*]: the appropriation [*Ereignis*]" (GA2 51). As we shall see, this very same assertion of being as "the *transcendens* pure and simple" reappears in one of the central later texts, "What Are Poets For?" When we come to discussing this text a central aim will be to discover what this double transcendence amounts to—what, in other words, Heidegger means by "the *Ereignis*."

Dwelling and the Turning

Heidegger rightly saw, then, that he needed to reverse out of the "dead end" of *Being and Time*; he saw the need for a turning. But did he succeed in executing it, and if he did, what exactly is the character of the contrast between his earlier and later thought? And can it be said that the later thought succeeds, where *Being and Time* had failed, in "overcoming metaphysics," in "remembering being"? Of the various points of entry to the question of the nature of the turning, I shall choose the topic of "dwelling," a central word for the later Heidegger. Though this may seem remote from "the question of being," we shall see that the topics are, in fact, intimately linked. A way of expressing the link might be to say that "the question of dwelling" is the existential aspect of "the question of being."

It might be thought that the topic of dwelling makes its first appearance in the later thought and that, entirely absent from *Being and Time*, it is unsuitable as a point at which to compare post- with pre-turning Heidegger. But this is not so. There is a discussion of dwelling in *Being and Time*.

I am not in the world, *Being and Time* observes, as the water is in the glass or the dress is in the wardrobe (BT 54). The "in" of Dasein's "being-in" is not a matter of spatial containment. Rather, my being-in-the-world is a matter of concernful engagement, as is, for example, my being in the "world of the theater" or the "world of sport." This fact, *Being and Time* continues, is clued by language, since the "in" of being-in

stems from *innan-*, to dwell [*wohnen*], *habitare*, "to reside" [*sich aufhalten*]. An signifies "I am accustomed," "I am familiar with [*vertraut mit*]," I look after something. It has the meaning of *colo* in the sense of *habito* and *diligo*. This being to whom being-in in this meaning belongs we characterise as the being which I myself always am. The expression "*bin*" is connected with "*bei*." "*Ich bin*" [I am] means I dwell [*ich wohne*], I say near ... the world as something familiar in such and such a way. Being as the infinitive of "*ich bin*" ... means "to dwell near [*wohne bei*] ...," to be familiar with. ... (ET 54)

The important thing about this passage is that it appeals to much of the same linguistic data that reappears, almost a quarter of a century later, in one of the principal expressions of Heidegger's later thought, "Building Dwelling Thinking," and does so in order to arrive, at least verbally, at the same conclusion: the *bin* of *ich bin*, the later work tells us, comes (like *bauen*, "to build") from the old High German word *buan*, which means "to dwell," from which the suggestion follows that "man *is* insofar as he dwells" (PLT 145). There *is*, then, a discussion of dwelling in *Being and Time*, which means that we can legitimately compare and contrast the earlier and later accounts of what it is that constitutes dwelling.

As the passage from *Being and Time* makes clear, dwelling in the earlier thought is a matter of being "familiar" with, attuned to, the world in which one dwells, the world of equipment, of the "ready-to-hand." It is a matter of one's practical engagement with the world being smooth, effortless, and in a certain sense "mindless." To grasp the point, compare cooking in one's own kitchen with cooking in someone else's. In the home kitchen, the activity is smooth and relaxed—relaxed because it is almost entirely thoughtless. In the foreign kitchen, it is the opposite: jerky, tense, frustrated, expletive-ridden, replete with thought, with hypothesis-formation and hypothesis-refutation. The reason for the contrast is that in the home, but not the foreign kitchen, one knows, without having to think about it, just where the potato peeler—so frustratingly unlocatable in the foreign kitchen—is kept. *Unready*-to-hand in the foreign kitchen, equipment is truly *ready*-to-hand when one is at home. One no more has to think about the location of the potato peeler than one has to think about the location of one's hand. One might indeed regard the equipment in one's own kitchen as a prosthetic extension of one's body, metaphorically even a part of it. (The common accusation that Heidegger, this most "hand"-centered of all philosophers, "ignores the body" seems to me quite mistaken.)

This, then, is *Being and Time*'s account of dwelling: dwelling consists in attunement to one's world in the sense of being familiar with its equipment (and with one's co-dwellers too). It is important to notice what this account of dwelling does *not* include. *Being and Time*'s project, let us recall, is to answer "the" question of the meaning of being by providing the necessary, a priori, "transcendental," structure which defines our "being-in-the-world"—our, that is to say, *dwelling*-in-the-world. Having identified "ready-to-handness" as the being of the entities other than Dasein with whom we share our world, Heidegger comes, in section 15, to the question of nature, the question of whether his analysis is adequate to cover the seemingly *nonequipmental* status of beings belonging to the natural environment. His response to this problem is to suggest that natural objects show up as ready-made equipment: "The wood is a forest of timber, the mountain a quarry of rock; the river is water-power, the wind is wind 'in the sails'" (BT 70). This, then, is nature as "ready-to-hand." The same passage, however, identifies two other senses of "nature": "present-at-hand" nature, nature as it is studied by the geographer or botanist, and poetic nature, "the nature which 'stirs and strives' and enthrals us as landscape." Heidegger observes that, when nature shows up as the present-at-hand object of scientific description and research, poetic nature

remains hidden. The botanists plants are not the flowers of the hedgerow; the "source" which the geographer establishes for a river is not the "springhead in the dale." (BT 70)[14]

Oddly, he does not explicitly observe that poetic nature *also* "remains hidden" when nature is revealed as ready-to-hand, but it would be evident nonsense to hold that, while the geographer's identification of the river's source hides the "springhead in the dale," its identification as a power source does not. On the contrary, as another of the central texts of the later philosophy, "The Question Concerning Technology," points out, the Rhine as a "water-power supplier" is precisely *not* the Rhine as "uttered in Hölderlin's hymn of that name" (QT 16).

A certain unease can be perhaps detected in this omission, an unease that is even more visible in *Being and Time*'s discussion of the world of "primitive people" (BT 81–82). The problem, here, concerns what he calls "fetishism and magic." Under a less dismissive description it concerns "the holy"; in other words—since, as the later Heidegger learned from Hölderlin, "poetry founds the holy" (GA52 193, GA4 148, HH 137–140)—it concerns "the poetic."

The early Heidegger's problem with "primitive people" is that some of their "signs [*Zeichen*]" do not fit *Being and Time*'s analysis of signs as items of equipment that serve to "indicate" something else, as, for example, the indicator of a car indicates the intention to turn and the south wind indicates to the farmer the approach of rain. A "primitive" sign, however, does not indicate something other than itself but rather "*is* what it indicates." (Examples given in Heidegger's later works of such, as it were, transubstantiation are the statue in the Greek temple that "lets the god himself be present and thus *is* the god" [PLT 42] and the figure of the saint on the South German bridge before which we "visibly give thanks for [the] *presence*" of the "divinity" [PLT 151; my emphasis].) Faced with his inability to account for the world of "primitive" humanity in terms of the analysis of *Being and Time*, early Heidegger faces a choice. The first option is to admit that, since dwelling presupposes the poetic (just what this means we will come to shortly), he cannot accommodate dwelling in an account of the life-world that is restricted to the categories of equipment and ready-to-hand. The second option is to deny that dwelling presupposes the poetic while going on to admit that his account cannot accommodate the being-in of those whose world *is* of a holy, poetic character. Heidegger opts for the second alternative, admitting with some frankness that since the "signs" of the primitive world do not have "the kind of being that belongs to equipment" it perhaps follows that "readiness-to-hand and equipment have nothing to contribute as ontological clues in interpreting the primitive world" (BT 82). At this point, in other words, he suggests that rather than being a "transcendental," quasi-Kantian account of *human being as such*, *Being and Time*'s analysis applies only to "our," Western Dasein—and even, perhaps, only to modern Western Dasein, since he knows perfectly well that his admired Greeks lived in a holy world. The consequence of this is that if, as later Heidegger will argue, dwelling indeed presupposes the holy, then *Being and Time* consigns the humanity whose existence it analyzes to "homelessness"—something other parts of *Being and Time* admit and even emphasize: in its "thrownness," its "abandonment" to a cultural world that is not of its choosing, Dasein is, *Being and Time* says, *unheimlich*, both in the sense of "uncanny" and in the sense of "not being at home [*Nicht-zu-hause-sein*]" that is suggested by the word's etymological components (BT 188).

The point we have now reached is this: *Being and Time* attempts to define being-in-the-world—that is, *dwelling*-in-the-world—in terms of equipmental attunement, familiarity with the ready-to-hand, alone.

Virtually explicitly—if uneasily—it excludes the poetic as relevan⁻ to dwelling. Dwelling is equipmental familiarity—and nothing besides.

Let us now turn to later Heidegger's account of dwelling. The first observation he makes, right at the beginning of "Building Dwelling Th_nking"—
an observation surely intended as self-criticism—is that to attem⊃t to give
an account of dwelling in terms of equipmental familiarity alone is a mistake: the truck driver is "familiar with [zu Hause auf]" the moto⊂way, the
engineer is familiar with the power station, but neither of then⊞ dwell in
those paradigmatic places of alienation (PLT 143). Familiarity with, zu-
Hause-sein, is an important—indeed, surely, necessary—condition of dwelling. But it is by no means sufficient. What more, then, is neede⊂? Via the
revered Hölderlin, Heidegger tells us over and over again: "Full of merit yet
poetically / man dwells upon this earth." Almost by itself, the qu⊃tation is
a critique of Being and Time's account of dwelling. For what it say⁻, at least
as Heidegger parses it, is, "full of merit (to be sure)," for his many achievements in getting to know his way around this world, yet … witnout the
"dimension" of the poetic he does not dwell (PLT 211–216). What we need
now to ask, is "the poetic," and what difference does it make?

In brief, to dwell, to live in the light of the poetic, is to live in the light
of the might, majesty, and "mystery" of poiesis, a word that means both
"bringing-forth" and "poetry" (QT 34). To dwell is to recapture the ancient
Greeks' sense of nature as physis, as the unaided "bringing-forth" of beings,
and of the proper role of human techne as allowing nature's "bringing-
forth" to happen through the human hand (QT 10–13). To live in the light
of the poetic is to live in "wonder," "the wonder that around us a world
worlds, that there is something rather than nothing, that there are things
and we ourselves are in their midst" (GA52 64).

In "What Are Poets For?" Heidegger finds such wonder expressed in
Rilke's "valid [gültig]" poetry, poetry which pictures "nature," the primordial ground" of our being, as "throwing us forth" into the "danger "of its
"venture." Though we are thrown forth, we are at the same time held "in
the balance," since the venture retains us in a "gravitational attraction" to
itself as the concealed, "unheard center" that belongs to the "dar⁻," unil-
luminated side of the "globe of being" (PLT 94–139). (Heidegger surely
intends this talk of "throwing" to call to mind Being and Time's "thrownness" and the idea of a "gravitational attraction" breaking the ve⊃city of
the throw to tell us what is missing from Being and Time.) Rilke's talk of the
"venture," implying as it does the notion of "will," employs, Heidegger
observes, the "language of metaphysics." It needs, therefore, to be treated
with caution. Nonetheless, the underlying thought is not invalidated by

this metaphysical appearance, since in Rilke's use of "nature" "there echoes, still, the earlier word *physis*" (PLT 98).

Heidegger emphasizes that (unlike the "God" of the philosophers and theologians (QT 26) Rilke's "center" is not separate from its venture. What it ventures, rather, is itself. In Heidegger's own language—here the phrase from the introduction to *Being and Time* reappears—being, conceived as Rilke's "venture,"

is the unique which wholly surpasses itself (the *transcendens* pure and simple). But this surpassing, this transcending, does not go up and over into something else; it comes up to its own self. ... (PLT 129/GA5 286)

Being *is* the visible world of nature. But it is also that which "gifts" the visible world, that is, itself. Mark Johnston, in an interesting excursion by an analytic philosopher into Heidegger studies, describes this as "panentheism," a doctrine he ascribes to both Heidegger and to himself: "the highest one" is not separable from nature but is at the same time more than nature. Nature is "being's self-giving."[15] In my final section, I shall argue that this is a misreading of Heidegger. (Every "-ism," Heidegger writes, is commodification of thought, a sign that "one no longer thinks" [PM 242].) But it can serve as a temporary summation of the point in the discussion that we have now reached.

What has the provisionally named panentheistic account of being to do with dwelling? "To dwell," Heidegger writes, as the old Gothic *wunian* tells us, means

to be at peace, to be brought to peace, to remain in peace. The word for peace, *Friede*, means the free, *das Frye*, and *fry* means: preserved from harm and danger, preserved from something, cared-for [*geschont*]. (PLT 147)

To dwell is to be, in a deep ("ontological" rather than "ontic") sense, *safe* (PLT 101)—safe even in the face of our ultimate danger, that of death. To dwell, as Wittgenstein put it in his "Lecture on Ethics," is to feel oneself "safe whatever happens." Rilke describes it as being "able to read the word 'death' without negation." It is to be capable, in Heidegger's own language, of "the good death," to be capable of dying without terror because one has overcome the sense that the "end [*Ziel*]" of life is an "empty nothing" (PLT 148–149). Locked as it is into the "constant negation of death" by means of technology, modern humanity as such is incapable of the good death. To be capable of the good death there must be, Heidegger writes, a "turning [*Kehre*]' (QT 36), that is, a "reversal [*Umkehr*]" (PLT 137/GA5 318), within mortals, a turning toward the concealed side of the "globe of being." (It is hard to avoid seeing, here, an allusion to his own spiritual journey out of *Being and Time*'s "forgetfulness of being.") If we make the turning to the concealed side of being then, in the words of Rilke's poem, we will find that

… There, outside all [technological] protection
this creates for us a safety—just there
where the pure forces' gravity rules …
(PLT 97)

To fully live in the light of the might and wonder of the "venture"- is to surrender our "will" to that of the venture and thereby to dissolving out identity into that of the venture. In this condition of, as it were, flowing with the "flow," we engage in *techne* rather than technology; we "accomplish but do not produce … accomplish in receiving" (PLT 118). If we return to this way of being we become, writes Heidegger, "without care [*ohne Sorge*], *sine cura, securum*—secure, safe" (PLT 101). Notice, here, the direct rejection of *Being and Time*'s identification of *Sorge* and *cura* as the human essence (BT 183). I shall return, shortly, to the significance of this rejection.

There is, then, no dwelling without *poiesis* and *physis*, without the "center" and the "venture," without the "*transcendens* as such" understood as the *double* transcendence of discussed earlier (p. 336). There can be no dwelling without what later Heidegger calls being's *Ereignis*—its "appropriation" of us to itself (TB 19), "appropriation" being the later Heidegger's own word for what Rilke calls the "gravitational attraction."

This hidden, poetic dimension to dwelling is radically unlike anything that appears in *Being and Time* as we have it. Yet the question might still be raised as to whether it could not simply be *added* to *Being and Time*'s account of dwelling as "familiarity," in which case the later thought would turn out, after all, to be a *supplement* to the earlier thought rather than a turning against it. Whatever Heidegger might have *claimed* about a "reversal" (it is not, after all, impossible for a philosopher to misrepresent his own philosophy), can the later thought not be regarded as continuous with and as a *completion* of the earlier? Can we not, in fact, conclude that *Being and Time*'s missing Division III, properly worked out, actually could have been added to the earlier divisions without plunging the work into radical self-contradiction?

The answer is that it could not. What precludes the grafting of the later thought onto *Being and Time*, precludes regarding it as the work's missing part, is the powerful presence of the "existentialist" element in *Being and Time*, the dominating fact that over and above Dasein and its world of the ready-to-hand there is, for Heidegger's earlier thought, *nothing*, an "absolute" nothing, *das Nichts* (BT 186–188, 276–277). This is what prevents *Being and Time* from acknowledging being's double transcendence. Being as something more than the being of beings cannot be added to *Being and Time* without eliminating the entire nexus of "thrownness," "abandonment," "homelessness," "uncanniness," "guilt," and "care [*Sorge*]," all of which is generated by Dasein's fundamental mood of "anxiety" before its inevitable absorption into the absolute void. What first drew attention to *Being and Time* as a major work was its articulation of the anguished mood of post-death-of-God, post-World-War-I European consciousness. ("No one born after 1914," claimed Bertrand Russell, "is capable of happiness.") In Germany this mood was significantly intensified by the distress of the Weimar period, a period of whose mood *Being and Time* is an important record. There is no "safety" in *Being and Time*. The only sense in which it can speak of a "good death" is that it is a death which is the terminus of an "authentic," that is to say, "resolute" life. "Resoluteness," as Heidegger describes it, is essentially dependent on the "empty nothing" because it is only by confronting it that one is rescued from existential alienation, rescued by the realization that, for all its alien character, one's "world" is the only game in town. Not until "the nothing" becomes, in Rilke's phrase, "something positive" (PLT 122) can Heidegger do justice to the fact that "poetically man dwells." Not until Heidegger overcomes his own "forgetfulness of being," not until he himself "turns," with Rilke, toward the realm of the doubly transcendent, can he dwell and his philosophy become a philosophy of dwelling.

From Metaphysics to "Meditative Thinking"

But, to return to Sheehan's worries, is not this doubly transcendent something precisely the "Big Being" which he rightly regards as "metaphysics in its most banal and vulgar form," a metaphysics that is not only "the destruction of everything Heidegger stood for" (he did, after all write an entire essay entitled "The Overcoming of Metaphysics") but also possibly fascist? Does not the idea of this double *transcendens* commit Heidegger to the "ontotheology" (GA9 449), the reduction of being to the "highest" of beings, that he tries so hard to overcome? What are we to say about Sheehan's worries?

Sheehan speaks satirically of Big Being's "performing a host of extraordinary activities"—concealing yet revealing itself, withdrawing, dispensing epochs of being, and so on (S 189). The intention is to expose Big Being as

"Teutonic bombast," as the kind of thing no one with any respect for Heidegger would wish to ascribe to him. Yet as we have seen, it is by no means only his interpreters who speak of being in these terms. It is Heidegger himself—copiously and in many texts. Since Sheehan knows this perfectly well, this is the reason I suggested earlier that his intention is to reconstruct— or purify—Heidegger rather than to interpret him. Given, however, that the present project is to understand Heidegger, should we not, then, grit our teeth and admit that he is indeed committed to Big Being—though we might prefer some less satirical description—for example, "God"?

I think not. To see that Heidegger is not, in fact, committed to "vulgar metaphysics" we need to attend more closely to the point we saw him making in relation to Rilke that to speak "the language of metaphysics" is not necessarily to commit oneself to metaphysics. Of his own "Letter on Humanism" Heidegger makes the later comment that (like Rilke's poetry) it "continues to speak in the language of metaphysics" (PM 239). Since he surely does not wish to convict this central, post-turning text of the "metaphysics" which, as Sheehan emphasizes, he wishes to "overcome," we need to attend to the question of how one can speak the language of metaphysics without being a metaphysician. A central text in answering this question is the 1962 *On Time and Being*.

Heidegger begins the lecture by saying that "the point is not to listen to a series of propositions but rather to follow the movement of showing" (TB: 2). The aim, then, as Heidegger's exact contemporary, Ludwig Wittgenstein, puts it, is to "show" rather than "say"; or better, to show through saying.

"Being," Heidegger begins by saying, while "a matter," in fact "*the* matter of thinking," is "not a being." (To think of being as a being, to attempt to capture it within some scheme that defines what a being is—some account of the "being of beings"—is, after all, exactly what "metaphysics" does.) And so we cannot say "Being is" (TB 5), since "anything of which we say 'it is' is thereby represented as a being" (TB 8). Rather, it seems, we must prefer the locution *Es gibt Sein*: "There is being," but, taken literally, "It gives being." We will now, Heidegger says, capitalize the "It" ("Big Being" with a vengeance, one might suppose) and try to "bring it into view" (TB 5). In order to "think being explicitly" we must "relinquish being as the ground of beings in favor of the giving which prevails, concealed in uncon-cealment, that is, in favor of the It gives" (TB 6). But what is this "It"? It is hard to say, since "it withdraws in favor of the gift which it gives."[16] Yet Heidegger persists with his questioning: "how is the 'It' to be thought?" (TB 10). Since *that* beings are disclosed to human beings and the fundamental shape of *how* they are disclosed is never "human handiwork" (QT 18), the

"It," presumably, is the "source" of the presence of things to us *as* things of a certain sort. But now there arises the "growing danger that when we speak of the 'It' we arbitrarily posit an indeterminate power which is supposed to bring about all giving of being "(TB 10). What is "dangerous"—or, as Sheehan would say, "vulgar"—about that? Heidegger does not explicitly tell us, but since he warns us against the error of supposing that every grammatical subject must refer to a being (TB 17–18), the answer is clear: taking being to be an indeterminate power turns it into a being, lapses, that is, into "metaphysics." The "It," then, that "gives" being (gives the "being of beings") is mysterious. For the moment, the word "names a presence of absence" (TB 18). The giving, Heidegger now says, he is going to call *Ereignis*, "event of appropriation." We must note, however, he adds, that although the German word ordinarily means "event," in the present context "this 'event' is not an occurrence, but rather that which makes any occurrence possible" (TB 19). Once again, in other words, by trying to "think being as the event of appropriation" we have ended up turning it into "a species of being." Formerly "philosophy thought being as *idea, energeta, actualitas*, will—and now, one might think, as appropriation." But that would simply be "a continuation of metaphysics" so that all we have really discovered is "how appropriation must *not* be thought" (TB 20–21).

So what is the upshot of this exercise in what later Heidegger prefers to call "meditative" rather than "philosophical" thinking (DT 46–56)? What we have discovered is that every attempt to say what being is—even to describe it as the "giver of the gift of intelligibility"—becomes a "metaphysics," reduces being to a being. All we can say is that "Appropriation appropriates," which, so long as we "hear a mere sentence," says nothing at all about that which appropriates (TB 24). Yet, as we know, the point of the meditation was not to "say" but rather to "show." The very form of his own lecture, the fact that it "has spoken merely propositional statements," is an "obstacle" that must be overcome in order to see what has been shown (ibid.). And something, Heidegger suggests, has shown itself, something over and above the negative knowledge that every attempt to capture being in language must fail. It is just that what has shown itself is something nonpropositional (ibid.).

"A regard for metaphysics still prevails," Heidegger writes, "in the intention to overcome metaphysics." And so "our task is to cease all overcoming and leave metaphysics to itself" (TB 24). Here we see further evidence of Heidegger's affinity with Wittgenstein. Having engaged in the meditative exercise of trying and failing to capture in words the "wonder" that is being, we move beyond that attempt. Following Wittgenstein, we must recognize propositions couched in the "language of metaphysics"—Rilke's talk of the "venture" and its "center," for instance—as ultimately "senseless," so that in the end "one must, so to speak, throw away the ladder away after one had climbed up it." In the end, "whereof we cannot speak we must remain silent" (Wittgenstein, *Tractatus Logico-Philosophicus* 6.54–57)—we must recognize, in other words, that "being is the *transcendens* pure and simple," that it transcends not just beings but also language as such.

In the "Letter on Humanism" Heidegger puts this by saying that to find our way into the "nearness of being," "we must learn to exist in the nameless" (PM 243). That is why he famously writes "being" with a crossing-out through it (GA9 385) and why he would, as I suggested earlier, reject "pan-entheism," along with every other "-ism," as an account of his fundamental insight. But this does not mean that all "being"-talk, talk of being as the "venture" which "comes to itself" in transcending itself, is useless. If it were useless then Heidegger would simply have *erased* "being" rather than allowing it to show through the crossing-out. Being-talk is useful in the way that ladders are useful: analogically, metaphorically, poetically, it can bring us into the forecourt of the wonder. But to fully come into its presence one must, at the right time, abandon the ladder, refrain from seeking to diminish the transcendent with the familiarity of names. This is why Sheehan is right: at least by the time that the turn has completed itself in the form of meditative thinking, there is no naming, no "vulgar" metaphysics—no metaphysics at all.

Heidegger had, during the 1950s, an intense, sometimes face-to-face engagement with Zen Buddhism.[17] The meditation conducted in "Time and Being" is, I think, carried out under the influenced of that engagement. And so one can, it seems to me, think of it as a kind of koan, a spiritual exercise that brings one into a special kind of tranquility—Heidegger calls it *Gelassenheit*, "releasement"—into, that is, a state of "dwelling." As he puts it at the end of "Building Dwelling Thinking," "as soon as man gives thought to his homelessness, it is a misery no longer" (PLT 159).

Notes

1. References are not to BT's page numbers but to the marginal page numbers of the seventh German edition.

2. William J. Richardson, *Heidegger: Through Phenomenology to Thought* (The Hague: Martinus Nijhoff, 1974). Hereafter abbreviated as R.

3. William J. Richardson, "Martin Heidegger," in *From Phenomenology to Thought, Errancy, and Desire*, ed. B. Babich (Dordrecht: Kluwer, 1995), 621.

4. Martin Heidegger, *Contributions to Philosophy (From Enowning)*, trans. P. Emad and K. Maly (Bloomington: Indiana University Press, 1999).

5. Thomas Sheehan, "A Paradigm Shift in Heidegger Research," *Continental Philosophy Review* 34 (2001): 183–202. Hereafter abbreviated as S. Sheehan's *Making Sense of Heidegger: A Paradigm Shift* (London: Rowman & Littlefield, 2014) appeared too late to be taken account of in this essay.

6. *Martin Heidegger: Gesamtausgabe*, ed. F.-W. von Herrmann (Frankfurt am Main: Klostermann, 1977–), vol. 65. As does Sheehan, I follow the standard practice of referring to volumes in these collected works as "GA" followed by a volume number.

7. Conceivably, that is, Sheehan might be reviving one side of the "Pantheism controversy" that preoccupied the German Idealists.

8. Jacques Derrida, *Of Spirit*, trans. G. Bennington and R. Bowlby (Chicago: University of Chicargo Press, 1989), 39.

9. PM 239–276: 249–250. Passages in square brackets are the marginal comments Heidegger wrote in his copy of the "Letter." To this translation, and to some of the others cited, I have sometimes made small adjustments.

10. A "dead end"—"albeit," Heidegger adds, "a necessary one" (necessary in the way that eliminating wrong turnings is "necessary" to finding the correct path). The apologetic use of "albeit" makes it evident that Heidegger is here using *Holzweg* in its standard German sense, rather than in the special, Heideggerian sense of a "path into a clearing." This latter is based on the fact that in the Black Forest region a *Holzweg* is a path through the forest into a clearing where villagers have cutting rights. It is a use of the word that, while familiar to Heideggerians, is unknown to most Germans.

11. (i) Matters are further confuse by the fact that sometimes "being" occurs within quote marks (is "mentioned") and sometimes not (is "used"), and by the fact that Heidegger switches back and forth between "the question of being [*die Frage nach dem Sein*" and "the question of the meaning of being [*die Frage nach dem Sinn von Sein*]" (BT 1–2). (ii) For those unacquainted with the sense–reference distinction: "Morning Star" and "Evening Star" have the same *reference* (viz., the planet Venus) but different *senses*. Senses are methods for identifying a referent, and sometimes two methods may end up with the same result. See "On Sense and Reference," in *Translations from the Philosophical Writings of Gottlob Frege*, ed. and trans. P. Geach and M. Black (Oxford: Blackwell, 1980).

12. Daniel Dahlstrom, *Heidegger's Concept of Truth* (Cambridge: Cambridge University Press, 2001), 23.

13. It might be thought that to allow being to be a referent is immediately to turn it into a being. But this is not so. Not all referents are beings. For example, the very statement "Being is not a being," if true, presupposes that some referents are not beings. Heidegger allows for referents that are not beings by distinguishing between "matters" and "beings." Being, while not a being is, he says, "the matter of thinking" (see p. 344 below), "the 'what' of thinking" (p. 332 above). Thinking is essentially *about* something. If there can be thinking that is not about beings, there must be referents other than beings (cf. GA29–30, 471).

14. "Springhead in the dale" is a free translation of *Quelle im Grund* but remains true, I think, to the spirit of the passage.

15. Mark Johnston, *Saving God: Religion after Idolatry* (Princeton: Princeton University Press, 2009), 113–128.

16. Heidegger adds: "a giving which gives only the gift, but in the giving holds itself back and withdraws … we call a sending" (TB 8). A "sending," then, is an "anonymous" gift and is to be distinguished from a "giving" in which the giver is present to the receiver in the act of giving.

17. See Heidegger, "Denken und Kunst," in *Japan und Heidegger—Gedenkenschrift der Stadt Messkirch zum hundertsten Geburtstag Martin Heideggers* (Sigmarinen: J. Thorbecke, 1989), and Heidegger, *On the Way to Language*, trans. P. D. Herz (San Francisco: Harper & Row, 1982), 1–54.

Contributors

Alain Badiou
Emeritus Professor at the Ecole Normale Supérieure

Lee Braver
University of South Florida

Daniel Dahlstrom
Boston University

Charles Guignon
University of South Florida

Graham Harman
American University in Cairo

Karsten Harries
Yale University

Theodore Kisiel
Northern Illinois University

Denis McManus
University of Southampton

Eric S. Nelson
University of Massachusetts, Lowell

Richard Polt
Xavier University

François Raffoul
Louisiana State University

Thomas Sheehan
Stanford University

Iain Thomson
University of New Mexico

Katherine Withy
Georgetown University

Julian Young
Wake Forest University

Index